D1075375

Protecting Society From
Sexually Dangerous Offenders

The LAW AND PUBLIC POLICY: PSYCHOLOGY AND THE
SOCIAL SCIENCES series includes books in three domains:

> *Legal Studies*—writings by legal scholars about issues of relevance to
> psychology and the other social sciences, or that employ social
> science information to advance the legal analysis;

> *Social Science Studies*—writings by scientists from psychology and
> the other social sciences about issues of relevance to law and public
> policy; and

> *Forensic Studies*—writings by psychologists and other mental health
> scientists and professionals about issues relevant to forensic mental
> health science and practice.

The series is guided by its editor, Bruce D. Sales, PhD, JD, ScD(hc),
University of Arizona; and coeditors, Bruce J. Winick, JD, University of
Miami; Norman J. Finkel, PhD, Georgetown University; and
Valerie P. Hans, PhD, University of Delaware.

* * *

The Right to Refuse Mental Health Treatment
  Bruce J. Winick
Violent Offenders: Appraising and Managing Risk
  Vernon L. Quinsey, Grant T. Harris, Marnie E. Rice, and
  Catherine A. Cormier
Recollection, Testimony, and Lying in Early Childhood
  Clara Stern and William Stern; James T. Lamiell (translator)
*Genetics and Criminality: The Potential Misuse of Scientific Information
in Court*
  Edited by Jeffrey R. Botkin, William M. McMahon, and
  Leslie Pickering Francis
The Hidden Prejudice: Mental Disability on Trial
  Michael L. Perlin
*Adolescents, Sex, and the Law: Preparing Adolescents for Responsible
Citizenship*
  Roger J. R. Levesque
Legal Blame: How Jurors Think and Talk About Accidents
  Neal Feigenson
*Justice and the Prosecution of Old Crimes: Balancing Legal, Psychological,
and Moral Concerns*
  Daniel W. Shuman and Alexander McCall Smith

Protecting Society From Sexually Dangerous Offenders

LAW, JUSTICE, *and* THERAPY

EDITED BY

Bruce J. Winick and John Q. La Fond

AMERICAN PSYCHOLOGICAL ASSOCIATION
WASHINGTON, DC

Published by
American Psychological Association
750 First Street, NE
Washington, DC 20002
www.apa.org

To order
APA Order Department
P.O. Box 92984
Washington, DC 20090-2984

Tel: (800) 374-2721; Direct: (202) 336-5510
Fax: (202) 336-5502; TDD/TTY: (202) 336-6123
On-line: www.apa.org/books/
E-mail: order@apa.org

In the U.K., Europe, Africa, and the Middle East, copies may be ordered from
American Psychological Association
3 Henrietta Street
Covent Garden, London
WC2E 8LU England

Typeset in Goudy by EPS Group Inc., Easton, MD

Printer: Port City Press, Baltimore, MD
Cover Designer: Berg Design, Albany, NY
Technical/Production Editor: Casey Ann Reever

The opinions and statements published are the responsibility of the authors, and such opinions and statements do not necessarily represent the policies of the American Psychological Association.

Library of Congress Cataloging-in-Publication Data
Protecting society from sexually dangerous offenders : law, justice, and therapy /
edited by Bruce J. Winick & John Q. La Fond.
     p. m.—(Law and public policy)
Includes bibliographical references and index.
   ISBN 1-55798-973-7 (hardcover : alk. paper)
   1. Sex offenders—United States.   2. Sex offenders—Legal status, laws, etc.—
United States.   3. Sex offenders—Rehabilitation—United States.   4. Sex crimes—
United States—Prevention.   I. Winick, Bruce J.   II. La Fond, John Q.   III. Series.

HV6592.P76 2002
364.15′3—dc21

2002015077

British Library Cataloguing-in-Publication Data
A CIP record is available from the British Library.

Printed in the United States of America
First Edition

Dedicated to the memory of my grandparents, Philip and Jennie Hurwitz
and Lill and Irving Winick, whose love and encouragement
were always there and still are.
—Bruce J. Winick

To Beth Smith
A woman of uncommon vision
For her friendship and support
—John Q. La Fond

CONTENTS

CONTRIBUTORS

Richard J. Bonnie, LLB, John S. Battle Professor, University of Virginia School of Law, and Director, Institute of Law, Psychiatry, and Public Policy, Charlottesville

John Kip Cornwell, LLB, Professor, Seton Hall University School of Law and Institute of Law and Mental Health, South Orange, NJ

Michalle E. Davis, BPsych (Honours), Griffith University Gold Coast, Queensland, Australia

Kim English, MA, Director, Office of Research and Statistics, Colorado Division of Criminal Justice, Denver

W. Lawrence Fitch, JD, Mental Hygiene Administration (Maryland), University of Maryland Medical School, and University of Maryland Law School, Baltimore

Alison Gray, MS, Sexual Abuse Counselling Service, Department of Families, Queensland, Australia

Debra A. Hammen, LCSW-C, Office of Forensic Services, Mental Hygiene Administration, Catonsville, MD

R. Karl Hanson, PhD, Department of the Solicitor General of Canada and Carleton University, Ottawa, Canada

Grant T. Harris, PhD, Mental Health Centre, Penetanguishene, Ontario, Canada; Queen's University, Kingston, Ontario, Canada; and University of Toronto, Ontario, Canada

Steven K. Hoge, MD, private practice, Charlottesville, VA

Eric S. Janus, JD, William Mitchell College of Law, St. Paul, MN

Linda Jones, MA, Manager, Office of Victims Programs, Colorado Division of Criminal Justice, Department of Public Safety, Denver

Roy B. Lacoursiere, MD, private psychiatric practice and visiting professor, Washburn School of Law, Topeka, KS

John Q. La Fond, JD, Edward A. Smith/Missouri Chair in Law, the

Constitution, and Society at the University of Missouri–Kansas City School of Law

Roxanne Lieb, MA, Washington State Institute for Public Policy, Olympia, WA

Robert D. Miller, PhD, MD, Professor of Psychiatry and Director of the Program for Forensic Psychiatry at the University of Colorado Health Sciences Center, Adjunct Professor of Law at the University of Denver College of Law and Institute for Forensic Psychiatry of the Colorado Mental Health Institute, Pueblo

Stephen J. Morse, JD, PhD, University of Pennsylvania School of Law and Department of Psychology, Philadelphia

Diane Patrick, MPA, Manager, Data Analysis, Colorado Division of Criminal Justice, Denver.

William D. Pithers, PhD, Professor of Psychology and Director of Clinical Psychology, Griffith University Gold Coast, Queensland, Australia

Marnie E. Rice, PhD, Mental Health Centre, Penetanguishene, Ontario, Canada; Queen's University, Kingston, Ontario, Canada; University of Toronto, Toronto, Ontario, Canada; and McMaster University, Hamilton, Ontario, Canada

Robert F. Schopp, JD, PhD, College of Law, University of Nebraska, Lincoln, NE

Jonathan Simon, JD, PhD, University of Miami School of Law, Coral Gables, FL

Leonore M. J. Simon, JD, PhD, East Tennessee State University, Johnson City

Bruce J. Winick, JD, Professor, University of Miami School of Law, Coral Gables, FL

Howard V. Zonana, MD, Department of Psychiatry at Yale University School of Medicine and Adjunct Clinical Professor of Law at Yale Law School, New Haven, CT

PREFACE

Protecting society from dangerous sex offenders has been a critical challenge in many countries, including the United States, Canada, and the countries of Europe, over the last decade. The United States has been at the forefront of this struggle to protect future victims by enacting innovative laws to prevent dangerous sex offenders from committing new sex crimes. These new laws rely on a broad array of strategies, including indefinite civil commitment of sex offenders after they have served their full sentence, mandatory registration of virtually all convicted sex offenders, community notification when dangerous sex offenders move into a neighborhood, and chemical castration of sex offenders as a condition of early release from prison. All are intended to prevent future sex crimes.

Proponents argue that special commitment laws (usually called *sexual predator laws*), activated only when a sex offender is about to be released from prison, will incapacitate especially dangerous sex offenders. In their view, these offenders suffer from a mental abnormality that makes them likely to commit sex crimes. Consequently, these individuals pose a high risk of reoffending and must be confined for the protection of the community. Proponents also argue that commitment provides treatment to those sex offenders who want to change their attitudes and criminal behavior.

Critics claim that these laws are unconstitutional because they are not bona fide civil commitment laws. They claim these laws really constitute preventive detention masquerading as involuntary treatment.

In any event, sexual predator laws assume that experts can identify which sex offenders are sick and dangerous and can effectively treat them. They also assume that experts can determine when these individuals are safe to be released. Not surprisingly, sexual predator laws are extremely expensive. Whether society can afford them or should spend its limited resources on other strategies that may be more cost-effective in protecting the community is an important question.

Registration laws require almost all sex offenders to register with law enforcement officials where they live. These laws, now in place in every American state, provide public officials with vital law enforcement information about dangerous sex offenders who live in the community. Notification laws provide the community, or selected members of the community, with this same information. Is the public better off knowing that dangerous sex offenders live in their neighborhood? Do these laws create their own unintended problems?

Changing an individual's biology to prevent potential crimes raises special concerns. Chemical castration laws are no exception. They require convicted sex offenders to take drugs that reduce their sex drive as a condition of parole from prison. These laws represent government use of medical technology and physicians for social control purposes. Do these laws violate the U.S. Constitution? Do they pervert the healing role of medicine and of doctors?

Needless to say, these new laws are controversial, testing the constitutional boundaries of state authority and the effective limits of law and public policy. They raise extremely important questions that need serious discussion.

We edited this book to provide readers with a thorough, balanced, and knowledgeable overview and analysis of these new strategies and the important questions they raise. To do this, we have assembled leading international authorities from many fields to examine these questions. Our authors are drawn from many different disciplines, including law, psychiatry, psychology, criminology, and sociology. These contributors describe what we know about sex offenders and what we don't know. They examine these new laws from a broad spectrum of perspectives, providing expert examination and discussion of these controversial strategies. They offer up-to-date information about these new legal approaches and how they are working, debate their wisdom, and consider the alternatives.

This book is essential for any reader interested in understanding the risk posed by sex offenders and in evaluating the novel legal strategies now being used in the United States and other countries to protect future victims of sex crimes. It is especially useful for policymakers, legislators, mental health professionals, program administrators, attorneys, judges, police, probation officers, and parole officers. Anyone, especially parents, interested in how society should protect their children against dangerous sex offenders will also find this book interesting and helpful. We have taken special care to ensure that this book was written to be clear and easily understandable.

We are especially grateful to our authors for their outstanding contributions to this important public policy debate. Our hope is to bring clarity to the discussion of issues that is often distorted by the strong emotional reactions that sexual violence inevitably produces. Law and public policy in this area need to be based on a firm scientific foundation, and our authors review and analyze the existing knowledge about the ability of clinicians to predict future sexual recidivism and to provide effective treatment. These new legal approaches raise an array of complex constitutional and ethical dilemmas that are probed by leading legal scholars, psychologists, psychiatrists, criminologists, social scientists, and ethicists. Sensible public policy in this area requires a full awareness of the costs imposed by these new legal models and whether their presumed benefits can be achieved. Our authors present the most current information available about these dimensions of these new laws. The authors also analyze the political and social forces that have produced these new legal approaches. They probe the therapeutic and antitherapeutic consequences of these new models for victims, members of the community, clinicians who work in sex offender programs, and sex offenders themselves. They also make recommendations for restructuring these laws and how they are applied to minimize the antitherapeutic effects and maximize the therapeutic potential. Finally, our authors analyze and propose alternative models for dealing with, reducing, and preventing sexual violence.

In short, this book presents cutting-edge information and analysis concerning how our society and laws should deal with the perplexing problem of sexual violence. We hope it will increase the quality of the debate and provoke further research and dialogue about these important issues.

ACKNOWLEDGMENTS

The editors especially wish to thank the contributors who wrote chapters for this book. These men and women are internationally known experts in their fields, and we know the demands that are continually made on their time and energy. We deeply appreciate their willingness to make time in their hectic schedules so that they could share their knowledge with our readers. We also thank Edward Meidenbauer, our editor at the American Psychological Association, whose insightful suggestions made this a much better book. Eileen Russell, Professor Winick's invaluable staff assistant, was an indispensable member of our team, and we thank her from the bottom of our hearts.

Professor Winick would also like to thank Jaymy Bengio, his work-study, for his many contributions, and Janet Reinke, a reference librarian at the University of Miami School of Law, for her extraordinary research assistance. Professor Winick also would like to thank Dean Dennis O. Lynch for his continued support and encouragement.

Professor La Fond would like to thank Burnele Powell, Dean of the University of Missouri–Kansas City School of Law, for his support and Norma Karn, his administrative assistant, for her invaluable contributions. Professor La Fond also would like to thank Kathleen Hall, a very talented research librarian at the University of Missouri–Kansas City School of Law, for her superb work under intense time pressure.

Protecting Society From
Sexually Dangerous Offenders

INTRODUCTION

BRUCE J. WINICK AND JOHN Q. LA FOND

Over the past decade, crimes committed by sex offenders have become a burning issue for society. The increasing number of sex crimes, especially those committed by released sex offenders against young victims, has struck the public nerve. The media has dramatized many of these crimes with sensationalist reporting. Every decent person recoils with horror when the person hears the graphic and terrifying details of a savage sex crime. Understandably, citizens are angry, vengeful, and fearful. It is not surprising that society demands both retribution and harsh measures to prevent these kinds of crimes from recurring.

NEW STRATEGIES TO PREVENT SEX CRIMES

These intense public demands for retaliation and protection have shaped law and public policy in the United States for the past dozen years or so. Since 1990, states across the country have enacted new laws designed to prevent convicted sex offenders from committing more sex crimes after they have been released from prison (Winick & La Fond, 1998). These new strategies include unique civil commitment laws that allow the state to confine mentally abnormal and dangerous sex offenders in secure mental health facilities until they are safe to be released. Every state has also enacted a mandatory registration law that requires sex offenders to register their home address with public authorities. States have also passed community notification laws that allow or require law enforcement agencies to disclose the names and addresses of registered sex offenders to potential victims in the community. These disclosures may be relatively narrow, including, for example, to schools or day care centers near a child molester's home, or they can be broad, include an entire neighborhood or city, if a serial rapist moves in. A number of states are now requiring some sex offenders to undergo "chemical castration" as a condition of their being paroled to the community. All of these laws have one thing in common: They are designed to prevent sex offenders from committing more sex crimes.

These new legal strategies raised serious constitutional questions. All are costly. The most important question, however, is whether they are effective in preventing sexual recidivism.

THE CONTEXT FOR LAW REFORM

Many of these new initiatives were enacted after heinous sex crimes against young children. Washington State's sexual predator law (Wash. Rev. Code Ann. § 71.09.01 et seq., 1992), the first sexual offender commitment law of this unique kind in the nation, was implemented in 1990 after Earl Shriner sexually assaulted a 7-year-old boy, cut off his penis, and left him to die. New Jersey passed a community notification law after Jesse Timmendequas, a released sex offender, lured Megan Kanka, a 7-year-old girl, into a house that he and two other discharged sex offenders rented in a New Jersey suburb. They sexually assaulted and killed young Megan. The community was outraged that Megan's parents and others on the block had not been told that these released sex offenders lived in their neighborhood and posed a threat to their children. The New Jersey law requires sex offenders to register with the police and also requires the state to notify communities when dangerous sex offenders move in (N.J. Stat. Ann. § 2C: 7-1, 1995). A federal law now requires all states to have sex offender registration laws or else lose significant federal funding for crime-fighting measures. Although courts have modified these laws in a number of important ways, these laws have, nonetheless, been upheld against constitutional challenges. As a result, every state in the country now has a sex offender registration law that requires most sex offenders to register with law enforcement authorities.

More recently, several states have introduced or enacted mandatory chemical castration laws (Cal. Penal Code § 645, 1996; Fla. Stat. Ann. § 794.0235, 1997; Ga. Code Ann. § 42-9-44-2, 1997; Mont. Code Ann. § 45-5-512, 1997; Wis. Rev. Stat. 980.12.062(b)(c), 980.08.(4)(5), and 980.12(2), 1998). These laws require many sex offenders seeking early release from prison on parole to take drugs that will reduce their sex drive. Offenders who refuse will not be released from prison until they have served their full prison terms. Under the Colorado law, a court *must* order certain child molesters to take antiandrogen treatment as a condition of parole without requiring a clinical examination to determine whether these drugs are medically appropriate for each offender. These drugs, though effective in reducing sex drive, can have serious side effects and have not been approved by federal regulatory agencies for this purpose. More states may enact similar laws.

The public is convinced that traditional reliance on the criminal justice system has not provided adequate protection against repeat sex offenders. It has demanded that new ways be found to keep the most dangerous sex offenders in confinement and to monitor other offenders more closely after their release from prison. Chemical castration laws are designed to literally change offenders' sexual behavior after they have been released from prison.

Legislatures enacted these laws in the heat of the moment. Although some efforts were made to bring experts and politicians together to examine the problem of sexual recidivism in depth, some state legislatures seemingly passed these laws to appease public anger and to assure the people that the government would do whatever was necessary to make them safe. Many states copied verbatim or with only minor changes the legislation enacted in Washington. These laws were passed without an examination of what is known—and not known—about sex offenders.

DO THE NEW STRATEGIES WORK?

Today, more than 12 years after these laws were first adopted, we now have acquired greater experience with how they work and what they cost. In some cases, especially in states that have enacted sexual predator commitment laws, the number of sex offenders committed has skyrocketed, and the costs have far exceeded initial estimates. The number of sex offenders required to register throughout the country has also increased significantly. Ironically, we also know more now about sex offenders, although there is a great deal we still do not know.

WHAT THE EXPERTS SAY

In this book we have assembled some of the foremost international experts in the field of sex offending, law, psychiatry, psychology, and public policy. They contribute chapters analyzing what we know—and what we do not know—about sex offending and these newly crafted strategies.

Chapter authors explain how sexual predator laws work, why states enacted them, how many sex offenders have been committed as sexual predators, and what problems states will face if they enact a predator law. One chapter provides a thorough explanation of how mental health professionals conduct sexual predator evaluations. Another chapter presents the findings and recommendations of a special task force of the American Psychiatric Association on the appropriate use of civil commitment and coercive therapy in controlling sexual violence. Another examines the pervasive patterns of sexual offending and questions the wisdom of these new laws. Most victims of sexual violence know their attackers, yet many of these new laws target sexual violence committed by strangers.

Some chapters are derived and updated from articles published previously in a special symposium issue, "Sex Offenders: Scientific, Legal and Policy Perspectives," in *Psychology, Public Policy, and Law* (Winick & La Fond, 1998). Some of these new or revised chapters discuss the most current research in risk assessment and treatment efficacy. Others consider the impact of *Kansas v. Crane* (2002), a very recent and important decision of the United States Supreme Court (decided *after* publication of the special issue) narrowing the state's authority to commit sex offenders. This case requires the government to prove that an individual suffers from a serious inability to control his sexual behavior before he can be committed as a sexual predator. Mental health professionals, lawyers, judges, and juries must now take this important element into account. Another chapter provides new and useful advice to states on how to keep the number of individuals committed as sexual predators from overwhelming their institutional capacity to house and treat them.

Experts also explore other strategies that could prove more cost-effective, protective, and rehabilitative than those recently enacted. Our authors canvass important topics such as whether sex offenders are especially dangerous, whether we can identify those offenders who pose special risk, whether treatment is effective in reducing sex crimes, whether we can tell when sex offenders are safe to live in the community, and what we know about sex offenders and their victims. Other contributors thoroughly examine the constitutionality and wisdom of sex predator commitment laws. Other authors examine important opportunities to prevent sex offending that are not receiving adequate public attention, such as treating children with inappropriate sexual behaviors. Others probe the therapeutic consequences of these laws and propose reforms calculated to increase their rehabilitative potential. Let us now turn to our individual authors and highlight their contributions. Together, our experts address important questions that need to be answered to fashion an effective and sensible public policy to reduce sex crimes.

SEXUALLY VIOLENT PREDATOR LAWS:
PROBLEMS AND SOLUTIONS

What are sexually violent predator laws and how do they work? In chapter 1, "The New Generation of Sex Offender Commitment Laws: Which States Have Them and How Do They Work?" Lawrence Fitch and Debra Hammen describe in some detail how various state predator laws work. Their chapter discusses eligibility for commitment and the review and referral process. They then analyze the frequency with which sex offenders are committed as predators in several states. Fitch and Hammen then present some useful data on the number of patients committed under predator laws. The National Association of State Mental Health Program Directors opposes these laws, and Fitch and Hammen describe the basis for its position. The chapter then explores alternative measures that might be used instead of predator laws. Legislators in the many states currently considering the adoption of these laws will find this chapter especially interesting, as will program administrators, mental health professionals working in public mental health systems, prosecutors and defense attorneys, students of public policy, and families with mentally ill members.

Why did states pass the new sexual predator laws? Roxanne Lieb, in chapter 2, "State Policy Perspectives on Sexual Predator Laws," explains why Washington State in 1990 became the first state to enact a sexually violent predator law. She reviews the history of the state's old sexual psychopath statute and its repeal by the state legislature in 1984. Lieb then describes the horrible sex crime committed by Earl Schreiner in 1989 and a brutal murder by a sex offender while on work release in Seattle. She explains how the Washington governor and legislature responded to these terrible crimes and the public anger the crimes spawned. She then describes why policymakers concluded that the state must enact a unique sexual offender commitment law to ensure that dangerous sex offenders would not be released into the community even after they had served their full prison terms.

Lieb then compares sexual predator commitment laws enacted by a number of states, discussing their similarities and differences. She candidly describes some of the major problems Washington State has encountered in implementing its predator law and the key lessons that other states should learn from the Washington experience. This chapter is valuable for the many states currently considering whether to adopt the new sexual predator law model. Administrators of public mental health institutions, attorney generals, civil rights attorneys, legislators, families of sex offenders, and others who are concerned with the difficult problems of implementing a sexual predator law, providing constitutionally adequate treatment, and starting a community release program will consider this a "must read."

SEX OFFENDERS AND DANGEROUSNESS

All of these new legal strategies are built on a primary premise: that experts can accurately identify those sex offenders who are most likely to commit another sex offense. R. Karl Hanson, in chapter 3, "Who Is Dangerous and When Are They Safe? Risk Assessment With Sexual Offenders," provides an up-to-date analysis of whether experts can, in fact, make this type of risk assessment. He reviews the "science" of predicting sexual dangerousness. He describes what we know about recidivism base rates for sex offenders, that is, the expected recidivism rate for the average sex offender. Contrary to popular opinion, Hanson concludes that sex offenders, as a group, are not especially dangerous. He then explores historical factors that tend to predict sexual reoffense. Hanson then explains how experts can convert these risk factors into actuarial risk scales. These scales have some established ability to identify a group of sex offenders who are more likely to commit another sexual offense than other groups of sex offenders who do not possess these characteristics. Hanson concludes that experts can predict sexual dangerousness with sufficient accuracy for their testimony to be used in deciding whether some sex offenders should be confined to prevent them from reoffending. He cautions, however, that mistaken predictions of dangerousness are inevitable. Hanson also concludes that experts have not yet demonstrated any special ability to determine when sex offenders have benefited from treatment and are safe to be released. Thus, experts appear more competent at identifying dangerous sex offenders who should be confined than they are at identifying those who have been rehabilitated and whose release would not threaten public safety.

This chapter is invaluable for lawyers, judges, and mental health professionals involved in any legal proceeding that requires a prediction of dangerousness or safety. It is also important reading for legislators, policymakers, graduate students, and anyone else concerned with whether experts can accurately identify offenders, including sex offenders, who pose a special risk to public safety. Mental health professionals will find this chapter a "state-of-the-art" explanation of how experts predict dangerousness. This field is undergoing a revolution in methodology, which generates more confidence in what can be done and more recognition of what cannot be done.

In chapter 4, "Evaluating Offenders Under a Sexually Violent Predator Law: The Practical Practice," Roy Lacoursiere, a practicing psychiatrist who has conducted numerous sexual predator evaluations, provides a detailed blueprint for mental health professionals on how to conduct a thorough evaluation of sex offenders being considered for commitment under predator laws. He describes the various contexts in which such evaluations might occur and the varying questions that a mental health expert must address. This chapter provides useful information on how to conduct the initial evaluation, including a discussion of how up-to-date and complete records and other information about the offender can be obtained.

Lacoursiere also explores the difficult task mental health professionals must undertake when they examine individuals committed under these laws to determine if they can safely be released back into society. He points out a number of practical issues, including ethical concerns, which an evaluator encounters when evaluating and testifying in these cases. This chapter is extremely useful for mental health professionals who conduct these evaluations and for attorneys and judges who will examine these evaluators and their reports in the courts.

Lawyers and judges who participate in sexual predator cases must be familiar with how these evaluations should be conducted. Mental health professionals who are involved in implementing sexually violent predator laws in any capacity, including not only clinical evaluations but also records review, treatment, and release decisions, will find this chapter an indispensable reference.

SEX OFFENDERS AND TREATMENT

Many mental health professionals maintain that we can effectively treat sex offenders and, thereby, significantly reduce the probability that they will commit new sex offenses. Of course, others remain skeptical on both counts. In an era in which experts claim new expertise, it is especially important that policymakers fully comprehend the power and the limits of this emerging knowledge. If these new laws designed to prevent sexual reoffending are not based on sound knowledge, they may not accomplish the goals policymakers expect them to achieve. Indeed, they may actually make matters worse. At the very least, they will consume scarce public resources that could be better spent on other policy initiatives.

In chapter 5, "What We Know and Don't Know About Treating Adult Sex Offenders," Marnie Rice and Grant Harris review the research on treatment of adult men who have committed rape and child molestation crimes. Their goal is to determine whether treatment is effective. They explain the methodology used by researchers in analyzing whether treatment actually works to reduce new sex crimes. They provide a detailed explanation of the limitations in making an accurate study of this question. Rice and Harris briefly describe the various types of treatment available for sex offenders, including nonbehavioral psychotherapy, castration and pharmacological treatments, and behavioral and cognitive–behavioral treatments. They then thoroughly review the available research on whether treatment is effective for sex offenders. In their view, the jury is still out on this important question. Simply put, we do not yet know if treatment is effective in reducing sex offending. Nonetheless, Rice and Harris believe that therapists should continue this important undertaking, using innovative methods based on emerging research and also rigorously evaluating whether these new techniques are effective.

Mental health professionals, judges, lawyers, legislators, policymakers, graduate students, and others who want to know if treatment reduces sexual reoffending will find this chapter illuminating.

Eric Janus, in chapter 6, "Treatment and the Civil Commitment of Sex Offenders," examines the role that treatment plays in civil commitment law and policy. He uses the recent enactment of sexual predator laws as the context for his analysis. Janus's primary interest is to determine whether individuals committed under the state's police power have a constitutional right to treatment.

Janus concludes that treatment can serve as a justification for civil commitment only when two principles are satisfied: the autonomy principle (when patients are incompetent to decide whether to accept treatment) and the beneficence principle (when the treatment serves the individual's "best interests"). When both conditions are satisfied, the state is justified in exercising its *parens patriae* authority to take away a person's liberty because the individual is unable to make an autonomous decision and the person will receive significant benefit. Janus argues that treatment is not a justification for police power commitments, such as those authorized by sexual predator laws, in which the primary purpose is to keep dangerous sex offenders in confinement. Treatment is, at best, a secondary purpose for these laws. Moreover, Janus notes, it is not clear that treatment is effective in reducing sex offense recidivism.

Janus explores the implications of the *Hendricks* case on the role of treatment as a constitutional justification for police power commitment. He contends that *Hendricks* establishes that treatment is not the constitutional justification for police power civil commitment. Rather, these commitments are justified because they benefit society by protecting it from dangerous persons whose violence is a product of their mental disorder. However, the case does establish that commitment itself gives rise to a constitutional right to treatment.

A question that has been the frequent subject of litigation concerning the new predator laws is whether they constitute punishment in violation of the constitutional ban on *ex post facto* laws or on double jeopardy, or instead, serve valid government purpose other than punishment. Janus points out that one way to test whether the purpose of the commitment scheme is to protect the public or to punish the individual is to see if the state actually provides available professional treatment. In addition, Janus concludes that the state is required by substantive due process to minimize the deprivation of liberty necessary to protect the public. Thus, the state must provide whatever professional treatment is available to ensure that commitment lasts no longer than is necessary to achieve the state's compelling interest in community protection. Although treatment may not be the principal justification for sex predator commitment, Janus concludes that sex offenders committed under these new laws enjoy a right to receive available treatment that can be enforced in the courts if not honored in practice. Lawyers, legal scholars, judges, state legislators, and policymakers will find this insightful chapter provocative. A major issue in the short history of sexually violent predator legislation remains open: Must states provide treatment to offenders committed under sexually violent predator laws?

In 1993, as state legislatures were beginning to enact new initiatives to deal with sexual violence, the American Psychiatric Association appointed a Task Force on Sexually Dangerous Offenders. This task force prepared a thorough scholarly analysis of sexual offending and the new legal responses. The task force focused major attention on the new generation of sexual predator commitment laws.

In chapter 7, "In the Wake of *Hendricks*: The Treatment and Restraint of Sexually Dangerous Offenders Viewed From the Perspective of American Psychiatry," Howard Zonana, Richard Bonnie, and Steven Hoge, the chairperson of the task force and two of its participants, present its major findings and recommendations on the use of these civil commitment statutes. The task force examined in depth the history and use of involuntary hospitalization in the United States, analyzing the purposes that civil commitment should serve. It also reviewed the U.S. Supreme Court's 1997 decision in *Kansas v. Hendricks*, which had upheld against constitutional attack the Kansas sex predator law. The task force concluded that the sex predator commitment laws are an inappropriate use of psychiatry. In particular, it criticized these laws' definition of mental disability and their clinical conditions for compulsory treatment.

The task force was especially concerned with the use by these laws of involuntary hospitalization for essentially a nonmedical purpose. In its view, this undermines the legitimacy of the medical model of commitment, the principal justification for involuntary hospitalization. In this chapter, Zonana, Bonnie, and Hoge summarize and comment on the task force's analysis and conclusions, presenting in detail the reasons why organized psychiatry finds these laws so troubling. Mental health professionals, policymakers, students, and others interested in whether civil commitment is an appropriate model for dealing with dangerous sex offenders will find this chapter extremely provocative.

THE RATIONALE, CONSTITUTIONALITY, AND MORALITY OF SEXUAL PREDATOR COMMITMENT LAWS

Many of the new strategies adopted in the 1990s assume that most sex crimes are committed by strangers who do not know their victims.

Some of the most severe legal measures for dealing with sex offenders, such as civil commitment laws, cannot be used against those who commit sex crimes within the family or against victims known to the offender. Do these laws target those offenders who do the most harm? Or do they ignore what we know about the patterns of sexual offending?

Leonore Simon, in chapter 8, "Matching Legal Policies With Known Offenders," thoroughly analyzes the available research on sex crime victimization. She demonstrates that most sex crimes against children are committed by family members or acquaintances. A similar pattern emerges when one looks at sex crimes committed against women. The vast majority of rapes, for example, are committed by acquaintances of the victims. Simon makes a cogent argument that current policy overestimates the risk of sexual violence by strangers and grossly underestimates and undervalues the harm committed by sex offenders who know their victims. She focuses extensively on how the criminal justice system processes rape crimes and concludes that significant reform is required if women are to be adequately protected against the dominant mode of sexual violence. Simon also argues that current sex offender legal policies have harmful effects of their own, and she notes their failure adequately to prevent sexual violence before it happens and to prosecute sex crimes after they occur. In short, Simon's chapter makes a persuasive case for the conclusion that much of our current sex offense policy is misdirected. In her view, public policy must be reoriented to recognize the patterns of victim–offender relationship that are pervasive in sex crimes today. Parents, police officers, prosecutors, advocates for women and children, graduate and undergraduate students in criminology and women's studies, and policymakers will find this chapter stimulating, challenging many of our common assumptions about sex offenders and their victims.

These laws also expand our traditional conceptions of civil commitment in ways that many regard as inconsistent with constitutional values and ethical theory. Others disagree and support these laws. Involuntary commitment to a psychiatric facility has traditionally been reserved for those suffering from a major mental illness or disability and has reflected a medical model and a treatment orientation. Is it appropriate to consider those who commit repeated sex offenses as mentally ill or disordered? Many in this category receive the psychiatric diagnosis of pedophilia or one of the other paraphilias, or they are thought to have an antisocial personality disorder. Are these "conditions" sufficiently like the major mental illnesses such as schizophrenia, depression, and bipolar disorder that are the usual bases for involuntarily hospitalizing someone? Legislatures enacting the new sex predator laws did not rely on a characterization of sexual predators as mentally ill. Instead, these new laws authorized this new form of commitment for those with a "mental abnormality" that makes them likely to reoffend.

This expansion of the state's civil commitment authority was challenged on several constitutional grounds. But, the Supreme Court in *Kansas v. Hendricks* (1997) upheld the constitutionality of this form of civil commitment. The Court's decision has generated considerable criticism and controversy. Are sex offenders truly unable to control their conduct as a result of a mental abnormality, or are they responsible agents who should be treated no differently from other criminal law violators? Is sex predator commitment merely a form of preventive detention, or can it be squared with our traditional rationales for involuntary hospitalization? Can the *Hendricks* decision be used to justify civil commitment for other categories of violence or antisocial conduct for which we have traditionally relied on the criminal law? What role does treatment play in the new commitment schemes, and do sex offenders subjected to commitment have a right to treatment? The authors in the remainder of this section tackle these complex questions of constitutional theory and morality.

Stephen Morse, in chapter 9, "Bad or Mad?: Sex Offenders and Social Control," describes the two dominant models for analyzing and responding to sexual predation: the medical and the moral models. Society, in its understandable rage over violent sexual offenses, has resorted to adopting sexual predator laws. Morse makes a powerful argument that these laws inappropriately use the medical model of illness rather than the criminal model of punishment that he contends justice demands. The medical model views sexual offending as a symptom of an underlying disorder for which the offender is not responsible. Treatment is the appropriate response to such illness. In contrast, the moral model assumes that sexual misconduct is intentional action by a responsible agent and therefore merits punishment. In Morse's view, sex offenders are capable of controlling their behavior and therefore should be dealt with by the criminal justice system. He persuasively demonstrates the lack of empirical or conceptual support for the conclusion that sex offenders are unable to control their behavior. Labeling them as "mentally abnormal" people unable to control their actions as a justification for their civil commitment, he argues, impermissibly enlarges state authority in ways that threaten our historic conceptions of liberty.

Instead, Morse contends, sex offenders should be punished, and those who reoffend should be incapacitated through enhanced criminal sentences. This means that sex offenders who have served their full prison term are entitled to their freedom. Under our constitutional system, all citizens are entitled to their liberty unless and until they commit a crime. Morse argues that the criminal justice system is fully capable of protecting the community from dangerous sex offenders. He concludes that in approving the use of civil commitment for sex offenders, as it did in the *Hendricks* case, the Supreme Court has inappropriately blurred the line between "bad" and "mad," and thereby has endangered the constitutional liberty of all citizens. Morse's chapter is a powerful criticism of the Supreme Court for giving the states excessive power to expand the class of citizens who may be incapacitated preventively. This chapter will challenge scholars, policymakers, and anyone interested in public morality.

Robert Schopp, in chapter 10, "'Even a Dog . . .': Culpability, Condemnation, and Respect for Persons," examines the impact that the recent enactment of sexual predator laws has on public morality. In his view, our public morality legitimately expects responsible adults to obey the law. If they commit crimes, our collective morality resents and blames them for their harmful actions. The criminal law captures and expresses this shared morality by holding most offenders accountable for their crimes and using condemnation and blame to express this morality. As a necessary corollary, in our democratic society, responsible adults are allowed to go about their business free of government interference so long as they do not harm others. The criminal law announces a set of rules forbidding wrongful behavior. Only *after* an individual has violated those rules, hurt others, and breached the common morality may the state use the criminal law to take away his or her liberty. And only in clear cases in which adults were incapable of acting as responsible human beings does our legal system not condemn or blame them as criminals for their harmful actions.

In Schopp's view, sexual predator commitment laws violate our shared morality precisely because most sex offenders are responsible adults who should be blamed and held accountable for their intentional chosen wrongdoing through punishment. He argues that civil commitment should be used only to take away the liberty of individuals who do not have the capacity to act as competent and responsible human beings. Misusing civil commitment to respond to our fears of sex offenders, Schopp contends, undermines our basic legal institutions and our respect for persons. In so doing, he warns, predator laws pose a serious risk that we will inappropriately expand the power of the state to intrude into the lives of every citizen and subvert both our liberty and our shared common morality. His chapter will appeal especially to mental health professionals, scholars, civil libertarians, students, and policymakers.

John Kip Cornwell, in chapter 11, "Sex Offenders and the Supreme Court: The Significance and Limits of *Kansas v. Hendricks*," takes issue with Schopp and other critics of the *Hendricks* decision. He examines *Hendricks* and other Supreme Court cases to ascertain current constitutional limits on the use of civil commitment to prevent harm. In his view, commentators who believe that this case confers unbounded authority on the state to deprive individuals of their liberty to prevent possible future crime need not be concerned. Cornwell concludes that important safeguards are now in place that will prevent such terrible possibilities from occurring. These include a heightened standard of judicial review, precision in defining mental disorder, a requirement that states provide treatment to those committed and return them to the community as soon as possible, and a prohibition on the use of civil commitment merely to prevent minimal harms.

Cornwell thus seeks to provide a thorough constitutional map of the current terrain of involuntary civil commitment in the United States. He argues that *Hendricks* need not be understood as rejecting a number of significant constitutional limits on commitment. As a result, this chapter suggests that the concerns voiced by many of the critics of *Hendricks* may be exaggerated and that the theory of commitment it adopts to sanction the new sex predator laws cannot be extended to authorize commitment for other categories of violence. Both critics and supporters of sexually violent predator laws will learn a great deal from this chapter.

ALTERNATIVE STRATEGIES FOR PROTECTING THE COMMUNITY

Although the new sex predator laws have been the focus of worldwide attention and legal challenges, they are not the only strategies for dealing with sexual violence that have emerged in recent years. Not every sex offender can be confined indefinitely in a prison or a psychiatric facility. Most will be released from these institutions into the community. What measures can be taken in the community to reduce the risk of sex offense recidivism by released sex offenders?

The chapters in this section analyze the new approaches that have been developed or suggested to prevent future sexual violence. They analyze new registration and community notification laws that have been passed throughout the United States, emerging intervention strategies for children exhibiting sexual behavior problems to prevent them from becoming adult offenders, chemical castration mandated in several states as a condition for parole, and an intensive community monitoring and containment approach pioneered in Colorado that seems to hold great promise for preventing reoffending.

Bruce Winick, in chapter 12, "A Therapeutic Jurisprudence Analysis of Sex Offender Registration and Community Notification Laws," describes how these laws work and analyzes their therapeutic and antitherapeutic consequences. Using the approach of *therapeutic jurisprudence*, Winick examines the effects these new laws are likely to produce. By giving people in the community information control over a salient risk in their environment, these community notification laws can have positive consequences for their emotional well-being. However, as Winick shows, they may also produce negative effects. They can produce fear and even hysteria. For people given this information whose children or spouses are subsequently victimized by discharged sex offenders, the result can be intense feelings of self-blame and guilt. In addition, because the great majority of sex offenses are perpetrated by family members and acquaintances, these reporting and notification laws may be highly embarrassing for victims, discouraging them from reporting their abuse to authorities. From a therapeutic perspective, Winick shows, these new approaches are a mixed bag.

Winick also documents the antitherapeutic consequences these laws may produce for discharged offenders. Offenders who have served their prison terms and paid their debt to society are subjected to a perpetual form of stigmatization and social ostracism that can make community reintegration and redemption impossible. This can also occur for offenders discharged from hospitals or community treatment programs who may have been rehabilitated. The public sex offender label these laws attach to them will severely limit their employment, educational, and social opportunities in the community, may produce anger and a sense of hopelessness, and may also produce self-attributional effects that can undermine rehabilitative efforts.

Winick acknowledges that as a political matter, these registration and community notification laws, now on the books in every state, are unlikely to be repealed as a result of the antitherapeutic effects that this chapter identifies. He therefore proposes a number of ways of minimizing their antitherapeutic consequences and maximizing their rehabilitative potential for offenders. Winick distinguishes between prediction models for assessing the risk of reoffending and risk assessment or risk management approaches. A prediction model is dichotomous—the individual is predicted to be either dangerous or nondangerous and static, the prediction is based on historic information, and once made, no new information is considered. By contrast, a risk assessment model sees risk as falling along a continuum and is dynamic in character, allowing new information about risk to be considered in light of changing circumstances. Winick shows that many state notification laws, because they use only one tier of risk, are in effect based on a prediction model. Moreover, he shows that even in jurisdictions using several tiers of risk with varying notification consequences, the reality that tier classification decisions made by the authorities will be unchangeable makes it appropriate to view even such reporting and notification schemes as essentially reflecting a prediction model.

Winick criticizes prediction models as inaccurate and as undermining the motivation of offenders to seek rehabilitation. By contrast, he suggests that risk assessment or risk management models are more accurate and more likely to motivate offenders to obtain treatment and to participate in it more effectively. Winick proposes that we change the way in which community notification laws are administered so as to apply a risk management rather than a prediction model. He suggests that jurisdictions use various tiers of risk and continually reevaluate the risk a discharged offender presents in light of changing circumstances, including the results of community monitoring and participation in rehabilitative efforts. He also proposes the use of hearings for risk classification and reclassification decisions, thereby allowing offenders a sense of participation in these important decisions that can be therapeutic for them and can help to break down cognitive distortions that may perpetuate their reoffending. Not only can the use of a risk management approach better achieve the community protection purposes of these notification laws, but also, if properly applied, this approach can provide an important incentive for discharged offenders to participate meaningfully in treatment and control their antisocial conduct. Winick thus proposes a broad restructuring of community notification laws and makes other suggestions for minimizing their antitherapeutic effects and increasing their therapeutic potential for both the community and the offender. State agencies managing registration records and community notification programs, mental health professionals treating sex offenders in the community, police, policymakers, and others interested in how registration and notification laws can have enhanced impact on public safety will find this chapter very informative.

In a provocative chapter, chapter 13, "Investing in the Future of Children: Building Programs for Children or Prisons for Adult Offenders," William Pithers, Alison Gray, and Michalle Davis bluntly suggest that far too much of our energy and resources have been spent on punishment of sex crimes after they have occurred. In their view, far too little attention has been paid to strategies that can *prevent* those tragedies from occurring in the first place. They focus on children with sexual behavior problems and examine the treatment strategies that show promise for changing the attitudes and behavior of these young victims, thereby preventing them from victimizing others as they grow older.

Pithers, Gray, and Davis provide some astounding information about young children who engage in sexually inappropriate behavior. They point out that a vast majority of children with sexually inappropriate behaviors have themselves been victims of sexual abuse. Many of these children will go on to victimize others if effective intervention does not occur. In their view, treatment of as well as research on young victims/offenders is woefully insufficient. Instead, America seems content to wait for these individuals to become adults and commit more sex offenses and, then, to convict and incarcerate them in prisons for long periods of time.

Pithers, Gray, and Davis argue that early intervention and prevention is much more cost-effective than warehousing adult offenders indefinitely. They discuss what is known about the etiology of sexual behavior problems in children, analyzing the types of mental disorders that early sexual abuse can cause in youngsters. The authors then describe effective treatment programs for children with sexual behavior problems and for their parents. They believe that carefully designed treatment can be effective in eliminating sexually inappropriate behavior in children, thereby preventing them from becoming future sex offenders. Failure to invest significant resources in such treatment efforts, they convincingly argue, is a tragic misallocation of resources and abandonment of young victims. Parents, advocates for children, and anyone interested in preventing future sex crimes will find this chapter compelling.

Robert Miller, a psychiatrist, in chapter 14, "Chemical Castration of Sex Offenders: Treatment or Punishment?" analyzes the emerging use of sex-drive-reducing drugs to control sex offenders after their release from prison. He evaluates recent legislation popularly known as *chemical castration laws*, which require sex offenders to take these drugs as a condition of probation or parole. Although the use of these drugs to control sex offenders is not new, what is unique about these new laws is that they require judges to impose treatment based solely on the crime the offender has committed. These laws often do not require medical evaluation to determine if these drugs are clinically indicated, safe, or effective for a particular offender. Miller briefly reviews the history of surgical sterilization in castration in the United States. He then thoroughly explains how chemical castration works, examining the drugs that are used and their effect on humans. Miller then describes the various laws that states have enacted or are considering enacting. In his view (and the view of the American Psychiatric Association), the use of sex-drive-reducing medications is ethically appropriate, but only after a thorough clinical evaluation as part of a comprehensive treatment plan. Miller is concerned about the use of psychiatry and drugs for social control rather than as appropriate medical treatment of an underlying mental disorder. He notes that none of these medications have been approved by the Federal Food and Drug Administration for this purpose. Moreover, the use of these drugs raises significant questions. For example, they have adverse side effects, and only a small minority of sex offenders respond effectively to them. Very few psychiatrists have experience prescribing, and administering these drugs and imposing these laws require that these drugs be administered to whole classes of sex offenders based on the crime they have committed rather than on a diagnosis of mental disorder.

Miller examines extremely important issues that these statutes generate. He explores the problem of obtaining informed consent as well as significant constitutional issues such as possible violations of due process, the First and Eighth Amendments, and individual privacy. Finally, Miller analyzes whether these new laws will compromise the integrity of the medical profession. In sum, this chapter raises profound concerns about this new use of drugs and medical expertise for social control rather than for treatment. Psychiatrists, doctors, state legislators, policymakers, and individuals intrigued by chemical castration laws will learn a great deal from this chapter.

Kim English, Linda Jones, and Diane Patrick in chapter 15, "Community Containment of Sex Offender Risk: A Promising Approach," describes *community containment*, an innovative method for intensively monitoring adult sex offenders while they live in the community on probation or parole in order to prevent them from committing new sex offenses. This systemwide approach to public safety is based on a multidisciplinary collaboration that has as its primary goal the protection of victims. The heart of this approach is a specially trained case management team that closely cooperates in reducing the risk of sexual reoffending by individual offenders. The basic strategy is to eliminate the offenders' opportunity to reoffend and their access to potential or past victims. This requires the team to thoroughly know the offender's past history, his potential victims, and unique high-risk behavior. Extensive use of lie detector tests, intensive supervision of the offender's daily routine, gathering and sharing of information about the offender, and ongoing treatment are used to prevent sexual reoffending.

This strategy adopts a risk management approach to public safety. Rather than making a one-time prediction that the offender will or will not commit another sex crime, this approach continually monitors the offender's behavior in the community, compiling past and present information about the offender and adjusting the restraints imposed on him in light of an ongoing evaluation of the probability that the offender will commit another sex crime. It offers a promising alternative to lifetime confinement in an expensive mental health facility as an effective method of preventing sex offenders from committing new sex crimes. Parole and probation officers, police officers, mental health professionals, victims, legislators, and public policymakers must read this chapter.

EVALUATING THE WISDOM OF SEXUALLY VIOLENT PREDATOR LAWS

Any attempt to understand these new initiatives for dealing with sexual violence must include a thorough analysis of how much money they cost. It must also seek to place them within the wider context of social and political forces that seem to be reshaping penological practices generally. Moreover, any attempt to understand their wisdom and how they can be improved must fully consider the therapeutic and antitherapeutic consequences they are likely to produce. The three chapters in this last section analyze these dimensions of our new legal strategies for dealing with sex offenders, and in the process, increase our understanding of their policy implications and of how they can be reformed.

In chapter 16, "The Costs of Enacting a Sexual Predator Law and Recommendations for Keeping Them From Skyrocketing," John La Fond thoroughly canvasses the costs that states can expect to incur in enacting and implementing a predator law. He provides a detailed review of the experience that selected states have encountered in screening records, conducting prefiling evaluations, trying cases and appeals, running institutions for sexual predators, including building or renovating facilities, hiring and training a sufficient number of professional staff, providing professionally appropriate treatment, preparing individualized treatment plans, and providing for transitional release for predators thought to be safe for release into the community.

La Fond offers extremely valuable information that states can use to identify and estimate costs that will be incurred if they enact a predator law. So far, most states have committed more offenders at greater cost than initially anticipated. Not only does this chapter document the high costs that sex predator laws generate, but it also makes several crucial suggestions on how states can keep the costs of a predator law from spiraling out of control. Governors and their staff, legislators and their staff, directors of state social service and mental health agencies, mental health professionals working in state agencies, and anyone interested in cost-efficient government must read this chapter.

Jonathan Simon, in chapter 17, "Sex Offenders and the New Penology," demonstrates how a new penology is unfolding in the United States today. This new penology is adopting different targets, strategies, and discourses than those previously in vogue. Most important, society is no longer interested in rehabilitating the individual offender. Rather, offenders are now seen as high-risk subjects in need of management. This shift, in turn, requires new technology and expertise.

The public discourse surrounding crime control measures is also changing dramatically. Simon describes it as "populist punitiveness." Simply put, the public has zero tolerance for crime and insists that crime should, and can, be totally eliminated. In his view, sexual predator laws blend the new penology with populist punitiveness. The new penology stresses "waste management." Populist punitiveness considers sex offenders as "modern-day monsters."

Contemporary predator laws reflect these social forces. They are not intended to change individual offenders; rather, they are designed to allow experts to "manage" this dangerous group. At the same time, predator laws reflect the public's demand for keeping these monsters confined as long as necessary to protect the community from potential crimes.

Simon also looks at sex offender registration and community notification laws. These laws use statistical evidence about recidivism rather than clinical judgments about individuals to categorize large groups of sex offenders and subject them to ongoing state regulation through risk management techniques intended to protect the community from harm.

Simon criticizes the Supreme Court for conferring a constitutional blessing on these new crime control measures. In his view, the Supreme

Court has reinterpreted its own past cases to emphasize the state's power to protect the community rather than provide constitutional protection for inappropriate state interference in individual liberty. Simply put, the Supreme Court in the *Hendricks* case has inappropriately expanded the state's power well beyond the criminal law to protect the public from individuals considered dangerous. Criminologists, political scientists, and sociologists, as well as those who are students in these fields or interested in them, will find this chapter intriguing.

Whether the expansion in the state's commitment power that *Hendricks* authorizes is justified as a matter of social policy requires a consideration of the many constitutional, philosophical, ethical, and fiscal issues that many of our authors probe in detail. In addition to these considerations, it is necessary to take into account the therapeutic impact of these new approaches. Bruce Winick in chapter 18, "A Therapeutic Jurisprudence Assessment of Sexually Violent Predator Laws," uses the powerful lens of therapeutic jurisprudence to examine the wisdom of the new predator laws. He explores whether these laws psychologically help or harm sex offenders, mental health professionals who work with offenders in these programs, and non–sex offenders who suffer from serious mental disorder.

Winick considers how law itself can label individuals, conveying messages for self-definition and creating behavioral expectations. He believes that punishing sex offenders and holding them accountable for their crimes in the criminal justice system conveys a strong signal that they are responsible for their behavior and can—and must—make choices not to offend. Using a civil commitment system, however, reinforces offenders' self-concept that they are "mentally abnormal" and, therefore, unable to control their sexual offending. Thus, labeling sex offenders as "sexually violent predators" may actually reinforce offenders' sexual misbehavior.

Winick also examines the effects these laws may have on treatment outcomes. Like most experts, he believes that treatment should be provided to sex offenders as soon as possible after they have been convicted. Treatment that is delayed is much less likely to be effective. Moreover, the threat of postsentence commitment will create disincentives to participate in prison-based treatment.

Winick believes that predator laws may also negatively affect clinicians who treat predators. Because these patients are involuntary, they may have less motivation to participate in treatment and to be fully candid with their therapists. Coerced treatment can also create ethical dilemmas for therapists. These professionals will be treating patients who are fully competent to decide whether they want treatment. Yet, this treatment regime is based on legal coercion and is primarily interested in social control rather than in the best interest of these patients. As a result, Winick warns that clinicians working in these programs may come to see themselves more as jailers than as therapists. He suggests that clinicians themselves may actually suffer psychological harm as a consequence of the function they are asked to play under these new laws.

Finally, Winick argues, these laws will drain enormous scarce resources away from the treatment of individuals who suffer from serious mental disorders. Publicly characterizing sex offenders as "mentally abnormal" may also have spillover effects. Individuals who are not sex offenders but have serious mental disorders already suffer from the stigma of dangerousness. Because the new sex predator laws label sexually violent offenders as mentally abnormal, the general public may consider all individuals with mental disorders to be extremely dangerous. Winick argues that this labeling may well exacerbate the stigma and low self-esteem that the truly mentally ill already suffer from.

Winick persuasively demonstrates how predator laws can actually do significant psychological harm to many people. He argues that these laws should be repealed or, if retained, modified in several important ways. Most important, Winick explains how society is better off using risk management strategies rather than prediction models of civil commitment in responding to the threat of sexual recidivism. Properly applied, these risk management strategies, as Winick demonstrates in chapter 12 on registration and community notification laws, can increase the accuracy of risk assessment, motivate offenders to achieve rehabilitation, and better protect community safety. Policymakers, scholars, social scientists, mental health professionals, and students will enjoy this chapter.

CONCLUSION

What do we know about sexual violence and its perpetrators, and what do we still need to know? Are the new legal models developed and tested in the 1990s just or unjust, wise or unwise, therapeutic or antitherapeutic? How can these models be improved, and what alternative approaches exist? Join us now for a tour of these fascinating questions conducted by the leading national and international experts in the field.

REFERENCES

Cal. Penal Code § 645 (West 1996).

Fla. Stat. Ann. § 794.0235 (West 1997).

Ga. Code Ann. § 42-9-44-2 (1997).

Kansas v. Crane, 122 S. Ct. 867 (2002).

Kansas v. Hendricks, 521 U.S. 346 (1997).

Mont. Code Ann. § 45-5-512 (1997).

N.J. Stat. Ann. § 2C:7-1 *et seq.* (1995 & West Supp. 2001).

Wash. Rev. Code Ann. § 71.09.01 *et seq.* (West 1992).

Winick, B. J., & La Fond, J. Q. (Eds.). (1998). Symposium on "Sex Offenders: Scientific, Legal and Policy Perspectives." *Psychology, Public Policy, and Law, 4*, 1–572.

Wis. Rev. Stat. 980.12.062(b)(c), 980.08.(4)(5), and 980.12(2) (1998).

I

SEXUALLY VIOLENT PREDATOR LAWS: PROBLEMS AND SOLUTIONS

1

THE NEW GENERATION OF SEX OFFENDER COMMITMENT LAWS: WHICH STATES HAVE THEM AND HOW DO THEY WORK?

W. LAWRENCE FITCH AND DEBRA A. HAMMEN

At the close of the 20th century, 15 states and the District of Columbia had laws for the special civil commitment of sex offenders.[1] Earlier in the century, more than half of the states had such laws. Reflecting the view that "sex offenders were ill and that psychiatrists could cure them" (American Psychiatric Association, 1999, p. 13), these early laws provided for treatment as an alternative to imprisonment for selected offenders. When cures proved elusive, these laws fell out of favor. Most were repealed (Fitch, 1998).

Their return in the 1990s reflects not so much a renewed optimism

---

[1] Jurisdictions with commitment laws and their effective dates: Arizona (1997), California (1996), District of Columbia (1948), Florida (1999), Illinois (1998), Iowa (1998), Kansas (1995), Massachusetts (1999), Minnesota (1939, 1994), Missouri (1999), North Dakota (1997), New Jersey (1999), South Carolina (1998), Virginia (enacted 1999; implementation date, January 2001), Washington (1990), and Wisconsin (1994). One state, Texas, has a law for the outpatient (but not inpatient) commitment of sex offenders. Not included in the list of 16, the Texas law is described infra (see p. 37).

about the efficacy of treatment as a frustration with the criminal justice system's perceived inability to keep sex offenders off the streets. Rather than provide a therapeutic alternative to prison, these new laws make no provision for treatment until an offender has completed his or her sentence and is about to be released from confinement. Many even go so far as to acknowledge that the individuals they target are "unamenable to existing mental illness treatment modalities . . . [and] that the prognosis for curing [them] is poor" (language appearing in the preamble to statutes in Washington, Kansas, and other states). "Thus, their primary purpose would appear to be incapacitative rather than therapeutic. No one has suggested that these new laws reflect a renewed faith in the power of psychiatry to cure sex offenders" (American Psychiatric Association, 1999, p. 12).

Without at least some pretense to treatment, however, laws for the special commitment of sex offenders may be vulnerable to attack on constitutional grounds. Authorities responsible for implementing these laws thus face the challenge to establish credible programs and meaningful services for the individuals in their charge. This chapter describes these laws and the states' efforts at implementation.

THE STATUTES

Of the 16 sex offender commitment statutes currently on the books, 14 were enacted in the 1990s. Minnesota's statute was enacted initially in 1939; however, it was amended in 1994 to include many of the provisions appearing in the newer statutes. The District of Columbia's statute, enacted in 1948, was never repealed and, although rarely used, remains in effect today.

Washington State was the first state to enact a statute expressly for the postsentence civil commitment of sex offenders. Prompted by the abduction, rape, and sexual mutilation of a 7-year-old boy by a recidivistic sex offender who was released from prison 2 years earlier, the law was part of a larger package of legislation—the Community Protection Act of 1990 —designed to protect the public from dangerous sex offenders. Another of the act's provisions, requiring sex offenders to register with law enforcement authorities on their release from confinement, also was the first of its kind and provided a template for legislation in other states (see this volume, chapter 12) and an impetus for federal legislation (the Jacob Wetterling Act of 1991) calling on all the states to enact sex offender registration laws.

Washington's sex offender commitment law has served as the model for legislation nationally. Indeed, the law in Kansas, "approved"[2] by the U.S. Supreme Court in *Kansas v. Hendricks* (521 U.S. 346, 1997), was taken nearly word for word from the Washington law. Careful to stay within constitutional parameters, legislatures in other states have followed this model closely. Whether states will amend their statutes in the wake of the U.S. Supreme Court's more recent opinion in *Kansas v. Crane* (534 U.S. 407, 2002), imposing a "lack-of-control" requirement for sex offender commitment, remains to be seen.

Washington's law provides for the indeterminate commitment of individuals found to be "sexually violent predators," a term coined by the Washington legislature and now used in most other states' sex offender commitment laws (as well as in virtually every state's sex offender registration law, and, increasingly, in common parlance). "Sexually violent predator" (or SVP) is defined by Washington law as "a person who has been convicted of or charged with a crime of sexual violence and who suffers from a mental abnormality or personality disorder which makes the person likely to engage in predatory acts of sexual violence" (1990 Wash. Laws 71.09.030). Offenses that qualify as "crimes of sexual violence" include forcible rape, statutory rape, indecent liberties by forcible compulsion or against a child under age 14, and other offenses determined to have been "sexually motivated" (1990 Wash. Laws 71.09.020 (4)). "Mental abnormality" is defined as "a congenital or acquired condition affecting the emotional or volitional capacity which predisposes the person to the commission of criminal sexual acts" (1990 Wash. Laws 71.09.020 (2)). "Personality disorder" is not defined.

Individuals subject to a petition for commitment under Washington's law include anyone convicted of a sexually violent offense whose sentence is about to expire; juveniles found to have committed a sexually violent offense whose confinement in the juvenile justice system is about to end; and individuals charged with a sexually violent offense, found to be incompetent to stand trial or not guilty by reason of insanity, and about to be released from confinement. (No provision is made for the commitment of any sex offender prior to his or her release from confinement.)

Commitment petitions may be filed by the prosecuting attorney for

---

[2] Note that in a concurring opinion, necessary to the majority vote of the Supreme Court Justices in *Hendricks*, Justice Kennedy, expressing reservations about Kansas's law, observed that the Court's opinion concerns *Hendricks* alone. "If [in another case] it were shown that mental abnormality is too imprecise a category to offer a solid basis for concluding that civil detention is justified, our precedents would not suffice to validate it. . . . In this case, the mental abnormality pedophilia is at least described in the DSM–IV [the *Diagnostic and Statistical Manual of Mental Disorders*]. Perhaps taking its lead from Justice Kennedy, the Supreme Court more recently declared that the standard for commitment in Kansas may provide insufficient grounds for distinguishing between dangerous sex offenders who belong in the mental health system and dangerous sex offenders who belong in the criminal justice system. The Court ruled that, to be constitutional, commitment of a sex offender requires proof of "serious difficulty controlling behavior," proof not expressly required by the Kansas law. (*Kansas v. Crane*, 534 U.S. 407, 2002).

the county where the individual was convicted (or charged) or by the state's Attorney General. Once a petition is filed, a court must determine whether there is probable cause to believe that the individual is a sexually violent predator. If probable cause is found, the individual is transferred to a facility for evaluation. The individual has the right to an additional evaluation by a qualified expert of his or her choice, provided at state expense for indigents. The individual may demand a trial by jury. If no such demand is made, a bench trial is held. For commitment, the state must prove beyond a reasonable doubt that the individual is a sexually violent predator. Commitment is to a facility operated by the Department of Social and Health Services. The commitment term is indeterminate: "until such a time as the person's mental abnormality or personality disorder has so changed that the person is safe to be at large" (1990 Wash. Laws 71.09.100).

Laws in other states prescribe essentially the same commitment protocol as Washington's. Differences include the following:

- Eligibility for commitment, by predicate offense: California requires previous conviction of a sexually violent offense against two or more victims. Minnesota and North Dakota require no previous criminal offense (but require a history of similar sexual misconduct).
- Eligibility for commitment, by age: Illinois, Washington, Wisconsin, and South Carolina permit commitment of juveniles; Arizona and Florida do not; other states' statutes are silent.
- Mental condition required: Arizona specifies "mental disorder," including paraphilias, personality disorders, or conduct disorder; California specifies "diagnosed mental disorder," defined precisely as Washington defines "mental abnormality."
- Precommitment confinement status: Missouri permits commitment of previously convicted individuals not currently in state custody who have committed a "recent overt act" or who have been in state custody within the preceding 10 years and meet criteria of a sexually violent predator.
- Standard of proof for commitment: "Clear and convincing evidence" (that an individual meets the commitment criteria) will suffice in Florida, Minnesota, and New Jersey.
- Duration of commitment: Commitment terms may not exceed 2 years in California, although subsequent commitments (in effect, extensions) are permissible.

Some newer statutes prescribe a detailed procedure for selecting offenders for a commitment petition. For example, Missouri law requires the directors of the Departments of Mental Health and Corrections to establish a multidisciplinary team to review all cases of individuals charged with or convicted of qualifying offenses and about to be released from confinement. The multidisciplinary team's "assessment" is given to the state's Attorney General for review. The Attorney General must appoint a five-member prosecutor's review committee to examine each case prior to the filing of a petition.

EXTRASTATUTORY CONSIDERATIONS

In some states, in an effort to narrow the class of individuals eligible for commitment, authorities with filing responsibility have established extrastatutory "filing considerations" to guide their decision making. In Washington State, for example, filing considerations promulgated by the Washington State Association of Prosecuting Attorneys call for a petition only if:

- a qualified mental health professional has determined that the offender "(a) currently suffers from the requisite mental abnormality or personality disorder and (b) because of that mental condition is likely to engage in predatory acts of sexual violence"
- the offender has a "provable pattern of prior predatory acts" (in practice, at least three prior acts are required)
- the offender was not paroled for his or her most recent offense
- all other civil commitment and/or criminal proceedings have been exhausted
- the victim and/or victim's family has been consulted and their willingness to testify has been considered (Sappington, 1998, p. 11)

An end-of-sentence review referral subcommittee (ESRRS) reviews the files of more than 2,000 adult sex offenders each year in Washington, referring approximately 20 for filing consideration (Schram & Milloy, 1998, p. iv). Prior to 1997, seven petitions (on average) were filed each year (Schram & Milloy, 1998, p. iv). A study released in February 1998 by the Washington State Institute for Public Policy found that, of 61 adult offenders referred by the ESRRS for possible commitment for whom petitions were not filed (during the period July 1990–June 1996), 59% were arrested for one or more new offenses during a follow-up period that ranged from 5 to 70 months (with a mean of 46 months); 28% were arrested for new sex offenses, 15% for violent felony offenses, 33% for nonviolent felony offenses, and 23% for misdemeanors (Schram & Milloy, 1998, p. i). The study, it appears, struck a nerve. In a 12-month period following the study, petitions were filed in 21 of 25 cases referred by the ESRRS (National

Association of State Mental Health Program Directors/Health Services Research Institute [NASMHPD/HSRI], 1999, pp. 22–23).

FREQUENCY OF COMMITMENT

The first generation of laws for the civil commitment of sex offenders generally were used infrequently. In Minnesota, for example, only 221 individuals were committed in the first 30 years (from 1939 to 1969; Minnesota Legislative Auditor, 1994). In the District of Columbia, under a statute in effect since 1948, only 8 individuals currently are committed (Fitch & Hammen, 2001).

Rates of commitment under the newer laws vary from state to state. In California, under a law enacted in January 1996, 4,116 cases had been referred for commitment consideration as of March 1, 2002. Of these cases, 3,692 had been resolved, 345 with commitment, 3,363 with no commitment. The rest were at various stages in the commitment process (California SVP Web site, 2002: http://www.dmh.cahwnet.gov/socp/ff.htm).

In the first 6 months after the effective date of Florida's law, 2,631 individuals were referred for consideration for commitment (Fitch & Hammen, 1999). By January 2002, that number had swollen to 9,307, with 385 committed (or detained pending commitment) and nearly 500 more awaiting further proceedings (Florida SVP Web site, 2002: http://www.folle.state.fl.us/sexual_predators/).

Using its careful review process to screen cases prior to filing, Washington State has managed to keep its commitment rate relatively low. As of spring 2000 (10 years after the statute took effect), 58 offenders had been committed; an additional 49 were institutionalized in the state's "Special Commitment Center" awaiting a commitment hearing (some waiting for as long as 3 years; Duran, 2000, p. A9).

Table 1.1 presents the results of a Fall 2001 survey of the jurisdictions with sex offender commitment laws (Fitch & Hammen, 2001).

PROVISION OF SERVICES

In most states with special sex offender commitment laws, the agency responsible for providing clinical care is the state's mental health authority (the Department of Mental Health). In Massachusetts, however, clinical care is the responsibility of the state's Department of Corrections (Fitch & Hammen, 2001). Washington State has established a special administration within its Department of Social and Health Services—apart from its mental health and corrections administrations—that has responsibility for these services (Duran, 2000).

TABLE 1.1
Jurisdictions With Sex Offender Commitment Laws; Number Committed (2001)

State	Year law effective	No. committed inpatient	No. committed outpatient	No. inpatient awaiting trial
Arizona	1997	70	0	65
California	1996	374	0	105
District of Columbia	1948	8	0	0
Florida	1999	35	0	310
Illinois	1998	92	3	78
Iowa	1998	22	0	12
Kansas	1995	53	2	8
Massachusetts	1999	9	0	88
Minnesota	1939, 1994	175	0	4
Missouri	1999	16	0	34
North Dakota	1997	3	0	0
New Jersey	1999	147	0	18
South Carolina	1998	37	0	23
Virginia	2001	N/A[a]	N/A[a]	N/A[a]
Washington	1990	68	6	69
Wisconsin	1994	207	9	52
Total		1208	20	866

[a] Not yet in effect or implemented at time of survey.

In most states, the agency responsible for clinical care also has responsibility for operation of the inpatient facility. In a few states, however, although clinical care is the Mental Health Department's responsibility, the facility is operated by the Department of Corrections (e.g., Florida and New Jersey; see Fitch & Hammen, 1999). In Washington State, services are provided at the "Special Commitment Center," in a former prison building on the grounds of the McNeil Island Correction Center. The Department of Corrections provides perimeter security. The program was moved to McNeil Island from the Washington State Reformatory in Monroe in April 1998. Services for sentenced offenders continue to be provided at the Monroe facility (Duran, 2000).

In California, committed sex offenders are served at Atascadero State Hospital, a secure psychiatric facility operated by the state's Department of Mental Health. With the influx of sex offenders, however, bed space at Atascadero has become scarce, threatening the displacement of other patients. To preserve Atascadero's beds for the treatment of psychiatric patients, officials in California reportedly are planning for the construction of a new and larger facility exclusively for sex offenders ("An Open Discussion," 1998). Laws for the civil commitment of sex offenders uniformly provide that treatment is one of the purposes of commitment (typically, "care, control, and treatment"). The availability of treatment, however, varies from state to state. In Minnesota and Wisconsin, a wide variety of services are offered, and offenders who participate, by program design, progress from stage to stage in the course of treatment. States with newly enacted laws, however, report difficulty recruiting qualified staff and establishing high-quality programs. In Illinois, state officials, after giving it their "best effort," contracted with a private, managed care organization to develop services for their sex offender population ("An Open Discussion," 1998). In California, officials report that hospital staff with years of experience serving other psychiatric patients have encountered significant difficulty acclimating to the facility's new population of sex offenders. Sources report incidents of sexual contact between staff and patients and at least one marriage ("An Open Discussion," 1998). In Washington, problems implementing the law have resulted in a 6-year court injunction to improve services, assignment of a special master to oversee the treatment program, a contempt citation (for failings ranging from poor living conditions to a lack of meaningful therapy), and a lawsuit that the state settled by paying 16 patients $10,000 each (Duran, 2000).

Recognizing the poor quality of care available in some programs and the need for staff to receive specialized training to cope with the challenges these patients present, professional associations such as the Association for the Treatment of Sexual Abusers (ATSA) have developed standards for practice and sponsor specialty workshops and conferences across the country (see, e.g., ATSA, 2000). Some states offer specialty training internally and require certification of all staff who work with sex offenders (NASMHPD, 1997). Despite these efforts, the standard of care in sex offender treatment programs is not well regulated. State-operated psychiatric hospitals in most states conform to established national standards and have received accreditation from the Joint Commission on the Accreditation of Hospital Organizations (JCAHO). Of the 16 jurisdictions with special sex offender commitment laws, however, only two, California and North Dakota, operate JCAHO-accredited facilities for this population (NASMHPD/HSRI, 1999). The staffing requirements for JCAHO accreditation contemplate hospital-level care, a higher level of care than is generally believed necessary for the "care, control, and treatment" of individuals committed under these special laws.

Staff-to-patient ratios in existing, inpatient sex offender treatment facilities vary from 1 staff per 1.5 patients (North Dakota) to 1.75 staff per patient (Minnesota; see NASMHPD, 1997). Staff composition on a ward typically includes a psychologist, a social worker, one or two activity therapists, and one or more security aides. Psychiatrists are used sparingly. Treatment programs generally follow a cognitive–behavioral/relapse preventive model (see chapter 5, this volume). Services address cognitive distortions (rationalizations that offenders may use to justify their acts), victim empathy, anger management, social skills, relapse prevention (identifying factors that place an offender at risk of reoffense and developing strategies for managing them), and in some cases hormonal therapy (to reduce sexual arousal).

States report that treatment is voluntary and that not everyone consents ("An Open Discussion," 1998). In Washington, approximately two thirds of committed patients participate in treatment (Hamilton, 2000). Those who do not participate remain confined, nonetheless. Some indicate they would prefer to return to prison. Officials in California report that on at least one occasion, a patient has assaulted a staff member for the express purpose of acquiring a criminal charge, hoping that it would lead (as it did) to his discharge from the treatment program and return to the more familiar environment of the penal system ("An Open Discussion," 1998).

ALTERNATIVES TO COMMITMENT

In the last decade, legislation for the special, postsentence commitment of sex offenders has been introduced in at least 42 states. In several states (e.g., Indiana, Maryland, Mississippi, and Tennessee), legislation has been introduced at repeated legislative sessions, never garnering sufficient support to pass (Fitch & Hammen, 2001). Although an effective means of preventing the release of dangerous offenders at the end of their sentence (and, thus, understandably attractive to the general public), these commitment schemes are not universally popular.

Indeed, they have drawn the ire of the mental health professions. In a monograph released in 1999, a task force of the American Psychiatric Association declared:

> [S]exual predator commitment laws represent a serious assault on the integrity of psychiatry. . . . [B]y bending civil commitment to serve essentially non-medical purposes, sexual predator commitment statutes threaten to undermine the legitimacy of the medical model of commitment. . . . [T]his represents an unacceptable misuse of psychiatry. (American Psychiatric Association, 1999, p. 173–174; see chapter 7, this volume)

The NASMHPD (1997) released a statement in opposition as well, observing that special sex offender commitment laws

> disrupt the state's ability to provide services for people with treatable psychiatric illnesses[,] . . . undermine the mission and integrity of the public mental health system[,] . . . divert scarce resources away from people . . . who both need and desire treatment[,] . . . and endanger the safety of others in those facilities who have treatable psychiatric illnesses. (p. 1)

Both the American Psychiatric Association task force and the NASMHPD implore states to shed their pretense that sex offenders require inpatient psychiatric care and address concerns about sex offender recidivism through sentencing reforms or other alternatives within the criminal justice system. Several states have done just that. As an alternative to special civil commitment, the Colorado General Assembly in 1998 enacted a law (captioned "Lifetime Supervision of Sex Offenders") authorizing indeterminate sentences for sex offenders and the possibility of lifetime probation or parole. The law directs the state's Department of Corrections to establish an "intensive supervision parole program" to include "the highest level of supervision that is provided to parolees, ... drug and alcohol screening, treatment referrals and monitoring, including physiological monitoring, and payment of restitution" (Colorado Sex Offender Lifetime Supervision Act of 1998, 16-13-805).

Some states have established task forces to examine all the options and make recommendations for legislation. An interagency committee appointed by the Governor of Connecticut to study that state's system for managing sexually violent offenders strongly advised against special commitment legislation, in favor of

- tougher upfront sentencing for adult sex offenders
- extended and enhanced community supervision for sex offenders on probation or parole
- more consistent reporting (by authorities supervising juveniles) of juveniles' predatory sexual behavior
- improved sex offender assessments (for use in presentence investigations and offender release determinations)
- enhanced treatment for incarcerated offenders

The committee observed that sex offender commitment laws enacted in other states all "share the same goal—to incapacitate sex offenders and to reduce recidivism" (Report of the Committee to Study Sexually Violent Persons, 1999, p. 2). The criminal justice system is best equipped to achieve this goal in the "quickest, most cost-effective" way, the committee reasoned, because public safety is its mission. To use civil commitment, the committee declared, "would collapse the important distinction between criminal punishment and mental health treatment and would result in detrimental effects on both the mental health system and the criminal justice system" (Report of the Committee to Study Sexually Violent Persons, 1999, p. 3). The Connecticut legislature agreed, rejecting proposals for civil commitment and enacting into law several of the committee's recommendations.

In a 1999 survey of state mental health authorities (Fitch & Hammen, 1999), officials in states where commitment legislation failed reported that "sentence enhancement" alternatives (e.g., lifetime parole, habitual offender "two strikes" provisions[3]) were factors that contributed significantly to the legislation's failure. Contributing even more significantly, however, was the fiscal impact of such legislation. (See this volume, chapter 16, for an analysis of the costs states incur in implementing an SVP law.)

The Texas legislature, after considering a variety of sex offender commitment proposals, enacted a law in 1999 for the involuntary commitment of sexually violent predators to outpatient treatment (Texas Civil Commitment of Sexually Violent Predators Act, 1999). The Texas law establishes procedures patterned on those found in other states' inpatient commitment laws, including a multidisciplinary, end-of-sentence review team; prehearing mental health assessments; and a trial at which a judge or jury must determine, beyond a reasonable doubt, that an offender is a repeat sexually violent offender and suffers from a "behavioral abnormality that makes the person likely to engage in a predatory act of sexual violence" (Texas Statutes, 841.003). "Behavioral abnormality" is defined in precisely the same terms as are used to define "mental abnormality" in other states' inpatient commitment laws. On a finding that an offender is a sexually violent predator, however, the disposition is not hospitalization but rather outpatient civil commitment, the requirements of which include supervision by a case manager, "tracking" by a tracking service provided by the Department of Public Safety, and "participation in a specific course of treatment." The treatment plan "may include the monitoring of the person with a polygraph or pletheysmograph" (841.083). The treatment provider may receive annual compensation in an amount not to exceed $6,000. Finally, and in stark contrast to all the other states' commitment laws, the statute expressly forbids housing of the individual "for any period of time" in a mental health facility (841.083).

CONCLUSION

What to do with dangerous sex offenders who complete a criminal sentence and prepare to leave secure confinement is a question that vexes corrections officials, mental health professionals, and law makers in every state. Powerless to extend an offender's sentence once served, officials in some states have looked to civil commitment for the answer. Ordinary commitment laws, however, provide little relief, as very few dangerous sex offenders have the kinds of mental disorders that these laws contemplate. Special commitment laws aimed specifically at sex offenders may enhance public safety, but they wreak havoc on public mental health systems and strain constitutional principles.

---

[3] "Two strikes" provisions ("three strikes" in some states) typically call for a longer (or life) sentence for individuals previously convicted of one or more qualifying sex offenses. In 1998, eight states had such laws specifically targeted at sex offenses.

In the year after the U.S. Supreme Court's decision in *Kansas v. Hendricks*, eight states enacted laws for the special, civil commitment of dangerous sex offenders. The following year, however, only three states joined their ranks, and one state—Oklahoma—repealed a commitment law it had enacted 2 years previously (Fitch & Hammen, 1999). As states with these laws labor to provide adequate services and scramble to fend off legal challenges, it is understandable that the press for legislation in other states has eased. But it has not ceased. Indeed, as this volume goes to press, legislation is pending in Michigan that would provide for the postsentence commitment of a variety of violent offenders found to be dangerous because of a mental abnormality or personality disorder—not just sex offenders (Fitch & Hammen, 2001). Should this legislation pass (and the inevitable legal challenges fail), the current trend to use mental health resources to contain society's misfits (Fitch & Ortega, 2000) will surely accelerate, leaving those with more serious mental disability to fend for themselves—on the streets and (ironically) in the nation's jails and prisons.

REFERENCES

American Psychiatric Association. (1999). *Dangerous sex offenders*. Washington, DC: Author.

"An Open Discussion Concerning Sex Offender Treatment Issues." (1998, October 7). Comments made by state mental health department representatives at the Annual Conference of the Forensic and Legal Divisions of the National Association of State Mental Health Program Directors (moderated by W. L. Fitch & J. Maher), St. Petersburg Beach, FL.

Association for the Treatment of Sexual Abusers (ATSA). (2000, November). *Putting it together: The art of integrating research and practice*. Paper presented at the 19th Annual Research and Treatment Conference, San Diego, CA.

Colorado Sex Offender Lifetime Supervision Act, 16-13-805 (1998).

Community Protection Act, Wash. Laws Ch. 3 (1990).

Duran, S. (2000, April 9). Unfinished treatment. *News Tribune*, pp. 1, 8, 9.

Fitch, W. L. (1998). Sex offender commitment in the United States. *Journal of Forensic Psychiatry, 9*, 237–240.

Fitch, W. L., & Hammen, D. (1999). *Sex offender commitment: A survey of the states*. Unpublished manuscript.

Fitch, W. L., & Hammen, D. (2001). *Sex offender commitment: A survey of the states*. Unpublished manuscript.

Fitch, W. L., & Ortega, R. J. (2000). Law and the confinement of psychopaths. *Behavioral Sciences and the Law, 18*, 663–678.

Hamilton, D. (2000, March 24). [Telephone conversation between R. D. Hamilton, clinical director, Center for Forensic Services, Western State Hospital, Washington State, and W. L. Fitch and D. Hammen, Office of Forensic Services, Maryland Mental Hygiene Administration.]

Jacob Wetterling Act of 1991, 42 U.S.C.A. § 4071 (West 1997).

Kansas v. Crane, 534 U.S. 407 (2002).

Kansas v. Hendricks, 521 U.S. 346 (1997)

Minnesota Legislative Auditor. (1994). *Psychopathic personality commitment laws.* St. Paul, MN: Office of the Legislative Auditor, Program Evaluation Division.

National Association of State Mental Health Program Directors (NASMHPD). (1997). *A tool kit for the SMHA commissioners and directors: Legislation for the psychiatric commitment of sexually violent predators.* Alexandria, VA: Author.

National Association of State Mental Health Program Directors/Health Services Research Institute (NASMHPD/HSRI). (1999). *Evaluation center survey on the civil commitment of sexually violent criminal offender legislation.* Alexandria, VA: NASMHPD.

Report of the Committee to Study Sexually Violent Persons. (1999, February). Report submitted to Governor John G. Rowland, State of Connecticut.

Sappington, S. (1998, April). *Sexually violent predator statutes: Current and future issues for prosecutors.* Paper presented before the National Conference of State Legislators, American Prosecutors Research Institute's National Center for Prosecution of Child Abuse, Washington, DC.

Schram, D., & Milloy, C. D. (1998, February). *Sexually violent predators and civil commitment: A study of the characteristics and recidivism of sex offenders considered for civil commitment but for whom proceedings were declined* (Document No. 98-02-1101). Olympia: Washington State Institute for Public Policy.

Texas Civil Commitment of Sexually Violent Predators Act, V.T.C.A. Health and Safety Code §§ 841 *et seq.,* enacted September 1, 1999.

Texas Statutes 841.003.

Texas Statutes 841.083.

Wash. Laws 71.09.020 (2) (1990).

Wash. Laws 71.09.020 (4) (1990).

Wash. Laws 71.09.030 (1990).

Wash. Laws 71.09.100 (1990).

2

STATE POLICY PERSPECTIVES ON SEXUAL PREDATOR LAWS

ROXANNE LIEB

In examining sexual predator laws, most commentators have concentrated on legal and mental health topics. In this chapter, I approach the issue from a policymaker's view. The chapter answers three questions: What problems are states trying to solve? How do state laws compare? What issues emerge after the laws have been passed?

WHAT PROBLEMS ARE STATES TRYING TO SOLVE?

The United States' first sexually violent predator (SVP) law went into effect in Washington State in 1990. Since then, 14 states have enacted similar laws. By reviewing the circumstances leading up to Washington's law, one can identify the policy dilemmas posed by dangerous sex offenders. Additionally, the purposes of Washington's sexual predator law can be clarified as (a) a narrow solution for a small group of sex offenders and (b) a remedy for a gap created primarily by the state's determinate sentencing system. In most instances, states with indeterminate sentencing systems have sufficient powers to control dangerous sex offenders without an SVP law.

Washington's History With Sex Offender Laws, 1950–1984

The 1990 civil commitment law was not Washington's first effort to confine and treat dangerous sex offenders under civil law. In the 1950s Washington passed a sexual psychopath law authorizing treatment in lieu of punishment for sexual psychopaths and psychopathic delinquents (Wash. Rev. Code § 71.060, 1957); similar laws were passed in about half the states. Sexual psychopath laws assumed that sex offenders suffered from a treatable mental disorder (Hacker & Frym, 1955).

Washington's statute required proof of a mental condition that made the person sexually dangerous. Commitment could only be initiated after the person's guilt or innocence was determined. Courts had the option to send the convicted offender to a state mental health hospital for evaluation of two conditions: (a) whether the person met the definition of sexual psychopathy and (b) whether the person was likely to benefit from the treatment. If met, criminal proceedings could be suspended, and the person was committed to the state hospital until he is "no longer a menace to . . . others" (Wash. Rev. Code § 71.06.020, 1985).

Throughout its history the sexual psychopath program was plagued with problems. Patients escaped and committed brutal rapes and murders. Studies concluded that less than one quarter of its participants were successfully discharged. Critics demanded that the sexual psychopath law be abolished. In 1984 Washington repealed its law.

Sexual psychopathy laws faced similar controversies in other states. California had also passed a sexual psychopathy law. It consistently led the nation in commitments, confining and treating approximately 1,000 sex offenders each year from 1949 through 1980 (Prager, 1982). Studies in the mid-1970s revealed that the sex offenders treated in the program spent considerably less time in confinement than those who were imprisoned (Dix, 1976). When successful graduates of the program committed headline crimes, political groups lobbied against the law. In the mid-1970s a prominent group of psychiatrists publicly criticized the law's therapeutic premises (Group for the Advancement of Psychiatry, 1977). In 1981, California repealed its sexual psychopathy statute, concluding that "the commission of sex offenses is not itself the product of mental disease" (Cal. Stat. Ch. 928 § 4, at 3485, 1981). By the late 1970s and early 1980s, 25 states had repealed or significantly changed their sexual psychopath laws. (Brakel, Parry, & Weiner, 1985).

At the same time, Washington's political leaders reformed the state's criminal sentencing framework. In the early 1980s, the state enacted a determinate sentencing system that emphasized statewide sentencing guidelines and the elimination of parole (Boerner & Lieb, 2001). In 1984, the state legislature enacted sentencing provisions for sex offenses, which created a treatment option for lower risk sex offenders found to be amenable for outpatient treatment. A voluntary prison treatment program was established, but it did not influence the participants' prison length.

1987: The Ground Shifts

In May 1987, Earl Shriner completed a 10-year sentence in Washington State for kidnapping and assaulting two teenage girls. Prior to his discharge, prison officials learned that he was planning to torture children after his release.[1] Because of his history and his stated intentions, prison officials tried vigorously in the late 1980s to civilly commit him at the end of his prison term ("System Just Couldn't Keep Suspect," 1989). Unable to demonstrate the necessary "recent overt act" to prove dangerousness, the state had to release Shriner when his sentence expired. Two years after his release, he raped and strangled a 7-year-old boy in Tacoma, Washington, severed his penis, and left him in the woods to die (Porterfield, 2000). The plight of the little boy and the state's inability to take preventative action earlier with Shriner became a significant news event. Public discussions quickly linked the state's inadequate laws with an earlier tragedy in Seattle involving the kidnapping, rape, and murder of a young businesswoman by a sex offender on work release (Siegel, 1990). In response to the significant public outcry over these crimes, then Governor Booth Gardner appointed a Task Force on Community Protection in 1989 to recommend changes to state laws (Brooks, 1992).

In late 1989, the task force concluded that sentence increases alone were an insufficient remedy to prevent dangerous sex offenders from committing new sex crimes after their release from prison, even when their mental condition, their prior crimes, or statements regarding planned crimes clearly indicated significant risk to the public (Task Force on Community Protection, 1989). Under an indeterminate sentencing system, lengthy parole periods frequently remain when offenders are released from prison, and therefore the state can set conditions and exercise control over the individual. Parole had been abolished under the new determinate sentencing law. Political leaders on the task force and in the legislature were wary of solutions undermining this reform.

Task force leaders, therefore, wanted a remedy that maintained the constructs of the sentencing reform: uniform statewide sentencing guidelines with relatively narrow ranges and strong incentives to prosecutors to accurately charge and prove crimes rather than relying on a parole board's discretion (Task Force on Community Protection, 1989). The task force was persuaded that sex offenders were a heterogeneous group and that

---

[1] During his last months in prison, Shriner designed plans to maim or kill children and made diary entries that identified apparatus he would use. In a conversation with a cell mate, he said he wanted a van customized with cages so he could pick up children, molest them, and kill them.

penalties needed to recognize a broad range of conduct, both in defining crime seriousness and in setting sentence ranges. Multidecade sentences for all sex offenses to ensure adequate public protection were rejected. Instead, the task force proposed proportional sentences for sex crimes, reserving the most powerful interventions for those posing the most serious threats to public safety.

The Task Force on Community Protection (1989) rejected revisions to the state's mental health laws. The state's general commitment law for the mentally ill had been significantly reformed in 1973, replacing long-term institutionalization with short-term treatment that emphasized medication (Washington Laws, 1973). Short-term periods of involuntary commitment were authorized for all but the most seriously impaired individuals. Commitment required a finding of "likelihood of serious harm," as well as a threat manifested by a recent overt act. General commitment standards could not be changed to allow indefinite hospitalization of someone like Earl Shriner while simultaneously excluding mentally ill individuals who did not pose immediate risks (Lieb, 1996).[2]

Thus, the task force crafted a narrow solution: a civil commitment law to confine and treat the most dangerous sex offenders that could be initiated only at the end of a prison term. It would be used very selectively, and fiscal projections were based on this narrow application. The task force also recommended registration and community notification laws (later known as Megan's Law) to protect the public. The Washington Legislature enacted these recommendations in 1990 as the Community Protection Act.

HOW DO SEXUAL PREDATOR STATUTES COMPARE?

Although Washington's SVP statute was not intended as a model for other states, it has served that role. As of 2002, 16 states have passed sexual predator statutes that authorize confinement and treatment following a criminal conviction. An additional state, Texas, requires outpatient treatment for persons committed as a sexual predator. (The remaining analysis does not include Texas because of the significant difference in this statute.) Table 2.1 lists the states and the number of persons detained or committed under SVP statutes as of spring 2002.[3]

The next two tables compare the state laws. Table 2.2 compares key elements of the commitment process and decisions; Table 2.3 covers decision points related to less restrictive alternatives and release. The comparisons reveal the following:

---

[2]New Jersey modified its mental health laws in 1994 to allow commitment of dangerous sex offenders but found this approach had significant disadvantages and enacted an SVP statute in 1998 (Lieb & Matson, 1998).
[3]Compiled in April 2002 by contacting program administrators via e-mail.

TABLE 2.1
Number of Persons Held Under Sexually
Violent Predator Statutes As of Spring 2002

State	No. detained or committed
Arizona	137
California	466
Florida	394
Illinois	150
Iowa	35
Kansas	96
Massachusetts	84
Minnesota	178
Missouri	17
New Jersey	212
North Dakota	8
South Carolina	46
Virginia	0*
Washington	161
Wisconsin	245
Total	2,229

Note. *Statute to be implemented in 2003.

- *Age*: About a third of the states allow commitment of juveniles; others restrict eligibility to persons convicted as adults or those over 18.
- *Offense pattern*: California requires two or more victims; other states require only a single offense.
- *Diagnosis or mental condition*: All states require proof of some mental condition, usually "mental abnormality" and/or "personality disorder."
- *Standard*: The most common standard is "likely to engage"; other variations include "will engage" (California); "substantially probable that the person will engage" (Illinois and Wisconsin); and "more likely than not" (Missouri).
- *Responsible agency*: Fourteen states have assigned responsibility to their human services/mental health agency. Massachusetts selected its Department of Corrections.
- *Setting*: Five states designated a hospital setting (Arizona, California, Florida, Minnesota, North Dakota). One specified a correctional facility (Massachusetts), and the remaining states specified some form of a secure facility. Six states require that the SVP population be segregated from other patients and/or prisoners.
- *Standard of proof*: Eleven states require the highest standard,

TABLE 2.2
State Comparison: Commitment and Treatment

State	Age criteria/eligible offenders	Mental condition/ Likelihood standard	Responsible agency	Setting	Standard of proof/Jury trial	Duration of confinement
Arizona	At least 18	Mental disorder Likely to engage in sexual violence.	Health Services	Hospital	Beyond a reasonable doubt Yes	Indeterminate
California	At least 18 Two or more victims	Currently diagnosed mental disorder The person is a danger to the health and safety of others in that he or she will engage in sexually violent criminal behavior.	Mental Health	Hospital	Beyond a reasonable doubt Yes; unanimous	2 years; can be extended by court with additional petition and trial
Florida	At least 18	Mental abnormality or personality disorder Likely to engage in acts of sexual violence if not confined in a secure facility.	Children and Family Services	Hospital; must be segregated from other patients	Clear and convincing evidence Yes; unanimous	Indeterminate
Illinois	Can include juveniles	Mental disorder Substantially probable that the person will engage in acts of sexual violence.	Human Services	Secure facility provided by Department of Corrections	Beyond a reasonable doubt Yes; unanimous	Indeterminate

State		Criteria	Responsible agency	Facility requirements	Standard of proof	Term
Iowa		Mental abnormality Likely to engage in predatory acts constituting sexually violent offenses if not confined in a secure facility.	Human Services	Must be segregated from other patients and criminal offenders	Beyond a reasonable doubt Yes; unanimous	Indeterminate
Kansas		Mental abnormality Likely to engage in predatory acts of sexual violence.	Social and Rehabilitative Services	Forensic mental health unit within Department of Corrections; must be segregated from other patients	Beyond a reasonable doubt Yes; unanimous	Indeterminate
Massachusetts	Can include juveniles	Mental abnormality or personality disorder Likely to engage in sexual offenses.	Adults: Department of Corrections Juveniles: Department of Youth Correctional facility	Must be segregated from other patients and in a separate building/facility	Beyond a reasonable doubt Yes; unanimous	Indeterminate

Table continues

TABLE 2.2 (*Continued*)

State	Age criteria/eligible offenders	Mental condition/ Likelihood standard	Responsible agency	Setting	Standard of proof/Jury trial	Duration of confinement
Minnesota		*Sexual psychopathic personality:* emotional instability, impulsiveness of behavior, lack of customary standards of good judgment; failure to appreciate the consequences of personal acts. *Sexually dangerous person:* engaged in harmful sexual conduct and manifested a sexual personality or other mental disorder or dysfunction. Likely to engage in acts of harmful sexual conduct to such a degree as to pose a threat to others.	Human Services	Hospital	Clear and convincing evidence No	Indeterminate
Missouri		Mental abnormality More likely than not to engage in sexual violence if not confined to a secure facility.	Mental Health	Appropriate secure facility; must be segregated from other mental health patients and prisoners	Beyond a reasonable doubt Yes; unanimous	Indeterminate

State	Age	Definition	Department	Facility	Standard of proof / Jury	Term
New Jersey	At least 18	Mental abnormality or personality disorder that makes the person likely to engage in sexual violence if not confined in a secure facility.	Human Services	Secure facility operated by the Department of Corrections	Clear and convincing evidence No	Indeterminate
North Dakota		Congenital or acquired condition that is manifested by a sexual disorder, a personality disorder, or other mental disorder or dysfunction Likely to engage in further acts of sexually predatory conduct.	Human Services	Hospital	Clear and convincing evidence No	Indeterminate
South Carolina	Can include juveniles	Mental abnormality or personality disorder Likely to engage in acts of sexual violence.	Mental Health	Secure facility	Beyond a reasonable doubt Yes; unanimous	Indeterminate

Table continues

TABLE 2.2 (Continued)

State	Age criteria/eligible offenders	Mental condition/ Likelihood standard	Responsible agency	Setting	Standard of proof/Jury trial	Duration of confinement
Texas	Can include juveniles	Behavior abnormality Behavioral abnormality that makes the person likely to engage in a predatory act of sexual violence	Council of Sex Offender Treatment	Outpatient treatment	Beyond a reasonable doubt Yes; unanimous	Indeterminate
Virginia		Mental abnormality or personality disorder So likely to commit sexually violent offense that the person constitutes a menace to the health and safety of others.	Mental Health, Retardation and Substance Abuse Services	Mental health facility within secure perimeter of Department of Corrections facility; must be segregated by sight and sound at all times from prisoners; conditional release to variety of settings also possible	Beyond a reasonable doubt Yes; unanimous	Indeterminate

Washington	Can include juveniles	Mental abnormality or personality disorder Likely to engage in predatory acts of sexual violence. Predatory defined as "acts directed toward strangers or individuals with whom a relationship has been established or promoted for the primary purpose of victimization." For individuals living in the community, a recent overt act is required.	Social and Health Services	Mental Health facility within the Department of Corrections	Beyond a reasonable doubt Yes; unanimous	Indeterminate
Wisconsin	Can include juveniles	Mental disorder Substantially probable that the person will engage in acts of sexual violence.	Health and Family Services	Secure mental health facility provided by Department of Corrections	Beyond a reasonable doubt Yes; unanimous	Indeterminate

TABLE 2.3
State Comparison: Less Restrictive Alternative and Release

State	Less restrictive alternative	Release authority	Jury trial	State's burden in opposing releasee
Arizona	Court can order conditional release to a less restrictive alternative at any point	Court	Yes	Beyond a reasonable doubt
California	After commitment, can be placed in forensic conditional release program for 1 year	Court	Yes	Not specified in statute
Florida	None specified in statute	Court	Yes	Clear and convincing evidence
Illinois	Petition for conditional release can be filed when 6 months have elapsed since initial commitment or subsequent petition for release	Court	No	Clear and convincing evidence
Iowa	Not specified in statute	Court	Yes	Beyond a reasonable doubt
Kansas	Court can order to transitional release after hearing	Court	Yes	Statute does not specify
Massachusetts	None specified in statute	Court	Yes	Unless court finds person remains a sexually dangerous person, it shall order discharge
Minnesota	Final program stages allow transitional release	Commissioner; appeal to court	No	Not specified in statute
Missouri	Not specified in statute	Court	Yes	Beyond a reasonable doubt
New Jersey	Court can order conditional discharge with community reintegration plan recommended by treatment team	Court	No	Clear and convincing evidence
North Dakota	None specified in statute	Court	No	Clear and convincing evidence
South Carolina	None specified in statute	Court	Yes	Clear and convincing evidence
Virginia	Court can order conditional release if institutional confinement unnecessary, outpatient treatment or monitoring needed, and conditional release does not present undue public safety risk	Court	No	Beyond a reasonable doubt
Washington	Conditional release after commitment possible; annual reviews necessary	Court	Yes	Beyond a reasonable doubt
Wisconsin	Supervised release possible 18 months after initial confinement	Court	No	Clear and convincing evidence

"beyond a reasonable doubt"; four authorize a standard of "clear and convincing evidence" (Florida, Minnesota, New Jersey, and North Dakota).

- *Jury trial for commitment*: Twelve states authorize a jury trial; 10 states require a unanimous jury verdict.
- *Duration of confinement*: In California, civil commitment under the SVP statute is for 2 years and can be extended with an additional petition and trial. Everywhere else, the confinement is indeterminate.
- *Less restrictive alternative*: Arizona and Virginia allow courts to order individuals to a less restrictive alternative than the initial placement. Most other states provide for this option only as an interim step toward release.
- *Release authority*: Minnesota delegates release decisions to a commissioner. All remaining states rely on the courts.

The process to identify potential SVP candidates varies greatly across the states. The key elements of this selection process include the following:

- *Reviewing sex offenders*: Several states have created screening committees to review prisoners due to be released who have convictions for sex crimes. Typically, structured risk assessment tools are used to screen this population; then, the committee decides which individuals will be referred to a prosecutor or Attorney General's unit, where the filing decision is made. Washington State has filing standards that assist its review committee in making the referral decision (Lieb & Matson, 1998).
- *Qualifications and affiliations of screeners*: For states with multiagency committees, membership is commonly set according to rules requiring representation by particular agencies rather than the individual's background or qualifications. California's statute, in contrast, specifically requires that two clinicians (licensed clinical psychologists or psychiatrists) evaluate each prisoner who appears to meet the statutory criteria and conduct a risk assessment that incorporates actuarial factors as well as clinical factors. Missouri relies on a review committee composed of five prosecutors representing a cross section of urban and rural counties.
- *Decisions to file petitions*: Many states have centralized these decisions in the state Attorney General's office to increase uniformity; others leave them to local prosecuting attorneys.

WHAT ISSUES EMERGE AFTER THE LAW IS PASSED?

Many states' laws are relatively recent, and the facilities are in early development. Washington, however, has over a decade of experiences, including operation in two locations and an extensive litigation history. The issues faced in Washington can be instructive regarding the operational challenges of an SVP statute.

As of spring 2002, Washington's Special Commitment Center (SCC) had 161 residents; two thirds of this population has been committed, and the remaining awaits court action. The program was initially located within the Washington State Reformatory in Monroe, but because of space needs, it was relocated to McNeil Island in 1998. The Island houses a state prison; SCC is located within the prison walls.

The Task Force on Community Protection's predictions of narrow application have been realized. Less than 1% of the released sex offender population has been committed under the law (Washington State Institute for Public Policy, 1998, p. 24). The costs of the law have not been insignificant (see Figure 2.1). For the fiscal years 2001–2003, the legislature allocated $43 million to operate the program, supporting a staff of over 200 (Washington State Department of Social and Health Services, 2001). A permanent 404-bed facility is under construction on McNeil Island, with over 200 beds scheduled for occupancy by 2003. The capital costs for this

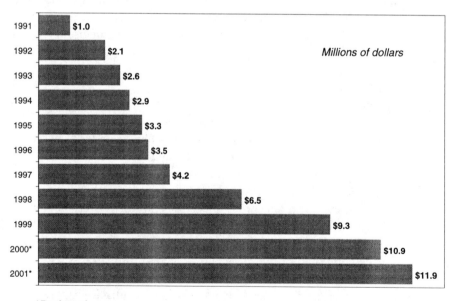

*Projected
Source: Department of Social and Health Services

Figure 2.1. The increasing cost of civil commitment for Washington State.

facility are estimated at over $50 million (Ith, 2001). (Chapter 16 analyzes the costs of an SVP law more extensively.)

Washington's SVP program has been subject to extensive legal challenges at both the state and federal levels. In a 1994 ruling, a federal district court found that Washington was not providing constitutionally required treatment. "The failure of the program to meet constitutional standards to date has contributed to a belief by residents that they have no chance of ever qualifying for release, i.e., that their confinement amounts to a life sentence" (*Turay v. Weston* 1994, p. 4). A 1994 injunction ordered SCC to correct its problems and appointed a special master to oversee compliance with five areas:

- improving staff competence
- rectifying the lack of trust and rapport between residents and treatment providers
- implementing a treatment program that includes all therapy components recognized as necessary key professional standards in comparable programs
- developing and maintaining individual treatment plans for residents with objective benchmarks of improvement
- providing an expert to supervise the clinical work of treatment staff

Between 1994 and 2001, the special master issued 19 reports to the court with numerous court hearings devoted to testimony from program staff, the special master, plaintiffs, and family members. In 1999, 5 years after imposing the injunction, the court found the state's response inadequate and determined that SCC did not meet constitutionally required minimum professional standards for the treatment of sex offenders. The judge found that the state's noncompliance was caused primarily by inadequate resources, as well as the center being treated as an "unwanted stepchild" of a prison. Finding the state in contempt, the court fined the state $50 per day per resident commencing May 1, 2000, unless the program was improved to the court's satisfaction.

Two days after the court's ruling, the state's Governor vowed to aggressively pursue additional funds from the legislature. Program officials were given immediate approval to spend $3 million for additional staffing and design work on a stand-alone facility. The 2000 Legislature appropriated an additional $4.6 million in operating expenses and $14 million in capital construction costs. The federal court continues to monitor the treatment program, and the message is clear that the state invest significant resources in a legitimate treatment facility.

The high costs associated with the SVP statute led lawmakers in 2001 to resurrect a version of indeterminate sentencing for sex offenders (Washington Sen. 6151). For violent sex offenders sentenced after September

2001, judges can find that the person is a sexually violent predator and impose a maximum sentence allowed by sentencing guidelines; the judge can also order the offender to serve a minimum prison term. When that minimum term has been served, the state's version of a parole board (the Indeterminate Sentence Review Board) reviews the case and determines whether the person can be released under supervision. If they decide not to release the person, the board sets another minimum term; this process can be followed up to the maximum term. Following release, offenders are eligible for lifetime parole.

Although this legislation does not repeal the SVP statute, sex offenders judged to pose high risks at sentencing will no longer be sentenced under the determinate sentencing system, and their release will be controlled by decisions about their risk to public safety. The number of likely candidates for commitment as an SVP should fall under this statute, and new commitments to the SCC should be significantly curtailed, if not cease altogether.

Fiscal conservatives were behind this new sentencing law. One of the cosponsors in the House of Representatives said that the legislation was "an attempt at cost avoidance in the future," noting that "all you have to do is look at the numbers to see why this is happening" (Carter, 2000, p. B-1).

WHAT CAN OTHER STATES LEARN FROM THIS HISTORY?

As states grapple with ways to control sexually dangerous persons, leaders should examine experiences from both the sexual psychopathy and the SVP laws. The lessons can be summarized in the following sections.

Sexual Psychopathy Laws

- The population of sex offenders selected for treatment in the civil system and those punished by criminal penalties are difficult to distinguish, resembling each other more likely than not.
- It is difficult to operate a treatment program for a population that includes offenders with very diverse characteristics, including sexual arousal to children, developmental disabilities, antisocial personality disorders, and sexual arousal to violence.
- Determining which program participants have benefited from treatment and/or confinement and are ready for conditional release will be extremely difficult. Some individuals will perform extremely well in the structured environment and be

able to verbalize significant advances in their thinking, behavior, and values. For some, however, these changes will be either superficial or only temporary, revealed later by a reoffense.

- The programs will move persons into less restrictive environments to test their readiness for release. Although partial releases are essential in the path toward full release, the public will expect tight controls on these persons, and failures will be closely scrutinized.
- Some individuals released from the program will reoffend, either during their partial release or after final release. Reoffenses will jeopardize public support for the underlying law and challenge the belief that sex offenders can be effectively treated.
- In the pursuit of fair application, courts will impose requirements and expectations on program management. The efficacy of a treatment law and the program's success will be judged principally by the answer to two questions: How many residents have been released? How many reoffended?

SVP Laws

Although the constitutionality of the SVP laws has been upheld, the courts will continue to scrutinize the day-to-day program operations. At a minimum, states need to pay attention to the following elements:

- The program must operate in a treatment-oriented and not a punitive environment.
- Services need to be consistent with current professional standards for sex offender treatment.
- Conditional release must be achievable.
- The program's operations and decision making must be open to external review through oversight mechanisms and grievance procedures.

CONCLUSION

It is clear that implementing a sexual predator law in a society committed to civil liberties is exceedingly difficult. The first steps are easy. Bills are drafted and passed, along with appropriations for the initial costs. The law will be upheld against constitutional challenges, bolstered by the long history in the United States of restraining persons with serious mental illnesses who pose grave danger to self or others.

The next steps are more precarious. What process will be used to identify and screen those who may meet the legal definition? Risk assessment instruments can guide this sorting process with far more precision than was possible under sexual psychopathy laws. (See this volume, chapter 3, for a more thorough discussion of these instruments and their use.) Even with these scientific advances, however, screening authorities and others will inevitably worry about false negatives, false positives, and the grave consequences of each error.

Once the courts commit individuals, a program must be developed that provides treatment required by the U.S. Constitution and that is effective in reducing the risk to reoffend. Individualized treatment plans are necessary and must be updated regularly. Progress in treatment will need to be charted and clear direction given to residents regarding their goals. In addition, educational, vocational, and recreational opportunities must be offered, with work compensated at the federal minimum wage.

The existing programs operate in a no-man's land between mental hospitals and prisons, mixing laws, procedures, and working cultures from each. Residents will need to be treated similarly to other individuals receiving mental health treatment. However, the public will expect facilities to maintain high-security environments. The courts have made it clear that a program that looks and feels too much like a prison will be declared unconstitutional.

It is clear that passing a sexual predator statute is the easy step. The real challenge for states is to create, fund, and sustain a credible treatment program.

REFERENCES

Boerner, D., & Lieb, R. (2001). Sentencing reforms in the other Washington. In M. Tonry (Ed.), *Crime and justice: A review of research* (Vol. 28, pp. 71–136). Chicago: University of Chicago Press.

Brakel, S. J., Parry, J., & Weiner, B. A. (1985). *The mentally disabled and the law* (3rd ed.). Chicago: American Bar Foundation.

Brooks, A. (1992). The constitutionality and morality of civilly committing violent sexual predators. *University of Puget Sound Law Review, 15*, 709–754.

Cal. Stat. Ch. 928, §4 (1981).

Carter, M. (2000, February 20). New rules for sex predators endorsed: Judges, parole board would get discretion. *Seattle Times*, p. B-1.

Community Protection Act, Wash. Laws Ch. 3 (1990).

Dix, G. (1976). Differential processing of abnormal sex offenders: Utilization of California's mentally disordered sex offender program. *Journal of Criminal Law and Criminology, 67*, 233–243.

Group for the Advancement of Psychiatry. (1977). *Psychiatry and sex psychopath legislation: The 30s to the 80s* (formulated by the Committee on Psychiatry and Law, Rep. No. 98). Dallas, TX: Author.

Hacker, F. J., & Frym, M. (1955). The sexual psychopath act in practice: A critical discussion. *California Law Review, 43,* 766–780.

Ith, I. (2001, January 18). Sex-predator law shifts to new phase. *Seattle Times,* p. A-1.

Lieb, R. (1996). *Washington's sexually violent predator law: Legislative history and comparisons with other states.* Olympia: Washington State Institute for Public Policy.

Lieb, R., & Matson, S. (1998). *Sexual predator laws in the United States: 1998 update.* Olympia: Washington Institute for Public Policy.

Porterfield, E. (2000, April 17). Sex predator law still stirs debate. *Seattle Post Intelligencer.* Retrieved from http://.www.Seattlepi.nwsource.com/local/pred171.shtml

Prager, I. (1982). Sexual psychopathology and child molesters: The experiment fails. *Journal of Juvenile Law, 6,* 49–79.

Siegel, B. (1990, May 10). Locking up "sexual predators." *Los Angeles Times,* p. A31.

System just couldn't keep suspect. (1989, May 23). *Tacoma News Tribune,* p. A-1.

Task Force on Community Protection. (1989). *Final report.* Olympia: State of Washington

Turay v. Weston, No. C91-664-WD (W.D. Wash., June 6, 1994) (order granting preliminary injunction).

Washington Laws Ch. 142 (1973).

Wash. Rev. Code § 71.060 (1957).

Wash. Rev. Code § 71.06.020 (1985).

Wash. Rev. Code § 71.05 (1989).

Washington Senate Bill 6151, enacted June 26, 2001.

Washington State Department of Social and Health Services. (2001). *SCC budget.* Retrieved from http://www-app2.wa.gov/dshs/budget/sccmain/shtm

Washington State Institute for Public Policy. (1998). *Sex offenses in Washington State: 1998 update* (Document No. 98-08–1101, 24). Olympia, WA: Author.

II

SEX OFFENDERS AND DANGEROUSNESS

3

WHO IS DANGEROUS AND WHEN ARE THEY SAFE? RISK ASSESSMENT WITH SEXUAL OFFENDERS

R. KARL HANSON

Nobody seriously questions the right of individuals to protect themselves from violent offenders. If we see somebody about to molest a child or rape a woman, we would try to stop him. But who is dangerous? It turns out that this question is more difficult than it initially appears. Not all sex offenders go on to commit new crimes, and those who do rarely announce their intentions to reoffend. Expert evaluators are often wrong. On average, the accuracy of expert opinion in predicting sexual recidivism is only slightly above chance levels (average $r = .10$; Hanson & Bussière, 1998). Despite the dismal performance of some commonly used assessment procedures, evaluators knowledgeable about recent research have the potential of providing risk assessment worthy of consideration in many applied contexts.

The recent introduction of civil commitment statutes, like those dis-

This chapter paraphrases some material first contained in Hanson (1998, 2000). Copyright 1998 by the American Psychological Association (APA). Adapted with permission of the author and APA.

cussed in chapters 1 and 2, has focused attention on the quality of risk assessments for sexual offenders. For these statutes, risk assessments are required to answer two central questions: (a) Initially, is the offender at sufficiently high risk to justify commitment? (b) Once committed, has the offender's risk level changed sufficiently to justify release? Although these questions are closely related, the answers require the consideration of different types of risk factors. The decision to commit can be based entirely on static, historical factors. If an offender has a long history of sexually offending despite all efforts to stop him, then this history can be sufficient justification that the offender is high risk. The release decision, however, requires the consideration of dynamic (changeable) factors. Before a high-risk offender is released, decision makers need to be convinced that the characteristics that predisposed the offender to sexual crime have diminished or have been effectively controlled.

As will be demonstrated, there is a substantial body of research on static risk factors that can be used to identify sex offenders with a long-term propensity to reoffend. In contrast, the research on dynamic factors is rather limited and allows for only the most tentative conclusions concerning changes in risk levels. The consequence is that there is much more evidence to justify committing offenders than there is for releasing them.

RECIDIVISM BASE RATES

Before considering characteristics that increase or decrease recidivism potential, it is useful to consider the expected recidivism rate for the average sex offender—the recidivism base rate. Contrary to common opinion, the observed recidivism rate of sexual offenders is relatively low. Based on a review of 61 recidivism studies involving close to 24,000 sex offenders, only 13.4% recidivated with a new sexual offence within 4 to 5 years (Hanson & Bussière, 1998). Approximately 12% of sex offenders recidivated with a nonsexual violent offence (e.g., assault), with rapists violently reoffending more often (22%) than child molesters (10%). When recidivism was defined as any reoffence, then the rates were predictably higher (36% overall).

The observed recidivism rates are underestimates of the actual rates because many sexual offences are never detected. The extent of the underestimation is the topic of active debate—a debate that is likely to remain active because definitive evidence is, by definition, unavailable. Nevertheless, we know that the observed sex offence recidivism rates can increase to 30%–40% as the follow-up period extends over 20 years (Hanson, Steffy, & Gauthier, 1993; Prentky, Lee, Knight, & Cerce, 1997). The inclusion of arrests and informal reports will also provide estimates substantially higher than those based solely on official convictions (e.g., Marshall & Barbaree, 1988; Prentky et al., 1997). However, even with long follow-up periods and thorough searches, studies rarely find sex offence recidivism rates greater than 40%. Any recidivism is troubling, but the available evidence does not support the popular belief that sexual offenders inevitably reoffend. The overall recidivism rate of sex offenders is, on average, less than the rate for nonsexual criminals (Beck & Shipley, 1989).

RECIDIVISM RISK FACTORS

Evaluators are most likely to provide valid assessments when they consider factors actually related to risk. The strongest evidence that a characteristic is a risk factor comes from follow-up studies. Follow-up studies compare the recidivism rate of offenders with a particular characteristic (e.g., married) with the rate of offenders with a different characteristic (e.g., single).

Follow-up studies have found that the factors that predict general recidivism are not identical to the factors that predict sexual recidivism. In general, the same factors predict nonsexual recidivism among sex offenders and nonsexual offenders. For both groups, the strongest predictors are prior criminal history, juvenile delinquency, antisocial personality, age, minority race, and substance abuse (Gendreau, Little, & Goggin, 1996; Hanson & Bussière, 1998). However, risk scales that effectively predict general recidivism typically have less success in predicting sexual offence recidivism. Because the procedures for assessing general recidivism are well described elsewhere (Andrews & Bonta, 1998; Quinsey, Harris, Rice, & Cormier, 1998), this chapter focuses specifically on sexual recidivism.

Table 3.1 presents the most well-established predictors of sexual offence recidivism drawn from Hanson and Bussière (1998). All of these factors have been replicated in at least four studies, allowing evaluators to be confident that they are valid risk factors. The results are presented as r, the correlation coefficient. The correlation coefficient can range from 0 to 1, with 0 indicating chance levels and 1 indicating perfect prediction. The values of r can be interpreted as the percentage difference in the recidivism rates of those offenders with or without a particular characteristic.

The strongest predictors of sexual offence recidivism are variables related to sexual deviancy, such as deviant sexual preferences, prior sexual offences, early onset of sex offending, and diverse sex crimes. The single strongest predictor in Hanson and Bussière's (1998) study was sexual interest in children as measured by phallometric assessment. Phallometric assessment involves the direct monitoring of penile response when the respondent is presented with various types of erotic stimuli (Launay, 1994).

Measures of criminal lifestyle, such as antisocial personality disorder and prior criminal history, are also related to sexual recidivism. Although

TABLE 3.1
Predictors of Sexual Offence Recidivism

Risk factor	r	n (k)
Sexual deviance		
PPG sexual interest in children	.32	4,853 (7)
Any deviant sexual preference	.22	570 (5)
Prior sexual offenses	.19	11,294 (29)
Any stranger victims	.15	465 (4)
Early onset	.12	919 (4)
Any unrelated victims	.11	6,889 (21)
Any boy victims	.11	10,294 (19)
Diverse sex crimes	.10	6,011 (5)
Criminal history/lifestyle		
Antisocial personality	.14	811 (6)
Any prior offenses	.13	8,683 (20)
Demographic factors		
Age (young)	.13	6,969 (21)
Single (never married)	.11	2,850 (8)
Treatment history		
Treatment dropout	.17	806 (6)

Note. This table was published previously in *Risk Assessment*, by R. K. Hanson, 2000, Beaverton, OR: Association for the Treatment of Sexual Abusers, and in "What Do We Know About Sex Offender Risk Assessment?" by R. K. Hanson, 1998, *Psychology, Public Policy, and Law, 4*, 50–72. The *r* is the average correlation coefficient from Hanson and Bussière (1998); *k* is the number of studies; *n* is the total sample size. PPG = penile plethysmography.

there is a debate about the extent to which treatment reduces recidivism (see this volume, chapter 5), it is clear that those offenders who drop out of treatment are higher risk than offenders who complete treatment programs.

COMBINING FACTORS INTO ACTUARIAL RISK SCALES

No single factor is strongly enough related to recidivism that it can be used on its own. Consequently, evaluators will want to consider a range of risk factors. There are three plausible ways in which risk factors can be combined: empirically guided clinical judgment, pure actuarial, and adjusted actuarial prediction.

In the guided clinical approach, evaluators consider a range of empirically validated risk factors and then form an overall opinion concerning the offender's recidivism risk (e.g., Boer, Hart, Kropp, & Webster, 1997). Although the accuracy of clinical judgment has generally been unimpressive, there are several examples in which empirically guided clinical judgments have yielded adequate results (Dempster, 1998; Epperson, Kaul, & Huot, 1995). In contrast, the actuarial approach not only identifies the relevant factors but also provides explicit rules for combining risk factors into specific probability estimates.

When actuarial tools are available, they have generally proved more accurate than clinical judgment (Grove & Meehl, 1996). The prediction of sexual recidivism is no exception (Hanson & Bussière, 1998). The major problem with actuarial approaches, however, is that no scale can claim to consider all relevant risk factors. It is always possible that an offender has special characteristics that mitigate the prediction provided by the actuarial scale. Consequently, many evaluators conduct clinically adjusted actuarial predictions in which the actuarial predictions are adjusted up or down on the basis of external factors. For example, the risk may be increased for a "low-risk" offender who stated his intention to reoffend, or it may be decreased for a "high-risk" offender crippled by disease.

The optimal approach to risk assessment depends, to a large extent, on the quality of the available research. In the murky, initial stages, simply identifying relevant risk factors is a significant advance. Given valid risk factors, evaluators can then consider how best to combine the factors into risk scales. The extent to which evaluators should deviate from the predictions provided by risk scales is a topic of active debate. Some experts argue that clinical prediction is so inferior to actuarial prediction that any adjustments should be avoided (Quinsey et al., 1998). Others argue that the existing scales neglect many important risk factors.

ACTUARIAL RISK SCALES

Table 3.2 presents the actuarial scales most commonly used to assess risk with sexual offenders. The first three scales were developed to predict general or violent recidivism, whereas the latter four scales focus on sexual offence recidivism. A detailed evaluation of the strengths and weaknesses of each measure is beyond the scope of this chapter; instead, only brief comments are provided on the measures' accuracy in predicting general, violent, and sexual recidivism. In the table, "moderate" levels of predictive accuracy correspond to correlations in the .25 to .30 range (Receiver Operating Characteristic [ROC] areas ~.70), and "high" accuracy corresponds to correlations in the .35 to .45 range (ROC areas ~.75). The area under the ROC curve can be interpreted as the probability that a randomly selected recidivist would have a more deviant score than a randomly selected non-recidivist. When considering the extent to which the scale has been successfully replicated, "high" indicates that consistent results have been found by several independent research teams, "moderate" indicates that the results have been found in at least two different settings, and "low" indicates that the results have been replicated, but all the samples were from the same setting.

The Violence Risk Appraisal Guide (VRAG; Quinsey et al., 1998) is among the most accurate risk measures for general violence, but it was not intended to assess the risk for sexual recidivism. The Sex Offender

TABLE 3.2
Risk Scales Commonly Used With Sex Offenders

Scale	No. of items	Type of items	Type of recidivism predicted	Strength of prediction	Strength of replication
VRAG	12	PCL–R, age, separation from parents, alcohol problems, childhood maladjustment, criminal history, marital status, victim injury, failure on conditional release	violent general	high high	high
SORAG	14	Similar to VRAG plus phallometric assessment	violent sexual	high moderate	low
PCL–R	20	Shallow affect, parasitic lifestyle, criminal versatility, impulsivity, lack of remorse, manipulative, glib, superficial	general violent	moderate moderate	high
MnSOST	21	Prior sex offences, violation of conditional release, use of force, age of victim, stranger victims, juvenile delinquency, substance abuse, employment, treatment drop-out, age	sexual	moderate	moderate
MnSOST–R	16	Similar to MnSOST but with empirically based weights	sexual	high	low
RRASOR	4	Prior sex offences, male victims, unrelated victims, age	sexual	moderate	moderate
Static–99	10	RRASOR items + nonsexual violence, total sentencing dates, stranger victims, unmarried, noncontact offences	sexual violent	moderate moderate	moderate

Note. This table is a simplified version of a table previously published in *Risk Assessment*, by R. K. Hanson, 2000, Beaverton, OR: Association for the Treatment of Sexual Abusers. VRAG = Violence Risk Appraisal Guide (Quinsey, Harris, Rice, & Cormier, 1998); SORAG = Sex Offender Risk Appraisal Guide (Quinsey et al., 1998); PCL–R = Psychopathy Checklist—Revised (Hare, 1991); MnSOST–R = Minnesota Sex Offender Screening Tool—Revised (Epperson, Kaul, & Hesselton, 1998); MnSOST = Minnesota Sex Offender Screening Tool (Epperson, Kaul, & Huot, 1995); RRASOR = Rapid Risk Assessment for Sex Offence Recidivism (Hanson, 1997); Static–99 (Hanson & Thornton, 1999).

Risk Appraisal Guide (SORAG; Quinsey et al., 1998) is a revision of the VRAG for sex offenders. The resulting scale is a good predictor of general violent recidivism and a moderate predictor of sexual recidivism (Barbaree, Seto, Langton, & Peacock, 2001). Both the VRAG and the SORAG include the Psychopathy Checklist—Revised (PCL–R; Hare, 1991) along with a number of other indicators of negative childhood adjustment, demographics, and criminal history. On its own, the PCL–R is a moderate predictor of both general and violent recidivism (Hemphill, Hare, & Wong, 1998).

The Minnesota Sex Offender Screening Tool (MnSOST; Epperson et al., 1995) was specifically designed to assess the risk of sexual recidivism among extrafamilial child molesters and rapists (incest offenders excluded). The revised version of the MnSOST, the MnSOST–R (Epperson, Kaul, & Hesselton, 1998), contains essentially the same items as the original version but uses an empirically based weighting system. A cross-validation of the MnSOST–R on a new sample of 220 offenders from Minnesota found moderate levels of predictive accuracy (r = .35; Epperson et al., 2000), although it did less well in a Canadian sample (r = .14; Barbaree et al., 2001). Further research is needed before the extent to which the MnSOST–R generalizes to diverse samples is known. Both the MnSOST and MnSOST–R were constructed from preestablished groups of recidivists and nonrecidivists, which makes it difficult to directly translate the scores into recidivism rates.

The Rapid Risk Assessment for Sex Offence Recidivism (RRASOR; Hanson, 1997) was developed to assess the risk for sex offence recidivism using a limited number of easily scored items. The initial pool of items was selected from Hanson and Bussière's (1998) meta-analysis and tested on seven different samples from Canada, the United States, and the United Kingdom. The scale is moderately accurate in the prediction of sexual recidivism but has little relationship to general or nonsexual violent recidivism (Barbaree et al., 2001).

Static–99 (Hanson & Thornton, 1999, 2000) combined the RRASOR items with the easily scored items from Thornton's Structured Anchored Clinical Judgement scale (SAC–J; Grubin, 1998). When tested in four diverse samples, the resulting scale predicted sex offence recidivism (average r = .33) better than either original scale (RRASOR or SAC–J). Static–99 also showed moderate accuracy in predicting any violent recidivism (average r = .32). In comparison, Hemphill et al. (1998) reported the average correlation between the PCL–R and violent recidivism to be .27.

HOW ACCURATE ARE THE RISK SCALES?

If a risk scale is to be used in applied contexts, then it is important that the degree of predictive accuracy is sufficient to inform rather than mislead. Critics could suggest, for example, that a correlation in the .30 range is insufficient for decision making because it only accounts for 10% of the variance. Even if such an argument is correct (and many argue that it is not), most decision makers are not particularly concerned about the "percentage of variance accounted for." Instead, applied risk decisions typically hinge on whether offenders surpass a specified probability of recidivism (e.g., more than 50%).

The relationship between Static–99 scores and sexual recidivism is presented in Figure 3.1 to illustrate the predictive accuracy of the available risk scales. The Static–99 scores from Hanson and Thornton (2000) were categorized as low (0, 1; n = 257), medium-low (2, 3; n = 410), medium-high (4, 5; n = 290), and high (6 plus; n = 129). The results are presented as survival curves, an analytic technique commonly used to track mortality in medical research. The curves present the cumulative probability of reconviction for a sexual offence over 20 years. As can be seen in Figure 3.1, Static–99 identified a substantial subsample (approximately 12%) of offenders whose long-term risk for sexual recidivism was greater than 50%. Most of the offenders, however, were in the lower risk categories, with long-term recidivism risk of 10% to 20%. Differences of this magnitude (10% to 50%) should be of interest to applied decision makers in many contexts.

DYNAMIC VARIABLES

A review of Table 3.1 and Table 3.2 shows that most of the established risk factors are static variables (e.g., offence characteristics) or highly

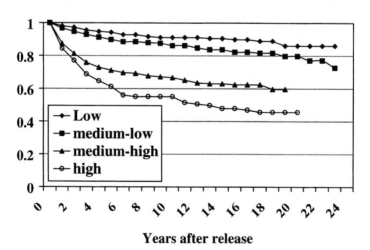

Years after release

Figure 3.1. The relationship between Static–99 scores and sexual recidivism (from Hanson & Thornton, 2000).

stable characteristics (e.g., personality disorders, deviant sexual preferences). All of the risk scales commonly used with sexual offenders contained predominantly static factors. Dynamic risk factors have been identified in a number of individual studies, but few have been replicated, and none have strong research support.

Recent research, however, suggests that the consideration of dynamic factors can increase the accuracy of risk assessments based solely on static factors (Hanson & Harris, 2000, 2001). For therapists interested in treatment targets, there are several dynamic factors worth considering. Recidivists, compared with nonrecidivists, tend to have intimacy deficits (i.e., problems in forming long-term love relationships). Furthermore, the social networks of recidivist sex offenders tend to be poor, comprising a disproportionate number of relatives and friends who support deviant lifestyles or inadequate coping strategies (Hanson & Harris, 2000). There is also some evidence that those offenders who hold attitudes tolerant of sex offending (e.g., "women in short skirts are asking to be raped" and "some kids enjoy sex with adults") are those most likely to recidivate. One of the more interesting problems associated with sex offending is the tendency to cope with stressful life events through sexual fantasies or behavior (Cortoni & Marshall, 2001). Another potential treatment target is impulsivity or poor general self-regulation. Offenders who have unstable lifestyles (e.g., frequent moves, unemployment, substance abuse, "partying") can be expected to have difficulty conforming to the demands of treatment and community supervision.

Although negative mood does not predict long-term recidivism, an acute worsening of mood is associated with increased recidivism risk. An offender who is chronically upset is at no greater risk than an offender who is generally happy, but both offenders become at increased risk when their mood deteriorates. Other acute risk factors include substance abuse, acute anger, and lack of cooperation with community supervision (Hanson & Harris, 2000, 2001).

CONCLUSION

Knowing that someone has committed a sexual offence is insufficient evidence that the offender is high risk. Most sexual offenders are never reconvicted for a new sexual offence. Consequently, blanket policies targeting all sex offenders (e.g., "one strike" laws) can be expected to expend resources on large groups of sexual offenders who would have stopped offending given even minimal interventions. Nevertheless, the available research evidence suggests that it is possible to identify a small group of high-risk sex offenders for whom the probability of eventual recidivism is greater than 50%.

The established risk procedures, however, are based almost entirely on static, historical factors. The neglect of dynamic risk factors for sex offenders contrasts sharply with the research on nonsexual criminals in which dynamic factors are among the strongest predictors of general criminal recidivism (Gendreau et al., 1996). An unfortunate consequence of our limited knowledge of dynamic risk factors is that we have better evidence for identifying sex offenders as dangerous than we have for determining when they are safe to be released. Not all sex offenders reoffend, and even high-risk offenders can change their ways. Previous research, however, has found that evaluators have had little success in determining when sex offenders have benefited from treatment. Pending the required advances in research knowledge, we can only hope that today's evaluators of treatment outcome are more accurate than their predecessors.

REFERENCES

Andrews, D. A., & Bonta, J. (1998). *The psychology of criminal conduct* (2nd ed.). Cincinnati, OH: Anderson.

Barbaree, H. E., Seto, M. C., Langton, C. M., & Peacock, E. J. (2001). Evaluating the predictive accuracy of six risk assessment instruments for adult sex offenders. *Criminal Justice and Behavior, 28,* 490–521.

Beck, A. J., & Shipley, B. E. (1989). *Recidivism of prisoners released in 1983* (U.S. Bureau of Justice Statistics Special Report). Washington, DC: U.S. Department of Justice.

Boer, D. P., Hart, S. D., Kropp, P. R., & Webster, C. D. (1997). *Manual for the Sexual Violence Risk–20.* Vancouver, British Columbia, Canada: British Columbia Institute Against Family Violence.

Cortoni, F. A., & Marshall, W. L. (2001). Sex as a coping strategy and its relationship to juvenile sexual history and intimacy in sexual offenders. *Sexual Abuse: A Journal of Research and Treatment, 13,* 27–43.

Dempster, R. J. (1998). *Prediction of sexually violent recidivism: A comparison of risk assessment instruments.* Unpublished master's thesis, Department of Psychology, Simon Fraser University, Burnaby, British Columbia, Canada.

Epperson, D. L., Kaul, J. D., & Hesselton, D. (1998, October). *Final report on the development of the Minnesota Sex Offender Screening Tool—Revised (MnSOST–R).* Paper presented at the Association for the Treatment of Sexual Abusers 17th Annual Conference, Vancouver, British Columbia, Canada.

Epperson, D. L., Kaul, J. D., & Huot, S. J. (1995, October). *Predicting risk of recidivism for incarcerated sex offenders: Updated development on the Sex Offender Screening Tool (SOST).* Paper presented at the Association for the Treatment of Sexual Abusers 14th Annual Conference, New Orleans, LA.

Epperson, D. L., Kaul, J. D., & Huot, S. J., Hesselton, D., Alexander, W., & Goldman, R. (2000, November). *Cross-validation of the Minnesota Sex Offender*

Screening Tool—Revised. Paper presented at the Association for the Treatment of Sexual Abusers 19th Annual Conference, San Diego, CA.

Gendreau, P., Little, T., & Goggin, C. (1996). A meta-analysis of the predictors of adult offender recidivism: What works! *Criminology, 34,* 575–607.

Grove, W. M., & Meehl, P. E. (1996). Comparative efficiency of informal (subjective, impressionistic) and formal (mechanical, algorithmic) prediction pocedures: The clinical–statistical controversy. *Psychology, Public Policy, and Law, 2,* 293–323.

Grubin, D. (1998). *Sex offending against children: Understanding the risk* (Police Research Series Paper 99). London, UK: Home Office.

Hanson, R. K. (1997). *The development of a brief actuarial risk scale for sexual offense recidivism* (User Report No. 97-04). Ottawa, Ontario, Canada: Department of the Solicitor General of Canada.

Hanson, R. K. (1998). What do we know about sex offender risk assessment? *Psychology, Public Policy, and Law, 4,* 50–72.

Hanson, R. K. (2000). *Risk assessment.* Beaverton, OR: Association for the Treatment of Sexual Abusers.

Hanson, R. K., & Bussière, M. T. (1998). Predicting relapse: A meta-analysis of sexual offender recidivism studies. *Journal of Consulting and Clinical Psychology, 66,* 348–362.

Hanson, R. K., & Harris, A. J. R. (2000). Where should we intervene? Dynamic predictors of sex offense recidivism. *Criminal Justice and Behavior, 27,* 6–35.

Hanson, R. K., & Harris, A. J. R. (2001). A structured approach to evaluating change among sexual offenders. *Sexual Abuse: A Journal of Research and Treatment, 13,* 105–122.

Hanson, R. K., Steffy, R. A., & Gauthier, R. (1993). Long-term recidivism of child molesters. *Journal of Consulting and Clinical Psychology, 61,* 646–652.

Hanson, R. K., & Thornton, D. (1999). *Static–99: Improving actuarial risk assessments for sexual offenders* (User Report No. 1999-02). Ottawa, Ontario, Canada: Department of the Solicitor General of Canada.

Hanson, R. K., & Thornton, D. (2000). Improving risk assessments for sex offenders: A comparison of three actuarial scales. *Law and Human Behavior, 24,* 119–136.

Hare, R. D. (1991). *The Revised Psychopathy Checklist.* Toronto, Ontario, Canada: Multi-Health Systems.

Hemphill, J. F., Hare, R. D., & Wong, S. (1998). Psychopathy and recidivism: A review. *Legal and Criminological Psychology, 3,* 139–170.

Launay, G. (1994). The phallometric assessment of sex offenders: Some professional and research issues. *Criminal Behaviour and Mental Health, 4,* 48–70.

Marshall, W. L., & Barbaree, H. E. (1988). The long-term evaluation of a behavioural treatment program. *Behaviour Research and Therapy, 26,* 499–511.

Prentky, R. A., Lee, A. F. S., Knight, R. A., & Cerce, D. (1997). Recidivism rates among child molesters and rapists: A methodological analysis. *Law and Human Behavior, 21,* 635–659.

Quinsey, V. L., Harris, G. T., Rice, M. E., & Cormier, C. A. (1998). *Violent offenders: Appraising and managing risk.* Washington, DC: American Psychological Association.

4

EVALUATING OFFENDERS UNDER A SEXUALLY VIOLENT PREDATOR LAW: THE PRACTICAL PRACTICE

ROY B. LACOURSIERE

Sexually violent predator (SVP) laws have been implemented by several states, and other states are considering them. (See this volume, chapters 2 and 3, for a general description of these laws.) These laws generally allow for the commitment of certain sexual offenders to a specialized mental health facility for an indeterminate period. Although the definition of an SVP can vary, it generally means a convicted sex offender who suffers from a mental abnormality or personality disorder that makes him (or her) likely to reoffend.

These SVP laws require mental health professionals (MHPs) to evaluate certain sex offenders currently serving time in prison to determine if they meet the criteria for being SVPs (Lacoursiere, Logan, & Peterson, 1998). The laws also require MHPs to later evaluate whether sex offenders previously committed as SVPs are subsequently less at risk to reoffend and are now safe to be released to a lesser level of restriction. Because the legal definition of an SVP is a relatively new concept and this is an area of fairly active litigation and appellate review, it is not entirely clear what the details of the SVP definition mean in practice for the law or for the mental health field.

This chapter sets out a general approach for conducting SVP evaluations for the initial commitment and for subsequent release-related purposes. It is a selective overview of SVP evaluations with an emphasis on practical forensic MHP practice in this area. The chapter concentrates on male pedophilic and rape perpetrators, the vast majority of offenders coming within the sweep of SVP laws. Female and adolescent offenders will generally not be included, not because they are excluded by these laws, but because their numbers in SVP settings are still small and their evaluations entail special considerations beyond the scope of this chapter. Although intended primarily for MHPs, attorneys, judges, and other readers interested in SVP evaluations should also find this chapter helpful. Before discussing SVP evaluations, I briefly provide some general definitions of terms commonly used and the legal processes in SVP cases.

SVP statutes: Each state's SVP law provides the relevant parameters for the evaluator. SVP laws vary, and an evaluator must know the details of the current state statute as well as case law developments. In view of these jurisdictional differences and the general nature of this chapter, specific state statutes and case law will not be cited. Nonetheless SVP laws in various jurisdictions have considerable commonality, except for Texas, where treatment in the community is used rather than commitment to a residential institution.

Screening procedures prior to prison release: Various procedures are generally triggered when a person convicted of a qualifying sexual offense is nearing release and may meet SVP statutory criteria. These procedures may include notifying the state attorney general and a multidisciplinary team established by the Department of Corrections (DOC). After receiving this notice, this team does a preliminary assessment, usually by means of a record review, as to whether the person apparently meets the SVP criteria, including the degree of reoffending risk. The team then notifies the relevant prosecuting attorney of its findings.

Probable cause hearing and subsequent trial: The prosecuting attorney then decides whether to file a commitment petition. If filed, a probable cause hearing will be held. If a judge finds probable cause, the state will conduct an SVP evaluation. If the state MHPs find that the person clinically meets the criteria for an SVP, the matter will then usually proceed to trial, in which in most states the government must prove beyond a reasonable doubt that the individual is an SVP. (For a review of burdens of proof in states with an SVP law, Table 2.1.) Most SVP laws authorize the individual to hire his own expert at state expense to conduct a forensic evaluation and to testify at trial.

There are some differences when the initial SVP evaluations are done by private MHPs or by the state. For example, between private and state

MHPs there may be differences in access to the evaluee, relative privacy for conducting the evaluation, resources available, and ease of availability of certain records. There may also be biases toward certain findings, with, for example, state evaluators having to resist returning the findings desired by the state's prosecutors.

Qualifications for SVP evaluators: It is important to insist on adequate MHP qualifications for SVP work. Because SVP laws are new and more states are enacting them (see this volume, chapters 1 and 2, for a summary of which states have enacted an SVP law), there is a shortage of qualified people to do evaluations. Presently, SVP statutes generally say little about standards for who may conduct these evaluations. For example, Kansas has not set minimal requirements, but California has done so (see La Fond, 1998). In any event, MHPs should not do SVP evaluations without adequate basic knowledge, skill, and experience with sex offenders. At a minimum, the evaluator must know sufficiently the professional literature on sexual and other offenders and on paraphilias and their treatment (see, e.g., Marshall, Fernandez, Hudson, & Ward, 1998; Schlank & Cohen, 1999; Schwartz, 1999) and must have experience in evaluating and usually treating sex offenders. The evaluator should know appropriate methods of investigating child abuse claims, the changing literature on normative child sexual behavior (e.g., Friedrich, Grambsch, Broughton, Kuiper, & Beilke, 1991; Wood & Wright, 1995), and the effects of rape on victims. And evaluators must be familiar with the literature on risk assessment. (See this volume, chapter 3, for a thorough discussion of risk assessment for sexual offenders.) This knowledge of risk literature needs to include the most recent information, which is often available on the World Wide Web, where updates and corrections of printed materials may be found (see, e.g., references below on risk assessment instruments). Because of the usefulness and need for this evaluative expertise, several professional organizations now provide courses on how to conduct SVP evaluations.

Because these evaluations may require MHPs to testify, evaluators must be skilled at appearing in court. Anyone who is too uncomfortable to testify should avoid this work if possible. (This may not be easy for some state MHPs because they may be the only available evaluators.)

Statutory definitions: A number of definitions are crucial for the forensic evaluator. Although specific definitions vary from state to state, most definitions of an SVP generally require (a) prior conviction for a qualifying sexually violent crime, (b) some particular type or types of mental condition, and (c) a nexus between the mental condition and sexual (mis)behavior that causes the individual to be a significant risk to reoffend in a sexually violent way if released from confinement. It is the causal nexus between mental abnormality and sexual dangerousness that justifies the use of civil commitment to confine and treat the individual to protect the public and to decrease the offender's risk of sexual violence recidivism.

Although all individuals being evaluated will have been convicted of a qualifying sex crime, the evaluator, nonetheless, must learn enough about the nature and details of that crime to understand the evaluee's behavior then and how it may be relevant to the offender's risk for future sexually violent criminal conduct. An additional condition required for commitment was recently imposed by the U.S. Supreme Court in *Kansas v. Crane* (2002)—that the offender's condition imposes a serious difficulty in controlling his behavior. Although state statutes do not yet reflect this condition, forensic evaluators will need to opine on whether the offender will be able to control his sexual (mis)conduct as a result of his abnormality.

SVP EVALUATIONS

SVP evaluations are discussed primarily for several main junctures: (a) postprobable cause or pretrial evaluation for the initial SVP commitment, (b) scheduled annual or other reviews after admission to the SVP treatment program, (c) release from the SVP inpatient program to the transitional release phase of the SVP program, (d) release from the transitional release phase to the conditional release phase of the SVP program, (e) final release after time in the conditional release phase of the program, and (f) other evaluations. For example, in Kansas the committed person may petition for release at other times even if the secretary of social and rehabilitation services has not recommended release (Commitment of Sexually Violent Predators Act of 1994). If the court authorizes a hearing on this issue, it may also authorize a private evaluation. Furthermore, if the secretary determines that "the person's mental abnormality or personality disorder has so changed that the person is not likely to commit predatory acts of sexual violence if placed in transitional release," the secretary shall authorize the person to petition the court for transitional release. The attorney general has the right to specify the conditions for this examination by an outside expert. An evaluation may also be conducted to determine if there is "probable cause" to hold one of these hearings. (For general references on SVP evaluations, see Abel, 1985; American Psychiatric Association, 1999; Schlank & Cohen, 1999.)

INITIAL SVP EVALUATION

The precommitment SVP evaluation will be different in emphasis in several ways from later, release-related evaluations. In the initial SVP evaluation, more emphasis should be placed on historical factors, especially the examinee's qualifying criminal convictions, and on whether he meets the definitions of the SVP statute. Conversely, subsequent release-related evaluations should emphasize whether changes have occurred in the person during the SVP treatment program. If the individual has improved, the evaluator should determine whether he is now safe enough to be placed in a less restrictive placement in the community or even given his final release.

The Initial Contact

For state evaluators, the initial contact with the evaluee may come when the suspected SVP is admitted to the evaluation unit. For a private SVP evaluation, the initial contact regarding the evaluation may come from an attorney, from the offender, or from his family. (Offenders often learn from each other who is doing private SVP evaluations.) If this initial contact for a private evaluation is not initiated by an attorney, the clinician should wait until the defendant is represented by an attorney before beginning the evaluation.

Regardless of who initiates an evaluation contact, clinicians must clearly and adequately explain the nature of the evaluation to the potential examinee. This includes telling him that the examination will have to be thorough and that the examiner will have to gather information from many sources. He must also explain that there are limits to confidentiality and risks in the evaluation. A private exam should not continue unless the examinee understands these conditions and agrees to them. Because of the usual reporting obligations, the examinee should also be told that if any new abuse victims are identifiable, the examiner may be legally required to report such cases to the police or prosecutors. This explanation may be especially important with evaluees who are not highly socially and intellectually endowed and who may excessively entrust information to an MHP without understanding these legal reporting requirements. The examinee should be advised to discuss all areas and behaviors asked about, but he should not specifically identify previously unknown victims. It may be helpful for the MHP to suggest ways for the examinee to do this, for example, "Say 'an unnamed boy at a camp'" or "Say 'some years ago.'"

For private evaluations, the attorney for the potential evaluee should have obtained all or most of the needed records. If other records are needed, such as those relating to prior treatment or employment, the examiner should obtain permission to access them. If permission is refused, this may be grounds for not doing the examination. In general, an examiner may not be able to conduct a useful evaluation of an uncooperative examinee, or if the evaluation is performed, the findings may be inconclusive.

Permission should also be requested to contact family members or others who may have relevant information (see below). If possible, the examinee should provide addresses, telephone numbers, and other contact information for these individuals. Even without the examinee's permission, the MHP may choose to contact them.

Record Review and Outside Information Gathering

There is a special need in SVP evaluations to obtain records and other outside information to corroborate offense and other background information. Details of the qualifying offenses should be obtained from witness statements and hearing transcripts if possible. This information provides the examiner with external evidence on the offender's sexual behavior and offenses. Outside corroboration is important even when there have been several sexual offense convictions so that any violent and predatory details of the offenses can be credibly known.

Several factors can make this corroboration difficult. There may be wide discrepancy between the number of offenses actually committed and those that led to criminal charges (see, e.g., Abel & Osborn, 1992; Berah & Myers, 1983; Bradford, Boulet, & Pawlak, 1992). Some relevant offenses may have occurred in distant jurisdictions or in those that are uncooperative in providing information. The original offense(s) may well have been years ago; this is usually the case when the examinee has served a long prison sentence before the SVP petition was filed. Complaining witnesses may not be easily traceable. If they are reachable, they may not be eager to talk to an evaluator, especially one retained by the offender. At times the original complainant may now be retracting and denying the complaint. Despite all these constraints, the evaluator must do his or her best to ultimately determine the nature of the sexual offense behavior, diagnose the examinee's current and prior mental condition (mental abnormality or personality disorder or whatever other statutory definition there is), and determine the likelihood that the examinee might repeat his sexually violent behavior. Under the requirement recently imposed by *Kansas v. Crane* (2002), the evaluator also must opine on whether the offender's abnormality(ies) and personality disorder(s) impose a serious difficulty in controlling sexually relevant behavior.

Outside information will also be helpful in determining, when relevant, if any relationship was developed primarily for the purpose of victimization or if the victimization was more opportunistic, perhaps occurring under conditions of increased stress or dysfunction in an ongoing heterosexual relationship. For example, did the offender appear to marry in order to have access to a stepchild for a sexual relationship, or was the sexual relationship primarily paternal with secondary, perhaps opportunistic, sexual behavior under specific circumstances of increased stress that is unlikely to be repeated? And what were the primary purposes of the examinee's jobs, volunteer work, or other activity that may have been associated with sexual offending opportunities?

All available preincarceration psychiatric, sexual, family counseling, and similar treatment records should be carefully reviewed, with special attention to treatment effects and compliance, mental disorders, and behaviors related to aggression, children, and sexual offenses. If such offending behavior was occurring during outpatient psychiatric treatment, was the treatment record silent because the examinee was not discussing or acknowledging such behavior? Conversely, treatment records may provide details of sexual misbehavior that are not found elsewhere. Prior medical records may also be of use.

DOC records should be reviewed. These will allow an assessment of the examinee's behavior during incarceration, including any violent or other significant disciplinary problems. At the time of this initial SVP evaluation, there may be few, if any, correctional sexual offender treatment records to review. If there was a DOC sexual offender treatment program, did the examinee attempt or succeed in getting into the program? Did any real change appear to occur, or did the examinee mostly "go through the motions"? Was such treatment satisfactorily completed, or was the offender dropped from the treatment program? (As will be seen later below, one objective factor for assessing risk recidivism is a failure to complete sexual offender treatment.)

In evaluating records and the examinee's participation in sexual offender treatment, the clinician should consider biases of whoever recorded the data. Do the records contain hints of such bias, for example, "Once a pedophile always a pedophile," "The poor guy was sexually abused as a child (otherwise he's okay)," and so on? For examinees who were potential candidates for other DOC programs, such as substance abuse treatment, were they in such a program and did they participate satisfactorily? This is especially important for evaluees for whom substance abuse increases risk (see below).

A private SVP evaluator will usually have access to the SVP evaluation conducted by the state examiners, including any psychological and other testing results. This material should be reviewed, with attention to who gathered what information and which information must be especially rechecked with the examinee or otherwise. Risk assessment instruments (see below) should usually be recalculated for accuracy.

Background History Information

This section briefly discusses general background history, but the emphasis is on the more specific sexual history in SVP evaluations and the approach the MHP should take to this material. As with all forensic MHP evaluations, one must constantly evaluate the data received from the evaluee for its credibility in view of what is known from the records, from other parts of the evaluee's examination, and from other sources. But the evaluator should also be alert to the possibility that some information is, in fact, not accurately "documented" in the records. This may become apparent when a more careful history is collected.

General Background

As in any mental health–related evaluation (American Psychiatric Association, 1995; Nicoli, 1999; Scheiber, 1999), the clinician should gather relevant background information on the examinee's parents, siblings, education, general and sexual developmental history, peer relationships, work, physical and mental health treatment, substance abuse, legal history, and so forth as needed. Is there a personal childhood abuse victim history? How abusive was any purported victimization, or was this "abuse" pursued and enjoyed, and maybe contributory to the subsequent paraphilic behavior? Why did the person leave jobs? Did the jobs offer access to children? Do they provide a basis for suspecting sexual misbehavior?

Information is also needed on adult relationships, marriages, children, and stepchildren, with details on the relationships with each of these. Why did relationships end? Was there family violence or possible sexual behavior with children or stepchildren?

Sexual History

The evaluator should expect that many examinees have engaged in perverse behavior of a diverse nature. Therefore, the evaluator must listen to the examinee discuss this type of behavior without reacting adversely. If the evaluator expects to hear this material, the examinee will be less inclined to deny that it occurred. Once the examinee gives an untruthful story, he will not be eager to retract what he said. Approaches to this expectant history gathering include, "What kinds of sex games did you play in your family?" "When you started to masturbate, what sexual fantasies did you have?" and "How much more excited did you get when you thought about boys?" (see Abel, 1985). (All sexually related and other terms used should be appropriate to what the examinee will culturally and intellectually understand.)

In spite of one's best clinical skills, the evaluee may adamantly deny behavior that others have reliably testified to. Under such circumstances, it is sometimes helpful to ask the examinee what others said the examinee did, for example, what the victim or the victim's parent(s) said occurred. At times this approach works: "If I call the victim (victim's mother/father, your ex-wife, etc.) after this interview, what will she/he say that you did to . . . ?"

Detailed descriptions are necessary to understand the exact behavior and the (likely) thought processes involved in various sexual criminal acts;

it will take time to get this information. Relevant questions include the following: "When did you first meet the person?" "How did you meet?" "What kind of things did you do together?" "Did she/he come on to you?" "When did you get a hard-on?" "What did you do then?" "What did she/he do?" "When was the first sexual activity?" "When did you ejaculate?" "What happened then?" "Did this happen more than (10, 50, etc. as appropriate) times?" "Did you give her/him money/presents?" "Did you ask her/him not to tell?" "Was a victim ever physically hurt?" Also ask about the victim's gender and age. Was there a childhood or adolescent sexual abuse perpetrator history? All of these questions should be asked with appropriate language.

When there are only a few known sexual offenses, details will be required on each offense to allow adequate conclusions to be drawn on a number of issues, such as the person's pattern of behavior. When there are many victims or episodes, details should be collected on at least a few sexual episodes, with emphasis perhaps on the first one, the most recent episode, and those that led to the criminal charges. This allows for the comparison of versions of the sexual behavior.

As part of the sexual history, the clinician should assess for the use of grooming behavior and for cognitive distortions. For example, does the examinee state or hint that he was "seduced" by the child or that the encounter was a "good learning experience" for the child?

The clinician should take a recent and contemporary sexual behavior history, evaluating it, as always, for credibility. What has been the examinee's sexual behavior history while incarcerated? Has there been sexual involvement with other inmates? If so, what has been the nature of the involvement and the relationship(s)? If there is no such involvement, why not? How often has masturbation occurred? To what fantasies? Has the examinee at any time, or even one time, been fantasizing about the victim(s)? If not, why not? Has he been using their picture or another object of theirs?

The evaluator will also need to take a broad lifetime sexual history, asking about all the potential paraphilias (voyeurism, exhibitionism, bestiality, obscene telephoning, e-mailing, etc.), if and when they occurred, their frequency, and number of victims. This can be done from a self-made listing, but available instruments for doing so are helpful so that nothing is forgotten (e.g., Langevin, 1990; Langevin, Handy, Paitich, & Russon, 1985). The responses to such an inventory can be compared for veracity against other parts of the examination.

Mental Status Examination

As with other parts of the exam, not every aspect of the mental status examination can be mentioned here. The evaluation must determine if there is a mental disorder or mental abnormality or personality disorder (however these are legally defined by the state SVP law) that makes the person likely to engage in the predatory or repeat acts of sexual violence. Standard diagnostic manual characterizations (American Psychiatric Association, 2000) will have to comport with legal characterizations.

The most obvious, relevant, and usual mental disorder diagnosis is pedophilia, but many other diagnoses are also highly relevant. Some clinicians would limit the mental disorder or "mental abnormality" to paraphilias (see, e.g., Becker & Murphy, 1998), but there are other mental disorders, alone or in combination, that may make the person "likely to engage" in predatory or repeat acts of sexual violence. Such conditions may include all mental disorders that can significantly impair understanding and behavioral or volitional control. This impairment can happen in a variety of ways, such as stronger than usual "sexually violent" impulses, with the offender acting on such impulses because of impaired thought process (e.g., "She looked 16 to me" or "The girl made me do it"), impaired control when under the influence of abusable substances, impaired judgment about the significance of the behavior (excessive rationalization or blatant denial), and callous disregard for others. These mental disorders or abnormalities can include (but are not limited to) bipolar disorders that impair impulse control, judgment-impairing dementias, personality disorders with antisocial and narcissistic traits that devalue others, and other disorders, including substance abuse disorders and borderline and lower intelligence. And, as Justice Thomas reminded us in Kansas v. Hendricks (1997), legislatures are constitutionally free to define mental disorders independently of what MHPs do.

Therefore, in addition to paraphilic behaviors and disorders, attention should be focused in the overall mental status exam on the range of abnormal mental behaviors that may be most likely associated with repetitive inappropriate sexual behavior (see Raymond, Coleman, Ohlerking, Christenson, & Miner, 1999). These latter determinations especially include findings associated with major depressive, bipolar, schizophrenic, dementing, substance abuse, and paranoid Axis I disorders, besides behaviors associated with certain Axis II conditions (American Psychiatric Association, 2000). Regarding these latter diagnoses, particular attention should be paid to narcissistic, antisocial, borderline, schizotypal, and schizoid features and disorders, conditions with, among other problems, impaired impulse control, distorted evaluations of others, and problematic relationships.

The examinee's general approach to the exam and examiner should be noted. Is the examinee's defensiveness within reasonable bounds under the circumstances? Is an attitude of excessive comfort reflective of glib denial and narcissism?

The MHP should evaluate the treatability of any Axis I disorders. This discussion with the examinee will help the clinician determine the examinee's understanding about his mental functioning. How treatment compliant has the examinee been or will likely be for the most relevant of these conditions? For example, an examinee with a bipolar disorder who is generally medication compliant may suggest less likelihood of repeat offending than a person not so compliant.

A discussion with the examinee about the possible use of antiandrogen drugs that reduce the secretion of the male hormone, testosterone, allows additional assessment of the offender's understanding of treatment and of his motivation. (See this volume, chapter 14, for a discussion of this treatment approach.) The examinee with a reasonable understanding of the risks and benefits of such treatment options, who is able to weigh and consider these issues relative to recidivism and release potential, will appear more motivated for changing his behavior. Conversely, an examinee who adamantly or unreasonably refuses to discuss such treatment will appear resistant and uninsightful. This is especially true if his comments reflect denial and minimization of his behavior and of the difficulties of changing sexual behavior patterns. Relevant discussion of disulfiram for treating alcoholism is similar.

Psychological Testing and Other Assessments

There are a large number of psychological tests and other assessment instruments that can be used with these evaluations (American Psychiatric Association, 1999; Wettstein, 1992; Zonana & Norko, 1999). Although some of the paper-and-pencil instruments can be self-administered, if that is done one has to be sure of the circumstances under which the tests are answered (e.g., did other SVP examinees help?). In state SVP pretrial evaluation programs in which there is essentially unlimited access to the offenders and substantial resources, administering more of these instruments may be feasible. If various instruments have been used in the state SVP pretrial evaluation program, the independent evaluator should obtain all such results so that they can be reviewed.

Independent evaluators may be under considerable time and financial constraints. Considering these and what testing is available elsewhere, the evaluator must decide what (additional) testing is most feasible. The Minnesota Multiphasic Personality Inventory (2nd ed., MMPI-II; Graham, 2000; Pope, Butcher, & Seelen, 1993)—if it has not recently been administered—is often useful because of its validity scales and attention to a range of Axis I disorders, helping to evaluate and corroborate parts of the examination. It is usually easier for an independent evaluator who is not a psychologist to learn how to administer this test and other "paper-and-pencil" tests to be discussed. This eliminates the need to hire a separate psychologist for this purpose. Obviously, for more specialized testing, the services of a psychologist or neuropsychologist are required.

Because of the strong association with recidivism (see, e.g., Quinsey, Harris, Rice, & Cormier, 1998; Quinsey, Rice, & Harris, 1995) and for general diagnostic purposes, the next most important test is likely the Hare Psychopathy Checklist—Revised (PCL–R; Hare, 1991). A variety of other instruments on examinee sexual interests, attitudes about women, and so on can be selectively used depending on the case, types of offenses, and whether similar information has already been gathered (see Salter, 1988, for a description of many of these instruments). Although these latter instruments suffer from self-report bias, they can nonetheless provide useful information. A test of cognitive distortion can be useful, such as the Abel and Becker Cognition Scale in pedophilia, as can the Burt Rape Myth Acceptance Scale in rape cases (see Salter, 1988, and references therein).

If there are questions of limited intelligence or reading difficulties that have not been adequately assessed, then these areas should be assessed further, either within the mental status exam or by screening tests available for preliminary evaluations, for example, the Shipley-Hartford test (Dennis, 1973; Institute of Living, 1940/1967) or Raven Progressive Matrices (Raven, 1958) for intelligence. (The standard MMPI–II cannot be administered with less than about an eighth-grade reading level.) When detailed intelligence or academic evaluation is necessary and not otherwise available, for example, in school records, then a qualified evaluator may be necessary.

More direct, physiological testing of sexual arousal and interest (penile plethysmography [PPG] and visual reaction time [VRT]) and veracity (polygraphy) may be indicated (if they have not already been done) if financial and testing resources are available, and if they are likely to produce probative test results in light of the overall information available. The evaluator must be able to evaluate any such testing that has been done (see, e.g., American Psychiatric Association, 1999; Becker & Murphy, 1998; Harris, Rice, & Quinsey, 1998; Johnson & Listiak, 1999; Kreuger, Abel, Kuban, Bradford, & Sasnowski, 2001). There is considerable literature on PPG, but the testing is expensive and selectively available around the United States (Lalumiere, 1998). VRT is newer and is also selectively available unless the evaluator becomes skilled in the procedure (Abel, Jordan, Hand, Holland, & Phipps, 2001). Interest in this testing is recent, and it remains to be seen if offenders will learn to confound the results. Polygraphy is more widely available and, like other physiological evaluative methods, may or may not be admissible in court.

Physical Exam and Standard Medical Tests

There are selected physical conditions that can be relevant for SVP evaluations; however, most examinees generally do not have a medically contributing condition. Nonetheless, the clinician should review the physical evaluation that is usually done as part of the DOC or state SVP pretrial evaluation, perform at least a minimal medical symptoms review, and note medications previously and currently being taken. For example, some anti-Parkinsonian drugs cause hypersexuality. If there is not a recent physical examination, consider the options, including the risks of not having a recent physical exam under the examinee's circumstances. A selective physical examination can be done quickly by a physician MHP or may be obtainable by the health services of the jail or other facility where the evaluee is being held.

Evaluation Conclusions and Recommendations

The evaluator should diagnose Axis I, Axis II, and relevant Axis III (physical medical) conditions (American Psychiatric Association, 2000). How treatable are any such disorders in this person? The evaluator should consider if there is a mental abnormality or personality disorder that makes the person likely to engage in the predatory or repeat acts of sexual violence or that predisposes the person to commit sexually violent offenses in a degree that makes him a menace to the health and safety of others.

The evaluator may well make various diagnoses but then not conclude that these disorders volitionally or otherwise "predispose" to sexually violent behavior unless the disorder is a condition like pedophilia that has been repeatedly acted on. Conversely, conditions like mania or dementia with or without antisocial or narcissistic personality disorders or traits may predispose to repeated relevant sexual misbehavior without a clear diagnosis like pedophilia. If the jurisdiction has other relevant definitional elements of its SVP law, such as on predation, then these elements also need to be considered.

Having reached the more clinical diagnostic conclusions, the evaluator should then assess the sexual recidivism risk, which is made taking into account any sexual offender treatment the offender has received. Assessing general violence risk is also indicated, especially in view of the strong association between this and sexual recidivism (Quinsey et al., 1995, 1998). Instruments to help such risk assessing are useful, whether it is less quantitative, more clinical instruments like the HCR–20: Assessing Risk for Violence (Version 2; Webster, Douglas, Eaves, & Hart, 1997) or the Manual for the Sexual Violence Risk–20: Professional Guidelines for Assessing Risk of Sexual Violence (SVR–20; Boer, Hart, Kropp, & Webster, 1997), or more quantitative actuarial methods that have fairly strong predictive power (see chapter 3). Such actuarial instruments include the Static–99 (Hanson & Thornton, 1999; Phenix, Hanson, & Thornton, 2000), an update and improvement on the popular Rapid Risk Assessment for Sexual Offense Recidivism (RRASOR; Hanson, 1997), the Sex Offender Risk Appraisal Guide (SORAG), the Violence Risk Appraisal Guide (VRAG; Quinsey et al., 1998), or the Minnesota Sex Offender Screening Tool—Revised (MnSOST–R; Epperson, Kaul, & Hesselton, 2000; Epperson et al., 2000a, 2000b).

These latter types of actuarial instruments provide numerical risk assessments for future time periods based on the database of the study; for example, in 5 years with a certain score on the Static–99, 33% of the sample sexually recidivated (Hanson & Thornton, 1999). The actuarial determinations are based primarily on so-called static or essentially unchangeable factors, such as offense history, gender, and relationship, if any, of the offender and victim(s), the current offender age, and so on, but the MnSOST–R also takes into consideration such so-called dynamic factors as discipline infractions, substance abuse, and sexual offender treatment while incarcerated.

Another actuarial instrument, the Sex Offender Need Assessment Rating (SONAR; Hanson & Harris, 2000), developed with released, community-supervised prior offenders, contains static and dynamic factors. The SONAR may be used when the individual lives outside of a secure institutional setting, such as with the Texas SVP community approach and after conditional release to the community in other state programs. (This instrument is yet to be replicated, but such research is under way [Harris, 2001].)

All of these risk assessment instruments also help the evaluator to keep in mind the various items found to have predictive value. Unlike the actuarial instruments, which provide recidivism percentage risks, the HCR–20 and SVR–20 provide only qualitative assessments of low, moderate, and high risk. These tests also provide a convenient listing and research citations for the most relevant items that generally need to be considered in sexual violence risk predictions.

The evaluator ordinarily should score several of these instruments because they are fairly easily scored and provide somewhat different information in view of their different items and of the different populations on which they were developed. The closer the evaluee in question comes to the population on which the instrument was developed, especially for the actuarial instruments, the better it is predictive of that evaluee's expected future behavior.

The SVP evaluator should not make the determination of predatory risk on the basis of the examinee's potential for participating in the SVP treatment program. The initial SVP evaluator's task is the SVP evaluation criteria and not whether the examinee might benefit from treatment. This is so even though an evaluation of possible future SVP sexual treatment motivation helps to assess the examinee's thinking processes, desire to change behavior, and reoffending risk.

The private clinician doing the initial SVP evaluation will usually make general treatment recommendations as indicated, in addition to specific recommendations for treatment of the sexual disorder(s) and other offending behavior. Although not limited by the treatment available in the SVP program, these recommendations should consider what is feasible. At times what is not available may be an issue, for example, a lack of specific treatment for a developmentally disabled evaluee (Brown & Pond, 1999; Stacken & Shevich, 1999), but this issue may not be easily addressed within the stricter confines of the SVP proceeding.

The evaluator should try to reach conclusions with an adequate degree of certainty (reasonable medical certainty [RMC], or a similar term) and not claim evaluative certainty beyond what can be obtained. This applies to both private and state evaluators. Axis I and III and often Axis II disorder diagnoses can be made with RMC, as can various treatment expectations for some of these conditions, but can RMC be achieved for other aspects of the evaluation? Can we say with RMC that relationships were developed primarily for "predatory" reasons if that is a standard? That certain diagnostic conditions, maybe a bipolar disorder now under satisfactory treatment control, still predisposes to "sexually violent" offenses? And opine on this with RMC?

RELEASE-RELATED SVP EVALUATIONS

Release-related SVP evaluations will examine primarily if there is now adequate change in the offender to protect public safety with the SVP in less restrictive confinement and with less intensive treatment. For example, is he changed enough to be placed in transitional release, and if so placed, is he unlikely to engage in sexually violent acts? We know more about how to conduct initial SVP evaluations to determine if the individual should be confined than we know about evaluating whether the individual has changed so that he can be safely placed in a less restrictive alternative setting or released outright. (It took some 3 years in Kansas for the first committed SVP to be released to the less restrictive transitional phase of the SVP program, and approximately another year for conditional release, and 2 more years for final release.)

Treatment Effects

It is hoped that SVP treatment will change the offender enough so that he no longer has a mental abnormality that predisposes him to committing sexually violent offenses and, consequently, renders him a menace to the health and safety of others. Even if inappropriate sexual urges remain, he may not act on them. This will usually mean that the offender has changed in a number of ways, such as having a better understanding of his abuse cycle and having less cognitive distortion in his abuse behavior, and his nonparaphilic (non-"sexual perversion"), comorbid psychiatric disorders are adequately treated or controlled (e.g., substance-related diagnoses, bipolar disorders, and antisocial or narcissistic personality traits). What has been the SVP's cooperation with treatment for these comorbid conditions? Was medication for a bipolar condition or other significant disorder willingly taken? Will compliance continue after release from the current treatment? Are there ways to assure compliance, such as blood checks of medication levels or long-acting medication injections?

The SVP who has spent most of his energy resisting the treatment program, whether by legal maneuvers or otherwise, will not likely have benefited much from the SVP treatment. The evaluator should, nonetheless, keep an open mind to consider if other factors may have made any significant differences (see below).

After considering paraphilic and other disorders, the evaluator should determine whether adequate community safety can be achieved after the individual is released from a secure institution by effective postrelease treatment, including continued counseling, avoiding unnecessary exposure to children, and other controls on the individual. In making this determination, the evaluator should consider the SVP's participation in, and completion of, sexual offender treatment, response to treatment, changes in sexual arousal, changes in cognitive distortions relative to sexual behavior, and anticipated postconfinement circumstances and stresses.

In using instruments in these later release evaluations, there is a need to emphasize "dynamic" factors instead of only "static" factors (see this volume, chapter 3). Important dynamic factors related to reduced recidivism are cooperation with treatment and treatment completion, seeing oneself as no risk, poor social influences, sexual entitlement, access to victims, anger, and noncooperation with supervision (Hanson, 1998). For securely confined SVPs, the only actuarial instrument currently available at this juncture that considers treatment effects is the MnSOST–R (Epperson et al., 2000b), but if other actuarial instruments were never previously used, they could also be considered.

Some states have not provided adequate SVP treatment programs; consequently, even motivated evaluees may have trouble with too frequent staff and program changes. If there have been multiple changes in the SVP treatment program, note should be made of it and how the person has dealt with these situations. The SVP who has been able to achieve personal changes despite less-than-optimal treatment will generally have better long-term potential.

In evaluating whether an SVP has changed sufficiently to be eligible for release, the state may use a range of assessment tools, including the PPG, VRT, and perhaps polygraph testing. The outside evaluator will need to evaluate all such assessments. When indicated, such assessments can be redone if possible. They should be redone especially if the state's tests are not sufficiently recent and yet are being used adversely to the SVP.

Treatment Risks

The SVP who is not sufficiently open and revealing of himself in treatment is likely to be viewed as not sufficiently cooperative with treatment. Yet, for many SVPs, being more cooperative and getting an optimal amount out of the treatment may mean discussing acts of sexual offending that are otherwise unknown to state authorities. This can raise the specter of a person in the program being viewed by the SVP evaluating staff as more of a reoffending risk than was initially thought.

This dilemma of open participation and full disclosure, which risk a longer stay, versus less openness and being seen as "not fully participating" is not easily avoidable. For SVPs with multiple unknown offenses, the best option may well be to reveal these matters early in treatment so they then can have time to work on their sexually offending behavior and risk and thereby effect some treatment change. When SVPs make these revelations late in treatment—after, for example, 1 or 2 years in treatment—they may be confined in a more restrictive treatment setting for additional years.

Other Factors

Other factors can affect the release risk evaluation. Unfortunately, new sexual or other offenses may occur in the SVP program that can have an impact on the reoffending risk. Aging may change reoffending risk. For example, antisocial behavior tends to decrease with age, but dementing conditions may appear or worsen. There may be health changes that occur during treatment, for example, prostatic cancer with treatment that includes antitestosterone drugs or surgical castration that can decrease reoffending risk. Other debilitating illness effects may make the sexual reoffending risk less, but a clinician should not too easily assume such; for example, even someone with advanced lung or cardiac disease may sexually reoffend.

Release Evaluation Conclusions

The evaluator will need to do his or her best to determine with some standard of certainty if the evaluee is now adequately safe for release from the more intense to lesser (or eventually no) sex offender treatment and less (and eventually no or almost no) supervision. (Offender registration laws can prolong some form of supervision for many years, in some cases indefinitely; see this volume, chapter 12.) Each such determination is done for the particular circumstances involved in the release in question, for example, from initial commitment to transitional release and so on. And this determination is made with consideration of the stresses to be faced under each of these conditions, for example, for adult relationships outside of confinement and for publicly dealing with an SVP history.

Population studies of pedophiles who have been incarcerated show that as a *group* they continue to be at risk to reoffend many years after release (e.g., Harris et al., 1998), but is *the person being examined* still at risk? What is his degree of risk? And with RMC? Is it "once a pedophile always a pedophile," or is there ever a time when he is no longer a pedophile? The *Diagnostic and Statistical Manual for Mental Disorders—Text Revision* (DSM–IV–TR; American Psychiatric Association, 2000) considers substance abuse in remission after an extended time without symptoms, but it has no such defined remission category for pedophilia. But, if the MHP, after a careful evaluation, determines that DSM–IV–TR criteria are no longer met, then the diagnosis should not be made. In the case of a person who has been confined and away from children for a protracted period, the MHP's diagnostic acumen may surely be tested. It may even be known from PPG or VRT studies that there continues to be sexual arousal interest in children. But more difficult yet will be the assessment of pedophilia diagnosis criterion B, "The person has acted on these sexual urges, or the sexual urges or fantasies cause marked distress or interpersonal difficulty" (American Psychiatric Association, 2000, p. 572). These questions of outright remission or the absence of the syndrome are easier to raise than answer at this stage of our knowledge, but the evaluator must reach the best available conclusion even if it is made without RMC.

And how about a statutory definition that requires behavior that is a menace to the health and safety of others? Studies show that not all sexually abused boys will say that they were harmed (Laumann, Gagnon, Michael, & Michaels, 1994; and see also Rind, Tromovitch, & Bauserman, 1998). Is the evaluator willing to grapple with this aspect of the SVP law, or might the courts only consider that, if the behavior is illegal and *defined* as a violent sexual offense, then nothing further is required, or admissible, on this element? It is clear that the grayer parameters of SVP evaluating and testifying are not decided but are still being worked out.

TESTIFYING, COUNTERTRANSFERENCE, AND ETHICS

As a practical matter, the evaluator must be aware of the realities of SVP laws and litigation. Even though the burden is on the state to establish the various elements of the statute (and the dyscontrol condition now required by *Kansas v. Crane*, 2002) beyond a reasonable doubt or by clear and convincing evidence (see this volume, chapters 1 and 2), most judges and juries will likely err on the side of safety. With hyperbole, some SVP attorneys have compared SVP cases with death penalty cases. In the forensic psychiatric evidence aspects of death penalty cases when reasonable doubt is raised, there are still options for the court that usually lead to confinement. Conversely, with SVP cases, if reasonable doubt is found, the examinee will be released, perhaps into the jurors' neighborhood. Many jurors will not easily take that risk.

Victims of sexual abuse are all around us in our schools, neighborhoods, and also often in our families (Finkelhor, 1986; Laumann et al., 1994). Unfortunately, often, so are the perpetrators. This means that the chance that an evaluator has been personally close to a victim or perpetrator is higher than is usual in most areas of forensic MHP work. If there have been especially painful or other personal experiences that might bias SVP evaluations, then the clinician must honestly face these issues and consider whether he or she can objectively do SVP evaluations or do a particular evaluation. This is not work that should be done to treat one's injured inner child (cf. Farrenkopf, 1992). The clinician must be ethically honest (American Psychiatric Association, 1998) and strive for objectivity (American Academy of Psychiatry and the Law, 1987).

The private SVP evaluator may discover additional sexual offense behavior that was not previously known and that heightens the risk of the examinee being considered an SVP. The defense attorney may decide not to use such an evaluation. Conversely, and of special note for state SVP evaluators, significant risk for violence recidivism that is not related to the SVP law may not be relevant to the evaluator's SVP conclusions.

Reviewing records and interviewing for private SVP evaluations will take several hours, and additional time is required for consulting with the attorney, report writing, testifying, and so on. A private SVP evaluation should not be undertaken if one is not prepared to put in this amount of time and commitment. Public authorities or others paying for these evaluations may be reluctant to pay a reasonable fee for the work required for a private evaluation. State MHPs also need adequate time to perform these complex and high-risk evaluations. If there are unreasonable constraints on their work in such cases, they need to realistically deal with such matters. This could mean that, under the conditions of the evaluation in question, they cannot reach diagnostic or other conclusions with sufficient professional certainty. The evaluator apprehensive about testifying would be unethical if he or she concluded that a person did not meet SVP criteria largely in an effort to avoid testifying in what could be a stressful matter.

The evaluator needs to decide in advance, whenever possible, if an independent, private SVP evaluation will be done for what one will be paid. It is ethical to refuse to start an evaluation for which there will not be reasonable compensation, but it is not ethical to do an inadequate job because payment is insufficient (American Psychiatric Association, 1998, Sections 6 & 1, respectively). (It is not inappropriate here to note the tradition of *pro bono* and reduced fee work.) In this compensation context, SVP cases are worse than death penalty cases in which payment is generally more appropriately available.

CONCLUSION

Our society, including legislatures, courts, corrections, and MHPs, among others, has been struggling with repeat sexual offenders for many decades. We are in a new phase of this struggle with recent SVP laws that are meeting constitutional standards. This chapter has endeavored to help both evaluators and other students of this area to get a firmer hold on SVP evaluations.

REFERENCES

Abel, G. G. (1985). A clinical evaluation of possible sex offenders. In *The incest offender, the victim, the family: New treatment approaches* (pp. 1–8). White Plains, NY: Mental Health Association of Westchester County.

Abel, G. G., Jordan, A., Hand, C. G., Holland, L. A., & Phipps, A. (2001). Classification models of child molesters utilizing the Abel Assessment for sexual interest. *Child Abuse and Neglect, 25,* 703–718.

Abel, G. G., & Osborn, C. (1992). The paraphilias: The extent and nature of sexually deviant and criminal behavior. *Psychiatric Clinics of North America, 15,* 675–687.

American Academy of Psychiatry and the Law. (1987, revised 1989, 1991, 1995). *Ethics guidelines for the practice of forensic psychiatry.* Bloomfield, CT: Author.

American Psychiatric Association. (1995). American Psychiatric Association practice guidelines: Practice guidelines for psychiatric evaluation of adults. *American Journal of Psychiatry, 152*(Suppl.), 66–77.

American Psychiatric Association. (1998). *The principles of medical ethics: With annotations especially applicable to psychiatry.* Washington, DC: Author.

American Psychiatric Association. (1999). *Task force report on sexually dangerous offenders.* Washington, DC: Author.

American Psychiatric Association. (2000). *Diagnostic and statistical manual of mental disorders—Text Revision* (4th ed.). Washington, DC: Author.

Becker, J. D., & Murphy, W. D. (1998). What we know and do not know about assessing and treating sex offenders. *Psychology, Public Policy, and Law, 4,* 116–137.

Berah, E. F., & Myers, R. G. (1983). The offense records of a sample of convicted exhibitionists. *Bulletin of the American Academy of Psychiatry and Law, 11*, 365–369.

Boer, D. P., Hart, S. D., Kropp, P. R., & Webster, C. D. (1997). *Manual for the sexual violence risk–20*. Burnaby, British Columbia, Canada: Simon Fraser University.

Bradford, J. M. W., Boulet, J., & Pawlak, M. A. (1992). The paraphilias: A multiplicity of deviant behaviors. *Canadian Journal of Psychiatry, 37*, 104–108.

Brown, J., & Pond, A. (1999). "They just don't get it": Essentials of cognitive–behavioral treatment for intellectually disabled abusers. In B. K. Schwartz (Ed.), *The sex offender: Theoretical advances, treating special populations and legal developments* (Vol. III, pp. 21-1–21-9). Kingston, NJ: Civil Research Institute.

Commitment of Sexually Violent Predators Act of 1994, 4 Kan. Stat. Ann. §§ 59-29a01–29a15 (Supp. 1998).

Dennis, D. M. (1973). Predicting full scale WAIS IQs with the Shipley-Hartford. *Journal of Clinical Psychology, 29*, 366–368.

Epperson, D. L., Kaul, J. D., & Hesselton, D. (2000). *Minnesota Sex Offender Screening Tool—Revised (MnSOST–R): Development, performance, and recommended risk level cut scores*. St. Paul, MN: Department of Corrections.

Epperson, D. L., Kaul, J. D., Huot, S. J., Hesselton, D., Alexander, W., & Goldman, R. (2000a). *Cross-validation of the Minnesota Sex Offender Screening Tool—Revised*. St. Paul, MN: Department of Corrections. Retrieved January 28, 2001, from http://www.doc.state.mn.us

Epperson, D. L., Kaul, J. D., Huot, S. J., Hesselton, D., Alexander, W., & Goldman, R. (2000b). *Minnesota Sex Offender Screening Tool—Revised (MnSOST–R): General instructions*. St. Paul, MN: Department of Corrections.

Farrenkopf, T. (1992). What happens to therapists who work with sex offenders? *Journal of Offender Rehabilitation, 18*, 217–223.

Finkelhor, D. (with Araji, S., Baron, L., Browne, A., Peters S. D., & Wyatt, G. E.). (1986). *A sourcebook on child sexual abuse*. New York: Sage.

Friedrich, W. N., Grambsch, P., Broughton, D., Kuiper, J., & Beilke, R. L. (1991). Normative sexual behavior in children. *Pediatrics, 88*, 456–464.

Graham, J. R. (2000). *MMPI–2: Assessing personality and psychopathology* (3rd ed.). New York: Oxford University Press.

Hanson, R. K. (1997). *The development of a brief actuarial risk scale for sexual offense recidivism* (Document No. 1997-04). Ottawa, Ontario, Canada: Solicitor General Canada.

Hanson, R. K. (1998). What do we know about sex offender risk assessment? *Psychology, Public Policy, and Law, 4*, 50–72.

Hanson, R. K., & Harris, A. (2000). *The Sex Offender Need Assessment Rating (SONAR): A method for measuring change in risk levels, 2000–1*. Ottawa, Ontario, Canada: Department of the Solicitor General of Canada. Retrieved June 2, 2000, from http://www.sgc.gc.ca/EPub/Corr/e200001b/e200001b.htm

Hanson, R. K., & Thornton, D. (1999). *Static–99: Improving actuarial risk assess-*

ments for sex offenders, 1999–02. Ottawa, Ontario, Canada: Department of the Solicitor General of Canada. Retrieved June 29, 2000, from http://www.sgc.gc.ca/epub/corr/e199902/e199902.htm

Hare, R. D. (1991). Manual for the Hare Psychopathology Checklist—Revised. Toronto, Ontario, Canada: Multi-Health Systems.

Harris, A. (2001). Improving the community supervision of sexual offenders. In Research summary: Corrections research and development (Vol. 6, No. 4). Retrieved January 7, 2002, from http://www.sgc.gc.ca/epub/corr/e200107/e200107.htm

Harris, G. T., Rice, M. E., & Quinsey, V. L. (1998). Appraisal and management of risk in sexual aggressors: Implications for criminal justice policy. Psychology, Public Policy, and Law, 4, 73–115.

Institute of Living. (1967). Shipley-Institute of Living Scale. Hartford, CT: Author. (Original work published 1940)

Johnson, S. A., & Listiak, A. (1999). The measurement of sexual preference: A preliminary comparison of phallometry and the Abel Assessment. In B. K. Schwartz (Ed.), The sex offender: Theoretical advances, treating special populations and legal developments (Vol. III, pp. 26-1–26-20). Kingston, NJ: Civil Research Institute.

Kansas v. Crane, 122 S. Ct. 867 (2002).

Kansas v. Hendricks, 117 S. Ct. 2072 (1997).

Kreuger R., Abel, G. G., Kuban, M., Bradford, J., & Sasnowski, D. (2001, October). Objective methods for assessing sexual interest: A critical appraisal. Paper presented at the annual meeting of the American Academy of Psychiatry and the Law, Boston.

Lacoursiere, R. B., Logan, W. S., & Peterson, S. E. (1998, October). Grappling with sexually violent predator evaluations in Kansas: Kansas v. Hendricks. Paper presented at the annual meeting of the American Academy of Psychiatry and the Law, New Orleans, LA.

La Fond, J. Q. (1998). The costs of enacting a sexual predator law. Psychology, Public Policy, and Law, 4, 468–504.

Lalumiere, M. L. (1998). Common questions regarding the use of phallometric testing with sexual offenders. Sexual Abuse, A Journal of Research and Treatment, 10, 227–237.

Langevin, R. (with Paitich, D., Russon, A., Handy, L., & Langevin, A). (1990). The Clarke Sex History Questionnaire for Males: Manual. Oakville, Ontario, Canada: Juniper Press.

Langevin, R., Handy, L., Paitich, D., & Russon, A. (1985). Appendix A: A new version of the Clarke Sex History Questionnaire for Males. In R. Langevin (Ed.), Erotic preference, gender identity, and aggression in men: New research studies (pp. 287–305). Hillsdale, NJ: Erlbaum.

Laumann, E. O., Gagnon, J. H., Michael, R. T., & Michaels, S. (1994). The social organization of sexuality: Sexual practices in the United States. Chicago: University of Chicago Press.

Marshall, W. L., Fernandez, Y. M., Hudson, S. M., & Ward, T. (Eds.). (1998). *Sourcebook of treatment programs for sexual offenders*. New York: Plenum Press.

Nicoli, A. M. (1999). History and mental status. In A. M. Nicoli (Ed.), *The Harvard guide to psychiatry* (pp. 26–40). Cambridge, MA: Belknap Press.

Phenix, A., Hanson, R. K., & Thornton, D. (2000). *Coding rules for the Static–99*. Ottawa, Ontario, Canada: Department of the Solicitor General of Canada. Retrieved June 29, 2000, from http://www.sgc.gc.ca/epub/corr/ecodingrules/ecodingrules.htm

Pope, K. S., Butcher, J. N., & Seelen, J. (1993). *MMPI, MMPI–2 and MMPI–A in court*. Washington, DC: American Psychological Association.

Quinsey, V. L., Harris, G. T., Rice, M. E., & Cormier, C. A. (1998). *Violent offenders: Appraising and managing risk*. Washington, DC: American Psychological Association.

Quinsey, V. L., Rice, M. E., & Harris, G. T. (1995). Actuarial prediction of sexual recidivism. *Journal of Interpersonal Violence, 10*, 85–105.

Rind, B., Tromovitch, P., & Bauserman, R. (1998). A meta-analytic examination of assumed properties of child sexual abuse using college samples. *Psychological Bulletin, 124*, 22–53.

Raven, J. C. (1958). *Raven's Standard Progressive Matrices*. San Antonio, TX: Psychological Corporation.

Raymond, N. C., Coleman, E., Ohlerking, M. A., Christenson, G. A., & Miner, M. (1999). Psychiatric comorbidity in pedophilic sex offenders. *American Journal of Psychiatry, 156*, 786–788.

Salter, A. C. (1988). *Treating child sex offenders and victims: A practical guide*. Newbury Park, CA: Sage.

Scheiber, S. C. (1999). The psychiatric interview, psychiatric history, and mental status examination. In R. E. Hales, S. C. Yudofsky, & J. A. Talbott (Eds.), *The American Psychiatric Press: Textbook of psychiatry* (3rd ed., pp. 193–227). Washington, D C: American Psychiatric Press.

Schlank, A., & Cohen, F. (1999). *The sexual predator: Law, policy, evaluation and treatment*. Kingston, NJ: Civic Research Institute.

Schwartz, B. K. (1999). *The sex offender: Theoretical advances, treating special populations and legal developments* (Vol. III). Kingston, NJ: Civil Research Institute.

Stacken, N. M., & Shevich, J. (1999). Working with the intellectually disabled/socially inadequate sex offender in a prison setting. In B. K. Schwartz (Ed.), *The sex offender: Theoretical advances, treating special populations and legal developments* (Vol. III, pp. 22-1–22-13). Kingston, NJ: Civil Research Institute.

Webster, C. D., Douglas K. S., Eaves, D., & Hart, S. D. (1997). *HCR–20: Assessing risk for violence* (Version 2). Burnaby, British Columbia, Canada: Simon Fraser University.

Wettstein, R. M. (1992). A psychiatric perspective on Washington's sexually violent predators statute. *University of Puget Sound Law Review, 15*, 597–633.

Wood, J. M., & Wright, L. (1995). Evaluation of children's sexual behaviors and incorporation of base rates in judgments of sexual abuse. *Child Abuse and Neglect, 19*, 1263–1273.

Zonana, H. V., & Norko, M. A. (1999). Sexual predators. *The Psychiatric Clinics of North America, 22*, 109–127.

III

SEX OFFENDERS AND TREATMENT

5

WHAT WE KNOW AND DON'T KNOW ABOUT TREATING ADULT SEX OFFENDERS

MARNIE E. RICE AND GRANT T. HARRIS

This chapter reviews research on the treatment of men who have committed sex offenses involving physical contact, specifically rape and child molesting. We know of no controlled outcome studies of the treatment of female sex offenders, who, in any case, form a very tiny proportion of the population of sex offenders (Abel, Rouleau, & Cunningham-Rathner, 1986).

How is treatment effectiveness best evaluated? First, it is necessary to compare the outcome of treated offenders against that of untreated offenders or with offenders given a different treatment (McConaghy, 1999; Quinsey, Harris, Rice, & Lalumière, 1993). Otherwise, there is no way to determine that change in offending following treatment is due to the specific effects of treatment rather than to other factors such as passage of time, increased age of the offender, or therapist expectancy. The presence of a

This chapter is a revised and updated version of material first published by the authors in Rice, Harris, and Quinsey (2001). Copyright 1998 by the American Psychological Association (APA). Adapted with permission of the authors and the APA.

control group is the most important methodological feature of a treatment evaluation; consequently, we concentrate on controlled studies.

Second, because the ultimate goal of sex offender treatment is the reduction of recidivism, some measure of that is the primary yardstick for evaluating treatment. But what measure of recidivism should be used—general, violent, sexual, or specific offenses, such as child molesting, rape, or sexual murder? Obviously, the more specific the measure, the lower will be the recidivism rate. Ought we use self-reports of recidivism or official arrest and conviction data instead? Unfortunately, the validity of self-reports has rarely been evaluated in treatment outcome studies. Among sex offenders specifically, denial, distortion, and minimization are extremely common (Abel, Mittelman, Becker, Rathner, & Rouleau, 1988; Pollock & Hashmall, 1991). Without special steps taken to ensure and evaluate their validity, offenders' self-reported recidivism cannot be trusted. Arrest and conviction data from police "rap" sheets are frequently used as outcome measures. On the one hand, both have the advantage of being "hard" in the sense that it is unlikely that an arrest or, especially, a conviction, will be recorded if nothing happened. On the other hand, both are conservative because many offenses do not result in an arrest or conviction. Moreover, because of plea bargaining, many men arrested for sex offenses are subsequently convicted of nonsexual offenses. Despite the fact that they underestimate offending, official records of sexual or violent reoffending (including sexual) are the best available measures to evaluate comparative recidivism rates among treated and untreated groups because they are least subject to bias related to treatment participation.

Risk of violent and sexual recidivism among sex offenders has been shown to persist over decades (Hanson, Steffy, & Gauthier, 1993; Prentky, Knight, & Lee, 1997; Rice & Harris, 1997); thus, longer follow-ups lead to higher rates of recidivism. Although official recidivism is the most important outcome measure, pre- and posttreatment changes on measures relevant to specific treatment components are also important. If pre–post changes on these measures are correlated with lower recidivism, then there is strong evidence that the treatment component is effective.

Treatment effectiveness will be grossly overestimated if treatment refusers and dropouts are ignored (e.g., Rice & Harris, in press). This happens when, for example, individuals who refuse treatment are excluded from the treatment group but individuals who would have refused treatment, had it been offered, are included in the comparison group. Similarly, counting as "treated" only those who remained in treatment until completion and ignoring the outcome of "dropouts" (or even worse, putting those who dropped out or refused into a control group) grossly inflates estimates of treatment effectiveness. Attrition is best handled by analyses in which all individuals initially assigned to each group are included (Chambless & Hollon, 1998; Flick, 1988). In other words, there are *general* effects of treatment participation: A treatment regimen selects relatively compliant and motivated individuals, and treatments induce expectancy bias for participants and therapists. The important social policy questions pertain to the *specific* effects of treatment: Does the treatment itself cause a reduction in offending? Consequently, the widely accepted practice standards (randomized control, unbiased outcome measures, double-blind administration, monitoring attrition, etc.) for evaluating any treatment are designed to measure its specific, causal effects.

Finally, there has been considerable work on the subtyping of child molesters and rapists (Knight & Prentky, 1990), and different treatments might be effective for different subtypes. The most important variables in discriminating among sex offenders and between sex offenders and other men, as well as the variables best predicting sex offender recidivism, are those based on history of victim choice (adults vs. children, male vs. female children, related vs. unrelated victims), history of antisociality (sex offense history, general criminal history, antisocial personality, and psychopathy), and sexual deviance (Hanson & Bussière, 1998; Harris, Rice, Quinsey, Chaplin, & Earls, 1992; Quinsey, Harris, Rice, & Cormier, 1998; Rice & Harris, 1999). Unfortunately, little is known about whether these variables affect response to treatment.

In addition to these methodological issues, narrative reviews of treatment suffer from other difficulties. For example, when positive effects are found in some studies and not in others, there is no quantitative way to evaluate whether the different results are due simply to sampling error or whether variables related to outcome (called *moderator* variables) such as client characteristics, setting, or treatment characteristics account for the differences. Meta-analysis is a method that allows data from many studies to be combined to determine the average effect and evaluates whether moderator variables can account for the disparate results. Although meta-analyses cannot make up for all of the inadequacies of individual studies, they do permit a more definitive conclusion about treatment efficacy. Unless there are enough high-quality studies, however, meta-analysis is not dependable (Chambless & Hollon, 1998). Unfortunately, as we will see later in this chapter, there are too few well-controlled studies of sex offender treatment to conduct an informative meta-analysis.

NONBEHAVIORAL PSYCHOTHERAPY

Until recently, the most common treatment for child molesters and rapists has been group or individual psychotherapy (Quinsey, 1977, 1984). Unfortunately, the treatment is seldom well described, usually seems to have been unstructured, and has rarely been evaluated in a controlled fashion. The few controlled evaluations that exist have provided no evidence that nonbehavioral psychotherapy reduces the likelihood of reoffending among child molesters or rapists. Frisbie (1969) and Frisbie and Dondis (1965) studied "sexual psychopaths" treatment in a humanistic, peer-led program in a maximum security psychiatric hospital and compared their outcomes with those of untreated sex offenders. The treated and untreated groups were neither matched nor randomly assigned; nevertheless, the rate of new sexual offenses was higher among the treated men. Sturgeon and Taylor (1980) followed a later cohort of 260 men treated in the same institution. Sexual and nonsexual violent reoffenses were compared with those of a group of 122 untreated sex offenders released from prison the same year. The untreated group included more rapists and were younger, had spent more time incarcerated, and had more serious violent and non-violent criminal histories (but less serious histories of sexual offenses). The treated men subsequently had fewer reconvictions for sex offenses, but there were no differences for nonsexual violent offenses. Romero and Williams (1983, 1985) conducted what is undoubtedly the best controlled treatment outcome studies for psychotherapy. Probationers (over 80% of whom were rapists or child molesters) were randomly assigned to either intensive probation or psychodynamic group therapy plus probation. Those assigned to psychotherapy had higher rates of rearrest for sex offenses (though not significantly) than those assigned to intensive supervision alone. Moreover, among those men who completed over 40 weeks of treatment, men who were treated were significantly more likely to be rearrested for a sex offense.

Thus, similar to findings for offenders in general (Andrews et al., 1990), humanistic and psychodynamic treatments do not reduce offending by rapists and child molesters. They might even increase the likelihood of recidivism.

CASTRATION AND PHARMACOLOGICAL TREATMENTS

Although its use is rare today, castration (surgical removal of the gonads) was used extensively in Europe to reduce sex drive and sexual recidivism. Castration might also reduce aggression more generally. Most human studies of castration have been completely uncontrolled, and many included men who are not now considered to be sex offenders (e.g., homosexual men with adult partners). Freund (1980) reviewed uncontrolled and partially controlled studies of castration and concluded that sexual recidivism rates among castrated offenders were very low even though offenders considered for castration were at high risk. In one partially controlled study, Cornu (1973, reported in Freund, 1980) compared the post-castration recidivism of 121 male sex offenders in Switzerland with 50 men also recommended for the procedure but who refused. In a 5- to 30-year follow-up, 7% of the castrated men and 52% of the uncastrated men committed another sex offense. Although the difference in outcome was striking, those who were recommended but refused may have been different from those who agreed in ways that made them higher risk. For example, they may have been less likely to admit they had a problem. In another study (Wille & Beier, 1989), 104 voluntarily castrated sex offenders were compared with 53 men, most of whom withdrew their consent before surgery. The sexual recidivism rate for the castrated men was 3% compared with 46% for the comparison sample.

In a partially controlled study of castration, Stürup (1968) studied the outcome of 38 men who had raped either adult women or female children and had been treated in a social therapy program. Eighteen men were castrated prior to release; another 18 were not (2 were never released). Over a follow-up lasting up to 25 years, 1 of the castrated and 3 of the noncastrated men were charged with additional sex crimes. There was no evidence that those considered for the procedure had worse sexual offense histories, but the noncastrated men had more psychiatric symptoms. Although Stürup reported that he considered the results of castration to be very positive, it would be difficult to recommend the procedure based on these results.

In conclusion, it seems beyond doubt that castration reduces sex drive and could reduce the risk of sexual reoffending among offenders whose offenses are limited to sexual ones and who freely consent to castration. The issue of consent has practical as well as legal and ethical implications, especially for incarcerated offenders or offenders who are given a choice between castration and incarceration (Alexander, Gunn, Taylor, & Finch, 1993). Offenders who were castrated under coercion might, for example, illicitly obtain testosterone or other anabolic steroids and thereby reverse the effects of castration. Although this has not been much of a problem to date, anabolic steroids are now easily available from the illicit drug market and are commonly used by body builders and other athletes (Brower, 1993). In any event, no one has argued that castration is appropriate for the large proportion of sex offenders (especially incarcerated offenders) who are diagnosed as personality disordered or have histories of diverse nonsexual offenses (see Eastman, 1993).

Pharmacological treatments are more popular than castration, especially in North America. Several drugs have been used to reduce deviant sexual behavior, including various serotonergic medications, but most common are drugs called antiandrogens (including cyproterone acetate, gonadotropin-releasing hormone analog, leuprolide acetate, and medroxyprogesterone acetate [MPA]) that reduce or block testosterone. (See this volume, chapter 14, for a thorough discussion of the legal and ethical issues raised by chemical castration.) Only MPA has been subjected to controlled outcome evaluations. Antiandrogens achieve the sex-drive-reducing effects of surgical castration with fewer ethical problems because their effects are completely reversible on withdrawal. However, they have unpleasant side effects, and most men strongly dislike taking them (Langevin, Wright, & Handy, 1988). Common complaints include weight gain, fatigue, head-aches, reduced body hair, depression, and gastrointestinal problems. As an example of the unpopularity of antiandrogens, Hucker, Langevin, and Bain (1988) studied child molesters randomly assigned either to MPA treatment or to a placebo. Of 100 offenders approached to participate, 48 agreed to complete the initial assessment and 18 agreed to take part in the study. Only 11 completed a 3-month trial, 5 MPA participants and 6 controls. Although there was evidence that MPA reduced testosterone levels, there was no evidence that MPA changed sexual behavior.

Fedoroff, Wisner-Carlson, Dean, and Berlin (1992) treated 46 para-philiacs (including 29 pedophiles) on an outpatient basis for 5 years with either group therapy or therapy plus MPA. The rate of relapse among those who received MPA was 15% compared with 68% for those not receiving MPA. Among the pedophiles, only 1 who received MPA relapsed, com-pared with 9 who did not receive MPA. However, 88 patients had been excluded because they refused MPA, and another 38 were excluded because they were arrested before completing 5 years of treatment. Thus, among child molesters who remained in long-term psychotherapy, those who also received MPA were less likely to reoffend. As Fedoroff et al. pointed out, participants were not randomly assigned to treatment; therapists were not blind as to which men were receiving MPA, and men in the MPA con-dition may have been more highly motivated by virtue of their willingness to volunteer for the drug.

Meyer, Cole, and Emory (1992) compared 40 men treated with MPA with 21 men who refused. Most were child molesters; the remainder were rapists, exhibitionists, and voyeurs. Both groups received outpatient psy-chotherapy, and all admitted their offenses and to having overwhelming deviant fantasies. Men who admitted their offenses but blamed alcohol or drugs were excluded, as were men who had histories of serious antisocial behavior. Twenty-nine of the 40 men started on MPA dropped out of the drug treatment, and 10 of these later reoffended. Also, 7 reoffended while taking the drug. Although only 18% of the men started on MPA reoffended while on the drug, 43% of the men started on MPA reoffended before the end of the study. By comparison, 12 of the 21 (or 58%) of the men who refused MPA treatment reoffended. The recidivism rates (which included self-reported and official arrests for sex offenses) were not significantly dif-ferent, and recidivism rates were surprisingly high considering that the men were relatively low risk and highly motivated. Similar findings showing no differences in recidivism between the MPA and comparison groups were obtained by other researchers (Maletzky, 1991; McConaghy, Blaszcynski, & Kidson, 1988).

In summary, it appears that very few sex offenders will voluntarily accept currently available drugs to reduce testosterone, and fewer still continue to take the drugs for extended periods. The available evidence suggests that reoffense rates are low among those few offenders who stay in treatment that includes such drugs. There is, as yet, no convincing reason to believe that the drugs cause reductions in reoffending. The small proportion of sex offenders who remain in drug treatment might just be especially highly motivated.

As a cautionary note, Hanson and Harris (2000) compared sex offenders who committed a new sex offense during parole supervision with sex offenders who were matched to the first group on several known risk factors but who had successfully completed parole supervision. The recidivists were much more likely to have been prescribed an antiandrogen. Of course, it is likely that those men perceived to be higher risk were more likely to have been seen as candidates for the drugs. Nevertheless, mandating antiandrogen drugs during community supervision neither eliminated recidivism nor reduced it to low levels.

BEHAVIORAL AND COGNITIVE–BEHAVIORAL TREATMENTS

Almost every published evaluation of behavioral or cognitive–behavioral treatment, and all but one of those described in this section, share one common component–behavioral technique to normalize deviant sexual preferences. The particular methods used to alter sexual preferences vary, but most (e.g., covert sensitization, masturbatory reconditioning, operant conditioning) attempt to associate aversive events with arousal to deviant stimuli or fantasies.

Most reports also indicate that training in social competence is a key treatment component. Many contain other components, including sex education (Rice, Quinsey, & Harris, 1991), anger management (Marshall & Barbaree, 1988), nonspecific counseling (Hanson et al., 1993), family systems therapy (Borduin, Henggeler, Blaske, & Stein, 1990), and relapse prevention (Marques, Day, Nelson, & West, 1994). Many contain noncognitive–behavioral elements such as insight-oriented psychotherapy (Davidson, 1984) or victim awareness and empathy (Marshall, Jones, Ward, Johnston, & Barbaree, 1991). This lack of standardization has unfortunate consequences: Treatments are abandoned (or at least greatly altered) before anything is known about their effectiveness, and measures of in-program change are seldom reported (for exceptions, see Marques et al., 1994; Rice et al., 1991), thus preventing the accumulation of knowledge about the effectiveness of individual components.

One preliminary study obtained positive results for *adolescent* sex offenders using community-based multisystemic therapy compared with individual therapy (Borduin et al., 1990). The treatment was problem-focused service aimed at family preservation by resolving school problems, social deficits, peer difficulties, and family contact. No treatment for deviant sexual preferences was provided. Treatment assignment was random, but no information was provided about treatment dropouts. Although the number of participants was small (eight in each group), officially recorded rearrest data for sexual and nonsexual offenses indicated a large positive effect of multisystemic therapy.

No methodologically adequate study of *adult* sex offenders has obtained large, or even moderate, positive treatment effects. Many of the studies that have obtained positive effects have used treatment refusers or dropouts as a comparison group. For example, Hildebran and Pithers (1992) evaluated a cognitive–behavioral program for adult rapists and child molesters. Fifty men who completed relapse prevention were compared with 40 men who dropped out. Men who completed the program were less likely to reoffend, but comparing treatment completers with treatment dropouts permits no conclusions about the efficacy of the specific treatment. Instead, completing treatment may be an indication that an offender (with or without the treatment) is low risk. Studies using dropouts or refusers as comparisons are not discussed further.

Marshall and Barbaree (1988) evaluated a community program that combined behavioral treatments to modify sexual preferences, social skills training, relaxation training, and counseling for child molesters. The comparison group were men who admitted their offenses and volunteered for treatment, but who lived too far away or later changed their minds about treatment. The outcome measure was the combination of official arrests plus unofficial reports of sexual recidivism. This measure indicated a positive effect of treatment. However, official recidivism data for men in this study were reported elsewhere (Marshall, Jones, et al., 1991) and yielded no statistically significant effects.

Several other evaluations of cognitive–behavioral or behavioral treatments have obtained no positive effects, mixed results, or negative effects (i.e., results in favor of the comparison group) of treatment (Davidson, 1984; Hanson et al., 1993; Quinsey, Khanna, & Malcolm, 1998; Rice et al., 1991). A study that deserves special comment is an ongoing, ambitious, cognitive–behavioral program for incarcerated child molesters and rapists that has so far been reported on in preliminary reports (e.g., Marques et al., 1994). The treatment combined relapse prevention training, relaxation training, social skills training, stress and anger management, counseling for substance abuse problems, behavioral treatment for deviant preferences, and aftercare. Random assignment to treatment was done from a larger pool of volunteers, and a second comparison group was formed by matching treatment refusers to treated participants. Offenders who dropped out of treatment were also recorded and followed. Attrition was high, and those participants who failed to complete treatment after beginning were especially likely to have a subsequent sexual or violent arrest (Marques et al., 1994). When participants assigned to treatment were compared with the untreated volunteers, there were no significant positive effects of treatment. When offenders who completed treatment were compared with untreated volunteers, treated men, especially child molesters, had significantly fewer subsequent arrests for nonsexual violent offenses than did untreated volunteers.

In summary, no data compel revision of the conclusions of earlier reviews of sex offender treatment (Furby, Weinrott, & Blackshaw, 1989; Quinsey et al., 1993). Simply put, the effectiveness of adult sex offender treatment has yet to be demonstrated. Although there have been some studies that have obtained positive results, the existing data provide no evidence about just what might have been responsible. The idea that current sex offender therapies are on the right track is further undermined by the finding that therapists' judgments about clinical progress are unrelated (or even positively related) to recidivism (Quinsey et al., 1998; Seto & Barbaree, 1999). The research literature is profoundly unhelpful in giving clues as to what treatment might be effective with what kinds of sex offenders. The preferred or recommended treatment continues to evolve (e.g., Hall, Shondrick, & Hirschman, 1993; Hollin & Howells, 1991; Marshall, 1993), but the evolution is not based on an empirical foundation of demonstrably effective treatment.

GENERAL DISCUSSION

In a meta-analysis of 12 sex offender treatment studies, Hall (1995) reported a small statistically significant positive effect and concluded that no variability in effect size could be attributed to methodological quality. However, we (Rice, Harris, & Quinsey, 2001) and others (McConaghy, 1999) have reported several problems with Hall's meta-analysis that compromise the conclusions. A closer examination of the studies in the meta-analysis revealed that the most methodologically rigorous studies demonstrated no treatment effect. By contrast, the studies that used treatment dropouts or refusers as controls obtained a large treatment effect. The most parsimonious conclusion is that the large effect obtained in the studies that used treatment dropouts or refusers as controls was due not to any specific effect of treatment but to the fact that volunteering for and persisting with treatment screens out high-risk offenders.

Hall (1995) compared three classes of treatment—behavioral, cognitive–behavioral, and hormonal (including castration)—and concluded that the latter two types of treatment were superior. Because his conclusion seemed to contradict more comprehensive meta-analyses of offender treatment (Lipsey, 1992), we examined the methodology of the studies more closely. We concluded that the classification of control groups yielded a more plausible explanation of the results: None of the evaluations of behavioral treatment, but all of the evaluations of hormonal interventions (reporting a positive effect) used the treatment-refusers-as-control design (Rice et al., 2001). It is clear that the number of well-controlled studies is too small to permit an informative meta-analysis. As an illustration, consider the evaluation of sex offender treatment in rural Vermont.

McGrath, Hoke, and Vojtisek (1998) reported that sex offenders on conditional release who chose specialized sex offender treatment (comprehensive assessment, cognitive–behavior therapy, behavioral treatment for deviant sexual interests, relapse prevention training, and coordinated community supervision) exhibited significantly less recidivism than those who chose nonspecialized treatment (little assessment, individual psychotherapy, and noncooperation between therapists and probation officials) from clinicians "whose experience with this population was typically minimal" (p. 208). This report is admirable for several reasons: Few sex offender therapists publish any empirical evidence pertaining to efficacy; the specialized treatment was very comprehensive and embodied the best current clinical advice; and the authors included a large number of participants, had a long follow-up (over 5 years), and used official recidivism data.

Unfortunately, this study also shows how difficult it is to reduce the uncertainty about the size of a specific effect of treatment without well-controlled research. For example, the nature of the treatment was clearly confounded with the quality and intensity of posttreatment supervision. Because the specialized treatment was compared with psychotherapy, it is possible, as discussed earlier, that the results were due to psychotherapy (especially delivered by naive and uncooperative clinicians) causing an increase in recidivism. Finally, participants chose their treatment condition and, as McGrath et al. (1998) stated, could have "avoided the specialized program and enrolled in less demanding treatment" (p. 207). It was clear that participants' selection of treatment was related to preexisting risk. For example, incest offenders, who exhibit the lowest risk among all sex offenders, were disproportionately more likely to choose the specialized treatment. None of this is meant to criticize the practice of McGrath and colleagues who, in our view, made responsible clinical decisions.

Nevertheless, this evaluation, though certainly better than most, does not reduce the uncertainty about the specific effect of sex offender treatment. It is possible that the specialized treatment caused a reduction in recidivism, but it is just as possible that other factors (all well-known threats to internal validity) were responsible for the differences observed. Indeed, the scientific principle of parsimony requires that we not accept the existence of an effect until empirical results demand it. Furthermore, a dozen or a hundred studies similar to this one would leave us no further ahead.

This fact is relevant to a recent meta-analysis of psychological treatment for sex offenders sponsored by the Association for the Treatment of Sexual Abusers (Hanson et al., 2002), which reported that random assignment studies showed a zero effect, but "incidental assignment" indicated that treated participants had lower recidivism rates than the untreated comparison participants. Incidental assignment studies were defined as those "in which equivalence was not assured, but where no obvious reasons for group differences" (Hanson et al., 2002, p. 172). In our view, however, inspection of the original studies reveals several obvious reasons. Most commonly, men in the treated group were those who completed treatment, whereas those in the comparison group were not offered treatment (e.g., Bakker, Hudson, Wales, & Riley, 1999; Looman, Abracen, & Nicholaichuk, 2000; Nicholaichuk, Gordon, Ga, & Wong, 2000); that is, the comparison group included an unknown number of men who would have refused or dropped out of treatment had it been offered. In addition, there were other obvious reasons to expect pretreatment group differences. These included (a) a longer follow-up period for the comparison group, (b) offenders who refused were excluded from the treated but not the comparison group (Allam, 1998; Worling & Curwen, 2000), (c) disproportionately high-risk offenders (i.e., exhibitionists) in the comparison group (Lindsay & Smith, 1998), (d) disproportionately low-risk offenders (i.e., incestuous child molesters) in the treated group (McGrath et al., 1998), or (e) the comparison group were offenders permitted to choose relatively undemanding counseling instead of specialized sex offender treatment (Guarino-Ghezzi & Kimball, 1998; Marshall, Eccles, & Barbaree, 1991; McGrath et al., 1998). The authors of the meta-analysis concluded "that the balance of available evidence suggests that current treatments reduce recidivism, but that firm conclusions await more and better research" (Hanson et al., 2002, p. 186). Obviously, it is just as empirically valid to say that the balance of available evidence suggests that current treatments *do not* reduce recidivism but that firm conclusions await more and better research. In our opinion, earnest wishes notwithstanding, epistemological standards require the latter statement with the former implied rather than the converse.

Because evidence of treatment efficacy is so weak, careful risk appraisal must be a cornerstone of the management of sex offenders (Quinsey et al., 1998). Because there is scant evidence that a high-risk offender can be turned into a low-risk offender by participation in any current treatment, the best advice is to use treatments that (a) fit with what we know about sex offenders specifically and about offenders more generally, (b) have been shown to produce pre- and posttreatment changes in empirically relevant measures, (c) are acceptable to offenders and ethically supportable, (d) are carefully described so that program integrity can be evaluated, and (e) can be incorporated into ongoing supervision programs. Community supervision programs (and empirically based ways to deny access to the community) are especially important given our lack of knowledge about effective treatments.

Among sex offenders specifically, the probability and type of recidivism are affected by victim age, sex, and relationship to the offender; the seriousness and nature of the sex offense; and the number of previous sex offenses (Hanson & Bussière, 1998; Harris et al., 2002). The most relevant of these for the design of treatment is probably sexual preferences (Hanson & Bussière, 1998). Some offenders have marked paraphilic (sexually deviant) interests in children or sadistic sexual assault, and these can be measured with varying degrees of adequacy by offender self-report, offense history, or phallometric assessment. Phallometric assessments are the most valid of these for sex offenders (Harris et al., 1992), although they are also undoubtedly intrusive and there are concerns about the ethics of their use (e.g., McConaghy, 1989). The measurement of these interests is important because it provides clues to motivation and ideas about the nature of possible future sexual aggression. Continued phallometric evidence of inappropriate sexual preferences is a bad prognostic sign, but a reduction in such interest is not necessarily a good sign (Proulx, Côté, & Achille, 1993). Notwithstanding recent research implicating a prenatal origin to deviant sexual preferences (Lalumière, Harris, Quinsey, & Rice, 1998), the discriminative and predictive validity of sexual preferences imply a focus for treatment (Harris & Rice, 1996).

Psychopathy is an important predictor of recidivism among sex offenders, as it is among offenders more generally. Moreover, the combination of psychopathy and sexual deviance predicts especially poor outcome (Harris et al., 2002; Rice & Harris, 1997). Although something is known about what treatment is harmful for psychopaths (Harris, Rice, & Cormier, 1994; Rice, Harris, & Cormier, 1992), there are no data about what will work. Nevertheless, because effective programs for psychopaths might be different from those for nonpsychopaths, and because psychopathy is a powerful risk factor, evaluations of treatment efficacy should assess sex offenders' psychopathy.

CONCLUSION

Based on what is known about sex offenders and about treating offenders in general, it is sensible for sex offender therapists to provide behavior therapy to reduce deviant sexual preferences, antisocial attitudes and values, procriminal peer associations, substance abuse, and unemployment. Drugs to lower sex drive may also make sense in some cases. However, the foregoing review indicates that these components (at least delivered at currently typical intensities) might be insufficient to decrease recidivism. The field of sex offender treatment urgently requires innovative treatments based on new research results on the etiology of sexual deviance and aggression, and rigorous high-quality research on therapeutic efficacy that includes random assignment to treatment, in-program change measures, and reliance on hard outcome data. Failure to meet these needs means that sex offender treatment will continue to change but not progress (Harris, Rice, & Quinsey, 1998; Quinsey, 1998; Quinsey et al., 1993; Rice et al., 2001).

REFERENCES

Abel, G. G., Mittelman, M., Becker, J. V., Rathner, J., & Rouleau, J. L. (1988). Predicting child molesters' response to treatment. In R. Prentky & V. L. Quinsey (Eds.), *Human sexual aggression: Current perspectives* (pp. 223–243). New York: Annals of the New York Academy of Sciences.

Abel, G. T., Rouleau, J. L., & Cunningham-Rathner, J. (1986). Sexually aggressive behavior. In J. Curran, A. L. McGarry, & S. A. Shah (Eds.), *Forensic psychology and psychiatry: Perspectives and standards for interdisciplinary practice* (pp. 289–313). Philadelphia: Davis.

Alexander, M., Gunn, J., Taylor, P. J., & Finch, J. (1993). Should a sexual offender be allowed castration? *British Medical Journal, 307,* 790–793.

Allam, J. (1998). *Community-based treatment for sex offenders: An evaluation.* Birmingham, England: University of Birmingham.

Andrews, D. A., Zinger, I., Hoge, R. D., Bonta, J., Gendreau, P., & Cullen, F. T. (1990). Does correctional treatment work? A clinically relevant and psychologically informed meta-analysis. *Criminology, 28,* 369–404.

Bakker, L., Hudson, S., Wales, D., & Riley, D. (1999). *"And there was light": An evaluation of the Kia Marama Treatment Programme for New Zealand sex offenders against children.* Unpublished report, Christchurch, New Zealand.

Borduin, C. M., Henggeler, S. W., Blaske, D. M., & Stein, R. J. (1990). Multisystemic treatment of adolescent sexual offenders. *International Journal of Offender Therapy and Comparative Criminology, 34,* 105–113.

Brower, K. J. (1993). Anabolic steroids. *Psychiatric Clinics of North America, 16,* 97–103.

Chambless, D. L., & Hollon, S. D. (1998). Defining empirically supported therapies. *Journal of Consulting and Clinical Psychology, 66,* 7–18.

Davidson, P. R. (1984, January). *Behavioural treatment for incarcerated sex offenders: Post-release outcome.* Paper presented at the The Sex Offender Assessment and Treatment Conference, Kingston, Ontario, Canada.

Eastman, N. (1993). Surgical castration for sex offenders. *British Medical Journal, 307,* 141.

Fedoroff, J. P., Wisner-Carlson, R., Dean, S., & Berlin, F. S. (1992). Medroxyprogesterone acetate in the treatment of paraphilic sexual disorders. *Journal of Offender Rehabilitation, 18,* 109–123.

Flick, S. N. (1988). Managing attrition in clinical research. *Clinical Psychology Review, 8,* 499–515.

Freund, K. (1980). Therapeutic sex drive reduction. *Acta Psychiatrica Scandinavica, 62,* 5–38.

Frisbie, L. V. (1969). *Another look at sex offenders in California* (Research Monograph No. 12). Sacramento: California Department of Mental Hygiene.

Frisbie, L. V., & Dondis, E. H. (1965). *Recidivism among treated sex offenders* (Research Monograph No. 5). Sacramento: California Department of Mental Hygiene.

Furby, L., Weinrott, M. R., & Blackshaw, L. (1989). Sex offender recidivism: A review. *Psychological Bulletin, 105,* 3–30.

Guarino-Ghezzi, S., & Kimball, L. M. (1998). Juvenile sex offenders in treatment. *Corrections Management Quarterly, 2,* 45–54.

Hall, G. C. N. (1995). Sexual offender recidivism revisited: A meta-analysis of recent treatment studies. *Journal of Consulting and Clinical Psychology, 63,* 802–809.

Hall, G. C. N., Shondrick, D. D., & Hirschman, R. (1993). Conceptually derived treatments for sexual aggressors. *Professional Psychology: Research and Practice, 24,* 62–69.

Hanson, R. K., & Bussière, M. T. (1998). Predicting relapse: A meta-analysis of sexual offender recidivism studies. *Journal of Consulting and Clinical Psychology, 66,* 348–362.

Hanson, R. K., Gordon, A., Harris, A. J. R., Marques, J. K., Murphy, W., Quinsey, V. L., & Seto, M. C. (2002). The First Report of the Collaborative Outcome Data Project on the effectiveness of psychological treatment for sexual offenders. *Sexual Abuse: A Journal of Research and Treatment, 14,* 169–194.

Hanson, R. K., & Bussière, M. T. (1998). Predicting relapse: A meta-analysis of sexual offender recidivism studies. *Journal of Consulting and Clinical Psychology, 66,* 348–362.

Hanson, R. K., & Harris, A. (2000). Where should we intervene? Dynamic predictors of sex offense recidivism. *Criminal Justice and Behavior, 27,* 6–35.

Hanson, R. K., Steffy, R. A., & Gauthier, R. (1993). Long-term recidivism of child molesters. *Journal of Consulting and Clinical Psychology, 61,* 646–652.

Harris, G. T., & Rice, M. E. (1996). The science in phallometric testing of male sexual interest. *Current Directions in Psychological Science, 5,* 156–160.

Harris, G. T., Rice, M. E., & Cormier, C. A. (1994). Psychopaths: Is a therapeutic community therapeutic? *Therapeutic Communities, 15,* 283–300.

Harris, G. T., Rice, M. E., & Quinsey, V. L. (1998). Appraisal and management of risk in sexual aggressors: Implications for criminal justice policy. *Psychology, Public Policy, and Law, 4,* 73–115.

Harris, G. T., Rice, M. E., Quinsey, V. L., Chaplin, T. C., & Earls, C. (1992). Maximizing the discriminant validity of phallometric assessment. *Psychological Assessment, 4,* 502–511.

Harris, G. T., Rice, M. E., Quinsey, V. L., Lalumière, M. L., Boer, D., & Lang, C. (2002). *A multi-site comparison of actuarial risk instruments for sex offenders.* Unpublished manuscript.

Hildebran, D. D., & Pithers, W. D. (1992). Relapse prevention: Application and outcome. In W. O'Donohue & J. H. Geer (Eds.), *The sexual abuse of children: Vol. 2. Clinical issues* (pp. 365–393). Hillsdale, NJ: Erlbaum.

Hollin, C. R., & Howells, K. (Eds.). (1991). *Clinical approaches to sex offenders and their victims.* Chichester, England: Wiley.

Hucker, S., Langevin, R., & Bain, J. (1988). A double blind trial of sex drive reducing medication in pedophiles. *Annals of Sex Research, 1,* 227–342.

Knight, R. A., & Prentky, R. A. (1990). Classifying sexual offenders: The development and corroboration of taxonomic models. In W. L. Marshall, D. R. Laws, & H. E. Barbaree (Eds.), *Handbook of sexual assault: Issues, theories, and treatment of the offender* (pp. 23–52). New York: Plenum.

Lalumière, M. L., Harris, G. T., Quinsey, V. L., & Rice, M. E. (1998). Sexual deviance and number of older brothers among sexual offenders. *Sexual Abuse: A Journal of Research and Treatment, 10,* 5–15.

Langevin, R., Wright, P., & Handy, L. (1988). What treatment do sex offenders want? *Annals of Sex Research, 1,* 353–385.

Lindsay, W. R., & Smith, A. H. (1998). Responses to treatment for sex offenders with intellectual disability: A comparison of men with 1- and 2-year probation sentences. *Journal of Intellectual Disability Research, 42,* 346–353.

Lipsey, M. W. (1992). Juvenile delinquency treatment: A meta-analytic inquiry into the variability of effects. In T. D. Cook, H. Cooper, D. S. Cordray, H. Hartmann, L. V. Hedges, R. J. Light, T. A. Louis, & F. Mosteller (Eds.), *Meta-analysis for explanation* (pp. 83–126). New York: Russell Sage Foundation.

Looman, J., Abracen, J., & Nicholaichuk, T. P. (2000). Recidivism among treated sexual offenders and matched controls. *Journal of Interpersonal Violence, 15,* 279–290.

Maletzky, B. M. (1991). The use of medroxyprogesterone acetate to assist in the treatment of sexual offenders. *Annals of Sex Research, 4,* 117–129.

Marques, J. K., Day, D. M., Nelson, C., & West, M. (1994). Effects of cognitive–behavioral treatment on sex offender recidivism. *Criminal Justice and Behavior, 21,* 28–54.

Marshall, W. L. (1993). A revised approach to the treatment of men who sexually assault adult females. In G. C. Nagayama Hall, R. Hirschman, J. R. Graham, & M. S. Zaragoza (Eds.), *Sexual aggression: Issues in etiology, assessment, and treatment* (pp. 143–166). Washington, DC: Taylor & Francis.

Marshall, W. L., & Barbaree, H. E. (1988). The long-term evaluation of a behavioral treatment program for child molesters. *Behaviour Research and Therapy, 26,* 499–511.

Marshall, W. L., Eccles, A., & Barbaree, H. E. (1991). The treatment of exhibitionists: A focus on sexual deviance versus cognitive and relationship features. *Behavior Research and Therapy, 29,* 129–135.

Marshall, W. L., Jones, R., Ward, T., Johnston, P., & Barbaree, H. E. (1991). Treatment outcome with sex offenders. *Clinical Psychology Review, 11,* 465–485.

McConaghy, N. (1989). Validity and ethics of penile circumference measures of sexual arousal: A critical review. *Archives of Sexual Behavior, 18,* 357–369.

McConaghy, N. (1999). Methodological issues concerning evaluation of treatment for sexual offenders: Randomization, treatment, dropouts, untreated controls, and within-treatment studies. *Sexual Abuse: A Journal of Research and Treatment, 11,* 183–193.

McConaghy, N., Blaszczynski, A., & Kidson, W. (1988). Treatment of sex offenders with imaginal desensitization and/or medroxyprogesterone. *Acta Psychiatrica Scandinavica, 77,* 199–206.

McGrath, R. J., Hoke, S. E., & Vojtisek, J. E. (1998). Cognitive–behavioral treatment of sex offenders. *Criminal Justice and Behavior, 25,* 203–225.

Meyer, W. J., Cole, C., & Emory, E. (1992). Depo provera treatment for sex offending behavior: An evaluation of outcome. *Bulletin of the American Academy of Psychiatry and Law, 20,* 249–259.

Nicholaichuk, T., Gordon, A., Gu, D., & Wong, S. (2000). Outcome of an institutional sexual offender treatment program: A comparison between treated and matched untreated offenders. *Sexual Abuse: A Journal of Research and Treatment, 12,* 139–153.

Pollock, N. L., & Hashmall, J. M. (1991). The excuses of child molesters. *Behavioral Sciences and the Law, 9,* 53–59.

Prentky, R. A., Knight, R. A., & Lee, A. F. S. (1997). Risk factors associated with recidivism among extrafamilial child molesters. *Journal of Consulting and Clinical Psychology, 65,* 141–149.

Proulx, J., Côté, G., & Achille, P. A. (1993). Prevention of voluntary control of penile response in homosexual pedophiles during phallometric testing. *Journal of Sex Research, 30,* 140–147.

Quinsey, V. L. (1977). The assessment and treatment of child molesters: A review. *Canadian Psychological Review, 18,* 204–220.

Quinsey, V. L. (1984). Sexual aggression: Studies of offenders against women. In D. Weisstub (Ed.), *Law and mental health: International perspectives* (pp. 84–121). New York: Pergamon.

Quinsey, V. L. (1998). Comment on Marshall's "Monster, victim, or everyman." *Sexual Abuse: A Journal of Research and Treatment, 10,* 65–69.

Quinsey, V. L., Harris, G. T., Rice, M. E., & Cormier, C. A. (1998). *Violent offenders: Appraising and managing risk.* Washington, DC: American Psychological Association.

Quinsey, V. L., Harris, G. T., Rice, M. E., & Lalumière, M. L. (1993). Assessing treatment efficacy in outcome studies of sex offenders. *Journal of Interpersonal Violence, 8,* 512–523.

Quinsey, V. L., Khanna, A., & Malcolm, B. (1998). Recidivism among treated and untreated sex offenders. *Journal of Interpersonal Violence, 13,* 621–644.

Rice, M. E., & Harris, G. T. (1997). Cross validation and extension of the Violence Risk Appraisal Guide for child molesters and rapists. *Law and Human Behavior, 21*, 231–241.

Rice, M. E., & Harris, G. T. (1999). Sexual aggressors. In D. L. Faigman, D. H. Kaye, M. J. Saks, & J. Sanders (Eds.), *Modern scientific evidence: The law and science of expert testimony* (Vol. 3, pp. 89–121). St. Paul, MN: West.

Rice, M. E., & Harris, G. T. (in press). The size and sign of treatment effects in sex offender therapy. In R. A. Prentky, M. C. Seto, & A. Burgess (Eds.), *Understanding and managing sexually coercive behavior*. New York: Annals of the New York Academy of Sciences.

Rice, M. E., Harris, G. T., & Cormier, C. A. (1992). Evaluation of a maximum security therapeutic community for psychopaths and other mentally disordered offenders. *Law and Human Behavior, 16*, 399–412.

Rice, M. E., Harris, G. T., & Quinsey, V. L. (2001). Treating the adult sex offender. In J. B. Ashford, B. D. Sales, & W. Reid (Eds.), *Treating adult and juvenile offenders with special needs* (pp. 291–312). Washington, DC: American Psychological Association.

Rice, M. E., Quinsey, V. L., & Harris, G. T. (1991). Sexual recidivism among child molesters released from a maximum security psychiatric institution. *Journal of Consulting and Clinical Psychology, 59*, 381–386.

Romero, J., & Williams, L. M. (1983). Psychotherapy and supervision with sex offenders. *Federal Probation, 47*, 36–42.

Romero, J. J., & Williams, L. M. (1985). Recidivism among convicted sex offenders: A 10-year follow-up study. *Federal Probation, 49*, 58–64.

Seto, M. C., & Barbaree, H. E. (1999). Psychopathy, treatment behavior, and sex offender recidivism. *Journal of Interpersonal Violence, 14*, 1235–1248.

Sturgeon, V. H., & Taylor, J. (1980). Report of a five-year follow-up study of mentally disordered sex offenders released from Atascadero State Hospital. *Criminal Justice Journal, 4*, 31–63.

Stürup, G. K. (1968). Treatment of sexual offenders in Herstedvester Denmark. *Acta Psychiatrica Scandinavica, 44*, 5–63.

Wille, R., & Beier, K. M. (1989). Castration in Germany. *Annals of Sex Research, 2*, 103–133.

Worling, J. R., & Curwen, T. (2000). Adolescent sexual offender recidivism: Success of specialized treatment and implications for risk prediction. *Child Abuse and Neglect, 24*, 965–982.

6

TREATMENT AND THE CIVIL COMMITMENT OF SEX OFFENDERS

ERIC S. JANUS

Recent litigation about the constitutionality of sex predator commitment laws addresses the role that treatment plays in both the law and policy of civil commitment. (See this volume, chapter 11, for a discussion of the constitutionality of sexually violent predator laws.) In this chapter, I examine these lessons about treatment, placing them into a context of constitutional law, morality, and social policy.

One can cautiously say that civilly committed sex offenders have a qualified, constitutional right to treatment. Without a treatment purpose, indefinite civil commitment would be punitive. Therefore, the U.S. Constitution requires states to make reasonable efforts to provide professionally acceptable treatment to those persons who are committed. However, because safety, not treatment, is the central justification for these commitments, states may be permitted to commit some dangerous, mentally disordered individuals for whom no effective treatment is available. I argue, however, that the logic of the Supreme Court's cases, though not their

---

The author has served as co-counsel in litigation challenging the constitutionality of Minnesota's Sexually Dangerous Persons Act.

explicit language, places a "reasonableness" limit on the confinement of persons for whom no effective treatment exists.

Despite the equivocal nature of the constitutional right, treatment-driven issues are critical to the public policy debates about sex offender commitments. Questions of the allocation of scarce mental health treatment resources (La Fond, 1998), the creation of treatment disincentives (Winick, 1998), and the generation of social meanings that distort and defeat therapeutic interventions are all raised by sex offender commitment schemes (Janus, 2000).

SEX OFFENDER COMMITMENTS

As we saw in chapters 1 and 2, sex offender commitments deploy civil-commitment-style confinement to address sexual violence. Because these laws are denominated "civil" rather than criminal, states claim they are not subject to the strict constitutional constraints of the criminal law.

State sexually violent predator laws generally confer a right to treatment for those committed. For example, the Minnesota law requires "treatment, best adapted, according to contemporary professional standards, to rendering further supervision unnecessary" (Minnesota Civil Commitment Act, 1998). More ambiguously, Kansas law mandates that the confinement "conform to constitutional requirements for care and treatment" (Kansas Commitment of Sexually Violent Predators Act, 1998).

Despite the legislative command for treatment, legislatures and courts have acknowledged that treatment is secondary to the primary purpose of sex offender commitments—the protection of the public (*In re Hendricks*, 1996; Washington Sexually Violent Predators Act, 1999). And, the actual performance of states calls into question the genuineness of the treatment purpose. Washington State's commitment law served as a national model, yet it has persistently refused to bring its treatment program up to constitutional standards (La Fond, 1999). On a national level, in the first decade of these laws' existence, only a handful of the hundreds of committed sex offenders have completed treatment and been discharged into the community (Janus & Walbek, 2000; Lieb & Nelson, 2001).

SEX OFFENDER TREATMENT

Arguments about the nature and efficacy of sex offender treatment are central to the constitutional debates about sex offender commitment statutes and are important in legal and policy contexts. Thus, a brief overview of sex offender treatment will assist in understanding these issues.

(See this volume, chapter 5, for a thorough review of various treatments for sex offenders and an analysis of whether they are effective.)

Sex offender treatment programs have evolved rapidly, and methods used 20 years ago are now considered inadequate and obsolete (Marshall & Pithers, 1994). Professional and public policy views about the efficacy of treatment have changed as well. In the early part of the 1900s, optimism about the powers of psychiatry produced a rash of sex offender commitment laws (Freedman, 1987). Pessimism about the efficacy of the treatment contributed to the demise of these laws in the 1970s and 1980s (Group for the Advancement of Psychiatry, 1977).

Currently, there is no consensus about the efficacy of sex offender treatment (see this volume, chapter 5). Some influential commentators believe that the evidence supports an "optimistic outlook" on the efficacy of treatment (Marshall & Pithers, 1994, p. 11). Others, conceding that "the jury is still out," find the evidence "encouraging" (Prentky, 1995, p. 167). Finally, some respected commentators pessimistically conclude that "there is little evidence that high-quality, state-of-the-art treatments significantly reduce recidivism" (Lieb, Quinsey, & Berliner, 1998, p. 93).

Even if one accepts the optimistic conclusions about treatment efficacy in general, sex offender commitment laws target the "most dangerous" sex offenders who are likely to be the least amenable to treatment (Lieb et al., 1998). Clinicians have no way to differentiate those individual offenders for whom treatment works (Grossman, Martis, & Fichtner, 1999).

Treatment for sex offenders falls into several categories. Although nonbehavioral psychotherapy treatment was the norm until recently, "the evidence suggests strongly that [these types of] treatments are ineffective" (Rice & Harris, 1997, p. 154). Surgical castration has not been shown to be effective for nonconsenting offenders or "the large proportion of sex offenders who have a history of diverse nonsexual offenses in addition to sexual ones" (Rice & Harris, 1997, p. 155).

Antiandrogen medications are used to achieve, through pharmacological means, the same sex-drive-reducing effects as surgical castration (Rice & Harris, 1997). (See this volume, chapter 14, for a discussion of the ethical and legal issues raised by the use of these drugs.) The American Psychiatric Association Task Force Report on Dangerous Sex Offenders concludes that these medications "can play an important role in the treatment of sexual offenders" (American Psychiatric Association, 1999). However, Rice and Harris (1997) concluded, "there is as yet no reason to believe that such drugs will reduce sexual recidivism among men who are coerced into taking the drugs" (p. 154). There has been some success reported with a class of drugs called selective serotonin reuptake inhibitors (SSRIs) for sex offenders with concurrent mood or anxiety disorders. But there have been no controlled studies, and conclusions about effectiveness of these drugs need further research (Grossman et al., 1999).

The most common contemporary approach to treatment of sex offenders is cognitive–behavioral treatment (Rice & Harris, 1997). Behavioral techniques are designed to decrease or eliminate deviant sexual arousal by "pairing" deviant fantasies with aversive consequences. Cognitive–behavioral techniques seek to change offenders' beliefs and attitudes and to increase their knowledge, skills, and empathy. Central to this form of therapy is "relapse prevention," which involves "strategies to anticipate and resist deviant urges" (Grossman et al., 1999, p. 335). The American Psychiatric Association Task Force concluded: "The treatment approach most likely to have an effect on recidivism is a combined pharmacological, cognitive, behavior, and relapse prevention approach" (American Psychiatric Association, 1999, p. 146).

HENDRICKS AND THE CONSTITUTIONAL ROLE OF TREATMENT

In *Kansas v. Hendricks* (1997), the U.S. Supreme Court upheld the constitutionality of Kansas' sex offender commitment law. Although the challengers raised a number of legal concerns about the statute, this chapter focuses on the role of treatment in the constitutional analysis.

As framed by the Court, the treatment argument took two alternative forms. The *treatment-amenability* alternative argued that Hendricks's commitment was unconstitutional because his condition (pedophilia) was not *amenable* to treatment. The *failure-to-provide-available-treatment* argument, on the other hand, assumed that the condition was amenable to treatment, but that the state *failed* to provide that treatment. In either event, the challengers argued that the lack of treatment rendered the commitment punitive and thus unconstitutional.

The Court dismissed both arguments. With regard to the first, the Court stated that treatment amenability was not a constitutional precondition to the civil commitment of dangerous individuals. Regarding the second argument, the Court stated that the "somewhat meager" treatment program initially offered to Hendricks had improved substantially. Given the "wide latitude" states enjoy in developing treatment regimens, the Court stated that "Kansas has doubtless satisfied its obligation to provide available treatment."

The Court's discussion suggests two possible lessons. First, at least for police power civil commitments, treatment is not the constitutional justification for confinement. When the state uses its civil commitment power to deprive a person of liberty *for the benefit of the society*, the justification must come from two sources other than treatment: the danger posed by the person (commitment is limited to a "narrow class of particularly dangerous individuals") and the nature of the person's mental disorder (commitment is limited to persons with "serious ... disorder[s]" that produce a "special and serious lack of ability to control behavior"; *Kansas v. Crane*, 2002). If these predicates are satisfied, it is arguable that states may commit individuals for whom no effective treatment exists. Note, however, that the precedential value of this lesson is weak because the Court characterized Hendricks himself as admitting that treatment for his condition was available. This characterization meant that the issue of treatment amenability was not squarely presented.

The second lesson is that civil commitment gives rise to a constitutional right to treatment. Even if treatment amenability is not a precondition for commitment, the state has an obligation to take reasonable steps to provide available, professional treatment to committed individuals. Referring several times to the state's "obligation" to provide treatment, the Court took some pains to enumerate the steps Kansas had taken to mandate and provide treatment. Although the record provided no occasion for the Court to judge the adequacy of the treatment, the Court cited *Youngberg v. Romeo* (1982), which required that professional medical judgment be exercised, and *Allen v. Illinois* (1986), specifically noting Illinois' undertaking to provide treatment "designed to effect recovery." In context, it seems clear that the Court's determination that Hendricks's confinement was not punitive turned heavily on this discussion of treatment. Four years later, in *Seling v. Young* (2001), the Supreme Court again hinted broadly that the Constitution provides some guarantee of treatment in sex offender commitments.

A CRITIQUE OF *HENDRICKS*: PUTTING THE *HENDRICKS* HOLDING IN A CONSTITUTIONAL AND ETHICAL FRAMEWORK

Context

Some context will help our assessment of the Supreme Court's treatment jurisprudence. Civil commitment is based on two distinct state powers. The *parens patriae* power describes the state's authority to protect individuals who are unable to protect themselves (*Addington v. Texas*, 1978). This power is based on two principles: autonomy and beneficence (Buchanan & Brock, 1989). In theory, these two principles ensure that *parens patriae* interventions are limited to individuals who are incompetent to make their own decisions (the autonomy principle) and that the intervention is designed to serve the individual's "best interests" (the beneficence principle).

The second state power is the police power, which authorizes the state to protect the public's health and safety (*Addington v. Texas*, 1978). This power, following the principle of utility, is based on a judgment that the burden on the detainee is outweighed by the benefits to others (Buchanan & Brock, 1989).

In actual practice, most civil commitments are directed at seriously mentally ill patients rather than seriously dangerous sex offenders. These "standard" mental health commitments are supported by both state interests. That is, the individual's interests and the public's interests are approximately coincident. Thus, the individual's incompetence to make life decisions gives the state the power to make decisions that simultaneously benefit both the individual and the public.

This chapter focuses on a different set of cases: those in which the only justification is the police power, because the *parens patriae* assumptions do not hold. These are cases in which the individual is competent to make life choices (but chooses a life of antisocial violence) or cases in which the individual is incompetent but society's interest in confining the individual exceeds the individual's interest in being confined for treatment. These civil commitments are not in the "best interests" of the detainee. Most committed sex offenders are competent, and therefore fall squarely within this non–*parens patriae* group. (Chapter 10 explores the relationship between the law and responsible individuals, on the one hand, and incompetent individuals, on the other.)

Rejection of a Treatment-Amenability Requirement

To the extent that *Hendricks* can be read as rejecting a treatment-amenability requirement, it is best understood as applying to police power cases but not to *parens patriae* cases. In *parens patriae* commitments, the principal justification for commitment is benefit to the individual, a benefit that will often come only from treatment. Treatment amenability is a precondition because the deprivation of liberty is justified only if the incompetent detainee is expected to receive some benefit from treatment.

Police power commitments are different. They are justified by the individual's dangerousness to the public and the nature of the mental disorder. To justify a police power commitment, the *safety* benefit to the public must outweigh the loss of liberty to the individual. *Treatment* benefit does not enter into this benefit-balancing equation.

For several reasons, I think that the Court's approach has some merit when applied to police power cases. A treatment-amenability requirement in police power commitments would undermine two important principles of medicine: autonomy and beneficence. Police power commitments are justified on the principle of utility: a determination that the benefit to society outweighs the harm to the detainee. A treatment-amenability requirement assumes that the utility scales tip toward the society only if treatment is effective. But when the detainee is competent, then "counting" a treatment benefit he or she has not chosen would violate the principle of autonomy. It inappropriately judges treatment to be a benefit to a competent individual irrespective of whether he or she would value it. If the detainee is incompetent, we know that the treatment benefit is not enough to outweigh the liberty deprivation (otherwise, this would be a *parens patriae* case, which, by hypothesis, it is not). So, the only way treatment amenability could tip the utility balance is by counting "cure" as an added benefit to the state. Such a move would be dangerous because it would introduce the principle that medical procedures can be forced on people to benefit the greater good, thus violating the principle of beneficence.

Some theorists suggest that a utility theory might justify the imposition of medical care in certain circumstances in which the costs to society from the individual's refusal to accept treatment are sufficiently great and the risk imposed on the patient sufficiently small (Buchanan & Brock, 1989). But where the "risk" to the patient is a massive deprivation of liberty for an extended period of time, and where the expected treatment benefits to any particular individuals are impossible to predict, it is doubtful that this balance is met.

This leads to a second problem with a treatment-amenability requirement: There is no way to determine which sex offenders will benefit from treatment. Even if one makes the optimistic assumption that sex offender treatment is effective, at best it reduces, but does not eliminate, recidivism. Treatment will benefit only an unknown subgroup of those committed. How can it serve to justify commitment for all the members of the group?

The actual reason the Supreme Court cites for rejecting a treatment-amenability requirement is less convincing. Theoretically, such a precondition could create a "gap" in the social control tools of the state, leaving the state unable to protect the public from dangerous individuals whose mental disorders are untreatable but excuse them from criminal responsibility. This theoretical "gap" is of small practical concern, because virtually all individuals found not guilty by reason of insanity suffer from psychiatric illnesses for which there is medical treatment (Winick, 1995), whereas the mental disorders of committed sex offenders virtually never excuse them from criminal responsibility (Winick, 1998).

A Right to "Reasonable" Treatment

To say that there is no treatment-amenability requirement in police power commitments is not to negate a right to treatment. Treatment is not a justification for commitment, but rather a right that commitment generates. The right to treatment that does arise is not an absolute right to effective treatment, but rather a right to reasonable, available treatment rendered according to professional standards. This right arises from the two legal theories that underlie the constitutionality of sex offender commitments: the punishment theory and the substantive due process theory.

Treatment and Punitive Intent

A central theme of the constitutional challenges is that sex offender commitments are really punishment in disguise, thereby violating the double jeopardy clause and the *ex post facto* clause. *Hendricks* teaches that the provision of treatment is one of the ways to measure the *bona fides* of the state's nonpunitive intent (*Kansas v. Hendricks*, 1997). Treatment is a traditional aim of civil commitment. A departure from this tradition raises suspicions that confinement is not really civil commitment. Thus, treatment can be understood to stand for a handful of conditions and values that identify a nonpunitive purpose and result.

This analysis results in a qualified right to treatment. The "punishment" label turns on an assessment of the state's intent. Intent is a subjective quality that permits some margin for the practicalities of execution. As in *Hendricks*, courts might consider the newness of a commitment program to be a relevant piece of evidence in judging whether a state's skimpy treatment performance evidences punitive intent. In a mature commitment program, actions and intent should be more in sync. Thus, *Hendricks* directs courts to examine "conditions surrounding . . . confinement" to determine whether they "suggest a punitive purpose on the State's part."

Further, intent is arguably a quality that attaches to the statutory scheme as a whole. Thus, it is possible that a state might provide a strong treatment program, establishing a nonpunitive overall intent even though effective treatment cannot be provided for a few individuals. Courts might measure intent by judging whether, averaged over the statutory scheme, state efforts to provide treatment adequately identify the scheme with traditional civil commitment and adequately distinguish it from criminal punishment.

In making these judgments, courts are constitutionally required to ask whether treatment complies with professional standards (*Youngberg v. Romeo*, 1982). A persistent departure from professional treatment standards supports an inference that the state's intent is punitive.

In *Seling v. Young* (2001), the Supreme Court added a complicated twist. Young sought release, arguing that the state's persistent failure to meet professional standards in treatment rendered the commitment law unconstitutionally punitive. The Supreme Court rejected his claim. Young's legal theories—*ex post facto* and double jeopardy—required proof that the law was punitive "on its face" rather than as applied in practice. But the Court did not decide whether a different legal theory, substantive due process, would provide redress in an "as applied" context.

On a different tack, some argue that the overwhelmingly cognitive nature of sex offender treatment is evidence that sex offender commitments exhibit a key feature of the criminal law—a reliance on deterrence—and are therefore unconstitutional. Cognitive–behavioral sex offender treatment works on the *will* of the individual rather than the body or the nervous system. Efficacy depends on the individual being convinced, by consequences that are severe enough, that attending to treatment and taking its messages seriously might be, for him, worthwhile. This does not happen "automatically" like the response to medication or behavioral programming, but rather is mediated through the individual's rational thought processes (Winick, 1981). By operating on the will of the individual, this treatment posits a rational mind, one that will respond at a cognitive level to the rather abstract incentives and disincentives of a system of control. This is, of course, precisely the kind of "deterrence" that is an identifying feature of the criminal justice system (*Kansas v. Hendricks*, 1997).

Treatment and Substantive Due Process

Substantive due process ensures that the state does not operate beyond the proper bounds of its power. A right to treatment arises from this doctrine in two ways. First, to deprive a person of liberty, the state must use narrowly tailored means to achieve a compellingly important end (*In re Linehan*, 1999; *State v. Post*, 1995). A state has no interest in confining a person who is not dangerous or who could become nondangerous through reasonable efforts on the part of the state. The command that intervention be "narrowly tailored" entails an affirmative obligation to minimize the individual's liberty deprivation to the extent it is reasonably possible. The provision of treatment is one way of ensuring that the confinement of the individual extends no longer than necessary (*Youngberg v. Romeo*, 1982).

Second, "the nature and duration of commitment [must] bear some reasonable relation to the purpose for which the individual is committed" (*Jackson v. Indiana*, 1972). Treatment is a purpose claimed by all states; arguably, the purpose is constitutionally necessary to ensure the nonpunitive status of commitment. Clearly, the "conditions" of confinement must advance this treatment purpose. Some cases suggest that the Constitution places a strict durational limit on nontreatment civil confinement and that the state has only a "reasonable" period to accomplish its commitment purpose (*Jackson v. Indiana*, 1972; *United States v. Salerno*, 1987; *Zadvydas v. Davis*, 2001). Though the Supreme Court's dicta suggest otherwise, these cases might forbid lifetime confinement of sex offenders for whom there is no reasonable likelihood of successful treatment (Janus & Logan, in press).

CONCLUSION

Treatment is an important right of civilly committed individuals. But the nature of the right varies depending on the justification for the commitment. In most mental health commitments, the individuals have severe mental illnesses that render them incompetent. For these individuals, the expected treatment benefit is the major justification for commitment. In contrast, most committed sex offenders are fully competent. Sex offender commitments must be justified by the need to protect the public and by the individual's inability to control dangerous behavior. Treatment is not a *justification* for these commitments, because using it as a justification would violate the important principles of autonomy and beneficence. Therefore, if detention is otherwise justified, states may commit "nontreatable" individuals. But the state is obliged to provide reasonably available treatment so that its intent is nonpunitive and to minimize the burden on detainees. Finally, some cases suggest that the Constitution limits the permanent detention of individuals for whom there is no reasonable likelihood of effective treatment.

REFERENCES

Addington v. Texas, 441 U.S. 418 (1978).

Allen v. Illinois, 478 U.S. 364 (1986).

American Psychiatric Association. (1999). *Dangerous sex offenders.* Washington, DC: Author.

Buchanan, A. E., & Brock, D. W. (1989). *Deciding for others: The ethics of surrogate decision making.* Cambridge, England: Cambridge University Press.

Freedman, E. B. (1987). Uncontrolled desires: The response to the sexual psychopath, 1920–1960. *Journal of American History, 74,* 83–101.

Grossman, L. S., Martis, B., & Fichtner, C. G. (1999). Are sex offenders treatable? A research overview. *Psychiatric Services, 50,* 349–361.

Group for the Advancement of Psychiatry. (1977). *Psychiatry and sex psychopath legislation: The 30s to the 80s.* New York: Author.

In re Hendricks, 912 P.2d 129 (Kan. 1996).

Jackson v. Indiana, 406 U.S. 715 (1972).

Janus, E. S. (2000). Civil commitment as social control: Managing the risk of sexual violence. In M. Brown & J. Pratt (Eds.), *Dangerous offenders: Punishment and social order* (pp. 71–90). London: Routledge.

Janus, E. S., & Logan, W. A. (in press). Substantive due process and the involuntary confinement of sexually violent predators. *Connecticut Law Review.*

Janus, E. S., & Walbek, N. H. (2000). Sex offender commitments in Minnesota: A descriptive study of second generation commitments. *Behavioral Sciences and the Law, 18,* 343–373.

Kansas Commitment of Sexually Violent Predators Act, Kan. Stat. Ann. § 59-29a09 (1998).

Kansas v. Crane, 122 S. Ct. 867 (2002).

Kansas v. Hendricks, 117 S. Ct. 2072 (1997).

La Fond, J. Q. (1998). The costs of enacting a sexual predator law. *Psychology, Public Policy, and Law, 4,* 468–504.

La Fond, J. Q. (1999). Can therapeutic jurisprudence be normatively neutral? Sexual predator laws: Their impact on participants and policy. *Arizona Law Review, 41,* 375.

Lieb, R., & Nelson, C. (2001). Treatment programs for sexually violent predators: A review of states. In A. Schlank (Ed.), *The sexual predator: Legal issues, clinical issues, special populations* (Vol. II, pp. 5-1–5-21). Kingston, NJ: Civic Research Institute.

Lieb, R., Quinsey, V., & Berliner, L. (1998). Sexual predators and social policy. *Crime and Justice, 23,* 43–114.

In re Linehan, 594 N.W.2d 867 (Minn. 1999).

Marshall, W. L., & Pithers, W. D. (1994). A reconsideration of treatment outcome with sex offenders. *Criminal Justice and Behavior, 21*(1), 10–27.

Minnesota Civil Commitment Act, Minn. Stat. § 253B.03, subd. 7 (1998).

Prentky, R. (1995). A rationale for the treatment of sex offenders: Pro bono publico. In J. McGuire (Ed.), *What works: Reducing reoffending—guidelines from research and practice* (pp. 155–171). New York: Wiley.

Rice, M. E., & Harris, G. T. (1997). The treatment of mentally disordered offenders. *Psychology, Public Policy, and Law 3,* 126–183.

Seling v. Young, 531 U.S. 250 (2001).

State v. Post, 541 N.W.2d 115 (Wis. 1995).

United States v. Salerno, 481 U.S. 739 (1987).

Washington Sexually Violent Predators Act, Wash. Rev. Code § 71.09.010 (1999).

Winick, B. J. (1981). Legal limitations on correctional therapy and research. *Minnesota Law Review, 65,* 331–422.

Winick, B. J. (1995). Ambiguities in the legal meaning and significance of mental illness. *Psychology, Public Policy, and Law, 1,* 534–611.

Winick, B. J. (1998). Sex offender law in the 1990s: A therapeutic jurisprudence analysis. *Psychology, Public Policy, and Law, 4,* 505–570.

Youngberg v. Romeo, 457 U.S. 307 (1982).

Zadvydas v. Davis, 121 S. Ct. 2491 (2001).

7

IN THE WAKE OF *HENDRICKS*: THE TREATMENT AND RESTRAINT OF SEXUALLY DANGEROUS OFFENDERS VIEWED FROM THE PERSPECTIVE OF AMERICAN PSYCHIATRY

HOWARD V. ZONANA, RICHARD J. BONNIE, AND STEVEN K. HOGE

Sexual predator commitment laws have been characterized as an "abuse of psychiatry" and an exercise in political diagnosis. In response to these critical concerns, the Board of Trustees of the American Psychiatric Association, an organization which represents the great majority of American psychiatrists (over 40,000), established a Task Force on Sexually Dangerous Offenders, charged with reviewing the state of scientific knowledge about treatment of sex offenders and evaluating sexual predator commitment laws and other legislative strategies pertaining to the treatment of these offenders. The task force was constituted to reflect the necessary expertise in sex offender research, forensic mental health services, criminal law, and mental health law. The three authors of this chapter participated in the deliberations of the Council on Psychiatry and Law and also served on the task force as chair, legal consultant, and member, respectively. The Task Force Report, issued in December 1996, and subsequently updated and reissued after the *Hendricks* decision, is summarized below (see "Findings and Policy Recommendations"). In the final section, we present our own reflections on the situation now confronted by American psychiatry in the wake of *Hendricks*.

This chapter discusses these issues from the perspective of the American Psychiatric Association. Nonetheless, these findings and recommendations speak not only to psychiatrists but also to other mental health practitioners, lawyers, policymakers, and others interested in this important public policy issue.

BACKGROUND: WHY THE AMERICAN PSYCHIATRIC ASSOCIATION APPOINTED A TASK FORCE

In 1993, American Psychiatric Association President John McIntyre appointed a Task Force on Sexually Dangerous Offenders in response to a growing national interest in the civil commitment of so-called "violent sexual predators." The American Psychiatric Association's Council on Psychiatry and Law had discussed the subject at length, recognizing that organized psychiatry had to respond to an increasing sentiment in favor of laws authorizing the commitment of sexual predators. Many states had once provided for the commitment of sex offenders, but these laws had been repealed or fallen into disuse in all but a few states. Moreover, many legal scholars regarded these decades-old statutes as illegitimate, on the grounds that they amounted to unconstitutional preventive detention. In 1984, the American Bar Association's (1989) Criminal Justice Mental Health Standards recommended repeal of the "sex psychopath" statutes that remained on the books in about one third of the states.

However, in the early 1990s, Washington State, followed by other states, enacted commitment laws with a cruel new twist: Imprisoned inmates who had committed sexual offenses could be committed to a psychiatric facility *after* the expiration of their criminal sentences (Wash. Rev. Code, 1992). Prior to this, the American Psychiatric Association had developed a strong position on the legal and ethical basis of civil commitment, one grounded in the paternalistic medical tradition and one which preserves psychiatrists' legal authority to facilitate hospitalization of severely mentally disordered individuals who cannot seek treatment on their own. The new laws implicated—and possibly endangered—this core interest of the American Psychiatric Association because they appeared to use the traditional, paternalistic model of civil commitment to achieve unmistakably nontherapeutic aims.

From the outset, the Council on Psychiatry and Law's discussions focused on a pivotal question: Is there a clinical justification for the involuntary treatment of sex offenders? If not, then commitment was being used for naked preventive detention, and psychiatric facilities would be transformed into prisons for the continued incarceration of sex offenders under a therapeutic pretext. Moreover, the statutory definitions of "sexual predator" were vaguely and broadly written (Wash. Rev. Code, 1992). Indeed, in some instances it was made clear that mental illness was not required for commitment. It was clear that such statutes implicated the integrity of the civil commitment model. Public confidence in psychiatric commitment might be undermined, weakening the ethical basis of the procedures for ordinary involuntary psychiatric hospitalization and reinvigorating more generalized charges of "abuse" that had been aimed at psychiatrists in the late 1960s and 1970s but had receded over the past 25 years.

The immediate and practical consequences of installing sexual predator programs were also of concern to the Council. It is widely acknowledged that forensic and correctional mental health systems are struggling to meet burgeoning demands with inadequate resources. Council members expressed concern that these resources would be drained or diverted from the treatment of seriously ill prisoners or forensic patients to the management of sex offenders who did not have an illness, or if they did, were not treatable. This misallocation of scarce resources should be strenuously resisted. (This volume, chapter 16, analyzes how much money selected states are spending to implement sexual predator laws.)

The Council registered strong concerns about the negative effects of the sexual predator commitment laws on traditional mental health services. At the same time, however, the Council recognized the American Psychiatric Association's obligation to give careful consideration to the treatment needs of sexual offenders. Undoubtedly, at least some of these individuals suffer from a diagnosable and treatable mental illness. And, even in those instances in which mental disorder is not present, some offenders are likely to be distressed by their criminal behavior and may seek psychiatric help. The American Psychiatric Association certainly would not want to discourage sex offenders from seeking treatment. Treatment of and research on correctional populations in general—and sex offenders particularly—have been marginalized in psychiatric services. The American Psychiatric Association has an institutional obligation to counteract these exclusionary tendencies in the treatment of sexual deviations, just as it has in relation to the treatment of addictions. Public and professional policies about the treatment of sex offenders should be based on clinical knowledge and experience, not on despair or distaste.

In sum, the American Psychiatric Association believes that sexual predator laws implicate core concerns of American psychiatry. These include the appropriate uses of the medical model of involuntary civil commitment and the responsiveness of the profession to the legitimate clinical needs of an emotionally disturbed population.

FINDINGS AND POLICY RECOMMENDATIONS OF THE AMERICAN PSYCHIATRIC ASSOCIATION TASK FORCE REPORT

The question whether all or some sexual offenders are mentally ill is complicated and controversial. Given the wide variety of behaviors and circumstances involved in sexual offending, it is not surprising that a plethora of theories, ranging from biological to cultural, have been proposed to explain this conduct. The degree of control that sex offenders have over their behavior—a question tied very closely to conceptions about the appropriate societal response—is in fundamental dispute. Clearly, many offenses occur in the absence of any mental or physical disorder or volitional impairment. Even when diagnosable mental disorder is involved, however, the relation between the disorder and the offense varies substantially. For example, some sexual offenses occur in the context of more systemic physical or mental disorders, such as mental retardation or traumatic brain injury. Other sexual offenses manifest primary sexual disorders, broadly categorized as paraphilias (e.g., pedophilia or exhibitionism), which can have obsessive and/or compulsive features. Finally, some offenders may have other mental disorders, ranging from disorders of psychotic proportions to substance abuse and personality disorders, which may have a derivative effect on specific sexual behavior or which may be unconnected with it.

The American Psychiatric Association Task Force reviewed the epidemiology of sexual behavior and sex offending and then summarized the research literature on evaluation, treatment, and recidivism, as well as prior American Psychiatric Association policy on civil commitment. The task force's major conclusions and policy recommendations are summarized below.

Research and Training

Although sound epidemiological data do not exist, it is clear that a significant number of people have paraphilic disorders, that these disorders cause substantial personal and social distress, and that only a small proportion of these individuals receive treatment in either community settings or correctional institutions. Although scientific understanding of the paraphilic disorders has improved in recent years, the societal investment in research has not been commensurate with the need for new knowledge relating to the diagnosis, treatment, and recidivism of persons with these disorders. Training programs for psychiatrists and other mental health professionals have devoted inadequate attention to the assessment and treatment of such persons. The task force recommended an increased investment in research on paraphilic disorders and in the clinical training of psychiatrists and other mental health professionals regarding assessment and treatment of persons with those disorders (American Psychiatric Association Task Force Report, 1999, p. 171).

Legal Control of Dangerous Sex Offenders: The Propriety of Civil Commitment

Sexual predator commitment laws represent a serious assault on the integrity of psychiatry, particularly with regard to defining mental illness and the clinical conditions for compulsory treatment. Moreover, by bending civil commitment to serve essentially nonmedical purposes, sexual predator commitment statutes threaten to undermine the legitimacy of the medical model of commitment. In the opinion of the task force, organized psychiatry must vigorously oppose these statutes to preserve the moral authority of the profession and to ensure continuing societal confidence in the medical model of civil commitment. The task force concluded that societal concerns about the need for punishment and incapacitation of dangerous sex offenders should be met through customary sentencing alternatives within the criminal justice system and not through involuntary civil commitment statutes (American Psychiatric Association Task Force Report, 1999, p. 176).

Misuse of Diagnostic Terminology and Methods

The sexual predator commitment laws establish a nonmedical definition of what purports to be a clinical condition without regard to scientific and clinical knowledge. In so doing, legislators have used psychiatric commitment to effect nonmedical societal ends. In the opinion of the task force, this represents an unacceptable misuse of psychiatry (American Psychiatric Association Task Force Report, 1999, p. 174).

Treatment of Dangerous Sex Offenders Within the Criminal Justice System

Legislatures and correctional agencies genuinely interested in providing therapeutic opportunities for dangerous sex offenders as a means of reducing the rate of recidivism should establish adequately funded programs within the correctional system that are based on current clinical knowledge. Legislatures interested in developing therapeutic dispositional incentives for sex offenders with paraphilic disorders should consider "special track" indeterminate sentencing arrangements for offenders who elect to participate and who are found clinically suitable. Under such a model, an administrative body similar to the bodies that now review and monitor insanity acquittees could determine conditions of confinement and release.

Sex offenders should have an opportunity to participate in treatment programs while serving criminal sentences whether or not such participation has any bearing on the nature and length of their sentences. Participation in such programs should not be mandatory (American Psychiatric Association Task Force Report, 1999, p. 178).

"Chemical Castration" Laws

Laws that predicate release from prison on chemical castration by surgery or antiandrogenic agents for broad classes of sex offenders are objectionable because they are not based on adequate diagnostic and treatment considerations and because they improperly link medical treatment with punishment and social control. Prescribing treatment based solely on offense improperly equates psychiatric diagnosis with criminal behavior. Antiandrogens have an appropriate role in the treatment of some types of convicted sex offenders, but they need to be selected on the basis of a clinical evaluation (American Psychiatric Association Task Force Report, 1999, p. 180). (See this volume, chapter 14, for a discussion of chemical castration.)

REFLECTIONS ON THE CURRENT SITUATION

A Backward Glance

To understand why sexual predator laws could undermine the legal basis for customary psychiatric care, it is helpful to examine the historical roots of the commitment process. Although the use of involuntary civil commitment in the United States has varied from time to time over this country's history, this examination will demonstrate that—prior to enactment of sexually violent predator laws—the contemporary system of civil commitment in the United States had struck an appropriate balance between individual liberty and legitimate state goals. The American Psychiatric Association has played an important role in striking this balance.

In colonial times, the mentally ill were either "warned out" of towns or confined in their homes, almshouses, or jails if their behavior was out of control (Dershowitz, 1974, p. 782). Beginning in the 19th century, civil commitment of the mentally ill in the United States has undergone pendular cycles of reform. These vacillations have depended on the perceived efficacy of mental health treatment, counterbalanced by the need to prevent abuses. In 1842, New York's statute required that mentally ill persons be hospitalized within 10 days of the onset of their illness. This was during a period when treatments were perceived to be effective and any delays in treatment were perceived to be harmful. During the same period, Dorothea Dix was urging construction of mental hospitals so that mentally ill persons would not be confined in jails and prisons. By the 1860s, when Elizabeth Packard was hospitalized under an Illinois statute permitting hospitalization of "wives without the usual evidence of insanity required in other cases," a new era of reform was initiated that introduced more substantial legal controls over this process (Dershowitz, 1974, p. 834). For example, many states required jury trials and transportation of patients to courts for hearings. This reform period lasted for 20–30 years.

By the early part of the 20th century, most legislatures settled on a strategy of conferring a great deal of discretion on physicians to determine whether a person was "a fit subject for confinement" (*Mayock v. Martin,* 1968). This, of course, was the legislature's way of permitting physicians to be the primary decision makers concerning the need for involuntary hospitalization. Eventually, the state hospitals during the first half of the 20th century became large total care institutions where the chronic mentally ill often stayed for years.

The rest of the story is well known. In the 1960s and 1970s, deinstitutionalization of persons with chronic mental illness was accompanied and accelerated by the civil rights movement. In the legal environment of the day, it was not surprising that a new generation of commitment laws took on a decidedly libertarian cast. *In re Gault* (1967) symbolized a deepening distrust of benevolent uses of coercive authority in its critique of the juvenile court system. In this context, a strong momentum built for a libertarian model of civil commitment reform, requiring proof of acts indicative of imminent danger and importing procedural safeguards from the criminal justice system. Some commentators argued for the outright abolition of civil commitment. The entire tradition of paternalistically based civil commitment that had been in place for the care and treatment of the mentally ill was under attack.

American Psychiatric Association Policy on Ordinary Civil Commitment

During the reform era of the 1970s, the American Psychiatric Association was faced with a challenging task. The organization was not opposed to legal safeguards in the commitment process, and it recognized the need to bring commitment procedures into congruence with modern human rights norms. However, the American Psychiatric Association was deeply concerned that the emerging libertarian model would undermine the therapeutic aims of involuntary hospitalization.

Under the leadership of Alan Stone, a psychiatrist on the faculty of the Harvard Law School, the American Psychiatric Association took two steps in the effort to preserve the paternalistic tradition of civil commitment. First, in 1974, the American Psychiatric Association established a Commission on Judicial Action to monitor constitutional litigation and to submit *amicus* briefs in important cases, mainly in the U.S. Supreme Court. Second, in 1979, the American Psychiatric Association established a Council on Governmental Policy and Law (subsequently renamed the Council on Psychiatry and Law) to take a proactive stance with legislatures and other governmental bodies on laws and policies relating to psychiatric care. After Dr. Stone completed his term as president of the American Psychiatric Association in 1980, he became chair of the Council. In that capacity, he initiated a project designed to produce a Model Civil Commitment Law as a counterforce to the libertarian model that had dominated the discourse in mental health law reform.

The American Psychiatric Association Model Civil Commitment Law, approved by the organization in 1982, represented one of several American Psychiatric Association actions emphasizing its support of the *parens patriae* model of commitment rather than a simple police power model (American Psychiatric Association, 1982). The American Psychiatric Association's amicus briefs also sought to persuade the Supreme Court to ratify a commitment system that rests on a paternalistic foundation and that is more relaxed procedurally than the criminal justice system, even though it is more carefully regulated than under the previous generation of statutes. In the American Psychiatric Association's view, hospitalization should not necessarily be predicated on a specific act but on clinical opinion, and decisions about length of hospitalization should remain in clinical hands.

The Supreme Court ultimately supported the American Psychiatric Association position and distinguished civil commitment from criminal incarceration. While hospitalization results in a significant deprivation of liberty, the Court acknowledged, treatment of mental disorders is grounded in benevolent rather than punitive motivations, and therefore does not warrant the same degree of procedural protection. (*Addington v. Texas*, 1979). Although the current generation of civil commitment legislation does not embrace all of the American Psychiatric Association views, it does reflect a more sensible balance between paternalistic aims and legal protections than the more libertarian approach that was being pressed on the courts and legislatures in the 1970s.

Most states have provided rather vague definitions for the types of mental illness or disorder needed to establish the predicate for civil commitment (e.g., "substantial impairment in thought, mood, cognition, or behavior"). This is hardly a scientific criterion, and its application ultimately requires a value judgment. The American Psychiatric Association Model Civil Commitment Law requires the presence of a severe mental disorder (i.e., generally of a psychotic magnitude) in making the judgment that a disorder must be serious enough to warrant involuntary confinement and treatment.[1]

In the main, although the lack of definition is problematic, ordinary civil commitment is rarely abused. There are significant pressures not to hospitalize (both public and private); the judgments are in the hands of psychiatrists (as initiators and determiners of the cutoff); and other criteria limit the scope (treatability, which is a prime consideration if not a legal requirement). Under the American Psychiatric Association model, the incompetence requirement also acts as a brake on overly broad commitment.

Since the advent of managed care in the 1990s, the use of formal civil commitment procedures has been further eroded, as lengths of stay have decreased dramatically (now usually less than 2 weeks). Long-term hospitalizations in state facilities are now increasingly limited to referrals from the criminal courts, for example, insanity acquittees, defendants referred for restoration of competency to stand trial, defendants needing presentence reports, and substance abusers in diversion programs.

Some states have moved toward "outpatient commitment" statutes in an effort to deal with the chronically mentally ill that gravitate to large cities. These statutes, designed to provide judicial leverage for outpatient follow-up treatment by patients with histories of noncompliance and deterioration, are highly controversial. The most recent example is "Kendra's Law" (New York Senate Bill 5762, 1999), an outpatient commitment statute that requires treatment attendance but does not allow the use of involuntary medication. The public remains highly ambivalent about the use of involuntary psychotropic medication as a part of these statutes (Gerbasi, Bonnie, & Binder, 2000). Again, what one sees is a balance being sought between the paternalistic aims of coercive mental health care and respect for the autonomy of individual patients.

Police Power Commitment Under the American Psychiatric Association's Model Law

Under the American Psychiatric Association Model Law, persons who are dangerous but not mentally ill (or who are not treatable) may not be

---

[1]Building on the foundation reinforced by the Supreme Court's decisions, the American Psychiatric Association Model Civil Commitment Law proposed the following criteria for hospitalization of involuntary patients: (a) The person is suffering from a severe mental disorder; (b) there is a reasonable prospect that his disorder is treatable at or through the facility to which he is to be committed and such commitment would be consistent with the least restrictive alternative principle; (c) the person either refuses or is unable to consent to voluntary admission for treatment; (d) the person lacks capacity to make an informed decision concerning treatment; and (e) as a result of the severe mental disorder, the person is likely to cause harm to himself or to suffer substantial mental or physical deterioration or likely to cause harm to others.

committed. Pedophiles and individuals with antisocial personality disorder are generally unsuitable for civil commitment as they do not have acute impairments of reality testing or emotional control and are not threatening immediate attacks on children or other crimes. Even though people addicted to cocaine are highly likely to abuse drugs sometime in the future, the laws of most states do not allow preventive detention in a psychiatric facility in the absence of some other psychotic disorder or immediate threats of imminent violence. In practice, of course, psychiatric confinement of individuals with sexual deviations and personality disorders does occur and presents a serious problem when it does. Fear of liability is a major concern for physicians if released patients become violent shortly after discharge. The American Psychiatric Association Model Law makes it clear that these individuals should not fall within the bounds of ordinary civil commitment.

Another scenario involving dangerous patients arises after a period of treatment has resolved acute illness, but there is a risk of harm on discharge. Most discharges do not now undergo judicial review, leading to the prospect of liability for negligent release and third-party liability for failure to protect. If one accepts the premise that medical judgment is involved, the apparent solution is that professional standards should be developed to address release decisions. This assumption is faulty. All patients pose some risk. Some risks (but not all) may be related in varying degrees to the presence of mental illness. However, the level of acceptable societal risk is not a matter of professional judgment, but one for social–political resolution. This is the path chosen by the Model Law. Under the Model Law, a judicial hearing would be held in which the psychiatrist or other clinical expert witness would present the relevant facts, but only a judge would have the authority to transfer or to discharge, driving home the point that patients' problematic behavior is a social control issue, not a therapeutic one.

Not Guilty by Reason of Insanity (NGRI) Commitment

Even police power commitments have a paternalistic grounding during the period of acute illness, but what of NGRI acquittees? To be brought to trial, these defendants must have been found to be "competent" or must have been treated until restored to competence. Following a successful insanity defense, a new evaluation of the defendant will typically be conducted to determine if the mental disorder present at the time of the crime continues and whether the defendant currently represents a danger as a result of the mental illness. In fact, at the time of acquittal—often a year or two after the offense—many NGRI patients do not have active, serious mental illnesses and would never be considered as candidates for routine, therapeutic hospitalizations absent the violence that precipitated the charges. In most cases, the patients' disorders cannot be cured but are merely ameliorated by controlling their symptoms. The presence of a severe mental illness coupled with the violent offense is generally ample ethical justification for the initial period of hospitalization. However, its therapeutic justification has often evaporated by the time of trial or evaporates after a short period of hospitalization in most cases, leaving preventive confinement as the primary aim.

The key question before the court in NGRI release cases is how these patients would handle the hazards of freedom in the community. Yet, in the absence of a trial of treatment in the community, there is little basis for predicting the patient's likely adaptation on release. In ordinary civil commitments, we generally accept a relatively high risk of relapse in deference to the patient's right to be free or (in the current fiscal climate) in an effort to contain costs. It is clear that the balance tips strongly on the side of social protection from insanity acquittees. Clinical judgments regarding the likelihood of relapse are needed, but ultimately the decision reflects a social judgment regarding the level of acceptable risk. A court or quasi-judicial body such as a psychiatric security review board, which has attorneys and lay members as well as professionals, must approve most insanity acquittee releases. In practice, the courts and boards are quite conservative and are willing to confine individuals for very long periods of time. Even with judicial approval, there still is significant threat of liability if an acquittee becomes violent shortly after release, which only adds to the conservatism of NGRI release decisions. As *Foucha v. Louisiana* (1992) indicates, physicians are reluctant to guarantee safety, especially when the underlying disorder that qualified the person for an insanity defense is resolved but long-standing character traits remain, increasing the likelihood of future dangerous behavior.

The sexual predator laws are often characterized as being similar to the handling of insanity acquittees, an analogy made plausible by the heavy tilt of NGRI dispositions toward preventive confinement and the absence of any therapeutic justification for extended hospitalization in most cases. In fact, the Supreme Court seemed to view the sexual predator laws as an acceptable extension of police power commitments. However, there are two significant differences between insanity acquittees and sexual predators. First, insanity acquittees have elected to raise the defense (which may no longer be imposed over a defendant's objection) and thereby have elected to submit themselves to the more restrictive features of the NGRI commitment law. Second, most insanity acquittees have serious mental disorders so severe as to render them nonresponsible for crimes they had committed. The disorders are usually amenable to treatment and suitable for psychiatric management, even though extended hospitalization may not be therapeutically required in most cases.

The *Hendricks* Decision: A Step Backward

Even though the Supreme Court (*Kansas v. Hendricks*, 1997) has held that the sexual predator statutes pass constitutional muster and do not constitute punishment or unwarranted preventive detention, it is hard for psychiatric professionals to view them in any other light. Despite the fact that these statutes provide substantial employment opportunities for psychiatrists (and long-term funding outside the influence of managed care), the American Psychiatric Association Assembly of District Branches and the Board of Trustees readily endorsed the findings and recommendations of the task force.

These laws are not animated by paternalistic aspirations, they do not require a diagnosis of major mental disorders, and they sweep aside claims of individual rights. They are, by statutory definition, designed to prevent future "crimes." In addition, the targets of these statutes do not appear to be "crazy" or "mentally ill" offenders, at least not in the same sense traditionally required for ordinary civil commitment. At least 15 states have adopted a sexual predator law. Some states like Kansas have used these statutes primarily to confine pedophiles. Other states like Wisconsin have used these statutes to confine a large number of individuals with antisocial personality disorder who have committed crimes such as rape. Even though the Supreme Court suggested that the Kansas law established a limited police power preventive detention scheme, the law on its face is without any meaningful limitations in scope. Although the law was technically upheld only as applied to *Hendricks*, it appears that most state courts will not construe these statutes as applying only to pedophiles or other offenders with paraphilias.

The statutory criterion of mental abnormality has been interpreted by courts to encompass disorders that are not even codified in the accepted classifications of mental disorders, for example, the *Diagnostic and Statistical Manual of Mental Disorders* (4th ed., DSM–IV; American Psychiatric Association, 1994) or the International Classification of Diseases (ICD-10). The statutes permit the original behavior that led to the arrest as justification for continued confinement even if it occurred 10–20 years before.

If antisocial personality disorder or other personality disorders become an adequate predicate for civil commitment, without severe psychiatric symptoms that affect cognitive processing, then psychiatry becomes an extension of the police power rather than a profession primarily directed toward alleviation of symptoms and the treatment of illness.[2] Under sex-

---

[2]More recently in *Kansas v. Crane* (122 S. Ct. 867, 2002) the Supreme Court acknowledged that the predator statutes had a potential for abuse if any diagnosis and a past crime were sufficient for civil commitment. They noted that "Hendricks underscored the constitutional importance of distinguishing a dangerous sexual offender subject to civil commitment from other dangerous persons who are perhaps more properly dealt with exclusively through

ually violent predator statutes, the predicate for hospitalization need not be a recognized disorder, much less one that could benefit from hospital treatment, for—as Justice Thomas so bluntly noted—the definition of a disease or disorder for legal purposes is a societal judgment, not a professional one. What Justice Thomas failed to understand, however, is that legal definitions of mental disorder must be based on scientific and clinical understanding. Legislatures should not have the prerogative to invent mental or emotional categories that are needed to justify involuntary treatment.

Sex offender commitment laws represent a perversion of the mental health system to solve a problem of sentencing structure. The systems of "indeterminate" sentencing—for example, one-day-to-life sentences that sexual offenders used to receive—came under sustained attack in the 1970s from all directions. Liberals were dissatisfied by the disparities that had emerged, whereas conservatives were concerned about the apparent failure of individualized sentencing and parole to prevent recidivism. In addition, overcrowding sometimes led to the premature release of offenders who had committed serious offenses. In short, "determinate" or fixed sentences were adopted in an effort to restore the public's faith in the sentencing and correctional system.

The "problem" with determinate sentences, of course, is that prisoners have to be released at the end of the prescribed period. It is no surprise that the public becomes outraged when an offender recidivates shortly after his release and commits a heinous crime, especially when children and women are the victims. Legislators have responded to these problems prospectively by enacting more severe sentences for sex offenders. Seen in this light, the main aim of the sexually violent predator commitment laws is to extend the period of confinement for prisoners whose terms have already expired under the laws in effect at the time of their offenses. What would otherwise amount to *ex post facto* punishment can be sustained only by declaring that the prisoner's continued incarceration is not punishment, but treatment instead. To deploy psychiatrists and other mental health professionals in such a deceptive scheme is an affront to the integrity of the professions.

Adding insult to injury, funding of these programs often comes directly from the State Department of Mental Health with legislatures appropriating no additional funds, thus taking away programming for the severely mentally ill. Sexual "predator" patients require maximum-security institutions that are extremely costly (three to six times the cost of cor-

criminal proceedings. That distinction is necessary lest civil commitment become a mechanism for retribution or general deterrence—functions properly those of the criminal law, not civil commitment" (p. 870). They concluded that in addition to a mental disorder there "must be proof of serious difficulty in controlling behavior . . . and the severity of the mental abnormality itself, must be sufficient to distinguish the dangerous sexual offender whose serious mental illness, abnormality, or disorder subjects him to civil commitment from the dangerous but typical recidivist convicted in an ordinary criminal case" (p. 870).

rectional incarceration), and the treatment programs, which have not been shown to reduce recidivism in any reliable way, are difficult to implement. These offenders also cannot be hospitalized on the same wards with the severely mentally ill as they tend to abuse and manipulate these patients. Although some treatments are beginning to look promising for some of the paraphilias, it makes no sense to professionals to withhold such treatment until the end of the penal sentence rather than offering it during the period of correctional incarceration.

CONCLUSION

The sexual predator commitment laws erode the ethical foundation of public policy governing mental health care. These laws are politically attractive, and, apparently, they pass constitutional muster. And some may view them as sound public policy. But they carry high costs for the psychiatric profession, the system of public mental health services, other mental health practitioners, and the ideal of honesty in government. What is most perplexing is that these costs can be entirely avoided by using the tools already available to the criminal justice system: greater use of intensive probation, extended term sentencing, registration, treatment during the primary incarceration, and a selective revival of parole. We hope that legislators will soon turn toward a more honest and less costly path.

REFERENCES

Addington v. Texas, 441 U.S. 418 (1979).

American Bar Association. (1989). *Criminal justice mental health standards.* Washington, DC: Author.

American Psychiatric Association. (1982). Guidelines for legislation on the psychiatric hospitalization of adults. *American Journal of Psychiatry, 140,* 672–679.

American Psychiatric Association. (1994). *Diagnostic and statistical manual of mental disorders* (4th ed.). Washington, DC: Author.

American Psychiatric Association Task Force Report. (1999). *Dangerous sex offenders.* Washington, DC: Author.

Dershowitz, A. (1974). The origins of preventive confinement law: Part II. The American experience. *Cincinnati Law Review, 43,* 781–846.

Foucha v. Louisiana, 504 U.S. 71 (1992).

In re Gault, 387 U.S. 1 (1967).

Gerbasi, J. B., Bonnie, R. J., & Binder, R. L. (2000). Resource document on mandatory outpatient treatment. *Journal of the American Academy of Psychiatry and Law, 28,* 127–144.

Kansas v. Crane, 122 S. Ct. 867 (2002).

Kansas v. Hendricks, 521 U.S. 346 (1997).

Mayock v. Martin, 245 A.2d 574 (1968).

New York Senate Bill 5762 (1999).

Wash. Rev. Code, § 71.09.010 *et seq.* (1992).

IV

THE RATIONALE, CONSTITUTIONALITY, AND MORALITY OF SEXUAL PREDATOR COMMITMENT LAWS

8

MATCHING LEGAL POLICIES WITH KNOWN OFFENDERS

LEONORE M. J. SIMON

Legal policies targeting sex offenders are appearing in an increasing number of states and on the federal level. These policies often result from widely publicized heinous sex crimes committed by stranger offenders. Washington State, for example, enacted its community notification legislation after a 7-year-old boy was raped and mutilated by a convicted sex offender (Siegel, 1990). New Jersey enacted similar legislation after a 7-year-old girl was raped and murdered by a twice-convicted sex offender who lived across the street ("Man Charged," 1994). (For a discussion of these statutes, see this volume, chapter 12.) In both cases, the resulting legislation was designed to protect children from strangers. Such legislation, however, promotes "a false sense of security, lulling parents and children into the big-bad-man mindset when many molesters are in fact trusted authority figures or family members" (Quindlen, 1994, p. 13).

This chapter examines the disjuncture between sex offender legisla-

This chapter is based in part on a paper presented in July 1998 at the First International Conference on Therapeutic Jurisprudence, Winchester, England. I wish to acknowledge the comments by John La Fond, Richard Lamma, and Jack Oakwright and the research assistance of Sharon Elliott and Yvette Deery.

tion aimed at stranger offenders and the empirical realities that most sex crimes against children and women are committed by family members and acquaintances. Disparate research findings are summarized demonstrating that the legal system consistently reserves the worst condemnation for the rare stranger sex criminal while treating more leniently the more prevalent family and acquaintance offender. The iatrogenic effects of current sex offender policies on victims are examined, and solutions are proposed for law reform.

SEX CRIMES AGAINST CHILDREN AND LEGAL POLICY

Although legal policy focuses on the stranger sex offender, fewer than 10% of all child molestations[1] are committed by strangers (Simon, 2000). The majority of sex crimes against children are committed by fathers (20%), stepfathers (29%), other relatives (11%), and acquaintances (30%; see Simon, Sales, Kaszniak, & Kahn, 1992). In fact, the stranger may be more rare than statistics indicate. The majority of child molestations by nonstrangers are not reported to police or on surveys (e.g., Widom, 1997). When they are reported to police, an arrest is made in, at most, 27% of the cases (Snyder, 2000). Given that at least 14% of men and 27% of women report sexual abuse during their childhoods by nonstrangers (Rind, Tromovitch, & Bauserman, 1998), policies targeting stranger sexual violence keep us from focusing on intervention and prevention strategies that would reach the majority of victims.[2]

The focus on the stranger offender belies the danger and harm posed by offenses committed by nonstrangers. Incest, for example, is of longer duration and is more extensive than stranger offenses, causing victims irreparable harm because of the betrayal of a trusted relationship (Fischer & McDonald, 1998). Nevertheless, in some statutes, family members and acquaintances appear to be explicitly excluded from recently enacted laws designed to prevent sexual violence. For instance, the Washington sexual predator law defines predatory crime as "acts directed toward strangers or individuals with whom a relationship has been established or promoted for the primary purpose of victimization" (Wash. Rev. Code § 71.09.020, 1998). Other state laws classify family sex offenses as family offenses and punish them less severely (Wash. Rev. Code § 9A.64, 1998) than child molestation offenses such as child rape (Wash. Rev. Code § 9A.44.073, 1998). More lenient treatment of family and acquaintance offenders also

---

[1]The terms *child molestation*, *child sexual abuse*, and *incest* and are used synonymously to refer to illegal sexual contact between adults and children.
[2]The statistics cited about the prevalence rates of childhood sexual abuse are based on a meta-analysis of most studies done on college students. Therefore, the statistics may underestimate the actual prevalence rates.

can be found in states that divert them into treatment while sentencing the stranger offender to prison (Berliner, Schram, Miller, & Milloy, 1995). The assumption underlying the differential treatment of family offenses, in particular, is that all attempts be made to keep the family together, although this may not always be in the best interest of children.

SEX CRIMES AGAINST WOMEN AND LEGAL POLICY

Harmful effects of legal policy on women victims of sex crimes are common (Schulhofer, 1998). Until recently, legal policy has been based on inaccurate statistics of the prevalence and incidence of rape.[3] As a result, rape has been viewed as uncommon, and women's fear of rape as irrational. For example, in 1994, there were 102,096 attempted and completed rapes reported to and believed by the police, resulting in 36,610 arrests (Federal Bureau of Investigation, 1994). These official statistics contrast sharply with the estimated 876,064 rapes reported on victim surveys (Tjaden & Thoennes, 2000). Rape appears to be more common in the lives of women than previously assumed. Victim surveys indicate that 17.6% of the female population in the United States have been raped at least once in their lifetime (e.g., Tjaden & Thoennes, 2000). Many American women are raped at an early age: Of the 17.6% of all women surveyed who said they had been the victim of a completed or attempted rape at some time in their life, 21.6% were younger than age 12 when they were first raped, and 32.4% were ages 12 to 17 (Tjaden & Thoennes, 2000). Thus, more than half (54%) of the female rape victims identified by victim surveys are younger than age 18 when they experience their first attempted or completed rape.

In addition to underestimates of the prevalence and incidence of rape, legal policies have relied on the same misleading police statistics to overestimate the proportion of stranger rapes (Bachman & Saltzman, 1995; Crowell & Burgess, 1996). It is not surprising, then, that fear of stranger rape accounts for a large part of women's fear of crime (Crowell & Burgess, 1996). Such fear belies the reality that over 80% of rapes of women are committed by acquaintances. Of these assaults, friends and acquaintances commit more than half (53%) of all rapes, intimate partners commit an additional 26%, and other relatives commit 3% (Bachman & Saltzman, 1995). In fact, the proportion of rapes perpetrated by acquaintances is likely to be higher than much survey data suggest. Surveys often provide underestimates of "hidden rape"—the 43% of women whose survey answers reveal that they have been raped by an acquaintance but who do not define

---

[3]The terms *rape* and *sexual assault* are used to refer to a man engaging in sexual contact (broadly defined) with any woman by the use or threatened use of force.

the experiences as such and who do not report the rape to anyone (Koss, 1995). Legal policy that emphasizes stranger rape may encourage women to take preventive measures against strangers while neglecting hazards associated with acquaintances.

VICTIM PERCEPTIONS OF RAPE AND SEXUAL ASSAULTS

Legal policy that focuses on the stranger offender produces many cases that fit the legal definition of rape but are not perceived as a crime. If the offender was an acquaintance and used moderate force, the victim might conclude that a rape did not occur. If she sees the perpetrator again, she may subject herself to further sexual assaults. If she initiates a relationship with a new person, she may not recognize new assaultive behavior.

Most rape victims are reluctant to report rape, and, if reported, the rape seldom results in conviction and imprisonment of the rapist. To illustrate, 16% of all rapes are reported, 36% of rape reports result in arrest, 20% of rape arrests result in conviction, and only 66% of those convicted of rape are sentenced to prison (Greenfeld, 1997). The problems faced by all rape victims are exacerbated by acquaintance rape victims. As the following sections indicate, acquaintance rapes are even less likely to be reported, or if reported, result in less conviction and imprisonment of the rapist than stranger rapes (Bryden & Lengnick, 1997).

POLICE PROCESSING OF RAPE CASES

If the rape is reported, police make the initial decisions on whether a woman's complaint is founded. The police decision to "unfound" rape cases (i.e., close them after determining that no crime occurred) is affected by the victim–offender relationship. Kerstetter (1990) found that rapes committed by strangers were less likely to be unfounded by police than were rapes committed by acquaintances. Bryden and Lengnick (1997) reviewed research on the police unfounding decision, concluding that unfounding in rape cases was more common when the victim and suspect were acquaintances than when they were strangers. Although the official national unfounding rate for rapes is 8% (Greenfeld, 1997), the proportion of acquaintance rape complaints that are unfounded has been found to be as high as 65% to 75% (Chappell & Singer, 1977). In one example, after unfavorable media publicity, the Oakland, California, police department decided to reopen 90% of the cases that they unfounded in 1989 and 1990 because police found the victims uncooperative, difficult to locate, engaged in prostitution, or known to their assailants (Cooper, 1991). Reexamination of the files led the Oakland police to conclude that of 203 of the unfounded cases, 184 rapes in fact had occurred ("Oakland Reexamines Sexual Assault Cases," 1991). Factors associated with police unfounding decisions include victim characteristics (e.g., drug use), inconsistencies in the victim's story, the absence of corroboration, and the victim–offender relationship (e.g., Bouffard, 2000; Holmstrom & Burgess, 1978; McCahil, Meyer, & Fischman, 1979). Unfounding decisions exacerbate rape trauma if the victim is blamed or not believed.

Older estimates of police unfounding rates in acquaintance rapes are dated and appear implausibly high. Critics suggest that the legal system may have the opposite problem: As many as a quarter of those charged with rape may actually be innocent (Greer, 2000). Although it does not address the acquaintance versus stranger disparity in unfounding of cases, a recent thought-provoking analysis suggests that law reforms favorable to acquaintance rape victims have actually increased "the number of rape reports that police deemed well-founded" (Futter & Mebane, 2001, p. 2). Future studies are needed to ascertain whether high rates of unfounding of acquaintance rape cases by police continue to be documented. If so, recent research on prosecutor decision making in rape cases may understate the problems faced by victims of acquaintance rapes.

PROSECUTOR PROCESSING OF RAPE CASES

Although recent data on police unfounding of acquaintance rapes are largely absent, prosecutorial decision making in rape cases continues to be studied. These studies indicate that even if an arrest is made, conviction is not guaranteed. Like police, prosecutors weed out a large number of rape cases based on victim characteristics and the victim–offender relationship (Frohman, 1991; Spohn & Holleran, 2001). Acquaintance rapes, especially those with unsympathetic victims, are less likely than stranger rapes to result in prosecution of the offender (e.g., Fairstein, 1993). Studies have found that the relationship of the victim to the offender and the circumstances of their initial contact are among factors considered most important in screening rape cases and obtaining convictions (e.g., Battelle Memorial Institute, 1977; Spears & Spohn, 1997). Prosecutors are significantly more likely to file charges if there is no question about the victim's moral character or behavior at the time of the incident (Spears & Spohn, 1997). Negative victim characteristics, such as victim's character or behavior at the time of the incident, are more likely to influence the outcomes of sexual assault cases if the victim and the offender are known to each other than if they are strangers, despite the fact that negative victim characteristics are more prevalent in cases involving strangers (Spohn & Holleran, 2001). Other research has found that 58% of all stranger cases resulted in indictments, compared with 29% of the cases among acquaintances and

47% among friends (Weninger, 1978). When the initial encounter was voluntary, only 33% of the cases resulted in indictment; when it was involuntary, the indictment rate was 62%.

JUROR DECISIONS IN RAPE CASES

Although very few rape cases proceed to a jury trial, decisions of jurors in these few cases provide insight into public attitudes toward rape. A classic study of jury verdicts found that juries convicted only 7% of acquaintance rape defendants; in sharp contrast, judges would have convicted almost half (Kalven & Zeisel, 1966). Most subsequent studies and anecdotal evidence have consistently found that jurors tend to acquit acquaintance rapists. Experimental studies have found that if the rapist knew the victim, participants are less likely to conceptualize the event as rape, less likely to consider the offense as serious, less likely to perceive the victim as truthful, and more likely to perceive the victim as responsible for the rape (e.g., Stacy, Prisbell, & Tollesfrud, 1992; Willis, 1992). Acquaintance victims also are blamed more than stranger victims if their sexual history violates traditional norms of female restraint or if they are intoxicated (e.g., Miller & Schwartz, 1995).

Because of misconceptions about the prevalence and nature of rape, jurors are likely to think they are wasting their time with rape cases involving individuals who know each other when they should be stringing up all the stranger sexual predators lurking in bushes and dark alleys. Police and prosecutors appear to anticipate this type of jury behavior when they decide not to bring acquaintance rape charges. In turn, to prosecute on this basis results in a vicious cycle that, at its core, represents public attitudes toward the majority of rape victims.

The views of jurors and legal actors toward rape victims reflect broader community attitudes toward women. A wide variety of Americans hold beliefs that can be used to justify rape (e.g., Burt, 1980). These attitudes that victims precipitate rape are partly responsible for low levels of rape reporting and for a "blame-the-victim" mentality that makes it difficult to prosecute rapists and to support victims (e.g., Russell, 1982; Stefan, 1994). As a result, rape victims are often victimized twice—once from the actual assault and a second time when they encounter negative, judgmental attitudes from the police, courts, and family and friends (Stefan, 1994).

HARMFUL EFFECTS OF CURRENT SEX OFFENDER
LEGAL POLICIES

Focusing on the stranger offender is misguided in that policymakers do not develop strategies to terminate or prevent sex crimes in the daily lives of women and children who are assaulted by nonstrangers. This may actually increase sex crimes because policymakers are using scarce criminal justice resources to target the stranger, lulling the public into a false sense of security. In Vancouver, Washington, for example, police apprehended a suspect believed to have committed a series of stranger rapes dating back to 1989 (Westfall, 1998). Prior to his capture, each time a rape was publicized, many women lived in heightened fear. At the same time, the numerous cases of acquaintance rapes seen by the local rape crisis center were, ironically, not publicized. When the serial rapist was arrested, women felt safer.

Current victims, the majority of whom have been victimized by a nonstranger, are likely to suffer in several ways. First, they are less likely to define their victimization as a crime.[4] This occurs because most individuals in society think of crime as a stranger phenomenon. When they are victimized by someone they know, particularly in a sexual manner, victims often are confused or in denial about what happened to them. Thus, it is not uncommon for a woman who has been raped or sexually assaulted by a man she knows to continue to see him after the assault (Koss, 1995). The confusion is more extreme in the case of children who are sexually abused by a family member or acquaintance. These children have been admonished not to talk with strangers but generally have not been schooled in refusing, for example, their fathers' sexual advances. In most cases, if the act is not defined by the victim as a crime, it will not be reported, thereby increasing the likelihood of continuing victimization by the perpetrator. Not defining an act as sexual abuse may be one of the reasons explaining why victims of childhood sexual abuse are at increased risk to experience victimization in adulthood (Tjaden & Thoennes, 1998a, 2000).

A second way current victims of sex crimes are adversely affected by legal policy occurs after a sex offense is reported. Police and prosecutors generally are more interested in going after the stranger offender because legal actors often do not define sex cases involving acquaintances as crimes. A woman who reports that she has been raped by her boyfriend raises legal eyebrows. If the victim resumes her relationship with the offender after the sexual assault, law enforcement and prosecutors may further doubt the victim's credibility. The same logic is not applied by police to the majority of aggravated assaults or attempted murders between men who resume their relationship with each other after the incident (Gottfredson & Hirschi, 1990). The credibility of these male victims is not an issue. These legal

[4]Some may assert that victims cannot truly be victims without subjectively feeling victimized. The studies that demonstrate this phenomenon use behaviorally specific language and legal criteria, finding that a substantial proportion of rape victims do not define their experiences as rape. The qualitative aspect of how that phenomenon works has not been explored. As with any other psychological phenomenon, individual differences in response to traumatic events do occur. Not defining their experiences as rape may serve as a survival mechanism for women. Clearly, this would be a fruitful area of future research.

policies and double standards hinder the ability of current rape victims to receive justice and protection from the legal system.

Current victims of sexual offenses are neglected by legal policies in yet another way. Efforts to reach out to individuals in high-risk situations to terminate ongoing victimization are limited. In the area of child sexual abuse, the 1980s saw the growth of sexual abuse prevention education programs for children. The availability of such programs has been reduced since then, due to cost-cutting measures affecting schools and community groups (T. Lufkin, personal communication, January 29, 1998). This is especially unfortunate because many of these programs elicited early disclosure of abuse, thereby preventing continued abuse (Daro, 1994). Although the literature in the area has not addressed the issue, arguably programs that educate parents about the prevalence and incidence of child sexual abuse may prompt parents to evaluate their own parenting practices. For parents who themselves were sexually abused or raised in dysfunctional families, this training could help them distinguish among appropriate, potentially troublesome, and inappropriate sexual interests or behaviors toward and by their children, leading them to better monitor their children's behavior and activities.

Current laws and policies toward sex offenders also have antitherapeutic effects on prospective victims of nonstrangers. As long as the public focus is on the stranger sex criminal, prevention of the majority of sex offense cases is not undertaken. As long as parents worry about the stranger child molester lurking in alleys, they are not in a position to protect their children from the nonstranger. This is because most parents do not know that their children are at higher risk of being sexually victimized by a family member or acquaintance. It is not uncommon for a mother whose child tells her about the sexual abuse perpetrated by her husband to deny it (Glendenning, 1995). This may be because her home is the last place she has been socialized to expect predatory behavior. Parent education efforts can strengthen parents' protective instincts and capacities so that they do not negligently allow spouses or others to abuse their children. Parent education programs also can emphasize communication skills to create a context in which secrets or manipulation by another adult becomes more difficult (Daro, 1994).

Prevention efforts also are thwarted by the paucity of information by the public on the prevalence of forcible rape by nonstrangers. Parents do not educate their daughters about the dangers of dating relationships or avoiding high-risk situations with males they know. Parents also fail to educate their daughters about how to resist pressure to have unwanted sex. Because sex is such an uncomfortable topic between parents and teenagers, if a rape does occur, the victim may be hesitant to tell her parents. Victims also may not tell their parents for fear of being blamed. All this is unfortunate because teenage girls have the highest rape victimization rate of any age group (Crowell & Burgess, 1996; Tjaden & Thoennes, 2000).

The failure to educate males and females to respect females is another example of how current legal policies toward sex crimes have antitherapeutic effects on prospective victims. Our society is suffused with a great deal of misogyny. Not only do men often dislike women, but women frequently dislike each other and themselves (Bowen, 1998). There are many messages that children receive about the relative worth of their gender. This may start with the family in which the mother is disparaged and abused. It continues in the school system in which girls may be neglected and discouraged from intellectual achievement (Lombardi, 1998). Occasionally, one reads an article about a boy in an elementary school who steals a kiss from a girl. This is dismissed as "boys will be boys" as opposed to "assaultive behavior starts early." Recently, cases have been publicized about the sexual harassment by male students of females in the schools (Biskupic, 1999; Bracey, 1999). Where girls and women are undervalued by themselves and others, they are more prone to victimization. Violence against women in the United States and the lukewarm legal response to it both reflect and contribute to the misogyny of our culture.

SOLUTIONS FOR FUTURE LAW REFORM TO ACHIEVE THERAPEUTIC EFFECTS ON VICTIMS

It is clear that current legal policy directed at stranger sex offenders adversely affects the majority of victims of sex crimes (i.e., nonstranger victims). Law reform is needed that seeks to prevent or terminate family and acquaintance sex offenses.

One approach to law in these cases, therapeutic jurisprudence, investigates the law's impact on the emotional lives of participants in the legal system by encouraging sensitivity to therapeutic and iatrogenic consequences that may result from the legal rules, legal procedures, and the roles of legal actors (Wexler & Winick, 1996; see also this volume, chapters 12 and 18). One can see most glaringly the adverse effect of the victim–offender relationship on the legal processing of criminal cases in the area of domestic violence (Simon, 1995; Winick, 2000). This is also true for sex offenses. Victims who have a prior relationship with the offender are not treated seriously and respectfully by social others and by the legal system. Even worse, these victims do not take themselves seriously. The legal system, in particular, further traumatizes victims of child molestation and forcible rape who have a relationship with the offender.

This chapter extends the reach of earlier work by arguing that laws, legal procedures, and legal actors in the criminal justice system must treat childhood incest and acquaintance sexual violence as seriously as (if not more seriously than) it does sexual violence perpetrated by strangers. Only by treating acquaintance sex offenses as seriously as stranger cases can these victims begin the healing process. If the legal system targets nonstranger sex offenders for rigorous arrest, prosecution, and conviction, victims will also define what happened to them as a crime. In turn, this realization may prevent its recurrence by the same offender or by someone else. Sensitive and empathic treatment by officials, ranging from the police to the judges and juries, in acquaintance rape cases will validate victims' often confused feelings about their victimization. Legal authorities such as child protection agencies, as well as legal actors, can treat intrafamilial child sexual abuse as a crime instead of as a "family" problem. Imposing sentences commensurate with those given stranger sex offenders will combat any distortions in the victim's mind that she was at fault. Prosecuting nonstranger offenders to the fullest extent of the law may also change public and jury attitudes about the victims in these cases. Therapeutic jurisprudence suggests that legal actors and policymakers can achieve therapeutic outcomes for victims of nonstranger sex crimes by shifting the legal focus from stranger to nonstranger sex offenses.

CONCLUSION

It is clear that current legal policy has deleterious effects on current and prospective victims of sex crimes committed by acquaintances and relatives. Because of myths and misconceptions, policymakers are afraid of the stranger while ignorant of the danger to children and women that resides closer to home. Educating the public about the nature and magnitude of sex crimes would be a first step in mitigating the trauma to current victims while also protecting prospective victims. An important step would be to encourage newspapers and television news programs to highlight the danger of nonstranger sex crimes by reporting them more frequently and putting into perspective the rare stranger sex crimes they report.

Future research should focus on the links between different forms of violence toward women and the victim–offender relationship. For example, a recent study provides compelling evidence of a link between stalking and other forms of violence in intimate relationships. Eighty-one percent of the women who were stalked by an intimate partner were also physically assaulted by the same partner, and 31% of the women who were stalked by an intimate partner were also sexually assaulted by the same partner (Tjaden & Thoennes, 1998b). Consequently, in acquaintance rape victimizations, there are likely to be other forms of violence perpetrated by the same or different intimates. To fully understand the fear and terror instilled in many acquaintance victims, a more holistic picture of the relationship needs to be established at all stages of legal processing. With more thorough knowledge of the full gamut of violence existing in a rape relationship, legal actors may alter their decision-making processes and more vigorously prosecute these cases, facilitating healing of the victims.

One factor underlying the legal neglect of sexual violence against women by acquaintances and family members has been that crime control policy is premised on countering stranger violence (Simon, 2000). Policies that target stranger violence address violence against males at the expense of violence against females (Tjaden & Thoennes, 2000). Because men and women generally engage in different lifestyles (Gottfredson & Hirschi, 1990), men are more likely to be victimized by strangers and women are more likely to be victimized by acquaintances and family members (Rennison, 2001). Future policy needs to reflect the reality that children and women are more likely to be victimized by family members and acquaintances than by strangers.

The disjuncture between actual sex offender policies and the empirical realities of most sex crimes discussed in this chapter has implications for future policies affecting sex offenders and their victims. Current sexually violent predator (SVP) legislation and Megan's Law approaches seem to target only a small proportion of sex offenders and to ignore the vast majority of them who are acquaintances and family members. Because of their focus on stranger sex offenders, such policies lull the public into a false sense of security and fail to terminate ongoing offenses or prevent future ones perpetrated by acquaintances and family members. SVP statutes specifically target stranger sex offenders. Moreover, they rely on predictions of future sexual violence, a process that may be fraught with false positives and false negatives (see this volume, chapter 3). Overprediction results in harm to erroneously incarcerated sex offenders. False negatives may result in harm to future victims. Future research is needed to measure the accuracy of the prediction process in these cases.

Megan's Law statutes similarly target stranger sex offenders released into communities (see this volume, chapter 12). When public attention is riveted by the sensational publicity accompanying release of a stranger sex offender into the community, individual families are not protecting their children from family members and acquaintances. Future research is needed to examine whether Megan's Law statutes protect children from people they know.

Future law reform may want to integrate the paradigm of therapeutic jurisprudence by enacting legislation that aims to achieve therapeutic outcomes for nonstranger sex crime victims (see this volume, chapter 12). One way of accomplishing this goal is for policymakers to focus less on current sex offender legislation targeting strangers and more on laws to protect women and children from the people they know.

REFERENCES

Bachman, R., & Saltzman, L. (1995). *Violence against women: Estimates from the re-designed study*. Washington, DC: U.S. Department of Justice, Bureau of Justice Statistics.

Battelle Memorial Institute. (1977). *Forcible rape: A national survey of the responses by prosecutors*. Seattle, WA: Law and Justice Center.

Berliner, L., Schram, D., Miller, L. L., & Milloy, C. D. (1995). A sentencing alternative for sex offenders: A study of decision making and recidivism. *Journal of Interpersonal Violence, 10*, 487–502.

Biskupic, J. (1999, January 13). A big test on taunts at school: Justices hear case over harassment. *Washington Post*, p. A4.

Bouffard, J. A. (2000). Predicting type of sexual assault case closure from victim, suspect, and case characteristics. *Journal of Criminal Justice, 28*, 527–542.

Bowen, A. (1998, August 14). Misogyny may be "out" but it's alive and well in many guises. *Seattle Post–Intelligence*, p. A16.

Bracey, G. W. (1999, May). The culture of sexual harassment. *Phi Delta Kappan, Bloomington*, p. 725.

Bryden, D. P., & Lengnick, S. (1997). Rape in the criminal justice system. *Journal of Criminal Law and Criminology, 87*, 1194–1384.

Burt, M. R. (1980). Cultural myths and support for rape. *Journal of Personality and Social Psychology, 38*, 217–230.

Chappell, D., & Singer, S. (1977). Rape in New York City: A study of material in the police files and its meaning. In D. Chappell, R. Geis, & G. Geis (Eds.), *Forcible rape: The crime, the victim, and the offender* (pp. 245–271). New York: Columbia University Press.

Cooper, C. J. (1991, February 1). Oakland admits 184 rapes ignored. *San Francisco Examiner*, p. A1.

Crowell, N. A., & Burgess, A. W. (1996). *Understanding violence against women*. Washington, DC: National Academy Press.

Daro, D. A. (1994). Prevention of child sexual abuse. *Future Directions, 4*, 198–223.

Fairstein, L. A. (1993). *Sexual violence: Our war against rape*. New York: William Morrow.

Federal Bureau of Investigation. (1994). *Crime in the United States*. Washington, DC: U.S. Department of Justice.

Fischer, D. G., & McDonald, W. L. (1998). Characteristics of intrafamilial and extrafamilial child sexual abuse. *Child Abuse and Neglect, 22*, 915–929.

Frohman, L. (1991). Discrediting victims' allegations of sexual assault: Prosecutorial accounts of case rejections. *Social Problems, 38*, 213–226.

Futter, S., & Mebane, W. R. (2001). The effects of rape law reform on rape case processing. *Berkeley Women's Law Journal, 16*, 72–131.

Glendenning, C. (1995). When you grow up an abused child. In P. Searles & R.

Berger (Eds.), *Rape and society: Readings on the problem of sexual assault* (pp. 246–249). Boulder, CO: Westview Press.

Gottfredson, M. R., & Hirschi, T. (1990). *A general theory of crime*. Stanford, CA: Stanford University Press.

Greenfeld, L. (1997). *Sex offenses and offenders: An analysis of data on rape and sexual assault*. Washington, DC: U.S. Department of Justice, Bureau of Justice Statistics.

Greer, E. (2000). The truth behind legal dominance feminism's "two percent false rape claim" figure. *Loyola of Los Angeles Law Review, 33*, 947–972.

Holmstrom, L. L., & Burgess, A. W. (1978). *The victim of rape: Institutional reactions*. New York: Wiley.

Kalven, H., Jr., & Zeisel, H. (1966). *The American jury*. Boston: Little, Brown.

Kerstetter, W. A. (1990). Gateway to justice: Police and prosecutorial response to sexual assaults against women. *Journal of Criminal Law and Criminology, 81*, 267–313.

Koss, M. P. (1995). Hidden rape: Sexual aggression and victimization in a national sample of students in higher education. In P. Searles & R. Berger (Eds.), *Rape and society: Readings on the problem of sexual assault* (pp. 35–49). Boulder, CO: Westview Press.

Lombardi, K. S. (1998, November 29). Girls wrestle with peer pressure. *New York Times*, p. 15.

Man charged in 7-year-old neighbor's killing. (1994, August 1). *New York Times*, p. B5.

McCahil, T. W., Meyer, L. C., & Fischman, A. M. (1979). *The aftermath of rape*. Lexington, MA: Lexington Books.

Miller, J., & Schwartz, M. (1995). Rape myths and violence against street prostitutes. *Deviant Behavior, 16*, 1–23.

Oakland reexamines sexual assault cases. (1991, February 4). *Herald Times*, p. A3.

Quindlen, A. (1994, August 8). So what if law isn't fair to sex offenders? Children come first. *Chicago Tribune*, p. 13.

Rennison, C. M. (2001). *Criminal victimization 2000: Changes 1999–2000 with trends 1993–2000*. Washington, DC: U.S. Department of Justice, Bureau of Justice Statistics.

Rind, B., Tromovitch, P., & Bauserman, R. (1998). A meta-analytic examination of assumed properties of child sexual abuse using college samples. *Psychological Bulletin, 124*, 22–51.

Russell, D. E. H. (1982). The prevalence and incidence of forcible rape of females. *Victimology, 7*, 81–93.

Schulhofer, S. J. (1998). *Unwanted sex: The culture of intimidation and the failure of the law*. Cambridge, MA: Harvard University Press.

Siegel, B. (1990, May 10). Locking up "sexual predators." *Los Angeles Times*, p. A1.

Simon, L. M. J. (1995). A therapeutic jurisprudence approach to the legal processing of domestic violence cases. *Psychology, Public Policy, and Law, 1,* 43–79.

Simon, L. M. J. (2000). An examination of the assumptions of specialization, mental disorder, and dangerousness in sex offenders. *Behavioral Sciences and the Law, 18,* 275–308.

Simon, L., Sales, B., Kaszniak, A., & Kahn, M. (1992). Characteristics of child molesters: Implications for the fixated-regressed dichotomy. *Journal of Interpersonal Violence, 7,* 211–225.

Snyder, H. N. (2000). *Sexual assault of young children as reported to law enforcement: Victim, incident, and offender characteristics.* Washington, DC: U.S. Department of Justice.

Spears, J. W., & Spohn, C. C. (1997). The effect of evidence factors and victim characteristics on prosecutors' charging decisions in sexual assault cases. *Justice Quarterly, 14,* 501–524.

Spohn, C., & Holleran, D. (2001). Prosecuting sexual assault: A comparison of charging decisions in sexual assault cases involving strangers, acquaintances, and intimate partners. *Justice Quarterly, 18,* 651–685.

Stacy, R. D., Prisbell, M., & Tollesfrud, K. (1992). A comparison of attitudes among college students toward sexual violence committed by strangers and by acquaintances. *Journal of Sex Education and Therapy, 18,* 257–263.

Stefan, S. (1994). The protection racket: Rape trauma syndrome, psychiatric labeling, and law. *Northwestern University Law Review, 88,* 1271–1345.

Tjaden, P., & Thoennes, N. (1998a). *Prevalence, incidence, and consequences of violence against women: Findings from the National Violence Against Women Survey.* Washington, DC: National Institute of Justice and Centers for Disease Control and Prevention.

Tjaden, P., & Thoennes, N. (1998b). *Stalking in America: Findings from the National Violence Against Women Survey.* Washington, DC: National Institute of Justice and Centers for Disease Control and Prevention.

Tjaden, P., & Thoennes, N. (2000). *Full report of the prevalence, incidence, and consequences of violence against women.* Washington, DC: National Institute of Justice and Centers for Disease Control and Prevention.

Wash. Rev. Code § 71.09.020 (Supp. 1998).

Wash. Rev. Code § 9A.64 (Supp. 1998).

Wash. Rev. Code § 9A.44.073 (Supp. 1998).

Weninger, R. A. (1978). Factors affecting the prosecution of rape: A case study of Travis County, Texas. *Virginia Law Review, 64,* 357–397.

Westfall, B. (1998, May 15). Gallatin charged with other rapes. *Columbian,* p. A1.

Wexler, D., & Winick, B. (1996). *Law in a therapeutic key: Developments in therapeutic jurisprudence.* Durham, NC: Carolina Academic Press.

Widom, C. S. (1997). Accuracy of adult recollections of early childhood abuse.

In J. D. Read & S. Lindsay (Eds.), *Recollections of trauma: Scientific evidence and clinical practice* (pp. 49–70). New York: Plenum Press.

Willis, C. E. (1992). The effects of sex role stereotype, victim and defendant race, and prior relationship on rape culpability attributions. *Sex Roles, 26,* 213–226.

Winick, B. (2000). Applying the law therapeutically in domestic violence cases. *University of Missouri–Kansas City Law Review, 69,* 33–91.

9

BAD OR MAD?: SEX OFFENDERS AND SOCIAL CONTROL

STEPHEN J. MORSE

Sex offenders arouse intense anger and fear (Garland, 2001). Their assaults are not only invasions of autonomy and bodily privacy but also intrusions on a person's ability to control the conditions of cherished intimacy or an interference with a child's emotional and sexual development. The question for both society and the law is how to control the dangers sexual offenders present consistent with the demands of justice.

This chapter argues that understandable resentment and fear of sexual offenders too easily lead to inappropriate confusion between the two dominant models for analyzing sexual predation—the medical and the moral models—and that this confusion in turn leads to injustice. I begin with an exploration of the two dominant models and the relation between them. I then turn to a discussion of the two dominant rationales for involuntary confinement—desert and disease—and indicate how they inevitably leave gaps that permit dangerous people to remain at large, gaps that the law tries to narrow by adopting preventive confinement schemes that confuse the two rationales. Next, I consider the most recent, striking examples of

Portions of this chapter are adapted from Morse (1998b). Copyright © 1998 by the American Psychological Association (APA). Adapted with permission of the author and the APA.

the confusion—the United States Supreme Court's decisions in *Kansas v. Hendricks* (1997), in which the court upheld the constitutionality of a state statute that provided for indefinite civil commitment for so-called "mentally abnormal sexually violent predators" *after* such predators had completed a prison term for such predation, and *Kansas v. Crane* (2002), in which the Court held that involuntary civil commitment of sexual predators was justified only if the predator had serious difficulty controlling himself. I contend that the Court went too far to protect public safety, thereby undermining important understandings of responsibility and justice. I conclude by suggesting that although the medical model may have great value, the law would be wiser to adopt a fully moral model to respond to sexual predation.

MEDICAL AND MORAL MODELS OF SEXUAL MISCONDUCT

The medical model treats the insistent, sexually aberrant desires and conduct of sex offenders as signs and symptoms of an underlying disorder. These "disorders of desire" have received the official imprimatur of inclusion in the American Psychiatric Association's *Diagnostic and Statistical Manual of Mental Disorders* (4th ed., Text Revision [DSM–IV–TR]; American Psychiatric Association, 2000). No causal model for these disorders can claim uncontroversial validity, but medical modelers agree that people with abnormalities of sexual desire are sick and that they are not responsible for having the underlying disorder. The signs and symptoms of most diseases are not intentional human actions but instead are simply mechanistic biophysical effects of the underlying pathology. The medical model is mechanistic, and it is easy to conclude by analogy that the diseased agent is not responsible for sexually aberrant desires and behavior. The appropriate response, it seems, is nonjudgmental and therapeutic rather than evaluative and punitive.

Many people influenced by the medical model recognize that sexual disorders (and addictions, impulse disorders, and the like) are unlike many other disorders in significant respects. Sexually aberrant conduct is intentional behavior rather than simply the state or movement of a body. It is plausible to assume that the sufferer might be able to exert some degree of intentional control over the aberrant behavior and that encouraging the agent to "take responsibility" for the conduct might be therapeutically efficacious. Thus, the medical model of disorders of sexual desire is not necessarily inconsistent with moral evaluation of at least the conduct that is a sign of the disorder. Nonetheless, the lure of mechanism powerfully impels medical modelers to conclude that sufferers have little if any control over their desires and conduct and are not morally responsible for them.

The foremost treatment implication of the medical model is that a therapeutic response is clinically and morally warranted. The interesting question is whether treatment can be imposed without the sufferer's consent and as a condition for the release of potentially dangerous predators who have been preventively confined. Answering this complex question goes beyond the scope of this chapter, but most people who suffer from sexual abnormalities are perfectly competent to make treatment decisions. If treatment is imposed on them, it must be justified by hard parentalism or by a pure police power rationale.

The moral model, in contrast, focuses on the reality that sexually aberrant conduct is intentional action. All moral theories agree that intentional human action is an appropriate object of moral assessment; therefore, sexual conduct, although arguably also a sign of a disorder, may properly be morally evaluated. Moreover, the law's concern is conduct, not thoughts and desires, because only conduct violates or threatens the rights of others. The question for morality and law, then, is whether a person with a disorder of sexual desire is morally responsible for the conduct motivated by the desire.

In our moral and legal system, responsibility is a necessary, crucial variable for making decisions concerning liberty and autonomy. Judgments of moral and legal responsibility are only possible, however, according to some implicit or explicit theory of responsibility. Theories of responsibility are highly contested, differing substantially about the criteria for both responsibility and excuse. Nevertheless, it is clear that our legal system at least implicitly—and sometimes explicitly—adopts a theory of responsibility that makes an agent's general capacity for rationality and the absence of unjustified compulsion or coercion the touchstones of responsibility. In turn, if the agent's general capacity for rationality was compromised or the agent acted under compulsion, excuse and nonresponsibility may be warranted. Responsibility is often discussed as if it were a question of free will or free choice, and the compulsion or coercion criterion for excuse is sometimes characterized as a "volitional" question. These are misleading characterizations, however, that do not and cannot explain the criteria for responsibility and excuse that both the law and ordinary morality adopt (Morse, 1998a).

The identified moral and legal criteria for responsibility—the general capacity for rationality and lack of unjustified compulsion—are normative and not self-defining. A legal system must provide justifiable criteria that decision makers can fairly apply. Differing definitions will produce different outcomes. Some may excuse many sexual offenders and others may excuse few, but rationality and compulsion will provide the parameters of the decision. Moreover, as Fingarette and Hasse have persuasively shown (1979), the presence of a disease per se does not answer the question of responsibility, even if the presence of the disease and its signs and symptoms are uncontroversial. Although human action may perhaps be properly considered the sign of an underlying disorder, it is nevertheless true that the effect of disease on responsibility must be cashed out in terms of rationality and compulsion. Having a disease is not an excuse per se when human action is at stake.

Viewed from the perspective of the moral model, many and perhaps most agents who exhibit aberrant sexual conduct seem responsible for their sexual behavior. Most sex offenders exhibit no defect of rationality. They understand what they are doing, their instrumental rationality is intact, and they understand the moral and legal rules governing sexual conduct. Indeed, they may fully endorse those rules. One might try to claim that sexually aberrant desires are irrational, but it is virtually impossible to make sense of the claim that desires are per se rational or irrational (Nozick, 1993). Finally, I have argued that some people with impulse problems may have a plausible irrationality claim because on occasion the desire becomes so insistent that it substantially compromises the agent's capacity for rational deliberation (Morse, 2000, 2002). This claim would be strong in few cases, however, and even then the moral modeler might argue that the agent had a duty to take steps to bind himself to the mast when his desires were less insistent.

The sexual offender's essential claim is thus that his desires are so strong, so powerful, that he cannot control them, that he cannot help himself. Thus, the primary excusing condition sexually aberrant conduct presents is some type of compulsion problem. Again, however, even if the desires are the product of a disorder, that does not per se imply that the agent must be excused. Here, too, the moral modeler may be skeptical. The sexual offender is not an automaton, and sexual conduct is far more calculated than the ticlike conduct associated with disorders like Tourette's syndrome. A desire is just a desire, whatever its cause may be, and causation is not an excuse (Moore, 1985). Both "normal" and "abnormal" desires can be strong or weak, constant or sudden and transient. When anyone is in the grip of a powerful, insistent desire of any type, it is frustrating and even painful not to satisfy it. But having a strong desire is not an excuse in general for engaging in prohibited behavior, and the moral modeler asks why a strong desire for forbidden sexual conduct in particular should furnish an excuse. We may feel sympathy for people tortured by strong and often unwanted desires for forbidden conduct, and we may provide help to such unfortunate people, but the moral modeler nonetheless expects such agents to control themselves and holds them responsible if they do not. So, for example, few sexual offenders are able successfully to raise the insanity defense, even in cases of the most "compelling" desires.

The treatment implications of the moral model depend on the applicable theory of punishment. On a purely retributive theory, the appropriate "treatment" is proportionate blame and punishment. Even if an offender agreed voluntarily to undergo some type of biological or behavioral intervention that would substantially reduce the probability of reoffending, there would be no justification for reducing the offender's condign sentence. If, however, a mixed theory blending retributive and consequential concerns is regnant—as it is today in most American jurisdictions—then interventions that reduce the likelihood of recidivism might reduce the offender's sentence to the lower end of a range set by desert. Prisoners are not entitled to treatment, so offering interventions under such conditions would probably not be considered coercive because it is an offer and not a threat. The imposition of treatment, especially invasive treatments, on unconsenting, competent prisoners might be justified by specific prevention, but almost certainly this rationale would yield to the prisoner's liberty right to be free of treatments that seek to change thoughts, feelings, and behaviors.[1]

The medical and moral models have attractive features and the potential for abuse. Treating people as sick rather than bad, as the medical model does, can produce kinder, more understanding treatment. The medical model also is likely to spawn research to identify the causes of undesirable behaviors and the types of interventions that may reduce their frequency. On the other hand, applying the medical model to intentional behavior can lead to unwarranted demeaning of the dignity and personhood of human agents and parentalistic treatment. It may create injustice by treating responsible agents as not responsible.

The moral model has the great virtue of treating people as subjects rather than as objects and thus endowing them with dignity and respect. Also, if justice demands that people be held responsible, only a moral model can properly do this. On the other hand, moral models can become harshly moralistic or punitive, and their application can blind people to the virtues of rehabilitation.

The medical and moral models need not be inconsistent. Let us assume both that sexual offenders, or anyway many of them, are properly characterized as suffering from a disease and that many such offenders are nonetheless morally responsible for their conduct. Responsible offenders might be fairly convicted and punished for sexual offenses, but society might also encourage research and provide various treatment programs to potential offenders and those being punished for their offenses. As Justice Marshall recognized in his opinion in *Powell v. Texas* (1968), which upheld

---

[1]Compare the United States Supreme Court's recent decision, *McKune v. Lile* (2002). Lile was a prisoner who had been convicted of rape. Some years before his scheduled release, the prison authorities ordered him to participate in a treatment program. As part of participation in the program, inmates had to agree to admit to all previous sexual activities, including those that would be chargeable as sexual offenses. Such admissions were not privileged and could be used against the prisoner in future criminal prosecutions. Failure to agree to make such unprivileged admissions constituted refusal to participate and could result in the automatic curtailment of desirable privileges and the imposition of onerous conditions. Lile challenged this scheme as an infringement of his Fifth Amendment right to remain silent, but the Court held that the choice imposed on Lile was not sufficiently compulsive to violate this right.

the constitutionality of punishing an undoubted alcoholic for being drunk in public, a criminal justice response may be useful in dealing with conduct a disease in part produces. On the other hand, if sexual offenders as a class are not responsible for their conduct, then blame and punishment would never be warranted. Or, if sexual offending is deemed not to be the sign of an underlying disorder and no excusing condition is otherwise found, it is possible that an entirely moral response might be appropriate and that civil commitment would never be justified. But even then, a nonmedicalized program of research to identify the causes of sexual offending would be justifiable.

LIBERTY, JUSTICE, AND INVOLUNTARY CONFINEMENT

American society has an enormous preference for liberty, for allowing citizens to pursue their projects. Because deprivation of liberty is a maximal exercise of the state's coercive power, our legal system is morally legitimate only if it is willing to give public, justifiable reasons to confine citizens involuntarily either civilly or criminally. Our society does not preventively confine for dangerousness alone (*Kansas v. Hendricks*, 1997). The central criteria for involuntary confinement are desert and disease (Morse, 1999; Robinson, 1996; Schulhofer, 1996; but see Robinson, 2001). If a responsible agent has violated the criminal law, the agent deserves and may fairly receive blame and punishment as a matter of retributive justice. With minor exceptions, the state may not preventively confine a responsible citizen, no matter how dangerous the agent might be, unless the agent has violated the criminal law because the liberty interest of responsible agents trumps society's interest in public safety. If an agent suffers from a disorder that renders him both dangerous and nonresponsible concerning the dangerous behavior, then criminal conviction for actual conduct is unjustified, and preventive confinement by involuntary civil commitment is justified. Retributive justice does not demand blame and punishment of nonresponsible agents, and the need for social safety trumps the liberty interest of those incapable of rational self-governance.

Despite its constitutional and theoretical credentials, the civil–criminal distinction is neither logically nor practically required to guide confinement. We might adopt a purely preventive regime in which confinement is authorized for dangerousness alone, untied to culpability or nonresponsibility (Robinson, 2001). This would be a scheme of "behavioral quarantine," analogous to medical quarantine to prevent the spread of infectious disease (Corrado, 1996). If society decided that safety outweighs the usual culpability and nonresponsibility limitations, only epistemological anxieties about accurate prediction would hinder such a regime. For now, however, the liberty interests enshrined in our constitutional law do not permit long-term pure behavioral quarantine. Confinement for dangerous behavior must therefore be premised on either culpability or nonresponsibility.

Society thus has two options for detaining potentially dangerous agents: criminal conviction and imprisonment *after* a responsible agent has violated the criminal law and involuntary civil commitment of a blameless agent who may or may not have engaged in dangerous conduct. In the former case, punishment must be proportionate to the offender's desert and offenders must be released when their sentence is complete, even if they have a substantial criminal history and remain dangerous. Despite theoretical proportionality constraints, however, the United States Supreme Court has held that there are virtually no constitutional limits on a state's power to impose for most crimes any term of years, including terms that are harshly punitive (*Harmelin v. Michigan*, 1991). Finally, states are free to impose enhanced sentences on recidivist offenders—so-called "three strikes and you're out" laws (Zimring, Hawkins, & Kamin, 2001). Such sentencing schemes have the consequential virtue of incapacitating potentially dangerous offenders for periods longer than the sentence permitted for the current crime, but whether such enhancements are retributively just is controversial (see *Brown v. Mayle*, 2002, holding that application of three-strikes laws for petty theft is a violation of the Eighth Amendment prohibition of cruel and unusual punishment). In sum, by various means, states can accomplish lengthy and even lifelong incapacitation through the criminal justice system.

In principle, involuntary commitment may be indefinite, although periodic review of commitment is required. The agent is being confined because the disorder makes him incapable of rationality concerning potentially dangerous conduct. In principle, the commitment should continue as long as the agent remains irrationally dangerous (*Jones v. United States*, 1983), and, as the United States Supreme Court held in *Foucha v. Louisiana* (1992), it should terminate if the agent regains his rationality or is no longer dangerous. A rational agent must be released because the disease/ irrationality precondition for involuntary commitment no longer obtains. Even if the agent remains irrational, however, preventive confinement is not necessary and justified if the agent no longer presents a danger. If the agent remains irrationally dangerous, justice places no limit on the length of civil preventive confinement. Although the state may not be able to offer treatment, an incapacitation rationale supports the continued civil confinement of agents who are irrationally dangerous. Nonetheless, in the pure civil commitment system, concerns about the substantial deprivation of liberty for innocent agents who may not have actually acted dangerously and about the efficacy and cost of long-term hospitalization have caused most states to limit the length of confinement substantially.

Sexual offenders who are likely to recidivate present a substantial danger to public safety. The question is which form of social control—criminal or civil confinement—is most appropriate. Sexual offenses are terrible wrongs, and if sexual offenders are responsible for their conduct, retributive justice requires that they should be convicted and punished proportionately to their culpability. Harsh sentences for such offenses are constitutional, and sexual offenders may thereby be incapacitated for lengthy periods. Once they have completed their deserved prison sentences, however, sexual offenders, like offenders in general, should be released, even if we are certain that they will recidivate. Indeed, the case of a child molester about to be released from prison who threatened to kidnap and mutilate a young boy after his release and then did so was the motivation for Washington State's mentally abnormal sexually violent predator law that has been the model for the spate of similar legislation in other states (La Fond, 1992). Some released sexual offenders will recidivate, but this is unavoidable unless states are willing to impose life sentences without possibility of parole or other onerously lengthy sentences. Once again, however, it is within the state's power to reduce sexual offense recidivism by criminal sentences.

In contrast, if some sexual offenders are genuinely not responsible for their conduct, they do not deserve criminal blame and punishment and they should be civilly committed. Because there is no necessary term limit on the permissible period for civil commitment, and courts will rarely overturn the judgments of clinicians concerning future dangerousness—especially if there is a history of sexually aberrant conduct—the state has the power to keep potential sexual offenders confined for as long as the state wishes. The Supreme Court made clear in *Hendricks* that an incapacitation rationale justifies confinement in such cases. Even if efficacious treatment does exist, the Supreme Court has never decided that there is a right to treatment for people whose civil confinement is justified by disease and consequent nonresponsibility. The Court has implied, however, that *if* a state claims that treatment is at least one rationale for civil confinement, due process might be violated if it is not provided (*Jackson v. Indiana*, 1972; *Seling v. Young*, 2001).

The analysis just offered suggests that states have nearly unlimited power in both the criminal and civil justice systems to confine sexual offenders for as long as necessary reasonably to limit public danger. If so, why should we care which system is used? The first reason is that the law should attempt to do justice, and it would be unjust to convict the innocent or to confine civilly those who are responsible. In addition to the inherent virtue of doing justice, the law should also teach citizens by example. The second reason to care is that the criminal and civil law work imperfectly to effectuate incapacitation of dangerous people. The criminal law must wait for a crime to occur, and then, for many reasons, conviction for the highest level of crime potentially chargeable and consequent lengthy incarceration may be difficult to obtain. Finally, although legislatures have the power to impose draconian sentences for sexual offenses, such penalties may appear unjust, and imprisonment is expensive. As a result of all these factors, lengthy sentences may not be imposed in cases involving the substantial probability of recidivism.

Pure civil commitment that does not follow an insanity acquittal also may provide only limited protection. Many potential sexual offenders are quite rational and may not satisfy the statutory criteria for pure civil commitment. Indeed, most states do not wish to confine an agent unless the disorder is severe and the agent is clearly nonresponsible. Moreover, as we have seen, pure civil commitment usually has limited terms. Finally, civil hospitals also do not prefer to provide expensive custodial care to apparently rational and untreatable patients who are confined primarily to protect the public. They would prefer to care for people who are uncontroversially severely disordered and who apparently cannot manage their lives without help. Thus, many sexually dangerous agents might not be civilly committable in theory or practice.

Although the criminal and civil confinement systems together might in principle effectively incapacitate most dangerous people, considerations of desert, constitutional limitations, and practical problems inevitably create a gap that permits some undeniably dangerous agents to remain at large because they fit neither the desert nor disease rationale (Schulhofer, 1996). The consequent public peril invites blurring of the distinction between the two rationales to narrow the gap, which increases the risk that society will accept pure civil preventive detention of responsible and dangerous but blameless agents. The commitment criteria that *Hendricks* and *Crane* addressed present a classic example of such dangerous blurring.

HENDRICKS, CRANE, AND THE POSSIBILITY OF PURE PREVENTIVE DETENTION[2]

The Kansas mentally abnormal sexual predator statute tried to fill the gap between traditional criminal and civil confinement by permitting the indefinite involuntary civil commitment of "any person who has been convicted or charged with a sexually violent offense and who suffers from a mental abnormality or personality disorder which makes the person likely to engage in the predatory acts of sexual violence" (Kan. Stat. Ann. § 59-29a02(a), 1994).[3] Serious sexual offenses meet the usual civil commitment

[2]This section of the chapter borrows extensively from portions of an earlier paper (Morse, 1998b).
[3]Kansas has since updated its statutory language, but it does not differ significantly from the statute the Court addressed in *Hendricks*. Therefore, I shall use and cite to the original language.

criterion of "danger to others." Moreover, unlike many standard civil committees, who only threaten harms prior to commitment, sexual predators by definition must be charged with or convicted of a sexual offense. Thus there is better evidence that sexual predators, as Kansas and like states define them, are in fact dangerous. The problem is the nonresponsibility justification. Using criteria for mental abnormality, Kansas sought to bring the statute within the allegedly nonpunitive, civil confinement disease rationale.

It is paradoxical, however, to claim that a sexually violent predator is sufficiently responsible to deserve the stigma and punishment of criminal incarceration but that the predator is not sufficiently responsible to be permitted the usual freedom from involuntary civil commitment that predictably dangerous but responsible agents retain. Even if the standards for responsibility in the two systems need not be symmetrical, it is difficult to imagine what adequate conception of justice would justify blaming and punishing an agent too irresponsible to be left at large. We need to be clear about whether sexually violent predators are mad or bad and respond accordingly.

An agent who is mad may be convicted of crime, but only if the agent is sufficiently culpable morally to warrant blame and punishment. If an agent is morally responsible, however, the agent should not be preventively detained. John La Fond, noting Washington State's insanity defense and civil commitment statutes (personal communication, September 12, 1998), has suggested in response that a state insanity defense might include only a cognitive criterion of responsibility, whereas the civil confinement system might also include volitional or control criteria. If so, an agent who suffered from a volitional defect might be criminally responsible *and* civilly committable. A state may constitutionally do this if it wishes. Nonetheless, such a scheme would be morally objectionable. If a state believes that a mental disability sufficiently compromises responsibility to warrant preventive detention, then such disability should surely be part of the criteria for the insanity defense because criminal blame and punishment are the worst afflictions the state can impose on citizens.

Sexual offenders can be extremely dangerous, which makes it easy to understand why Kansas grasped for a remedy, but not every problem has a solution that is morally, theoretically, or empirically defensible. Mentally abnormal sexual offender commitments provide some public safety, but they also threaten the civil liberty of legally innocent, responsible people to be left largely alone. In effect, *Hendricks* jettisons culpability *and* nonresponsibility as predicates for confinement and permits pure preventive detention without recognizing that it is doing this. To support this assertion, let me turn to an analysis of the criteria for mental abnormality in Kansas's predator statute and the Supreme Court's response to challenges to the constitutional adequacy of this standard.

States are not bound by the conceptions and definitions of any discipline when they create legal criteria (*Kansas v. Hendricks*, 1997). Nothing, for example, prevents a state from defining "mental abnormality" differently from traditional psychiatric or psychological definitions of mental disorder. And nothing in the abstract prevents a state legislature from finding that a class of citizens is not responsible for specific conduct, even if mental health professionals or ordinary citizens would disagree. Responsibility is a normative concept, and we empower legislators to create normative standards through legal rules. But to command respect and allegiance, such definitions and findings should comport with reasonable standards for conceptual coherence and empirical understanding of behavior. My claim is that the Kansas standard for "mental abnormality," which was accepted without critical analysis by the Supreme Court, falls far short of the standard for rational support, suggesting that Kansas and the United States Supreme Court filled the gap between criminal and civil confinement by a legal sleight of hand.

Recall that Kansas defines a sexually violent predator generally as "any person who has been convicted of or charged with a sexually violent offense and who suffers from a mental abnormality or personality disorder which makes the person likely to engage in the predatory acts of sexual violence" (Kan. Stat. Ann. § 59-29a02(a), 1994). A "mental abnormality" is defined as a "congenital or acquired condition affecting the emotional or volitional capacity which predisposes the person to commit sexually violent offenses in a degree constituting such person a menace to the health and safety of others" (Kan. Stat. Ann. § 59-29a02(b), 1994).

These provisions together are vague and even incoherent definitions of *abnormally* produced sexual danger. The former, which attempts to satisfy the critical nonresponsibility criterion for justifiable civil commitment, requires that an abnormality must produce the potential sexual predation. The terms *personality disorder* and *mental abnormality* must therefore do all the work. Personality disorder is a recognized diagnostic category, but people with such disorders are seldom psychotic and rarely can avoid responsibility for their deeds. This is not a promising predicate for nonresponsibility without a great deal of conceptual reason to believe that this recognized abnormality does sufficiently compromise responsibility. Mental abnormality is not a recognized diagnostic term, but, as mentioned, a statutory term creates a legal criterion and need not precisely track terms from other disciplines. But if the statutory definition does not make rational sense, it should not pass constitutional muster.

The definition states that a person is abnormal if any biological or environmental variable caused the person's emotional or volitional capacity to predispose the agent to engage in criminal sexual misconduct. But what else would predispose anyone to any conduct, sexual or otherwise, if not biological and environmental variables that affect their emotional and volitional capacities? In other words, the definition is simply a description of the causation of *any* behavior. The content of abnormality in the definition is entirely dependent on the requirement of "sexually violent offenses." Nothing else in the definition differentiates the sexual predator from *any* other person. *All* behavior, normal and abnormal alike, is the product of congenital or acquired conditions affecting emotional or volitional predispositions. But if anyone who has a tendency to engage in sexual violence is abnormal, then the term *mental abnormality* is circularly defined and does no independent conceptual or causal work. Moreover, such a definition collapses all badness into madness. Finally, it is strange, if not incoherent, to define an abnormality by reference to the penal code. If the penal code becomes more forgiving, do the people who now satisfy the definition become automatically "mentally normal"?

Assuming, probably erroneously, that the law could cabin the seemingly unconstrained reach of the vague term *mental abnormality*, why any particular abnormality should be excused remains unexplained. Simply because a mental abnormality may be causally related to other behavior does not mean that the behavior should be excused. This is to confuse causation and excuse. Causation, even by an "abnormal" variable, is not an excusing condition. To believe otherwise is to commit what I have termed "the fundamental psycholegal error" (Morse, 1994). Even if the potential predator suffers from some causal abnormality, it does not necessarily follow that the potential predator is not responsible. The causal abnormality must produce a genuine, independent excusing condition, such as irrationality, for a moral or legal excuse to obtain.

What actual theory to hold potential predators nonresponsible might be implicit, however? We have seen that irrationality is not a good candidate. We are thus left with some type of control theory of excuse. Indeed, this was precisely the theory of nonresponsibility that the Supreme Court accepted as sufficient to justify the *civil* commitment of mentally abnormal sexually violent predators generally. Commenting on criteria for civil commitment that depend on a control theory, the Court wrote:

> These added statutory requirements serve to limit involuntary civil confinement to those who suffer from a volitional impairment rendering them dangerous beyond their control. The Kansas Act is plainly of a kind with these other civil commitment statutes: It requires a finding of future dangerousness, and then links that finding to the existence of a "mental abnormality" or "personality disorder" that makes it difficult, if not impossible, for the person to control his dangerous behavior. . . . The precommitment requirement of a "mental abnormality" or "personality disorder" is consistent with the requirement of these other statutes that we have upheld in that it narrows the class of persons eligible for confinement *to those who are unable to control their conduct* [italics added]. (*Kansas v. Hendricks*, 1997, p. 358)

All the Justices subscribed to this part of the Court's opinion, which implicitly assumes that Kansas (and others) understand and can reliably and validly assess when an agent is "unable to control" *intentional action*.

Kansas v. Crane (2002) addressed whether a total lack of control was a necessary constitutional predicate for commitment of mentally abnormal sexual predators. The majority argued that a total lack of control was an unworkable standard but held that the state had to prove that the alleged predator had "serious difficulty" controlling himself to justify commitment. The required control defect allegedly differentiated abnormal predators from ordinary recidivists and thus rendered the commitment scheme genuinely civil. Thus, the Court reemphasized that commitment for dangerousness alone is unjustified, but it provided almost no guidance to the states about how a serious lack of control was to be defined. Because the Court had already accepted the incoherent Kansas definition of "mental abnormality" and because the Court is willing to grant the states great leeway to define the criteria for these commitments, the control requirement places essentially no limit on a state's ability by creative legislation or judicial decision to civilly confine a sexual recidivist offender. The control standard the Court adopted cannot successfully maintain the civil–criminal distinction.

Moreover, what good reason is there to believe that volitional problems are well understood and that "mentally abnormal" sexual predators specially lack the ability to control their sexual conduct? So-called volitional or control problems are generally and notoriously difficult conceptually to define and practically to apply. Just such difficulties led both the American Psychiatric Association and the American Bar Association to recommend the abolition of a control test for legal insanity in the early 1980s (American Bar Association, 1984; American Psychiatric Association Insanity Defense Work Group, 1983). Moreover, what is there about sexual desires that makes them more "compelling" than other equally strong desires, such as intense greed that may result in property crime?

Sexual urges, including "abnormal" sexual urges, and strong urges of other types are not irresistible forces that render human beings automatons. Consider the following analogy, which is often used to buttress the argument for volitional excuses, that powerful or abnormal impulses operate like mechanical reflexes and are therefore "uncontrollable." Imagine that a person is hanging by the fingernails from the edge of a cliff and cannot pull himself or herself back up. Depending on strength, the agent can hang on for some time, but ultimately the agent will fall. Impulses are allegedly like the pull of gravity in the example. To see why the analogy fails, however, imagine that another agent stands at the edge of a cliff with a gun and tells the hapless cliffhanger that if the cliffhanger starts to let go, the gunslinger will shoot and kill the cliffhanger. Despite this dreadful threat, sooner or later, all cliffhangers, no matter how strong they may be, will fall as a joint effect of gravity and muscle physiology. But now imagine that a similar gunslinger remains always at Hendrick's elbow and tells him that if he starts to molest a child, he will be killed instantly. Hendricks will not molest. The cliffhanger's fall is a genuine mechanism and not human action; it is ultimately unmodifiable by reason. In contrast, sexual molestation is human action and modifiable by reason. If it is not so modifiable, the agent is irrational but still not an "uncontrollable" mechanism. Most arguments that facilely suggest that sexual impulses or desires, or any other kind, are necessarily uncontrollable are conceptually and empirically unsupported (Morse, 1994, 2002). This conclusion cannot be altered just because the impulse is allegedly a symptom without begging the question.

In *Hendricks*, the Supreme Court deferred to the Kansas legislature's definition. In *Crane*, the Court signaled that it would give great deference to state criteria for "serious" control problems. But the conceptual and empirical basis is exceedingly scant for the "enormous deprivation of liberty" that civil sexual predator commitments permit. Of course, we might claim that people like Hendricks are not responsible because they suffer from a mental abnormality; they are also "victims" of their abnormality and their dreadful crimes are symptoms that do excuse. But, I contend, we do not really believe this, and it is easy to understand public fear and the plight of potential victims. Sometimes, however, there is no adequate remedy. This appears to be such a case because virtually all sexually violent predators are responsible agents. Although such offenders do not arouse much sympathy, when they complete their prison terms, no further punishment is deserved, and they should not be civilly committed unless their condition has deteriorated and they are currently not responsible. Some dangerous people may be released, but this is one of the costs of liberty. The only justifiable response to the danger they threaten is to lengthen the term of imprisonment for sexual offenses, consistent with proportionality.

Hendricks and *Crane* present a danger beyond their threat to the civil liberty of sexually violent predators. All people convicted of crime are potentially civilly committable according to the cases' logic. State legislatures are free within the widest limits to define mental abnormality as they wish and to find that mentally abnormal people so defined are unable to control specific conduct. The problem is that the definition of mental abnormality the Court found acceptable, even when coupled with a requirement of serious lack of control, cannot be logically limited to sexually violent predators. As I demonstrated above, the definition is so broad that it in fact can be applied to any behavior. The abnormality and its consequent control defect could be *any* antisocial or deviant conduct "in a degree constituting a menace to the health or safety of others." Interpreted narrowly, any crime against the person would constitute a menace to health or safety; interpreted broadly, any crime at all could constitute such a menace. In *Jones v. United States* (1983), for example, the Supreme Court was untroubled by the specter that relatively minor property crime was used as the predicate for the dangerousness component of commitment after an insanity acquittal.

Nothing, therefore, would seem constitutionally to bar a state from defining a class of "mentally abnormal violent predators," or more broadly, "mentally abnormal dangerous predators," and from providing for involuntary commitment of the class at the end of a prison term. The expanded definition of "mental abnormality" would be this: "a congenital or acquired condition affecting the emotional or volitional capacity which predisposes the person to commit violent [dangerous] offenses in a degree constituting such person a menace to the health or safety of others."

As long as this so-called condition "makes the person likely to engage in violent [dangerous] acts," the new criterion is a perfect analog to the Kansas sexually violent predator provisions found acceptable in *Hendricks*. And if a court found or if the legislative history or act preamble contained language indicating that the state found that such mentally abnormal violent [dangerous] people could not control themselves and presented a special threat to public safety, the analog to the constitutional requirement in *Crane* would be complete. Moreover, if the state found that these "violent predators" were, alas, untreatable, the failure of the state to provide anything more than pure incapacitation would not compromise the allegedly nonpunitive character of the commitment. Finally, as *Youngberg v. Romeo* (1982) makes clear, even if one purpose of the commitment is treatment and "violent predatory predisposition" is treatable, the state need not provide more than "professional judgment" deems minimally necessary. In sum, the pure behavioral quarantine of potentially violent predators would be justified, and little effective treatment would be provided, even if it were available.

No state would have difficulty finding mental health professionals who would opine that a particular violent or dangerous offender suffered from an abnormality that increased the likelihood of future harm-doing and that such people cannot control themselves. Moreover, a large number of present offenders already exhibit or could be diagnosed easily as manifesting the established "antisocial personality disorder" (see Lykken, 1995). When culpability "runs out"—when a responsible offender's proportionate, deserved prison term ends—virtually any convicted offender could satisfy the expanded, surely constitutional criteria for the indefinite, civil confinement of potential violent [dangerous] predators.

After *Hendricks* and *Crane*, if my interpretation of the implications is correct (cf. Krongard, 2002, concerning substance abusers), society need never worry again about the conflict between culpability and danger. Some justifiable form of incapacitation will always be available. Every person in prison would be at risk. This would be a fine result if the newly contiguous boundary between the two systems could be conceptually and empirically justified. Who can object to increased public safety in the abstract? But the purported meshing of the civil and criminal confinement systems cannot be justified. Either most sexual predators are responsible and deserve punishment or most are not responsible and should not be punished. Pure preventive detention, justified as ordinary civil commitment and by spurious nonresponsibility, is now a constitutional possibility. And unlike culpability, which sets some limit on the ambit of deserved punishment, "nonresponsible dangerousness" sets no limit.

CONCLUSION

The danger to civil liberty of an expanded medical model of deviance and its associated disease rationale for preventive confinement is apparent. The medical model and disease rationale have more potential for expansive preventive detention than the moral model and desert rationale. Although there are inevitable and difficult trade-offs in a free society between liberty and safety, a robust moral model robustly applied to sex offenders provides the greatest potential to achieve both justice and safety. Virtually all sex offenders are responsible for their sexually aberrant misconduct, even if it is the sign of a disease, and thus they deserve blame and punishment. Proportionate but lengthy prison terms will prevent much recidivism, although people who pose a clear danger will continue to be released. This will on occasion lead to tragic outcomes, but such tragedies can be entirely prevented only by exceptionally harsh and probably disproportionate sentences or by an expanded scheme of civil commitment. The former will be unjust and expensive. The latter will threaten the liberty of all and will be both unjust and expensive.

REFERENCES

American Bar Association. (1984). *ABA criminal justice mental health standards.* Washington, DC: Author.

American Psychiatric Association. (2000). *Diagnostic and statistical manual of mental disorders* (4th ed., Text Revision). Washington, DC: Author.

American Psychiatric Association Insanity Defense Work Group. (1983). Statement on the insanity defense. *American Journal of Psychiatry, 140,* 681–688.

Brown v. Mayle, 283 F.3d 1019 (9th Cir. [Cal.]) 2002.

Corrado, M. (1996). Punishment, quarantine, and preventive detention. *Criminal Justice Ethics, 15*(2), 3–13.

Fingarette, H., & Fingarette Hasse, A. (1979). *Mental disabilities and criminal responsibility.* Berkeley: University of California Press.

Foucha v. Louisiana, 504 U.S. 71 (1992).

Garland, D. (2001). *The culture of control: Crime and social order in contemporary society.* Oxford, England: Oxford University Press.

Harmelin v. Michigan, 501 U.S. 957 (1991).

Jackson v. Indiana, 406 U.S. 715 (1972).

Jones v. United States, 463 U.S. 354 (1983).

Kan. Stat. Ann. § 59-29a02(a) (1994).

Kansas v. Crane, 534 U.S. 407 (2002).

Kansas v. Hendricks, 521 U.S. 346 (1997).

Krongard, M. L. (2002). A population at risk: Civil commitment of substance abusers after *Kansas v. Hendricks. California Law Review, 90,* 111–163.

La Fond, J. Q. (1992). Washington's sexually violent predators statute: Law or lottery? A response to Professor Brooks. *University of Puget Sound Law Review, 15,* 755–779.

Lykken, D. T. (1995). *The antisocial personalities.* Hillsdale, NJ: Erlbaum.

McKune v. Lile, 122 S. Ct. 2017 (2002).

Moore, M. S. (1985). Causation and the excuses. *California Law Review, 73,* 201–259.

Morse, S. J. (1994). Culpability and control. *University of Pennsylvania Law Review, 142,* 1587–1660.

Morse, S. J. (1998a). Excusing and the new excuse defenses: A legal and conceptual review. In M. Tonry (Ed.), *Crime and justice: A review of research* (Vol. 23, pp. 329–406). Chicago: University of Chicago Press.

Morse, S. J. (1998b). Fear of danger, flight from culpability. *Psychology, Public Policy, and Law, 4,* 250–267.

Morse, S. J. (1999). Neither desert nor disease. *Legal Theory, 5,* 265–309.

Morse, S. J. (2000). Hooked on hype: Addiction and responsibility. *Law and Philosophy, 19,* 3–49.

Morse, S. J. (2002). Uncontrollable urges and irrational people. *Virginia Law Review, 88,* 1025–1078.

Nozick, R. (1993). *The nature of rationality.* Princeton, NJ: Princeton University Press.

Powell v. Texas, 392 U.S. 514 (1968).

Robinson, P. H. (1996). The criminal–civil distinction and the utility of desert. *Boston University Law Review, 76,* 201–214.

Robinson, P. H. (2001). Punishing dangerousness: Cloaking preventive detention as criminal justice. *Harvard Law Review, 114,* 1429–1456.

Schulhofer, S. (1996). Two systems of social protection: Comments of the civil–

criminal distinction, with particular reference to sexually violent predator laws. *Journal of Contemporary Legal Issues, 7,* 69–96.

Seling v. Young, 531 U.S. 250 (2001).

Youngberg v. Romeo, 457 U.S. 307 (1982).

Zimring, F. E., Hawkins, G., & Kamin, S. (2001). *Punishment and democracy: Three strikes and you're out in California.* New York: Oxford University Press.

10

"EVEN A DOG ...": CULPABILITY, CONDEMNATION, AND RESPECT FOR PERSONS

ROBERT F. SCHOPP

Consider three incidents in which individuals respond in similar yet distinctly different ways to perpetrators who have harmed third parties.[1]

Jones is the mother of a child who is abducted on her way home from school, sexually assaulted, and killed. The police arrest a suspect who is convicted of kidnapping, sexual assault, and murder. As the convicted perpetrator is led from the courtroom pending a sentencing hearing, Jones takes a gun from her purse and fires several shots, killing him.

The *Smiths* are the parents of a child who is abducted on her way home from school, sexually assaulted, and killed. The police arrest a suspect who is convicted of kidnapping, sexual assault, and murder. The Smiths confer with the prosecuting attorney's office throughout the trial, and they steadfastly support the prosecutor in seeking the death penalty. They attend

I am grateful to Ed O'Dowd and Marc Pearce for prior discussion of this chapter and to John La Fond and Bruce Winick for helpful editorial comments.

[1]All three incidents are based on reported events, but I have modified all three for expository and comparative purposes. I do not document the original events to make clear that these accounts are modified and to avoid calling unnecessary attention to the participants.

each day of the guilt and sentencing phases of the trial. When the jury returns a sentence of death, the Smiths wait outside the courtroom and thank the jurors as they leave, telling the jurors that they made the right decision. The Smiths explain to the jurors that nothing will end the pain or bring closure but the death sentence is a very important resolution—it helps.

Brown is a forest ranger whose responsibilities include monitoring and managing the interaction between people and bears in some of the campgrounds bordering a wilderness area. One problem bear has become more aggressive in seeking food in campgrounds and approaching humans. The rangers drug and relocate the bear to a remote area, but the bear returns to the area around the campgrounds and kills a child it encounters on the trail. Brown tracks and shoots the bear because the bear has become a serious danger to humans and the less drastic alternative of relocation has failed. Brown and others involved regret having to kill the bear and do so with a sense of failure and sadness.

These three incidents reveal certain common factors. In each case, a perpetrator kills an innocent human being. In each case, one or more other individuals respond to that harmful behavior in a manner that inflicts or encourages and endorses the infliction of severe harm on the perpetrator. Despite these common properties, however, important factors differentiate the three cases. Although the responders all engage in conduct intended to cause the death of the original perpetrators, they use different methods, and they act with markedly different attitudes and emotional correlates. Furthermore, many readers might react to the original perpetrators and to the responders with judgments and emotional responses that differ markedly across the cases.

Although individual readers might react in a variety of ways to the original perpetrators and to the responders, we also react collectively through legal institutions, including institutions of coercive behavior control that we establish and apply as a society. These institutions represent important components in our conventional public morality (CPM). A society's CPM consists of the widely accepted principles of political morality that provide the foundation for the legal institutions that order the public jurisdiction. These principles are moral in that they represent societal values that generate legal rules specifying the manner in which we should or should not behave. Although some of these rules serve merely to promote efficiency or convenience, the core rules of the criminal law, such as those prohibiting murder, assault, and theft, forbid certain categories of behavior because they are wrong. The CPM is conventional in that it consists of those principles that are widely endorsed in a particular society. These principles may or may not converge with those that are most defensible by normative argument. Finally, societies may differ regarding the aspects of human life they subject to legal regulation and those they reserve for the nonpublic domain. The CPM is public in that it addresses only the range of moral life that the society subjects to public regulation through law (Schopp, 1998).

Legal institutions representing the CPM are designed to serve practical functions such as prevention of crime through deterrence or incapacitation. They also serve important symbolic functions in that we express, reinforce, and shape central principles of the CPM through the manner in which we design and apply legal institutions. Legal institutions of coercive behavior control instantiate fundamental principles of the CPM. This chapter examines some of the expressive functions served by these institutions, and it applies that analysis to the contemporary generation of sexual predator statutes. This analysis reveals that these statutes distort the CPM and the expressive significance of important legal institutions.

The next section provides an initial interpretation of the three incidents described above, and it sketches preliminary criteria for a satisfactory analysis of these events. I then discuss the expressive functions of criminal punishment as one legal institution of coercive social control and apply this analysis to the three incidents. Finally, I address the significance of this analysis for the contemporary sexual predator statutes and the CPM.

INITIAL INTERPRETATION

Oliver Wendell Holmes asserted that "even a dog distinguishes between being stumbled over and being kicked" as part of his interpretation of the early common law forms of liability as directed primarily toward vengeance rather than compensation (Holmes, 1881/1995, p. 116). He interpreted these forms of legal liability as institutional methods for seeking vengeance for a wrong by a blameworthy wrongdoer. He argued that these early forms of liability were limited to intentional wrongs because only intentional wrongs were seen as deserving blame and vengeful responses. Many readers may find that Holmes's famous quote and his broader interpretation resonate with their intuitive responses to certain aspects of the three incidents discussed earlier. Our interpretations of the psychological states and processes of the perpetrators and of the responders in these incidents influence our practical and emotional responses to these individuals as well as our attributions of responsibility and blame. These interpretations influence our individual judgments and responses, as well as the manner in which we design and apply legal institutions.

Consider, for example, some likely responses to these incidents. Although we realize that we cannot condone actions by individuals who take justice as they understand it into their own hands, many readers might experience sympathy for Jones. Many can imagine wanting to do what she did, and many may think the perpetrator deserved it. Although we may agree that a society cannot allow such individual action, we may feel empathy with and sympathy for Jones rather than outrage or resentment toward her. We might make the judgment that we must repudiate her action without feeling the resentment that ordinarily accompanies repudiation of wrongs. We might agree that some punishment is necessary to maintain effective institutions of justice, but we may do so with sorrow or regret rather than anger.

Many readers understand the Smiths' anger and their desire for severe punishment, and many might share that experience of anger and resentment, particularly if they learn the details of the crime or learn more about the victim or the Smiths. That is, we may respond with increased anger and resentment toward the perpetrator as we come to know the Smiths as persons. Some readers might approve their decision to pursue capital punishment. Others might disapprove of that decision but empathize with their desire for severe punishment. The latter group may consist primarily of those who object categorically to capital punishment and who would not have misgivings if the penalty were life in prison without the possibility of parole. Thus, ambivalence experienced by some readers may reflect more general concern regarding capital punishment. In contrast to the Jones case, it seems unlikely that many readers will repudiate the Smiths' decision to participate in the institutional process to seek severe punishment. Finally, even those who do not endorse their seeking capital punishment are unlikely to resent or condemn them for doing so.

Some readers might endorse relocation of the bear in the third incident. If there is no alternative that will prevent further attacks, we might find broad agreement that the ranger must kill the bear, but many readers will share the ranger's sadness and regret regarding this decision. Insofar as we do, these emotional responses reflect the judgment that in some important sense this incident resulted from our collective failure. Anger at the bear would be understandable but misguided. Resentment and condemnation of the bear would be fundamentally misdirected and confused because these responses would reflect deep misunderstanding of important differences between culpable human criminals and the bear.

Compare common attitudes toward the bear with corresponding attitudes toward the initial perpetrators in the Jones and Smith incidents. Set aside attitudes regarding capital punishment because these seem to be primarily about capital punishment rather than about these perpetrators. Had both perpetrators been convicted and sentenced to life sentences in jurisdictions that did not practice capital punishment, expressions of anger, resentment, and condemnation toward these offenders would probably be widespread and noncontroversial.

Relocation of the bear to remote wilderness might receive wide acceptance if it seemed likely to prevent further attacks on humans. That is, our primary concern about the proper disposition for the bear is instrumental. Common attitudes toward the bear would include fear, concern, sadness, regret, and perhaps a sense of responsibility and failure, particularly among those who accept responsibility for managing our interaction with the remaining fragments of the wild.

Suppose that one were to propose a similar attitude and practical approach toward the perpetrators in the Jones and Smith cases. Rather than convicting and punishing them, should we diagnose them as disordered (pedophilia), find them not guilty by reason of insanity, and commit them to a true mental health facility (i.e., a facility that is run for the care of those committed rather than as a separate unit within the correctional system)? Assume that neither manifested any impairment beyond the pattern of sexual fantasy, arousal, and conduct supporting the diagnoses of pedophilia and antisocial personality disorder (American Psychiatric Association, 2000; *Kansas v. Hendricks*, 1997, pp. 2078–2079; *In re Young*, 1993, pp. 994–996). If security were comparable with that in correctional settings, and thus risk to the public was no greater than with imprisonment, would this disposition with an attitude of sadness, regret, and concern for the perpetrators be appropriate? Would this approach seem inadequate because it fails to express our anger, resentment, and condemnation? Would or should the Smiths accept this alternative?

A satisfactory analysis of these incidents and of common individual and collective responses to them must distinguish several levels of response. First, society needs a practical disposition reasonably expected to prevent recidivism by these perpetrators and to discourage others from committing similar crimes. Furthermore, this disposition must accurately represent the CPM, expressing condemnation of such conduct as wrongful and of perpetrators who culpably commit such offenses. The second and third levels of response serve these expressive functions. The second level expresses judgments of repudiation directed toward the criminal conduct and of culpability directed toward the guilty offender. The third level expresses the emotional responses of anger and resentment directed toward the culpable perpetrator of wrongful harm. Those who would endorse executing the Smith perpetrator and shooting the bear would probably recognize an important difference between capital punishment and extermination. That difference involves contrasting judgments regarding culpability and corresponding differences in the expression of blame, anger, and resentment. These contrasting judgments and expressions reflect the moral significance of the distinction between the mere harm caused by the bear and the wrong inflicted by the human perpetrators.

This expression of anger, resentment, and blame toward the culpable human perpetrators reflects the standing of responsible adults in the CPM. Our judgments and emotional responses directed toward these perpetrators and toward the responders reflect our understanding of the differences between a bear and a responsible human and between a mere injury and a wrong. Our individual judgments and emotional responses, as well as our legal institutions, reflect these differences. Like Holmes's dog, we distinguish between being stumbled over and being kicked. At our best, we might design legal institutions that reflect this distinction in a subtle and defensible form.

THE EXPRESSIVE FUNCTION OF LEGAL INSTITUTIONS OF SOCIAL CONTROL

If we were only instrumentally concerned with preventing recidivism by these perpetrators, we would be indifferent as to whether they were subject to criminal conviction and incarceration on the one hand or similarly secure postacquittal commitment on the other. If our judgments and emotional responses reflected only the harm done and fear of additional injury, they would be comparable across all three cases. Neither our practical interventions nor our judgments and emotional responses conform to these simple patterns, however, because they reflect a more complex set of considerations and serve a more complex set of functions.

In addition to providing a method of coercive social control, criminal conviction and punishment express condemnation, including judgments of disapproval and reprobation and attitudes of resentment and indignation. These moral judgments and accompanying emotional responses repudiate the defendant's conduct not merely as injurious but also as wrong. They also express vindictive resentment of the defendant as culpable and blameworthy for that wrongful conduct (Feinberg, 1970; Schopp, 1998). To wrong another is not merely to injure that person but also to treat him or her unjustly or unfairly. Thus, insofar as criminal conduct involves wronging another, it involves injurious conduct that constitutes an unjust or unfair violation against that person (wrong; New Shorter Oxford English Dictionary, 1993, pp. 3732–3733). By punishing criminal conduct, we express disapproval of that unjust violation of another as well as anger and resentment toward the perpetrator as responsible for that conduct. Thus, criminal punishment expresses anger, resentment, and indignation toward the perpetrator as one who has wronged and demeaned the victim through conduct for which the perpetrator is culpable and blameworthy (indignation; resentment; New Shorter Oxford English Dictionary, 1993, pp. 1350, 2559).

In addition to serving as an instrumental regulatory device, criminal conviction and punishment express this complex set of social judgments and attitudes central to the function of the criminal law as an institutional representation of the CPM. The criminal law adopts offense definitions that prohibit certain categories of conduct as wrongful violations of the

CPM rather than merely as counterproductive, inefficient, or inconvenient. By prescribing punishment rather than only compensation, education, or treatment, the criminal law repudiates such conduct as wrongful. By punishing particular individuals for particular criminal offenses, the criminal justice system holds them culpable and blameworthy for engaging in wrongful conduct as responsible participants in the CPM. That is, the criminal justice system establishes and applies criteria of personal responsibility in the CPM, differentiating the culpable perpetrators in the Smith and Jones incidents from the bear.

By establishing and applying standards of criminal responsibility, the criminal justice system fulfills a critical function for the CPM of a society that represents the Western liberal tradition of political morality. Societies in this tradition establish political institutions that provide a fair system of social cooperation among citizens who may endorse a variety of comprehensive moral theories. These institutions establish distinct public and nonpublic domains of jurisdiction, and they respect individual self-determination within each of these domains. They do so in the public domain by establishing a relationship between the individual and the government in which the government accords equal respect to all competent adults by recognizing their equal standing in the democratic political process and in the legal institutions that establish and apply the law that regulates this domain. These political and legal institutions respect individual self-determination in the nonpublic domain by identifying and protecting a sphere of sovereignty within which each individual can direct his or her own life through the exercise of discretion. By protecting equal standing and self-determination, these institutions provide competent adults with the opportunities to define the central values and projects that give meaning to their lives and to develop self-respect as members of a community of equal, sovereign citizens (Schopp, 1998).

The criminal justice system protects individual self-determination and equal standing by proscribing and punishing conduct that violates the rights and interests of others. Thus, the criminal law not only represents the conventional public morality that orders cooperative social interaction in the public domain but also articulates certain contours of each individual's protected domain of individual discretion by proscribing specified types of intrusions as crimes. When a liberal state enforces the core rules of the criminal law, it articulates the substantive standards of the CPM and the criteria of criminal responsibility that partially define the capacities required for full standing in the public jurisdiction. By exercising coercive social control through the criminal justice system, the state vindicates the standing of the victims by recognizing that the crime wrongs them, and it vindicates the standing of the perpetrators by recognizing that they possess the capacities of responsible participants in the public jurisdiction.

Liberal states respect the standing of competent adults as capable of directing their lives through reasoned choice, and those states establish rule-based criminal justice systems as the form of coercive behavior control that is uniquely appropriate to such beings. Criminal punishment is limited to those who qualify for this status by possessing the capacities needed to comprehend moral and legal reasons and to direct their conduct through a process of practical reasoning. Rule-based criminal justice systems with appropriate criteria of culpability provide the only legitimate form of coercive state behavior control for these persons (Schopp, 1998). The systemic criteria of culpability embodied in the voluntary act requirement, the culpability elements, and excuses such as the insanity defense define the standards of responsibility under the criminal law (American Law Institute, 1985). In doing so, they partially define the criteria of equal standing in the public jurisdiction.

In contrast to justification defenses that exempt certain instances of prohibited conduct from the condemnation ordinarily directed toward conduct of that type, excuses retain the systemic condemnation of the conduct as wrongful but exempt the individual from responsibility and blame for that conduct (Schopp, 1998). Thus, excuses do not express approval or acceptance of the injury to the victim, but they withhold punishment and condemnation of the defendant who lacks the capacities needed to participate in the public jurisdiction as a fully responsible agent. In doing so, the criminal justice system reaffirms respect for persons as responsible participants in the public jurisdiction, and it reflects the differences in capacities, guilt, and desert that justify differential treatment of and attitudes toward the perpetrators in the Jones and Smith cases as compared with the bear.

THE THREE CASES: PRACTICAL AND EXPRESSIVE FUNCTIONS

From a practical perspective, we require protection in the form of isolation or incapacitation of all three perpetrators in the cases discussed in the introduction. Insofar as we are concerned only with this function, either confinement or execution suffices. The dispute regarding the choice between execution and life imprisonment for the perpetrator in the Smith case emphasizes important questions about the substantive content of the CPM rather than practical considerations of effective protection from this perpetrator. That is, we can effectively prevent recidivism in most cases through either execution or extended imprisonment, but choosing between these alternatives requires that we address important questions regarding the principles of political morality underlying the criminal justice system.

The decision to relocate or kill the bear, in contrast, depends heavily on practical considerations regarding the likely effectiveness of relocation.

Because the bear is not a responsible agent, we address that problem primarily from a practical perspective. Although some of the humans involved may experience a sense of responsibility, regret, or failure, expressions of condemnation directed toward the bear would reflect a fundamental misunderstanding of the moral status of the bear and of the significance of the criteria of criminal responsibility for standing as a responsible agent in the public jurisdiction ordered by the CPM. The proper response to the third incident depends primarily on practical considerations rather than expressive functions, because we address concerns of harm and risk reduction relatively uncomplicated by wrongs, the substantive standards of the CPM, or the moral standing of the participants.

The Smith and Jones incidents present much more complex questions precisely because they raise concerns regarding the substantive standards of the CPM, the moral standing of the participants, and the expressive functions of the criminal law. The dispute between those who would endorse capital punishment for the perpetrator in the Smith incident and those who would endorse life imprisonment involves fundamental questions regarding the principles of political morality that the CPM should embody and express. Setting aside these substantive issues regarding capital punishment, the Smiths experience the anger and resentment elicited by the perpetrator as one who culpably inflicts wrongful injury. Furthermore, they express that anger and resentment through the institutional structure appropriate to the coercive behavior control of responsible agents.

Jones expresses anger and resentment similar to that expressed by the Smiths, but she does so in a manner that violates the institutional structure that orders the public jurisdiction. Many readers might empathize with Jones. Many might understand why she would want to do what she did and feel hesitant to condemn her. Many would also agree, however, that society cannot allow individuals to take such matters into their own hands. We might attempt to excuse her or to mitigate her responsibility by claiming that she "snapped" or "lost control," but we are unable to provide any clear account of these notions. They seem to represent intuitive attempts to express repudiation of such behavior without expressing condemnation of Jones as one who merits blame or resentment for conduct that is wrong. The intuitive inclination to exempt Jones from punishment exposes the ragged border between justification and excuse insofar as it becomes very difficult to distinguish the claim that she was not responsible for her conduct from the claim that she did no wrong. Perhaps this difficulty reveals the judgment that although she violated the rules of a just social institution, she did not wrong the perpetrator (see Schopp, 1998, chapter 5). That is, her wrong may involve her violation of a just institution that regulates interaction among responsible participants in the public jurisdiction rather than an unjust injury to the perpetrator.

SEXUAL PREDATOR STATUTES

The Washington Sexually Violent Predators Act (Wash. Rev. Code Ann. § 71.09 Supp., 1998) provides the prototype for several recently enacted sex offender commitment statutes (see this volume, chapter 1), including the Kansas Sexually Violent Predators Act (Kan. Stat. Ann. § 59-29 Supp., 1997) at issue in *Kansas v. Hendricks* (1997) and *Kansas v. Crane* (2002). Commitments of convicted sex offenders at the end of their prison terms provide the most controversial applications of the sexual predator statutes. These commitments frequently involve individuals who lack the severe impairment usually associated with civil commitment but who are considered likely to commit additional sexual offenses following their criminal sentences. The subjects of the petitions for commitment in recent cases had completed, or were completing, sentences for repetitive violent sexual offenses. None of these offenders carried diagnoses that indicated serious impairment of orientation, consciousness, perception, comprehension, reasoning, or reality testing. They carried diagnoses, including antisocial personality disorder and the paraphilias, that can be based heavily on the demonstrated propensity to commit such offenses. The appellate opinions indicate that the testimony regarding the diagnoses as well as regarding the findings of mental abnormality or personality disorder and of likelihood of reoffending emphasized the pattern of criminal conduct that generated the conviction and sentences (*In re Hendricks*, 1996, pp. 137–138; *In re Young*, 1993, pp. 994–996). This pattern continues beoynd the early cases. Recent commitments reveal diagnoses that emphasize substance abuse, paraphilia, and personality disorders (Janus & Walbek, 2000).

These statutes raise difficult questions regarding the justification for ostensibly civil commitment of an individual who previously has been criminally convicted and punished as fully responsible. The *Hendricks* Court emphasizes the inability to control sexual conduct as the justification for addressing these offenders through civil commitment rather than exclusively through the criminal justice system (*Kansas v. Hendricks*, 1997, p. 2081), a justification recently reiterated by the Court in *Kansas v. Crane* (2002). The *Hendricks* Court provides no account of the purported inability to control, however, and it provides no reason to believe Hendricks's unsubstantiated assertion that he was unable to control his extended pattern of planned, organized, and goal-directed conduct. Perhaps most important, the Court provides no explanation reconciling Hendricks's putative inability to control his criminal conduct with the criminal conviction that held him fully responsible for it (see this volume, chapter 9).

The fundamental problem with the sexual predator statutes does not involve a claim of excessively harsh treatment. Many of these offenders would be subject to extended sentences under repeat offender statutes (*In re Hendricks*, 1996, pp. 136–137). The most important defect in the sexual predator statutes involves the manner in which they distort the CPM that orders the public jurisdiction. Legal institutions representing the CPM in a liberal society promote cooperative interaction among citizens capable of participating as equals in the public jurisdiction, and they protect discretionary control by each competent adult in the nonpublic jurisdiction. Minimally adequate psychological capacities, including consciousness, orientation, comprehension, reasoning, and reality testing, enable the individual to function as a competent and responsible participant in the public jurisdiction.

The criminal justice system provides an institution of coercive social control uniquely appropriate to responsible adults in the public jurisdiction of a liberal society because it allows them to direct their lives through the exercise of uniquely human capacities that enable them to pursue their own values, projects, relationships, and interests without subjecting themselves to coercive intervention by the state. Their intact psychological capacities enable them to comprehend the requirements of the criminal law as well as the moral and prudential reasons for complying with those requirements. These capacities enable them to anticipate the aversive consequences of violating the law and to direct their conduct in light of these reasons for action without actually experiencing those consequences. They may commit crimes of passion, self-interest, or conscience despite this understanding, but they do so with understanding of the risks they incur and of the reasons for acting or for refraining from such action. Thus, they partially define their lives through the reasons for acting that they treat as persuasive, and they do so as accountable subjects of the criminal justice system.

Criminal punishment appropriately expresses condemnation of criminal behavior and of culpable criminals precisely because these responsible adults possess the capacities needed to participate competently in the public jurisdiction ordered by the criminal justice system. These capacities of practical reasoning enable them to define and pursue the lives they have chosen in the nonpublic domain and to function as responsible participants in the political and legal institutions that order the public domain. By providing an institution of social control uniquely suited to persons with these capacities, the criminal law maximizes the opportunity for such persons to define and direct their lives in such a manner as to develop and pursue those aspects of their lives in which they vest value and to conduct themselves in the public jurisdiction in a manner designed to remain free from coercive intrusion by the state.

The mental health system provides alternative institutions of social control, such as police power civil commitment, for those who lack the capacities that enable persons to competently define and pursue their own lives, to function as responsible participants in the public jurisdiction, and to qualify as appropriate subjects of condemnation when they commit culpable wrongs (see this volume, chapter 9). By applying these complementary institutions of social control according to the capacities of the individual, the state expresses respect for persons who possess the capacities to comprehend reasons for action and to direct their conduct through the exercise of reasoning (Schopp, 2001; chapter 7).

The sexual predator statutes undermine these institutions and the respect for persons represented by these institutions by convicting these offenders in the institution applicable to those who possess the capacities needed to direct their conduct through competent practical reasoning and then committing them on the premise that they lack these capacities. Some readers might reasonably ask whether we should be concerned about expressing disrespect for these repeat violent offenders by confining them under an inappropriate statute. The fundamental defect of these statutes is not, however, that they express disrespect for these offenders. These provisions undermine respect for persons by violating the status of persons as those who are subject to coercive control in the public jurisdiction only through the criminal justice system because they possess the capacities that allow them to participate in the public jurisdiction as competent practical reasoners. By undermining the significance of this status in the liberal society, they subvert the CPM that protects equal standing in the public jurisdiction and discretionary control in the nonpublic jurisdiction for those who possess the capacities to direct their own lives for reasons and through reasoning.

CONCLUSION

The fundamental flaw in the sexual predator statutes involves the manner in which they distort the parameters of state authority to intrude into the lives of persons who possess the capacities needed to function as practical reasoners in the public jurisdiction. By doing so, these statutes undermine the status of persons as those who possess these capacities, and they dilute the respect for such persons expressed by the CPM. These statutes authorize confinement of a small number of offenders, but in doing so, they subvert the principles that support the standing of persons as accountable participants in the public jurisdiction, justify the punishment of these offenders, and render coherent the different judgments and emotional responses elicited by the three incidents described at the beginning of this chapter. Thus, by undermining the distinction between criminal justice and mental health institutions of social control, they blur the lesson taught by Holmes's insightful dog.

REFERENCES

American Law Institute. (1985). *Model penal code and commentaries*. Philadelphia: Author.

American Psychiatric Association. (2000). *Diagnostic and statistical manual of mental disorders* (4th ed., Text Revision). Washington, DC: Author.

Feinberg, J. (1970). *Doing and deserving*. Princeton, NJ: Princeton University Press.

In re Hendricks, 912 P.2d 129 (Kan. 1996).

Holmes, O. W., Jr. (1995). The common law. In S. M. Novick (Ed.), *Collected works of Justice Holmes: Complete public writings of Oliver Wendell Holmes* (pp. 115–134). Chicago: University of Chicago Press. (Original work published 1881)

Janus, E. S., & Walbek, N. H. (2000). Sex offender commitments in Minnesota: A descriptive study of second generation commitments. *Behavioral Sciences and the Law, 18*, 243–274.

Kansas v. Crane, 534 U.S. 407 (2002).

Kansas v. Hendricks, 117 S. Ct. 2072 (1997).

Kansas Sexually Violent Predators Act, Kan. Stat. Ann. § 59-29 (Supp. 1997).

The New Shorter Oxford English Dictionary. (1993). Oxford, England: Clarendon Press.

Schopp, R. F. (1998). *Justification defenses and just convictions*. Cambridge, England: Cambridge University Press.

Schopp, R. F. (2001). *Competence, Condemnation, and Commitment*. Washington, DC: American Psychological Association.

Washington Sexually Violent Predators Act, Wash. Rev. Code Ann. § 71.09 (Supp. 1998).

In re Young, 857 P.2d 989 (Wash. 1993).

11

SEX OFFENDERS AND THE SUPREME COURT: THE SIGNIFICANCE AND LIMITS OF *KANSAS V. HENDRICKS*

JOHN KIP CORNWELL

Sexually violent predator (SVP) laws represent a return of the civil commitment model for people who commit repetitive acts of sexual violence. These statutes and how they came about are described in chapters 1 and 2 of this book. The constitutionality of these laws was broadly endorsed by the United States Supreme Court in *Kansas v. Hendricks* (1997). Other chapters in this book (chapters 7, 9, and 10) criticize *Hendricks* on a variety of clinical, political, and philosophical grounds. Does the Supreme Court's deferential approach to these new laws suggest a future expansion of the civil commitment power to categories of dangerous or nondangerous individuals beyond sex offenders?

Portions of this chapter are reprinted from "Understanding the Role of the Police Power and Parens Patriae Powers in Involuntary Civil Commitment Before and After Hendricks," by J. K. Cornwell, 1998, *Psychology, Public Policy, and Law, 4,* pp. 317–413. Copyright © 1998 by American Psychological Association. Reprinted with permission.

A HEIGHTENED STANDARD OF REVIEW

In her petition for certiorari to the U.S. Supreme Court in *Hendricks*, the Kansas Attorney General asked the justices to clarify the relevant substantive due process principles applicable to that state's SVP Act (Kansas Commitment of Sexually Violent Predators Act, Kan. Stat. Ann. § 59-29a02 *et seq.*, 1998). This was an eminently reasonable and appropriate request, because the Court had provided no clear guidance to lower courts grappling with the critical issue of what level of judicial scrutiny applies to sexual predator commitment statutes.

Citing the fundamental liberty interests implicated in sexual predator commitment proceedings, lower courts have generally applied strict scrutiny (see *In re Blodgett*, 1994; *In re Linehan* [*Linehan III*], 1996; *Kansas v. Hendricks*, 1996; *Wisconsin v. Post*, 1995; *Young v. Weston*, 1995). *Foucha v. Louisiana* (1992), which addressed the constitutionality of state statutory procedures governing the commitment of insanity acquittees, provides the strongest support for this position. There, the majority stated that because "[f]reedom from physical restraint is a fundamental right, the State must have a particularly convincing reason" for committing sane acquittees. The fundamental rights language does indeed suggest strict scrutiny; however, the fact that the state need not proffer the "compelling state interest" traditionally required in this context indicates less exacting review. Justice O'Connor, whose concurrence provided a crucial fifth vote for the majority in *Foucha*, likewise seemed to eschew strict scrutiny in favor of a more deferential standard that permitted commitment where the nature and duration of detention are "tailored to reflect pressing public safety concerns related to [an individual's] continuing dangerousness." Earlier Supreme Court case law signals even greater deference, requiring only that classifications affecting involuntary psychiatric detention be rationally or reasonably related to legitimate governmental concerns (see *Humphrey v. Cady*, 1972; *Jackson v. Indiana*, 1972; *Jones v. United States*, 1983).

Justice Thomas has been particularly critical of the application of higher level review to involuntary commitment statutes, arguing that there is no fundamental right to "freedom from bodily restraint" applicable to all persons, regardless of the circumstance (*Kansas v. Hendricks*, 1997). In his dissent in *Foucha*, he accused the majority of dodging the scrutiny question, adding that the imposition of strict scrutiny would wreak "a revolution in the treatment of the mentally ill" (*Kansas v. Hendricks*, 1997). He likewise lambasted Justice O'Connor for advocating "a heightened standard of review heretofore unknown in our case law." In light of the foregoing, one would have expected Justice Thomas to have taken the opportunity to resolve the scrutiny conundrum once and for all in his majority opinion in *Hendricks*. Paradoxically, he did not do so. The decision is devoid of any clear indication of what level of scrutiny applies. Instead, it ambiguously states that involuntary civil commitment statutes that "[narrow] the class of persons eligible for confinement to those who are unable to control their dangerousness" are constitutional, provided "the confinement takes place pursuant to proper procedures and evidentiary standards" (*Kansas v. Hendricks*, 1997).

In the 5 years since *Hendricks* was decided, lower courts have varied widely in their approach to scrutiny in evaluating sexual predator commitment statutes. The Supreme Court of Minnesota, deciding a sexual predator commitment case remanded by the U.S. Supreme Court for reconsideration in light of *Hendricks*, applied strict scrutiny (*In re Linehan* [*Linehan IV*], 1999). While *Hendricks's* reference to "narrowing" the class of persons eligible for commitment provides some support for this understanding, the failure to require a "compelling state interest" suggests less exacting review, consistent with Justice Thomas's previous commentary on this matter. Other courts have identified different standards of review, depending on the type of constitutional challenge. The Supreme Court of Washington, for example, has applied strict scrutiny to its sexual predator commitment statute "as a whole" but has used the rational basis test for equal protection claims based on the differential treatment of mentally disordered sexual predators and other mentally ill persons, noting that such distinctions need only have "some relevance to the purpose for which the classification is made" (*In re Turay*, 1999). The U.S. Court of Appeals for the Ninth Circuit, by contrast, has applied intermediate scrutiny in the same context, thereby requiring the state to show that its classifications are substantially related to important government interests (*Young v. Weston*, 1999).

Justice Thomas's assertion that freedom from bodily restraint does not necessarily implicate a fundamental right meriting strict scrutiny seems correct (see *Chapman v. United States*, 1991). By the same token, rationality review, which more or less "rubber stamps" government conduct (*Lindsley v. Natural Carbonic Gas Co.*, 1911; *McGowan v. Maryland*, 1961; *New Orleans v. Dukes*, 1976), is inappropriate where the legislation at issue produces such a massive curtailment of liberty. Instead, intermediate scrutiny should apply and should require, accordingly, an "exceedingly persuasive justification" for substantive provisions pertaining to the involuntary civil commitment of sexual predators.

Several factors mandate heightened scrutiny. First, as mentioned above, classification as a mentally disordered sex offender engenders a substantial infringement of bodily liberty, the seriousness of which the Court has consistently recognized (see, e.g., *Addington v. Texas*, 1979; *In re Gault*, 1967; *O'Connor v. Donaldson*, 1975). Second, labeling sex offenders as mentally disordered persons subjects them to well-documented, stigmatizing stereotypes that undermine their respect and dignity (see Skinner et al., 1995). Third, the public antipathy engendered by the heinousness of sexual predators' prior misconduct diminishes their political power and increases their social isolation.

Moreover, while the Court did not specify the standard of scrutiny it was applying in *Hendricks* or in its more recent consideration of the Kansas statute in *Kansas v. Crane* (2002), the analysis of those cases suggests more searching review than that provided by the rational basis test. In *Hendricks*, in upholding the Kansas statute, the Court seemed to impose a condition that was not set forth in the statute itself by referring to the Kansas statute as requiring a mental abnormality or personality disorder "that makes it difficult, if not impossible, for the dangerous person to control his dangerous behavior" (*Kansas v. Hendricks*, 1997). In *Kansas v. Crane* (2002), Kansas had contended that the Constitution permits the commitment of SVPs without any lack of control determination, but the Court rejected this contention, insisting instead that "there be proof of serious difficulty in controlling behavior." In effect, the Court found that the Kansas statute, which did not contain this difficult-to-control-behavior requirement, swept too broadly to meet the requirements of substantive due process. By mandating proof of volitional impairment, the Court was applying a standard of scrutiny more exacting than the minimal rational basis test, which would have required upholding the statute as written. *Hendricks* and *Crane* thus reflect the Court's willingness to apply a form of heightened scrutiny to measure the constitutionality of sexual predator commitment statutes.

THE MEANING OF MENTAL ABNORMALITY

The sufficiency of Leroy Hendricks's mental abnormality for purposes of involuntary civil commitment was at the heart of the *Hendricks* case. Although he did not dispute that he suffered from pedophilia, Hendricks claimed that this disorder, standing alone, was not constitutionally sufficient to justify the loss of his liberty. The State of Kansas countered that, as a matter of substantive due process, psychotic illness was not constitutionally necessary for psychiatric detention. It was enough that an individual suffer from "a mental abnormality or personality disorder which makes the person likely to engage in an act of predatory sexual violence" (Kan. Stat. Ann. § 59-29a02(a)). Thus, because Hendricks's disorder satisfied this standard, the state could constitutionally detain him, even though he was not eligible for commitment under its general commitment law.

The U.S. Supreme Court unanimously agreed that Hendricks's pedophilia was sufficient to commit him involuntarily to a state forensic hospital. Justice Thomas explained that "the term mental illness is devoid of any talismanic significance," as is reflected by the Court's use of various expressions to denote "the mental condition of those properly subject to civil confinement" (*Kansas v. Hendricks*, 1997). The majority focused less on the precise terminology used and its acceptance by the psychiatric community, and more on its functional significance, noting that the mental conditions recognized by the Court "serve to limit involuntary civil confinement to those who suffer from a volitional impairment rendering them dangerous beyond their control" (*Kansas v. Hendricks*, 1997).

But what exactly does it mean for a mental abnormality to render individuals "dangerous beyond their control?" In *Kansas v. Crane* (2002), the Court required "serious difficulty in controlling behavior" to justify sexual predator commitment but declined to define "serious difficulty" with any specificity. The majority noted simply that states "retain considerable leeway in defining the mental abnormalities and personality disorders that make an individual eligible for commitment."

This deference to state authority supports the constitutionality of statutes such as Minnesota's Sexually Dangerous Persons Act (1994), which requires that an individual lack "adequate" control over sexual impulses, making it highly likely that he will engage in sexual misconduct in the future. A sexual predator may retain some control over his conduct and still be sufficiently dangerous to justify commitment, as in the case of an individual who is able to "plan, wait and delay the indulgence of their maladies until presented with a higher probability of success" (*Linehan III*, 1996). Thus, an individual who does not lack total control over harmful sexual impulses may nonetheless have a degree of volitional impairment such that they are unable to control their dangerousness, as *Hendricks* requires.

Crane's vindication of the breadth of states' authority to detain mentally disordered sex offenders accords with the spirit of *Hendricks*. If the *Hendricks* majority intended to require that mental abnormality be characterized by the inability to control sexual impulses, it could have relied on the Court's earlier decision in *Minnesota v. Pearson*, which upheld a separate Minnesota statute providing for the involuntary psychiatric detention of "psychopathic personalities" who "manifest an utter lack of power to control their sexual impulses" (*Minnesota v. Pearson*, 1940). The decision to rely instead on broad conceptualizations of the state's police power prerogative to defend itself against persons "unable to control their dangerousness" suggests a desire to extend the outer limits of civil detention beyond *Pearson*.

Hendricks is no more specific than *Crane*, however, in clarifying the extent to which state officials may determine which of its citizens have a mental illness sufficient to justify their involuntary detention. While the justices were unanimous in approving the mental abnormality formulation contained in the Kansas SVP Act, their reasoning varied significantly. For four members of the Court, who dissented from the Court's decision on other grounds, the prescription was constitutional, as applied to Leroy Hendricks, because he suffered from "a serious mental disorder," recognized by many mental health experts, that rendered him dangerous because of a "specific, serious, and highly unusual inability to control his actions." Justice Kennedy, who provided the critical fifth vote for the majority, concurred separately to caution that involuntary detention would be impermissible if mental abnormality proved to be "too imprecise" a category to "offer a solid basis" for confinement.

Clearly, then, a majority of the Court is concerned about the potential reach of a mental illness standard that authorizes civil commitment based on volitional impairments that make individuals dangerous. Although there is little disagreement about the sufficiency of Leroy Hendricks's disorder, sex offenders are not always diagnosed with impairments as "specific, serious and highly unusual" as pedophilia. Many, for example, carry a diagnosis of antisocial personality disorder by virtue of their chronic impulsivity, irresponsibility, aggressiveness, and unlawful behavior. The defendant in Crane, for example, was diagnosed as having antisocial personality disorder and exhibitionism. Because researchers have speculated that a majority of prison inmates suffer from antisocial personality disorder (Abram, 1989; Arboleda-Florez & Holley, 1991; Ogloff, Roesch, & Hart, 1994), constitutionalizing the commitment of those with antisocial personalities would give states broad authority to civilly detain prisoners at the end of their sentences.

Endeavoring, perhaps, to avert such a result, the dissenters specified that the adequacy of Hendricks's abnormality turned, in part, on the fact that it did not "consist simply of a long course of antisocial behavior." Likewise, Justice Kennedy's aforementioned admonition that detention would cease to be justified if mental abnormality proved "too imprecise a category," coupled with his emphasis on the "dangers inherent when a civil confinement law is used in conjunction with the criminal process," suggests strongly his disapproval of allowing the routine use of postincarceration civil commitment. The fact that many sex offenders carry a diagnosis of antisocial personality disorder (In re Blodgett, 1994; Hammel, 1995; Linehan III, 1996) does not, moreover, require recognition of this "abnormality" as a legitimate basis for commitment for all individuals to prevent their release; on the contrary, it is sufficient ground only for those persons for whom it evidences a lack of control predisposing them to commit violent sexual offenses.

Likewise, noting that from 40% to 60% of the male prison population is diagnosable with antisocial personality disorder, the Crane Court underscored the need to distinguish between dangerous sexual offenders subject to civil commitment from other dangerous individuals more properly dealt with through the criminal law (Kansas v. Crane, 2002). Otherwise, the majority noted, endorsing the concern previously voiced by Justice Kennedy in his concurring opinion in Hendricks, civil commitment could become a mechanism for retribution and general deterrence. The Court thus painted a border between civil commitment and criminal punishment, requiring "a special and serious lack of ability to control behavior" in which the state relies on a volitional impairment to justify involuntary psychiatric commitment (*Kansas v. Crane*, 2002). Although Leroy Hendricks's pedophilia satisfied this volitional impairment standard, the Court did not decide whether Crane's condition (antisocial personality disorder and exhibitionism) produced a sufficiently serious difficulty in controlling behavior to justify involuntary commitment. Instead, they remanded that case back to the state courts, thereby leaving for future resolution which other conditions would meet the test.

BEYOND PERSONALITY DISORDERS AND PARAPHILIAS

Although paraphilias and personality disorders figured prominently in *Hendricks*, the Court's discussion of mental abnormality has relevance both beyond these particular disorders and for populations other than sexual predators. If a majority of the justices would approve a mental illness standard characterized by volitional impairment rendering an individual dangerous beyond his control, what, for example, about arsonists who cannot suppress the urge to set fires?

Although the Court does not discuss the confinement of any group other than sexual predators, its citation of *Heller v. Doe* (1993), which addressed the parameters of the state's authority to detain those with mental retardation, suggests that applying the volitional impairment standard to other classes of mentally abnormal, dangerous individuals may be constitutionally permissible. Justice Kennedy's concern as to definitional imprecision could be satisfied through narrow drafting tailored to SVP Act terminology; thus, commitment could be available only for those persons suffering from "a mental abnormality or personality disorder making them likely to engage in acts of impulsive arsony."

The fact that this definition does not, in and of itself, describe a disorder contained in the *Diagnostic and Statistical Manual of Mental Disorders* (4th ed., Text Revision, *DSM–IV–TR*; American Psychiatric Association, 2000) is immaterial under *Hendricks*. More significant in this regard is the *DSM–IV–TR*'s inclusion of "pyromania," which is classified as an "impulse-control disorder" characterized, *inter alia*, by "deliberate and purposeful fire setting on more than one occasion" to achieve "pleasure, gratification, or relief" (p. 669). Presumably, most individuals meeting the mental abnormality standard defined above would be found to suffer from pyromania, much as sexual predators committed under the SVP Act typically suffer from one or more of the paraphilias, described elsewhere in the *DSM–IV–TR*. This availability of an extant diagnostic category describing a volitional impairment clearly influenced the dissenters' acceptance of Hendricks's pedophilia as sufficient to justify detention. While seemingly less reliant on the existence of DSM classifications, the majority did note that Hendricks's pedophilia was "a condition that the psychiatric profession itself classifies as a serious mental disorder." In light of the danger inherent in impulsive fire-setting behavior, pyromania may be similarly classified.

If the state may legitimately commit arsonists based on a mental abnormality formulation similar to that approved in *Hendricks*, what about other individuals who pose a danger to society due to a mental impairment of a different sort? Consider, for example, women who suffer from a particularly acute form of "premenstrual dysphoric disorder" (PMDD). Unlike premenstrual syndrome, which affects an estimated 70% of menstruating women and does not necessarily impact mood, PMDD occurs in an estimated 2% to 5% of women and often produces overwhelming stress that precludes normal functioning (Knowlton, 1996; Solomon, 1995). In addition, some PMDD sufferers grapple every month with difficult and sometimes frightening struggles to control unpredictable mood swings that lead them to acts of violence against family members.

In one British case, for example, a 30-year-old woman, whose behavior was otherwise nonviolent, reportedly experienced a marked onset of irritability culminating in aggressive and violent conduct toward her husband and her children 7 days prior to the onset of menses each month (Taylor & Dalton, 1983). In addition, in at least two British cases, extreme premenstrual distress has diminished criminal responsibility for brutal homicides. In one, the prosecution mitigated murder to manslaughter where a woman pinned her boyfriend to a car and killed him (Carney & Williams, 1983). In the other, an appellate court did the same, where a woman bludgeoned her mother to death with a hammer (*Regina v. Reynolds*, 1988).

Although American courts have historically been skeptical of permitting criminal defenses based on premenstrual status (Carney & Williams, 1983), increasing psychiatric recognition of the PMDD classification may well change this. If PMDD sufferers' difficulty in controlling behavior is sufficient to exonerate or mitigate responsibility for criminal acts, then, *a fortiori*, it should serve as an adequate basis for civil commitment. Even if PMDD evidence is not admissible in criminal trials, the disorder would appear to satisfy nonetheless the mental abnormality standard of *Hendricks* and *Crane*, which simply requires "a special and serious lack of ability to control behavior" (*Kansas v. Crane*, 2002). Inasmuch as one might attempt to distinguish PMDD from disorders such as pedophilia by arguing that the former is an emotional as opposed to a volitional impairment, the salience of this contention is speculative at best in light of the Justices' comment in *Crane* that ordinarily they do not distinguish "among volitional, emotional and cognitive impairment" for constitutional purposes in the civil commitment context (*Kansas v. Crane*, 2002).

Assuming *arguendo* that PMDD would satisfy the Court's civil commitment requirements, Justice Kennedy and the dissenters in *Hendricks* would likely object, at any rate, to the potential breadth of civil commitment engendered by recognizing a disorder suffered by as many as 5% of women of childbearing age. To placate these concerns, states could extend commitment only to those PMDD sufferers who manifested repeated, violent behavior toward others, just as antisocial personality disorder could be deemed sufficient only where characterized by a predisposition toward acts of sexual predation.

Limiting PMDD in this way may be required, at any rate, under prior Supreme Court precedent. In *Foucha v. Louisiana* (1992), Justice O'Connor opined that it would be permissible to confine in a psychiatric hospital an insanity acquittee who regained sanity, provided there was a "medical justification" for his confinement; however, where the only evidence of dangerousness is the commission of "a nonviolent or relatively minor crime," the liberty interest of a "sane" but dangerous acquittee "might well outweigh the government's interest in detention." Thus, although a state may choose to define the impairment sufficient for psychiatric commitment as a "mental illness," a "mental abnormality," a "medical justification," or something else, Justice O'Connor believes that, in determining its sufficiency, it is appropriate to analyze the nature and severity of the danger the mental disability produces.

The case of Terry Foucha himself may be used to illustrate this principle. Foucha was not mentally ill in such a way as to make him an appropriate candidate for ordinary civil commitment; rather, like sexual predators, arsonists, and certain women suffering from an acute form of PMDD, he had an impulse-control disorder that rendered him dangerous. As such, Justice O'Connor recognized both the potential necessity of detaining Foucha and those like him and the dangers inherent in sanctioning a standard as broad as the Louisiana statute at issue in that case, which risked transforming psychiatric hospitals into warehouses for the socially dangerous. To steer out of this difficulty, she relied on a civil commitment "calculus" that, in balancing governmental and individual liberty interests, would allow the confinement of "sane" yet mentally "abnormal" people like Terry Foucha who endangered the community's physical safety but would not permit detention where their mental dysfunction posed solely a risk to property.

Hendricks's majority opinion, which Justice O'Connor joined, is in accord inasmuch as the confinement it approves is expressly predicated on proof of "past sexually *violent* behavior and a present mental condition that creates a likelihood of such conduct in the future if the person is not incapacitated." This focus on violence serves not only to limit the scope of commitment based on disorders such as PMDD but also eliminates others entirely. For example, while kleptomania is a classified impulse-control disorder in the *DSM–IV–TR*, its danger is limited to property. Thus, kleptomaniacs are not subject to involuntary commitment under *Hendricks* and *Foucha*, even though its sufferers are unable, due to a volitional impairment, to control their dangerousness.

A NEED FOR TREATMENT

If *Hendricks* permits states to commit dangerous individuals to psychiatric hospitals involuntarily based on mental abnormalities that might or might not be found in the *DSM–IV–TR*, clinicians may encounter significant difficulty in defining and implementing appropriate treatment. In the case of Leroy Hendricks, for example, Kansas had no individualized treatment program in place for sex offenders at the time of his commitment, even though the state acknowledged that he could be treated and that his confinement was based, at least in part, on the desire to provide treatment. This failure to provide treatment led four of the nine Justices to conclude that Hendricks's detention was punitive and therefore unconstitutional.

But what if no treatment exists for the particular mental abnormality on which an individual's involuntary detention is based? All nine Justices agreed that, in this instance, civil incapacitation, standing alone, provides a sufficient justification. Taken to the extreme, this would allow states to declare entire classes of dangerous, mentally ill individuals "untreatable" and leave them to languish indefinitely in psychiatric hospitals. Moreover, inasmuch as their release from detention is predicated on some degree of recovery from the mental impairment that renders them dangerous, the state's failure to develop any treatment program will effectively prevent recovery. Where deficits in the provision of treatment are attributable to patient conduct, the state should not be held responsible; if, however, state officials do not attempt, in good faith, to provide the patient with such an opportunity, he should not suffer the inevitable consequences of their inertia.

Justice Kennedy's concurrence in *Hendricks* underscores these concerns about the SVP Act's "practical effect" of converting civil detention into "confinement for life." He cautions that psychiatrists "may be reluctant to find measurable success in treatment even after a long period and may be unable to predict that no serious danger will come from release of the detainee." In the face of such realities, he warns state officials not to use the civil system "to impose punishment after the State makes an improvident plea bargain on the criminal side"; while incapacitation is a legitimate objective of psychiatric hospitalization, deterrence and retribution are not.

This juxtaposition of civil and criminal justifications begs the question of what might convert an acceptable system of incapacitative psychiatric detention into unlawful, punitive confinement. As noted above, the fact that long-term commitment may occur under a given statutory scheme is not determinative for Justice Kennedy, nor should it be, as states routinely commit dangerous, mentally disturbed persons indefinitely. If, however, facilitating lifelong detention is the statute's apparent *intention*, as opposed to its "practical effect," the confinement it prescribes is indistinguishable from criminal incarceration.

A contrary purpose is demonstrated, first and foremost, by the provision of treatment. To what extent, however, must a state endeavor to create treatment programs for the dangerous persons it commits whose mental illness is presently untreatable? And, if an illness is treatable, who decides how much and what kind of treatment is necessary? These questions raise important substantive due process issues that were not resolved by the Supreme Court in *Hendricks*. In fact, the majority's discussion of treatment focused on the petitioner's *ex post facto* and double jeopardy claims without reference to specific due process requirements. Justice Breyer did comment, however, that providing treatment that is "potentially available" necessarily satisfied due process concerns. Inasmuch as this dicta might signal the Court's thinking on this important issue, it bears scrutiny.

The use of presently available treatment as a constitutional benchmark is not without judicial precedent. In the seminal case of *Rouse v. Cameron* (1967), for example, a federal appellate court held that, to justify psychiatric detention, a state need not demonstrate treatment efficacy but must endeavor instead to provide treatment that is "adequate in light of present knowledge." While relieving the state of its obligation to demonstrate the ameliorative potential of a given course of treatment, *Rouse* nonetheless required that the state's treatment efforts be "*bona fide.*" This, in turn, necessitated exploration into whether hospital staff had made "initial and periodic inquiries . . . into the needs and conditions of the patient with a view to providing suitable treatment for him" and whether a program had been created that was "suitable to his particular needs." Thus, the provision of presently available treatment was constitutionally sufficient under Rouse provided medical personnel were, at the same time, reviewing and refining treatment regimens to ensure that they were appropriate for the particular individuals involved.

This understanding of the right to treatment fairly accommodates both the state's interest in detaining psychiatrically impaired individuals for whom there is not, as yet, effective treatment and its corresponding obligation to attempt, in good faith, to create therapeutic regimens tailored to patients' needs. As such, *Rouse* provides a ready framework for interpreting the treatment standard suggested in *Hendricks*. Indeed, obligating state officials to fashion "appropriate" treatment for those who are involuntarily committed is of particular importance in cases such as *Hendricks*, in which providing "available" treatment might be tantamount to providing nothing at all. *Rouse's* emphasis on individual patient's needs and the development of a specialized treatment regimen prevents state officials from relying indefinitely on nonspecific treatments, such as "milieu" or group therapy, which may not serve patient interests. Rather, for their efforts to be *bona fide*, medical personnel must endeavor to enhance existent therapies or develop new ones where none presently exists.

This formulation is consistent with *Youngberg v. Romeo* (1982), the Court's most definitive pronouncement to date of patients' right to treatment. In *Youngberg*, which addressed institutionalized mentally retarded persons, the justices required not only that treatment be made available but also that it be "minimally adequate . . . to ensure safety and freedom from undue restraint," adding that lower courts should bestow "presumptive validity" to the judgments of "qualified professionals" in this regard. *Youngberg* would accommodate, moreover, the use of certain factors, including those cited in *Rouse*, in assessing whether the exercise of professional judgment was proper in a given case. For example, in *Janet D. v. Carros* (1976), a state appellate court relied on *Rouse* in assuming responsibility for determining what constituted appropriate treatment. It specified a variety of factors, including periodic patient reevaluation and the development of individualized treatment programs, which would be used to assess the propriety of professional judgments. Incorporating these considerations serves not to usurp medical judgment but rather "to ensure that professionals . . . apply their knowledge and skills" in determining the sufficiency of the state's treatment efforts.

CONCLUSION

Kansas v. Hendricks is a watershed decision in mental health law. Its primary significance lies not, however, in its holding but in its reasoning. In permitting the postincarceration, civil detention of mentally disordered sex offenders, the majority opinion used sweeping language that, standing alone, appears to give states unbridled discretion to define mental illness with such breadth that most, if not all, dangerous social outcasts could be taken off the streets and deposited into state psychiatric hospitals. The unavailability of treatment for their mental abnormality likewise erects no barrier to confinement because, under that opinion's reasoning, civil incapacitation justifies the detention of the dangerous mentally disordered whether or not they are amenable to therapeutic interventions.

Fortunately, *Hendricks* cannot be fully understood by reading the majority opinion alone. The concurring and dissenting opinions, subscribed to by five Justices, temper significantly the analytical harshness of Justice Thomas's decision. Hendricks must also be read in light of relevant legal authority and other case law, especially *Foucha v. Louisiana* and *Kansas v. Crane*, both of which addressed the authority of states to civilly detain dangerous, mentally disordered individuals who do not presently suffer from major mental illness. Considering these lines of authority together, the potential for widespread warehousing of those who are socially undesirable is undermined significantly by various requirements, including the following: a heightened standard of review that requires an "exceedingly persuasive justification" for involuntarily committing individuals to state psychiatric hospitals; precision in defining and labeling mental illness; a *bona fide* effort to provide meaningful treatment tailored to each patient's individualized needs; and the use of a commitment "calculus" that determines the sufficiency of a given mental impairment for commitment by balancing its severity against the gravity of the danger it may produce. Thus, although the new millennium may well witness an expansion in the reach of involuntary psychiatric detention, *Hendricks* is not an Orwellian prophecy.

REFERENCES

Abram, K. M. (1989). The effect of co-occurring disorders on criminal careers: Interaction of antisocial personality, alcoholism, and drug disorders. *International Journal of Law and Psychiatry, 12,* 133–148.

Addington v. Texas, 441 U.S. 418 (1979).

American Psychiatric Association. (2000). *Diagnostic and statistical manual of mental disorders* (4th ed, Text Revision). Washington, DC: Author.

Arboleda-Florez, J., & Holley, L. H. (1991). Antisocial burnout: An exploratory study. *Bulletin of the American Academy of Psychiatry and the Law, 19,* 173–183.

In re Blodgett, 510 N.W.2d 910 (Minn. 1994).

Carney, R. M., & Williams, B. D. (1983). Recent decisions. *Notre Dame Law Review, 59,* 253–269.

Chapman v. United States, 500 U.S. 453 (1991).

Cornwell, J. K. (1998). Understanding the role of police power and parens patriae powers in involuntary commitment before and after Hendricks. *Psychology, Public Policy, and the Law, 4,* 317–413.

Foucha v. Louisiana, 504 U.S. 71 (1992).

In re Gault, 387 U.S. 1 (1967).

Hammel, A. (1995). Comment: The importance of being insane: Sexual predator civil commitment laws and the idea of sex crimes as insane acts. *Houston Law Review, 32,* 775–813.

Heller v. Doe, 509 U.S. 312 (1993).

In re Hendricks, 912 P.2d 129 (Kan. 1996).

Humphrey v. Cady, 405 U.S. 504 (1972).

Jackson v. Indiana, 406 U.S. 715 (1972).

Janet D. v. Carros, 362 A.2d 1060 (Pa. Super. 1976).

Jones v. United States, 463 U.S. 354 (1983).

Kansas v. Crane, 534 U.S. 407 (2002).

Kansas v. Hendricks, 521 U.S. 346 (1997).

Kansas Commitment of Sexually Violent Predators Act, Kan. Stat. Ann. § 59-29a02(a) (Supp. 1998).

Knowlton, L. (1996). *Female gender mood disorders are historically related.* Retrieved from http://www.mhsource.com/edu/psytimes/p961060.html

Lindsley v. Natural Carbonic Gas Co., 220 U.S. 61 (1911).

In re Linehan, 557 N.W.2d 171 (Minn. 1996) ("Linehan III").

In re Linehan, 594 N.W.2d 867 (Minn. 1999) ("Linehan IV").

McGowan v. Maryland, 366 U.S. 420 (1961).

Minnesota Sexually Dangerous Persons Act, Minn. Stat. § 253B.185 (1994).

Minnesota v. Pearson, 309 U.S. 270 (1940).

New Orleans v. Dukes, 427 U.S. 297 (1976).

O'Connor v. Donaldson, 422 U.S. 563 (1975).

Ogloff, J. R. P., Roesch, R., & Hart, S. D. (1994). Mental health services in jails and prisons: Legal, clinical, and policy issues. *Law and Psychology Review, 19,* 109–136.

Regina v. Reynolds, Crim. L.R. 679 (C.A.) (1988) (LEXIS, Enggen Library, Cases file).

Rouse v. Cameron, 373 F.2d 451 (D.C. Cir. 1967).

Skinner, L. J., Berry, K. K., Griffith, S. E., & Byers, B. (1995). Generalizability and specificity of the stigma associated with the mental illness label: A reconsideration twenty-five years later. *Journal of Community Psychology, 23,* 3–17.

Solomon, L. (1995). Premenstrual syndrome: The debate surrounding criminal defense. *Maryland Law Review, 54,* 571–600.

Taylor, L., & Dalton, K. (1983). Premenstrual syndrome: A new criminal defense? *California Western Law Review, 19,* 269–287.

In re Turay, 139 Wash. 2d 379 (1999).

Wisconsin v. Post, 541 N.W.2d 115 (1995).

Young v. Weston, 898 F. Supp. 744 (W.D. Wash. 1995).

Young v. Weston, 176 F.3d 1196 (9th Cir. 1999).

Youngberg v. Romeo, 457 U.S. 307 (1982).

V

ALTERNATIVE STRATEGIES FOR PROTECTING THE COMMUNITY

12

A THERAPEUTIC JURISPRUDENCE ANALYSIS OF SEX OFFENDER REGISTRATION AND COMMUNITY NOTIFICATION LAWS

BRUCE J. WINICK

In the past 10 years, every American jurisdiction has adopted a sex offender registration and community notification law. In 1994, Jesse Timmendequas, a released sex offender, lured Megan Kanka, a 7-year-old girl, into a house that he and two other discharged sex offenders rented in a New Jersey suburb, and they sexually assaulted and killed her. The community reacted with outrage that Megan's parents and others on the block had received no official notification that these discharged sex offenders resided in their neighborhood and posed a threat to their children. The result was Megan's Law, a registration and community notification statute requiring such notification that quickly was adopted throughout the country, including a federal version enacted in 1995.

This chapter describes how these new laws work and conducts a ther-

This chapter is a revised and updated version of material first published by the author in Winick (1998). Copyright 1998 by the American Psychological Association (APA). Adapted with permission of the author and the APA.

apeutic jurisprudence analysis (Stolle, Wexler, & Winick, 2000; Wexler & Winick, 1991, 1996; Winick, 1997) of their consequences for parents, police and prosecutors, the community in general, and the offender. It also proposes changes in the way these laws are applied to decrease their antitherapeutic effects on offenders and the community, to increase their ability to manage the risk of reoffending, and to increase their potential to facilitate the rehabilitation of offenders.

HOW REGISTRATION AND COMMUNITY NOTIFICATION LAWS WORK

These laws require sex offenders to register their place of residence and authorize notification designed to supply information to interested members of the community concerning sex offenders who are discharged from either criminal confinement or civil commitment (Winick, 1998). These statutes require discharged sex offenders to register with local police departments in the areas in which they reside. Those required to register must complete a form eliciting their name, social security number, age, race, sex, date of birth, height, weight, hair and eye color, permanent address and any temporary address, date and place of employment, date and place of each conviction and the form of adjudication thereof, indictment number, a brief description of the offense(s), and any other information required by the state attorney general. The form also requires the individual's fingerprints, and some states require submission of a picture, blood sample, and hair sample.

This information is kept on file by the police department and is available for inspection by interested members of the public. Sometimes the police chief is required to notify residents within a defined area. Sometimes the information is placed on the Internet or is maintained at the police department for computer or manual inspection by interested members of the public. In at least one state, sex offenders must place an ad in the local newspaper providing information about their offense and criminal background and mail it to neighbors within a 1-mile radius of their residence (La. Code Crim. Proc. Ann. art. 895(H), 2002; La. Rev. Stat. Ann. § 15: 542, 2002). The prosecutor in this state also may take other measures of providing notification to the community, including requiring offenders to affix a bumper sticker to their car, place signs on their residence, and display labels on their clothing.

In most states, the degree and method of notification depend on offenders' placement in one of several tiers, reflecting the degree of risk of reoffending that they are thought likely to present. Typically, the prosecutor in the district in which the offense occurred and in which the discharged offender will reside, together with other law enforcement officials, will make an initial determination concerning the tier in which the offender will be placed. About 25% of jurisdictions use only one tier, but a majority use three. In those using only one tier, all discharged sex offenders are treated alike with regard to community notification. New Jersey's Megan's Law is representative of the three-tier model (N.J. Stat. § 2C:7-1, 1995 & West Supp. 2001). Sex offenders presenting a low risk of reoffending are placed in Tier 1. Those presenting a moderate risk are placed in Tier 2, and those presenting a high risk are placed in Tier 3. The statute provides criteria for the local prosecutor to consider in making tier classification determinations. The prosecutor must review the offender's criminal history and consider whether the offender's conduct was "characterized by repetitive and compulsive behavior"; whether the offender served the maximum prison term of imprisonment; whether the offense was committed against a child; whether the offender had a prior relationship with the victim; whether the offense involved a weapon, violence, or serious bodily harm; the number, nature, and recency of prior offenses; the offender's response to any treatment received; and the offender's recent behavior, including any recent threats or expressions of intent to commit additional crimes.

Guidelines adopted by the New Jersey attorney general supplement these statutory criteria. These contemplate preparation of a criminal and behavioral history of the offender to facilitate an appropriate decision about the risk of reoffense. The guidelines list factors to be considered by prosecutors in deciding in which tier offenders should be placed. In Tier 1, the factors include whether the offender is under the supervision of probation or parole, is receiving treatment, is under the supervision of a home or halfway house to which he or she has been released, is employed or attending school or a vocational program, and presents no evidence of alcohol or drug abuse. The factors for Tier 2 include whether the offender failed to seek therapeutic counseling, to comply with conditions of supervision including the taking of prescribed psychotropic drugs, to obtain employment, and to refrain from alcohol or drug use. They also include whether the offender has a history of making threats against people who are not family members, of stalking locations where children congregate, or of arson or animal mutilation. The factors for Tier 3 include whether the offender's crime was characterized by repetitive and compulsive behavior, whether the offender failed to respond to previous treatment and currently is refusing treatment, whether the offender failed to show remorse for the crime, whether the offender served the maximum term, whether the offender committed the offense against a child who was a stranger, whether the offense involved physical force or violence, whether the offender has a history of violent and aggressive behavior toward others, whether the offender expressed continued threats to engage in criminal sexual conduct, and whether at least one of the offender's prior offenses was brutal and violent in nature. The guidelines also contain a psychological profile to be used in rating the offender's risk of recidivism.

The prosecutor must weigh these factors in determining into which tier the offender should be placed. Offenders wishing to challenge their tier designation may petition for judicial review. The judicial hearing is an evidentiary one, but judicial practice thus far suggests that the likelihood of the court's overruling the prosecutor's discretionary determination is small.

All offenders are placed in Tier 1 at a minimum, and details concerning their identity and prior offenses are given to all law enforcement agencies in the state that are likely to encounter them. For offenders placed in Tier 2, those who present a moderate risk of reoffending, notice is given to organizations in the community, including schools and religious and youth organizations with which the offender is likely to have contact. For offenders placed in Tier 3, those who present a high risk of reoffending, notice also is given to members of the community likely to encounter the offender. The New Jersey statute appears to be the model for most of the states using three tiers, although the method of notification varies somewhat.

THERAPEUTIC IMPLICATIONS OF REGISTRATION AND COMMUNITY NOTIFICATION STATUTES

What are the therapeutic implications of registration and community notification statutes? To answer this question, one must consider their therapeutic effects on both members of the community and the offender.

Effects on the Community

The parents of Megan Kanka, the 7-year-old victim of a sex offense for whom the New Jersey statute was named, testified at the state legislature that had they known that a sex offender resided on their block, they would have taken appropriate precautions to prevent their daughter from venturing near his house. The Megan's Law model seeks to afford parents information about sex offenders discharged to their neighborhoods to empower them to take action to protect their children. Without such information, parents may experience a sense of powerlessness, a feeling that can create great anxiety and fear. Providing parents with this information, therefore, predictably reduces their level of fear and anxiety and enhances their feeling of control over their environment.

This psychological value can be explained in terms of what the social cognition literature describes as "information control," the perception of personal control that results from obtaining information related to stressful situations and events (Fiske & Taylor, 1984, p. 122). The information provided by registration and community notification statutes thus can give members of the community a sense of control over a salient and frightening hazard in their environment. Using the concept of locus of control, psychological research demonstrates a relationship between perceptions of control and mood and feelings of psychological well-being (Lefcourt, 1982). Individuals who perceive themselves as having an internal locus of control are vital, lively, and essentially happy. Those who have an external locus of control—the feeling that they do not have power over the forces that affect their world—lose the sense of mastery and effectiveness and become demoralized and depressed.

These laws may also have positive psychological effects for law enforcement officials. Police and prosecutors must experience a heightened sense of helplessness, despair, and depression at their inability to protect the community from the actions of sex offenders, particularly those highly cruel, grotesque, and sometimes fatal crimes that involve young children. Registration and community notification laws give the police and prosecutor the opportunity to provide concrete assistance to the community that can help to prevent such atrocities. In the process, law enforcement officials can earn the gratitude of the community rather than its blame. Megan's Law thus can be an oasis of job satisfaction in what otherwise often is highly frustrating work. By providing this information to the community, law enforcement officials diffuse their responsibility for community protection and share their crime prevention and deterrence functions with members of the public. If a sex offense should be committed by an offender about whom notification has been provided, the tendency of the community to blame the police will be reduced.

These laws, however, also may impose negative psychological effects on members of the community. The provision of information itself can increase the saliency of the risk of a sex offense, causing fear, anxiety, and sometimes even hysteria. People aware that a dangerous sex offender has been released to their neighborhood might be afraid to venture outside their homes or may do so only with great stress and anxiety. This may be particularly true for the elderly. Children may be forbidden from playing outside or even from going to school or visiting friends unescorted. The heightened sense of fear and suspiciousness of strangers that these laws may produce can contribute to the breakdown of the sense of community that already characterizes modern urban and suburban life. These laws can breed a sense of paranoia and even hysteria that can be psychologically debilitating for both the individual and the community.

For parents who fail to take precautions or take inadequate ones, the feelings that might result should their child be sexually victimized might include a measure of self-blame or guilt. Self-blame and guilt could also be produced for adult victims of sex offenses who fail to take sufficient precautions after notification of the discharge of a sex offender to their community. Moreover, the husband of a woman victimized by such a sexual assault may blame himself for not having prevented it and also blame his wife for not having avoided it.

These registration and community notification laws are based on the assumption that sex offenses are committed by strangers. In reality, most sex offenses are perpetrated by family members and people known to the victim (see this volume, chapter 8). More than 75% of cases involving the sexual abuse of children are perpetrated by someone the child knows (Butler, 1985). Many such offenses happen within the family, involving child sexual abuse and domestic sexual violence. Those who commit acts of sexual abuse against their child or spouse may pose no risk or only a minimal risk of victimizing others sexually. To the extent that the sex offender required to register under these statutes has committed an act of sexual abuse against a member of the family, community notification may be unnecessary to protect those who are not family members but will be extremely embarrassing to the family and to neighbors who learn of these highly personal family secrets. Sexual abuse within the family is an intensely private and sensitive matter, the exposure of which can shroud the family in feelings of shame, guilt, and embarrassment. Much sexual abuse within the family already goes unreported. These strong feelings brought on by community notification concerning sexual abuse within the family will further inhibit the reporting of these offenses, perhaps thereby perpetuating intrafamily sexual abuse.

Community notification laws thus may produce both positive and negative effects for the emotional well-being of members of the community. Whether the public is better or worse off knowing that discharged sex offenders live in their neighborhood is a complex empirical question that requires further research and public policy debate. Can we prevent the antitherapeutic consequences that these laws might produce—fear and hysteria, perhaps self-blame and guilt—and for sex crimes perpetrated against victims by family members or acquaintances, and exacerbation of public embarrassment that will likely discourage the disclosure that might be a necessary precondition for ending the abuse? If anything, as a result of the identification of these antitherapeutic consequences, consideration needs to be given to limiting community notification to situations raising a high risk of sexual violence by a stranger. If we are to be more selective in the use of the community notification remedy, we need to develop better risk assessment tools for sexual violence (see this volume, chapter 3) and techniques and strategies for managing the risk of such violence in the community, including more widespread availability of community treatment and preventive resources (see this volume, chapters 5 and 13), ways of using the law to motivate previous offenders to avail themselves of these services and to refrain from reoffending, and innovative probation and parole monitoring approaches (see this volume, chapter 15).

Effects on the Offender

Registration and community notification laws would seem to present both positive and negative therapeutic effects for offenders. Requiring offenders to write out the facts of their offense will help break down the denial from which many sex offenders suffer and that tends to perpetuate their criminal behavior. This requirement can help offenders understand that their conduct has imposed significant negative consequences on their victim and to develop a sense of empathy with the victim that can reduce the risk of reoffending. Moreover, requiring the sex offender to open up in this way could produce a variety of positive psychological consequences for the individual and reduce the negative psychological consequences of repressing these events (Pennebaker, 1990).

However, these laws also pose negative therapeutic consequences on offenders required to register. Offenders who have served their term in prison and have been rehabilitated may nonetheless be required to register and to have the facts of their prior sexual offenses made public. Notification will predictably cause neighbors to shun these persons and prospective employers to refrain from hiring them. These consequences, which will continue during the period of notification—lasting for many years and, in some states, a lifetime—may have a strongly negative effect on individuals' response to treatment. Although criminal punishment serves other ends, in part it is designed to rehabilitate the offender. A prison sentence provides offenders an opportunity to reflect on their past and an incentive to undergo change and forsake their antisocial attitudes and behavior patterns. Offenders are offered a second chance after they have paid their debt to society and, at least in principle, are eligible for reintegration into the community. The possibility of redemption and forgiveness may be a powerful incentive for the offender to expend the effort needed to achieve rehabilitation.

This basic framework of offender rehabilitation, however, is violated by registration and community notification laws. Individuals are publicly labeled as sex offenders, a label that must be worn for many years and sometimes for a lifetime. The label indicates that they are not redeemed and not forgiven by the community. They are characterized as deviants and ostracized by the community in ways that may seem impossible to overcome. By denying them a variety of employment, social, and educational opportunities, the sex offender label may prevent these individuals from starting a new life and making new acquaintances, with the result that it may be extremely difficult for them to discard their criminal patterns. Furthermore, the continued shaming and stigmatization that the registration and community notification laws impose may produce anger in the discharged sex offender, further norm deviance, and, in extreme cases, even physical violence.

In addition, the continuation of the sex offender label may pose strongly negative self-attributional effects for individuals, who may come to feel that their essential identity is as a sex offender (see this volume, chapter 18). They have been a sex offender in the past, they know, and the requirement that they wear the stigmatizing label for 10 or more years, and in some states in perpetuity, may suggest that their character as a sex offender is essentially unchangeable. Many sex offenders may feel that they are unable to control their strong urges to reoffend. To the extent that sex offenders experience a strong measure of uncontrollability concerning their conduct, the continued sex offender label may make them feel that their uncontrollability is causally related to an internal deficit that is stable rather than changeable, producing the feeling that improvement or change is hopeless (Seligman, 1980).

Attribution theory suggests that individuals who experience failure or lack of control may posit the existence of an internal deficit that is responsible for their problems. Jones and Berglass (1978) used the term *self-handicapping* to describe this pattern. According to self-handicapping theory, individuals may seek or create reasons for inhibiting future performance to avoid potential failure, thereby reducing the threat to their self-esteem that failure can create. An individual who engages in self-handicapping "reaches out for impediments, exaggerates handicaps, and embraces any factor reducing personal responsibility" for failure (Jones & Berglass, 1978, p. 202). Individuals in general thus tend to discount their own responsibility for failure, attributing it instead to a real or imagined handicap. If self-handicapping occurs even when individuals are not subjected to labeling, affixing public and durable sex offender labels to offenders who have completed their term of imprisonment will predictably increase the tendency of offenders to perceive themselves as handicapped in regard to their ability to control their sexual behavior. By communicating that attempts to control behavior will likely be useless, the sex offender label imposed by registration and community notification laws will predictably inhibit attempts on the part of sex offenders to control their behavior or seek treatment designed to help them learn how to do so. To the extent that the label attributes their difficulty in controlling their sexual urges to a lack of ability that is inherent in their character, the likelihood is high that they will internalize this self-conception in ways that may make change difficult, if not impossible. By producing or reinforcing expectancies of failure, the publicly applied, durable sex offender label imposed by registration and community notification laws may actually frustrate one of the primary goals of the law in this area: to prevent recidivism by sex offenders by encouraging them to take responsibility for their actions and undergo rehabilitation.

RESTRUCTURING SEX OFFENDER NOTIFICATION LAWS TO REFLECT A RISK MANAGEMENT RATHER THAN A PREDICTION MODEL

Sex offender registration and community notification laws thus can produce both therapeutic and antitherapeutic effects for both the community and the offender. In view of the strong public support for these laws, which have been adopted in all 50 states and endorsed in federal legislation, it seems unlikely that their antitherapeutic consequences for sex offenders and the community will lead to their repeal. The question is: How can these laws be changed to minimize their antitherapeutic effects, and how can they be applied to maximize their therapeutic potential?

There are basically two models for assessing risk in this and other areas in which legal issues turn on a prediction of future dangerousness: a prediction model and a risk management model (Winick, 2000). Predicting future dangerousness is an important task in several legal contexts. When a sex offender registers pursuant to a Megan's Law-type statute, in jurisdictions that use three tiers of risk with differing notification consequences, the prosecutor must determine into which tier a particular offender should be placed. This determination is based largely on an assessment of the risk of future recidivism presented by the offender. Similarly, under sexually violent predator statutes, the determination as to whether a sex offender at the expiration of his or her prison term should be subjected to civil commitment is based largely on an assessment of the likelihood of the individual's reoffending. A similar assessment of the risk of future dangerous behavior arises in other legal areas, including civil commitment generally; criminal sentencing, including capital punishment; and preventive detention and parole decision making.

Traditionally, the law has relied on what has been described as a *prediction model* for making these determinations (Monahan, 1984). A prediction model seeks to determine the probability of the occurrence of a specified event within a future time period. Under a prediction model, the determination is dichotomous—the individual is determined to be either dangerous or not—and static—involving a one-time prediction based on factors existing at the time the prediction is made.

Until recently, under the prediction model, predictions about future dangerousness were made by processes that relied almost exclusively on the recommendations of clinical evaluators after an examination of the individual in question. The accuracy of clinical predictions, however, has been seriously questioned (Winick, 2000). Several problems contribute to this concern about clinical predictions. Such predictions often are based on opinions grounded in clinical observations and experiences that have not been scientifically tested and validated. These observations may be idiosyncratic, and the theories underlying such predictions may be invalid. Moreover, the clinical judgment that forms the basis for these predictions may be contaminated by the evaluator's own biases and the heuristics that he or she relies on. In practice, clinicians often use unstated criteria in predicting dangerousness. Accuracy of clinical predictions has consistently been poor (Steadman et al., 1993).

In recent years, there has been increased interest in statistical or actuarial methods of assessing risk (see this volume, chapter 3). These approaches have long been used in predicting the potential for recidivism among released prisoners in decision making about parole. These actuarial techniques have now been applied to predicting violence among people with mental disorder (Monahan, 1997). They have also been used in the area of predicting recidivism by sex offenders (Becker & Murphy, 1998; see also this volume, chapter 3). The accuracy of prediction models that rely on clinical evaluation can be enhanced when evaluators are aware of risk factors that have been validated actuarially. Clinical judgment is improved through the use of actuarial information concerning risk, which is used to anchor and structure clinical discretion (Monahan, 1997).

Building on these actuarial models, but moving beyond them, scholarly thinking about the prediction of violence has begun to reject the prediction model in favor of what has been termed the *risk assessment model* or *risk management model* (Steadman et al., 1993; Winick, 2000). A paradigm shift has occurred in which the focus has moved from dangerousness to risk. The major elements of this "emergent reconceptualization" are the movement away from "a focus on the legal concept of dangerousness" to "the decision-making concept of risk"; the concept that prediction issues should be viewed as being on a continuum rather than as dichotomous; the shift from "a focus on one-time predictions about dangerousness" made for the court to "ongoing day-to-day decisions about the management and treatment" of those presenting the risk of violence; and "balancing the seriousness of possible outcomes with the probabilities of their occurrence based on specific risk factors" (Steadman et al., 1993, p. 41; see also Carson, 1997; Heilbrun, 1997; Heilbrun, Nezu, Keeney, Chung, & Wasserman, 1998). Unlike the prediction model, which is essentially static, measuring risk at a particular date based on information then in existence, the risk management model is dynamic, factoring in information concerning the individual as it may develop over time in light of the individual's ongoing behavior and response to treatment interventions. Whereas the primary function of the prediction model is to assess dangerousness through predicting the probability of the event's occurring, the risk management model attempts to reduce the risk of such behavior. The focus is on managing and reducing risk through treatment and rehabilitative intervention.

In principle, the risk management approach should lead to greater accuracy inasmuch as it considers more data points and is continuously open to reevaluation of the degree of risk as it changes over time. The prediction model, in contrast, does not allow new information to be taken into account. Because the risk management model is more useful to legal decision makers, is likely to be more accurate, and includes an interactive component that is calculated to reduce the extent of risk, this approach seems to have several important advantages over the prediction model.

These advantages include a number of considerations valued by therapeutic jurisprudence (Winick, 2000). Because it involves a dynamic process that factors in new information about individuals as it unfolds, the risk management model provides a feedback loop to individuals that can help them shape their behavior to effect a reduction in the level of risk presented. Under a prediction model, individuals have little incentive to effect change in ways that will reduce the degree of risk they present. Because the prediction model is static, producing predictions of risk that will not change, nothing the individual may do after the determination will have the effect of altering the evaluation that initially was made. With a risk management model, individuals are provided with an incentive to alter their behavior to minimize or avoid interferences with their liberty that are justified as a result of the determination that they are dangerous. In this way, the risk management model is in effect a method of behavior management that harnesses principles of psychology to reduce risk.

Are sex offender registration and community notification laws examples of the prediction model or the risk management model? Thirteen states use only one tier of risk (Winick, 1998). These community notification statutory schemes can be seen as an example of the prediction model inasmuch as they are static, basing legal consequences on historic facts existing at a particular point in time. In contrast, community notification statutory schemes that use several tiers of risk (the majority use three) can be seen as examples of a risk management model, but only to the extent that individuals can freely move between tiers as the information concerning the risk they present changes over time. If, in practice, there is little opportunity to move among tiers, three-tier systems also can be seen as essentially reflecting a prediction model.

Given the therapeutic advantages of the risk management model, one-tier systems can be criticized as providing no incentive for change, as can three-tier models that, in practice, signal to offenders that a change in their tier designation is highly unlikely. This criticism suggests that states presently using only one tier should adopt a system using several tiers of risk, and those with several tiers should allow for periodic reassessment of the risk an individual presents and consequent movement between tiers.

Existing three-tier systems, following initial placement of the individual in a particular tier, provide for a change in placement only if the individual seeks judicial review of his or her tier designation. In practice, however, such judicial review would seem to present only a small likelihood of changing the individual's tier classification. Rather than limiting the possibility of changing an individual's tier classification to judicial review that is predictably unlikely to succeed, community notification statutes should build in several meaningful opportunities for such reconsideration, including at the prosecutorial classification decision-making level. Prosecutors should receive updated information concerning offenders, their conduct since the initial tier designation was made, and their participation in and response to treatment, if any. In jurisdictions using a community containment approach that relies on polygraph testing (see this volume, chapter 15), prosecutors can also use the results of such testing. On the basis of this information, the prosecutor should be able to periodically adjust individuals' tier designation in light of changing circumstances, perhaps based on a petition for reclassification filed by them. Restructuring community notification laws in this way will allow them to achieve the benefits that the risk management model has to offer. Indeed, these benefits would predictably be enhanced to the extent that the number of tiers was expanded beyond three. A larger number of tiers, graded in order of ascending assessment of risk, would provide more meaningful opportunities for individuals to change tiers and a corresponding increase in the incentive for them to attempt to do so by controlling their behavior and accepting and responding effectively to treatment interventions. To the extent that offenders are aware that there will be a payoff for controlling their behavior and engaging in treatment, they will be more willing to do so.

Because a risk management model utilizing several tiers of risk takes into account more information as it develops over time, it will predictably increase accuracy concerning the extent of risk and thereby better achieve the community protection purposes these laws are designed to accomplish. In addition to increasing accuracy, converting community notification laws from a prediction to a risk management model will give offenders an incentive to undergo attitudinal and behavioral change in ways that could earn them opportunities to demonstrate that the risk of reoffending has decreased. Whereas community notification laws that functionally perform and appear to be an example of a prediction model convey a message of hopelessness to the offender and a disincentive to change, converting these laws to a risk management model can provide a message of hope and an incentive to attempt change.

In restructuring community notification laws to reflect a risk management rather than exclusively a prediction model, consideration also should be given to the provision of hearings at various points at which classification and reclassification decisions are made. Rather than allowing state officials to make such decisions unilaterally, affording offenders an opportunity to participate through a hearing process can have significant therapeutic value (Winick, 1999, 2001). The literature on the psychology of procedural justice demonstrates the psychological value of giving people the opportunity to participate in hearings they perceive to be fair (Lind & Tyler, 1988; Tyler, 1990). Hearings can serve an important participatory or dignitary value that has been shown to have a significant impact on the attitudes of individuals who participate in them. People who are given a sense of "voice" (the opportunity to tell their story) and "validation" (the feeling that what they say is taken seriously by the hearing officer) and who feel that they are treated fairly, with respect for their dignity as human beings, have been shown to have greater satisfaction with the outcome of the hearing and a greater willingness to accept that outcome and to comply with it.

Although more empirical investigation is needed to determine the. extent to which these principles apply to people with serious mental illness (Cascardi, Poythress, & Hall, 2000), people diagnosed with pedophilia or one of the other paraphilias do not suffer from cognitive impairments or other psychotic symptoms. It therefore seems likely that sex offenders, if given a right to participate in what they come to see as fair hearings concerning their classification for community notification purposes under a state's Megan's Law, will experience psychological benefits that will help to make them accept and comply with the results of the hearing. These effects predictably will enhance the efficacy of treatment received. Adding hearings to the risk management model suggested here for community notification laws could therefore produce significant benefits that may increase the likelihood of rehabilitation and reduce sex offender recidivism.

Such hearings can have an additional benefit. They will place sex offenders in the position of advocating that they are amenable to treatment and rehabilitation and that their present risk of reoffending is reduced. The more persuasive their advocacy is on these points, the more likely they are to be placed in a lower tier of risk. To the extent that sex offenders remain in denial concerning their behavior or suffer from cognitive distortions about it, as will many, providing an incentive to offer effective advocacy on these points and impress the hearing officer with their genuineness can help break down such denial and cognitive distortions and make individuals more amenable to rehabilitative efforts.

Thus, for a number of reasons, hearings should be built into the administration of community notification laws. Not only will they increase the accuracy of the decision-making process, limiting the number of erroneous determinations, but they also will serve important participatory and dignitary values for offenders. Treating offenders with dignity and respect at a hearing that they perceive to be fair and that gives them the opportunity to tell their story can prove to be an important step in redemption, one that inspires hope and genuine efforts to change. Periodic hearings to consider the need for a change in risk classification for community notification purposes can also be an important means of producing additional information concerning offenders over time, enabling a more effective management of the risk they present and providing a tool that itself can help to reduce that risk.

CONCLUSION

Nathaniel Hawthorne's novel *The Scarlet Letter* (1850/1962) depicts a different kind of sex offender registration and community notification law applied in colonial Massachusetts. Hester Prynne, convicted of adultery, was required to wear a scarlet "A" prominently displayed on her clothing as a form of shaming (many variations of which were prevalent in colonial America). In time, however, the community came to know Hester as the good mother and helpful and caring community member she was. Notwithstanding the label she was required to wear, the possibility of redemption remained open. In time, the label itself became transformed in the mind of the community, its meaning shifting from a brand identifying her as an adulteress to a colorful ornament to her clothing that became associated with her qualities of goodness and kindness.

Modern-day sex offenders should also be offered the possibility of redemption. The perpetual stigma imposed by registration and community notification laws seems to signal that the possibility of redemption is foreclosed. Sex offenders are given a particularly stigmatizing deviancy label and subjected to social ostracism. Discharged sex offenders will be branded with a public sex offender label that suggests that a mental abnormality is responsible for their conduct and that they suffer from a deficit that is beyond their control and seems unchangeable. This is a message of hopelessness that can only diminish the individual's motivation and ability to change. Instead, community notification laws should be rewritten and applied in such a way as to offer a message of hope.

Under our present practices, when sex offenders are predicted to be likely to recidivate, they are cast off, either indefinitely committed to a psychiatric hospital for a lengthy period of incapacitation or released to the community with a brand that will prevent or seriously encumber their rehabilitation and redemption. If we genuinely wish to effectuate the rehabilitation of sex offenders, sex offender treatment should be made readily available in the community on a confidential basis to anyone wishing to engage in it. Behavioral techniques, social skills training, cognitive restructuring approaches, empathy training, and relapse prevention training should be offered and encouraged for anyone who would like help in learning how to control his or her sexual desires. Preventive approaches in the community also should be offered. When offenders are released, adequate postrelease programs should be available that include community treatment and probation or parole supervision.

Sex offender registration and community notification laws should be restructured to reflect a risk management approach for sex offenders discharged to the community. Several tiers of risk with corresponding degrees of community notification should be used, and there should be periodic review of tier classifications, allowing offenders who have demonstrated evidence of rehabilitation to obtain reclassification and, ultimately, to earn relief from the registration and notification requirements. Fair hearings, affording offenders a sense of participation and respect for their dignity, should be provided at various tier classification, reclassification, and review of classification decision points. Converting existing registration and community notification schemes so as to reflect a risk management model with periodic hearings can provide a meaningful incentive for discharged offenders to obtain needed treatment and to reduce the risk of their reoffending.

If implemented, these reforms could do much to minimize the present antitherapeutic consequences of registration and notification laws and increase their therapeutic potential. Instead of subjecting sex offenders to psychologically damaging labeling and perpetual stigmatization, we should offer meaningful treatment and incentives that motivate them to accept treatment and to learn how to control their behavior. Instead of hopelessness and continued ostracism, we should extend to sex offenders who are motivated to change a meaningful opportunity for rehabilitation and redemption.

REFERENCES

Becker, J. V., & Murphy, W. D. (1998). What we know and do not know about assessing and treating sex offenders. *Psychology, Public Policy, and Law, 4,* 116–137.

Butler, S. (1985). *Conspiracy of silence: The trauma of incest.* San Francisco: Volcano Press.

Carson, D. (1997). A risk management approach to legal decision-making about "dangerous" people. *Klauwer Law International, 255,* 255–269.

Cascardi, M., Poythress, N. G., & Hall, A. (2000). Procedural justice in the context of civil commitment: An analogy study. *Behavioral Science and the Law, 18,* 731–740.

Fiske, S. T., & Taylor, S. E. (1984). *Social cognition.* Reading, MA: Addison-Wesley.

Hawthorne, N. (1962). *The scarlet letter.* New York: Nelson. (Original work published 1850)

Heilbrun, K. (1997). Prediction vs. control models relevant to risk assessment:

The importance of legal decision-making context. *Law and Human Behavior, 21,* 347–359.

Heilbrun, K., Nezu, C. M., Keeney, M., Chung, S., & Wasserman, A. L. (1998). Sexual offending: Linking assessment, intervention, and decision making. *Psychology, Public Policy, and Law, 4,* 138–174.

Jones, E. E., & Berglass, S. (1978). Control of attributions about the self through self-handicapping strategies: The appeal of alcohol and the role of underachievement. *Personality and Social Psychology Bulletin, 4,* 200–206.

La. Code Crim. Proc. Ann. art. 895(H) (West Supp. 2002).

La. Rev. Stat. Ann. § 15:542 (West Supp. 2002).

Lefcourt, H. M. (1982). *Locus of control: Current trends in theory and research.* Hillsdale, NJ: Erlbaum.

Lind, E. A., & Tyler, T. R. (1988). *The social psychology of procedural justice.* New York: Plenum.

Monahan, J. (1984). The prediction of violent behavior: Toward a second generation of theory and policy. *American Journal of Psychiatry, 141,* 10–15.

Monahan, J. (1997). Clinical and actuarial predictions of violence. In D. Faigman (Eds.), *Modern scientific evidence: The law and science of expert testimony* (Vol. 1, pp. 287–318). Minneapolis, MN: West.

N.J. Stat. § 2C: 7-1 *et seq.* (1995 & West Supp. 2001).

Pennebaker, J. (1990). *Opening up: The healing power of confiding in others.* New York: Morrow.

Seligman, M. E. P. (1980). *Human helplessness: Theory and applications.* New York: Academic Press.

Steadman, H. J., Monahan, J., Robbins, P., Applebaum, P., Grisso, T., Klassen, D., et al. (1993). From dangerousness to risk assessment: Implications for appropriate risk strategies. In S. Hodgins (Ed.), *Mental disorder and crime* (pp. 39–62). Newbury Park, CA: Sage.

Stolle, D. P., Wexler, D. B., & Winick, B. J. (Eds.). (2000). *Practicing therapeutic jurisprudence: Law as a helping profession.* Durham, NC: Carolina Academic Press.

Tyler, T. R. (1990). *Why people obey the law.* New Haven, CT: Yale University Press.

Wexler, D. B., & Winick, B. J. (1991). *Essays in therapeutic jurisprudence.* Durham, NC: Carolina Academic Press.

Wexler, D. B., & Winick, B. J. (Eds.). (1996). *Law in a therapeutic key: Developments in therapeutic jurisprudence.* Durham, NC: Carolina Academic Press.

Winick, B. J. (2001). The civil commitment hearing: Applying the law therapeutically. In L. E. Frost & R. J. Bonnie (Eds.), *The evolution of mental health law* (pp. 291–308). Washington, DC: American Psychological Association.

Winick, B. J. (1997). The jurisprudence of therapeutic jurisprudence. *Psychology, Public Policy, and Law, 3,* 184–206.

Winick, B. J. (1998). Sex offender laws in the 1990s: A therapeutic jurisprudence analysis. *Psychology, Public Policy, and Law, 4,* 505–570.

Winick, B. J. (1999). Therapeutic jurisprudence and the civil commitment hearing. *Journal of Contemporary Legal Issues, 10,* 37–60.

Winick, B. J. (2000). Applying the law therapeutically in domestic violence cases. *University of Missouri–Kansas City Law Review, 69,* 33–91.

13

INVESTING IN THE FUTURE OF CHILDREN: BUILDING PROGRAMS FOR CHILDREN OR PRISONS FOR ADULT OFFENDERS

WILLIAM D. PITHERS, ALISON GRAY, AND MICHALLE E. DAVIS

The focus of this chapter is children with sexual behavior problems, who are youths younger than age 13 who have engaged in sexual behaviors that would be considered felony offenses if committed by an adult or whose sexual behaviors are developmentally unexpected, repetitive, and unresponsive to parental intervention. In several American states, children with sexual behavior problems cause 13%–18% of all substantiated child sexual abuse, with another 22%–27% being committed by youths age 13–18 years (Pithers & Gray, 1998). Research demonstrates that 65%–95% of children with sexual behavior problems have been sexually abused themselves (Araji, 1997), with up to 56% of the children having been multiply abused (e.g., sexually and physically abused; Gray, Pithers, Busconi, & Houchens, 1999). As their sexual victimization is proximal to their sexual acting out against other children, we refer to these children as *children with sexual behavior problems* rather than child sex offenders. This term of reference is more than just a matter of semantics. These children exhibit a diverse array of developmental needs that reach far beyond problematic sexual behavior, yet simultaneously influence its occurrence (e.g., family violence, poverty, learning disabilities, psychiatric disorders; Gray et al., 1999). The phrase *children with sexual behavior problems* implies that, if only as a result of developmental differences, children must be treated differently from adolescent or adult perpetrators. Given the unique needs of these children, it may be ineffective, if not unethical, to use interventions designed for adults to address highly sexualized behaviors in children.

One may be tempted to conclude that highly sexualized, developmentally unexpected behaviors are short-lived symptoms manifested by sexually abused children. If children with sexual behavior problems quickly desist from such behaviors, there may be no need to respond to their troubling conduct, though the need to respond to the burdens of their victims would remain. Although research has not yet been conducted to determine the proportion of children with sexual behavior problems whose behaviors persist into adolescence or adulthood, and it is doubtless true that intrusive sexual behaviors remit spontaneously in some maltreated children, the best data demonstrate that many aftereffects of child sexual abuse can persist into adulthood (Classen, Fielf, Atkinson, & Spiegel, 1998). Maltreated children have a higher rate of arrest as juveniles and adults than their nonabused peers (Widom, 1995, 2000). Further evidence of the criminogenic effect of childhood sexual abuse comes from adult sex offenders, 40%–80% of whom disclose their own childhood abuse during treatment (Pithers, 1999). Rather than interpreting these data as condemning child victims to a life of crime, the findings reflect the importance of providing timely and effective interventions for child victims of abuse and neglect.

Research has consistently shown that sexually abusive behaviors have an earlier onset than expected. In a study of adult sex offenders conducted under a federal certificate of confidentiality, which permitted offenders to fully disclose their abusive interests without fear of criminal prosecution, 50% of the men who had abused boys acknowledged they were aware of this preference prior to age 16 (Abel et al., 1987; Abel & Rouleau, 1990). In a retrospective study with adolescent sexual abusers, Burton (2000) found that 46% of 243 adolescent sexual abusers reported that they had begun to engage in sexually abusive behaviors prior to age 12. Based on the most sensitive research, there is substantial reason to believe that the onset of sexually abusive behavior occurs much earlier in development than was once believed.

The early onset of sexually problematic behavior is evident in government statistics. In one American state, sexual abuse performed by children younger than 14 increased 300% from 1984 to 1994 (Pithers & Gray, 1998). Nationally, between 1980 and 1995, while juvenile arrests for crimes committed by children age 12 and younger increased 24%, arrests of children younger than 12 soared 125% for sex offenses (excluding rape) and

190% for rape. Thus, in children under 12, arrests for sexually abusive acts have increased at a greater rate than arrests for general crime. Of all juvenile arrests of children under 12, 29% are for a sex offense (Butts & Snyder, 1997).

Another difference between children with sexual behavior problems and adult sex offenders emerges powerfully from the research data: Children generally have fewer victims. In our research on 6–12-year-old children with sexual behavior problems, the mean number of victims was 2.1 (Gray et al., 1999). In marked contrast, adult pedophiles have self-reported, when their disclosures were protected by a federal certificate of confidentiality, a mean of 75.8 and a median of 7 child victims (Abel et al., 1987). Given the traumagenic and criminogenic influences of childhood sexual abuse, the data argue strongly for the importance of early intervention when sexually problematic behaviors are discovered.

Some administrators may argue that treating pedophiles who have sexually abused 75 children will yield greater benefit than treating children who have "only" 2 victims. The argument is based on fallacy. If an adult pedophile has abused 75 children, this is an argument for natural life incarceration, not treatment. In contrast, if one relies on their mean numbers of victims, effective treatment for a child with problematic sexual behavior may prevent roughly 73 children from being sexually abused. Little can be done to alter history once it has been written; much can be done to transform a child's future adolescence and adulthood.

It should not be surprising that it is difficult to accept that children cause a substantial proportion of the sexual victimization of other children. Even esteemed researchers can be reluctant to accept this reality. One anonymous scientist, in a peer review of a research proposal, commented that conducting research on children with sexual behavior problems "represented yet another example of a psychologist attempting to pathologize normal childhood development." Because of our social discomfort with sexuality and aggression, it may be challenging to acknowledge that children may be equally as likely to exhibit problematic sexual behaviors as troublesome eating, sleeping, or learning disorders.

Reluctance to accept children's sexual behavior problems may seem to preserve a world in which childhood may remain a time of protected innocence. In reality, it accomplishes precisely the opposite. An unwillingness to acknowledge children's problematic sexual behaviors precludes a meaningful response to a significant social problem. To alter the prevalence and course of this problem, we need to accept the reality that children are nearly as capable as adults of engaging in inappropriate sexual behaviors against children. We can then provide early interventions for children who have been abused and for their parents, rather than waiting until the first disruptive behaviors of youths have become engrained criminal transgressions in adolescents and adults. As the following data demonstrate, investing in prisons and programs for adults does not yield the same return as early interventions with children and adolescents.

AMERICA'S PREDOMINANT RESPONSE TO CHILD SEXUAL ABUSE

Adults cause 60% of all childhood sexual abuse, yet a vastly disproportionate amount of money is spent to respond to the abusive acts of adults compared with those of adolescents and children. In 1998, 94,000 adult sex offenders were among the 1.8 million inmates in American prisons, an increase of 62.1% in comparison with the number of sex offenders in prison in 1988 (Beck & Mumola, 1999). Estimating the annual cost of incarceration per inmate at $24,000, American taxpayers spent $2.256 billion to house sex offenders in prisons in 1998. The $2.256 billion covered housing costs for only 1 year and excluded the cost of any treatment to alter the offenders' interests in sexual aggression.

By relying on the "offense of record," Beck and Mumola (1999) likely have significantly underestimated the number of sex offenders in American prisons. Conviction for a sex offense is widely known to make an inmate the target of hostility from nonsexual offenders. As a result, defendants charged with sex offenses may seek to avoid being assaulted in prison by accepting a plea bargain that results in incarceration for a nonsexual offense. Comparing the "offense of record" with the "actual offense" of inmates in one state's prison system, Pithers (1982) found that the offense of record underestimated by 20% the number of inmates whose incarceration was the direct result of a sex offense. Applying this percentage to the 1998 prison census, an estimated 112,800 inmates may have been incarcerated as a direct result of a sex offense, and the annual cost of incarcerating sex offenders in America in 1998 would be $2.707 billion. Of course, incarcerated sex offenders tend to remain in prison longer than 1 year.

The growing number of sex offenders have helped to make corrective services the fastest growing item in the budgets of most American states from 1995 to 1997 (American Bar Association, 1994). In 1995, 150 new American prisons were constructed. The State of California constructed 21 prisons in 20 years from 1978 to 1998. California's prisons contain more inmates than those of France, Great Britain, Germany, Japan, Singapore, and the Netherlands combined (Schlosser, 1998). The prison system in California operates at double its capacity, and California will expend $2.4 billion in prison construction in the next 10 years to remain at that level of overcrowding. California spent more on prisons than on higher education in 1995.

Schlosser (1998) noted that Eisenhower, in his Presidential farewell speech on January 17, 1961, warned Americans to resist "a recurring temptation to feel that some spectacular and costly action could become the miraculous solution to all current difficulties." Schlosser also observed, "In the realm of psychology a [prison-industrial] complex is an overreaction to some perceived threat." The prison complexes quickly becoming a common feature of the American landscape evince the fact that we have not heeded Eisenhower's wise admonition. There are better responses to the perceived threat of most sex offenders than prison sentences and the extreme economic sacrifice they impose on society.

Few compassionate human beings will dispute that child sexual abuse is an egregious, reprehensible act. Few would argue that adults who sexually abuse children deserve punishment. Most who advocate incarceration for adult sex offenders do so because it precludes a known offender from abusing children. However, even with indeterminate commitments for individuals deemed sexual psychopaths, most incarcerated sex offenders will eventually be released. If conditions of confinement breed anger rather than constructive personal change, the memory of prison will promote future sex offending, not deter it. The best available data demonstrate that, without effective treatment during incarceration, sex offenders recidivate at the same rate as nonsexual offenders (Furby, Weinrott, & Blackshaw, 1989). Given the exorbitant costs of building and operating prisons, and the lack of any evidence that prison serves as a deterrent to crime once a sex offender has been released, a new, evidence-based solution must be pursued. The definition of insanity is continuing to do the same things and expecting different results.

How might America respond more effectively to adult perpetrators of child sexual abuse? In one American state, we created a systemic, statewide response to adult sex offenders. This response began prior to sentencing when a specialized probation officer and psychologist conducted separate, court-ordered evaluations of the convicted offender. These reports addressed (a) the offender's strengths and weaknesses; (b) juvenile and adult criminal and sexual history; (c) distal and proximal situational, emotional, behavioral, and cognitive risk factors associated with criminal acts; (d) special conditions of probation that might restrict the offender's access to risk situations associated with past offenses; (e) risk factors that could be addressed through specialized, mandatory treatment; and (f) appropriate placement (e.g., prison, probation, or alternate sanctions). On the basis of these reports, supervision and treatment plans were tailored to each offender's risks and needs.

This procedure resulted in 25% of all convicted sex offenders being sentenced to a lengthy incarceration to protect community safety. The remaining 75% received lengthy probationary sentences with special conditions that restricted their access to risk factors and that required the offender to participate in specialized treatment as directed by the probation officer. Rather than being incarcerated at an annual cost to taxpayers of $24,000, 75% of all convicted sex offenders remained gainfully employed, continued to pay taxes, were required to pay their own treatment costs, had to adhere to other special probation conditions, and were monitored by specialized probation officers for a lengthy period of time. Offenders who received probationary sentences but who refused to adhere to treatment requirements were subject to probation violation hearings that could lead to incarceration (Pithers, 1997).

The recidivism rate for sex offenders on probation who received specialized treatment and supervision was lower than that of incarcerated sex offenders, regardless of whether the incarcerated offenders had received treatment (Pithers, 1997). The cost of probation was $4,000 annually. Thus, in addition to lowering the recidivism rate, taxpayers saved $20,000 annually for each sex offender placed on probation rather than in prison. If 75% of the estimated 94,000 adult sex offenders incarcerated in America in 1998 had received probationary sentences (along with mandated treatment), the annual cost savings to American society would be $1.410 billion. The cost savings and reduction in recidivism make self-evident the importance of specialized probation services with carefully screened sex offenders (see this volume, chapter 15).

AMERICA'S RESPONSE TO ABUSED AND NEGLECTED CHILDREN

In lamentable contrast to America's investment in prisons, our response to abused and neglected children appears meager and inconsistent. As a case in point, one can examine the standards followed by some child protective services (CPS) agencies in America. Once a report of suspected child sexual abuse has been made to CPS, most might assume that an investigation would follow and, if abuse was substantiated, the child and family would receive services responsive to their needs. In some CPS agencies, the reality is different from the expectation.

A study of one CPS agency found that workers did not provide any service in nearly 60% of the confirmed cases of child abuse (Meddin & Hansen, 1985). The neglect of abused children may be more dire in urban areas. In one study in New York, 56% of all child abuse cases were closed the same day they were officially substantiated (Salovitz & Keys, 1988).

In a similar vein, after a decade of significant annual increases in the number of substantiated victims of child abuse, Vermont's CPS agency (Social and Rehabilitation Services; SRS) reported a 20% decrease in child abuse in a single calendar year. However, this reported decrease was not solely the result of a network of effective treatment for victims and perpetrators but also due to a legislated change in the act that regulated the practices of SRS. One year prior to the 20% decrease, the legislature eliminated the requirement that SRS investigate all reports of suspected child abuse in favor of an act that provided that SRS "may" investigate suspected abuse. This bureaucratic method of reducing child abuse is not in the best interests of the children and families the agency is charged to protect. One might speculate the social outcry that would result if legislation was approved providing that police "may" investigate reported crimes when they choose to do so and, as a result, police informed every fifth caller that their victimization was not sufficiently severe to warrant their attention.

Our intention is not to indict CPS agencies. CPS line staff generally are dedicated and overworked. CPS workers face enormous challenges and emotional demands every workday. Greater funding is needed for CPS agencies so that they can meet their responsibilities to children and families. Enacting legislation to reduce their responsibility to abused children, rather than providing necessary increases in funding, is a deception, not an answer.

ETIOLOGY OF SEXUAL BEHAVIOR PROBLEMS

In one study, the age at which a child was first sexually abused was the strongest predictor of sexual behavior problems in children (McClellan et al., 1996). After categorizing children into one of five groups based on the age at which they were first sexually abused, McClellan et al. found that the prevalence of sexually inappropriate behavior ranged from 42.1% in children who were first abused when 13–17 years old to 79.5% in the children first abused when 0–3 year olds. When sexual abuse occurred during early childhood, children were also more likely to have experienced (a) a higher rate of physical abuse, chronic sexual abuse, and neglect by parents; (b) more family disruptions; and (c) a higher number of total victimizers.

Several findings have emerged consistently from our research program on children with sexual behavior problems (Gray et al., 1997, 1999; Gray & Pithers, 1993; Pithers, Gray, Busconi, & Houchens, 1998a, 1998b; Pithers, Gray, & Davis, in press). The children often have been catastrophically maltreated, having been abused by a mean of 2.3 perpetrators. More than half of the children (56%) have been multiply abused (sexually and physically). Further confirming the proportion of childhood sexual abuse performed by children, 18% of children had been abused by a child 5–10 years old, and an additional 15% were sexually maltreated by an older child or adolescent 11–18 years old. Maltreatment permeated their extended family, with 72% of the families containing at least one additional victim of sexual abuse and 62% having at least one additional perpetrator. The mean age at which the children were first abused was 4 years, precluding the child's opportunity to acquire a substantial foundation of normal experiences before encountering trauma. Special educational services were received by 59% of the children with sexual behavior problems, a significantly greater proportion than the 10% of all 6–12-year-olds receiving such services in America (U.S. Department of Education, 1994). Psychiatric diagnoses were common, with 96% of the children meeting the criteria for at least one *Diagnostic and Statistical Manual of Mental Disorders* (4th ed., *DSM–IV*; American Psychiatric Association, 1994) psychiatric disorder. Of the children who had been psychiatrically diagnosed, 74% were dually diagnosed. Children with sexual behavior problems most commonly acted out sexually with their siblings (35%) or friends (34%). Children who had been maltreated by more perpetrators tended to create more victims.

The children's families displayed many markers of chronic distress, including high rates of poverty (79% of the families) and parental arrest for criminal behavior (20%). More than half of the children (53%) had witnessed violence in their own home, with one parent hitting, punching, or striking the other. An objective measure of attachment identified an impaired parent–child attachment, with parents of children with sexual behavior problems being less attached to their child than 85% of all parents. Thus, parents and families of children with sexual behavior problems manifest characteristics that deter children's recovery from abuse and that exacerbate self-management problems.

In summary, children with sexual behavior problems exhibited an array of functional impairments commonly associated with maltreatment, including psychiatric and learning disorders, that may compromise their ability to make meaningful gains from standard forms of treatment. Given the high levels of distress in the families, maximally effective treatment must involve the children and their caregivers, not the child alone. By doing so, it may be possible to foster the creation of a new family culture that promotes a problem-preventing lifestyle. Assisting families to attain a prevention lifestyle requires an intervention that steps beyond the boundary of the therapy suite and enters the realms in which the families spend most of their time: their home, school, and community.

CONVERGENCE OF POSTTRAUMATIC STRESS DISORDER AND CONDUCT DISORDER IN ABUSED CHILDREN WITH DISRUPTIVE BEHAVIORS

Posttraumatic stress disorder (PTSD) is a common consequence of childhood sexual abuse. In one study, 48% of all sexually abused children met the *DSM–IV* criteria for PTSD (McLeer, Deblinger, Atkins, Ralphe, & Foa, 1988), and most sexually abused children manifest behaviors associated with at least one PTSD symptom cluster (McLeer et al., 1988).

One meta-analysis found only two symptoms that reliably differentiated child sexual abuse victims from nonabused children seeking clinical services from outpatient psychiatric clinics: a higher prevalence of PTSD and highly sexualized behaviors (Kendall-Tackett, Williams, & Finkelhor, 1993).

As some theorists have posited that PTSD might inhibit development of sexual behavior problems in abused children (Berliner, 1991), it may seem incongruous that child sexual abuse precipitates both PTSD and highly sexualized behaviors. Perhaps PTSD alone might inhibit sexualized behaviors, whereas the conjunction of PTSD and other factors (e.g., exposure to violence, conduct disorder) may be associated with highly sexualized behaviors.

Pithers et al. (2001) compared matched samples of abused children who had exhibited problematic sexual behaviors and abused children who had not acted out sexually. They found that the children with sexual behavior problems had (a) been sexually abused by more perpetrators, (b) a greater likelihood of having been physically abused, (c) a greater diagnosis of conduct disorder in conjunction with a high degree of trauma, (d) a higher mean score on a scale measuring the frequency of the children's sexual behaviors, and (e) higher mean scores on scales measuring internalizing (e.g., withdrawn, anxious) and externalizing (e.g., aggressive) behaviors. Abused children who did not display sexualized behaviors were more likely to respond submissively to provocation. Parents of children with sexual behavior problems were more likely to have an impaired attachment to their child than the parents of abused children who had not acted out. Pithers et al. concluded that PTSD and conduct disorder may share a common etiology in children with sexual behavior problems.

Data from a study that generated a taxonomy of children with sexual behavior problems (Pithers et al., 1998b) revealed that the comorbidity of PTSD and conduct disorder was 72.7% in the *highly traumatized* child type. Highly traumatized children were the youngest child type, yet had the highest mean number of victims of any child type. Highly traumatized children had been abused by a higher mean total of sexual and physical abusers than any other child type. Highly traumatized children had a short interval between their own maltreatment and their first instance of sexual acting out. Highly traumatized children's parents reported feeling significantly less attached to their children than any other child type.

A substantial body of research demonstrates that PTSD emerges most readily in individuals who have been subjected to previous stressors. Prior to their sexual abuse, children with sexual behavior problems typically have encountered a wide array of significant stressors, including physical victimization, exposure to violence, poverty, impaired parent–child attachment (which has been associated with inattentive parenting; Abidin, 1995), parental criminal conviction, and frequent expression of unmodulated anger

(Gray et al., 1999). The same array of variables has frequently been associated with the emergence of conduct disorder in children (Patterson, 1982).

Factors common to families of children with PTSD, conduct disorder, and children with sexual behavior problems include (a) poverty, (b) child's observation of violence within the family, (c) family members who have been arrested for criminal conduct, (d) a history of sexual abuse within the extended family, (e) substance abuse, (f) parental history of abuse or neglect during their own childhood, (g) impaired parent–child attachment, and (h) high levels of state and trait anger in the parents.

If at least one type of child with sexual behavior problems (i.e., highly traumatized; Pithers et al., 1998b) has comorbid PTSD and conduct disorder, he or she may vacillate between extremes of withdrawal and acting out. This hypothesis has been supported by Steiner (1999), who identified four distinct groups of children who express trauma in different ways. The most relevant of the four groups to this chapter consists of children who are both conduct disordered and high on internalizing behaviors (e.g., withdrawal). Steiner reported that these children were the most highly traumatized of his four groups. However, these children also had a high degree of restraint, enabling them to function in the face of distress. This finding is vital to comprehending how highly traumatized children are also able to act out aggressively. Their ability to function cognitively while feeling highly distressed makes it possible for them to engage in planned and purposeful behavior that is harmful to others, such as sexual abuse.

If the hypothesis holds true that PTSD and conduct disorder have a high degree of comorbidity in at least one type of child with sexual behavior problems, selective interventions may be used with the children and their caregivers. Such an intervention would need to incorporate elements of treatment protocols for PTSD and conduct disorder. Of at least equal importance, intervention with the children and families will need to assist the family to alter its lifestyle. Interventions that respond only to the psychopathological aspects of the child's and family's functioning are almost certain to be found wanting.

THE STEP PROGRAM: AN EMPIRICALLY VALIDATED INTERVENTION FOR CHILDREN WITH SEXUAL BEHAVIOR PROBLEMS AND THEIR PARENTS

Many treatment providers grew up in middle-class homes. When family members in such homes gathered around the dinner table each night, our families discussed the events of each person's day. We discovered the difficulty, followed by relief, of talking about troubling events. We experienced the soothing emotional balm of support from family members who love us and, in turn, the warm satisfaction derived in offering our compassion to them. As a result of the fortune of our childhood experiences, in our adult lives the process of disclosing stresses, and accepting and giving support, seems as natural as taking a seat at the dinner table.

Many of the families with whom we work have not had similar experiences. There are numerous indications that the children with sexual behavior problems and their families are highly distressed, and, depending on their age, income, and personal resourcefulness, families of children with sexual behavior problems may haven fallen through the holes in the social safety net.

In our research, although few of the families had been referred by a CPS agency, most had previously been involved with CPS because of their child's abuse or neglect. If one universal sentiment existed among the families, it was their disdain for the CPS agency. The parents felt harshly criticized by CPS procedures that focused on finding faults before seeking to build on strengths. The parents felt put under a microscope, objectified, dehumanized, and denigrated. As a consequence, many families entered therapy with a palpable distrust and resentment, even though the treatment program was not associated with a CPS agency.

Families in this research were under no legal mandate to attend therapy. The only incentives they received to remain in therapy were support and respect that empowered the families to build on their strengths and, through that process, address their shortcomings. Clients needed to know confidently that treatment providers respected their human dignity, personal rights, and the strength that resides within distressed families regardless of the nature of their problems. A dismissive statement by even the most compassionate professional may last a lifetime in the memory of a distressed family.

Our research was known formally as the Vermont Sexual Abuse Research Project but became known as the "STEP Program" because our treatment model discussed, as one of its elements, "Safety Steps" that can be taken to help children with sexual behavior problems refrain from further harmful acts. The final treatment session associated with this research was conducted in 1996, and our research program has since moved to Australia. The continued existence of several STEP Programs in Vermont represents a sincere compliment to the integrity of our work.

In the STEP Program, families participated in one of two interventions. Sex Abuse Specific Treatment (SAST) adhered to a modified relapse prevention framework (Gray & Pithers, 1993; Pithers, 1990), including the creation of sexual safety rules and a safety team. The second treatment was an expressive therapy designed by a panel of national experts as the modal form of therapy conducted with sexualized children. Therapy sessions involved $1\frac{1}{2}$-hour parallel child and parent groups. Children's groups were conducted separately for children ages 6–9 and 10–12 years. Treatment duration was 32 weeks.

As little leverage existed to mandate treatment of children with sexual behavior problems, it should be immediately evident that treatment of these children does not follow the same rules and expectations as treatment with juvenile or adult sex offenders. Juvenile and adult sex offenders are more likely to have (a) a longer history of positive reinforcement (e.g., orgasm fused with abusive behaviors) and negative reinforcement from abusive behaviors (e.g., relief from negative emotional states), (b) a constellation of abusive fantasies that have been sculpted over time, (c) a disordered sexual arousal pattern, (d) a repertoire of cognitive distortions justifying abuse, and (e) less of a naturally occurring social support system (e.g., school personnel, parents, and other family). Thus, children with sexual behavior problems have different treatment needs than adolescent and adult sexual abusers. However, the most important reason why interventions for children with sexual behavior problems must differ from those of juveniles and adults is obvious: These are children.

As children, the targets and methods of intervention differ from those used with adolescents and adults. One must consider the educational needs and achievement of each child. Parental characteristics that promote or inhibit therapeutic change may coexist within the same parent. Therapeutic goals must be devised in light of developmental norms. Meaningful modeling and connectedness can have a strong influence on child development.

EMPIRICALLY DERIVED TYPES OF CHILDREN WITH SEXUAL BEHAVIOR PROBLEMS

Every treatment outcome study finds that the magnitude and valence of treatment effects differ across participants. To determine the children for whom SAST was most effective, we needed to discover whether different types of children with sexual behavior problems exist. This research has been detailed elsewhere (Pithers et al., 1998b), but a synopsis of the findings follows.

Five distinct types of children with sexual behavior problems emerged from a theory-driven cluster analysis: nonsymptomatic, highly traumatized, abuse reactive, rule breakers, and conduct disordered. Significant differences among the five child types existed on a large number of historical, diagnostic, behavioral, and demographic variables, including number of victims, degree of aggression used during sexual acting out, sexual penetration, psychiatric diagnosis, and internalizing and externalizing behaviors (see Table 13.1).

Clinical relevance of the child types was examined by analyzing

TABLE 13.1
Significant Differences Between Five Types of Children With Sexual
Behavior Problems

Variable	Significant differences between child types		
Child's age at intake	1 > 2, 3, 5	4 > 3	
% males in type	1, 5 > 2, 4		
No. of sexual abusers to child	3 > 1		
No. of physical abusers to child	3, 5 > 1, 2, 4		
No. of emotional abusers to child	3 > 1, 4		
Total no. of abusers to child	3 > 1, 2, 4, 5	4, 5 > 1	
Additional sex abusers in extended family	4 > 1, 3		
Age/onset of sexual behavior problem	1, 4 > 3	1 > 2, 5	
Years from abuse to behavior problem	4 > 5		
No. of sexual victims by child	5 > 1, 2, 4	3 > 2	
M sex aggression rating	1, 4, 5 > 2, 3		
% high in sex aggressive (>4)	1, 4 > 2, 3		
% children engaging in penetration	1, 5 > 2, 3, 4		
M no. of penetrative acts	1 > 2, 3, 4, 5		
M no. of psychiatric diagnoses	3, 5 > 1, 2, 4	1, 4 > 2	
% conduct disorder (CD) diagnosis	1, 5 > 2, 3		
DSM–IV CD: aggression	1, 3, 4, 5 > 2		
DSM–IV CD: property damage	4 > 2		
DSM–IV CD: deceitfulness	1, 3, 4, 5 > 2		
% ODD diagnosis	5 > 1, 2, 3, 4		
% PTSD diagnosis	3 > 1, 2, 4, 5		
% ADHD diagnosis	3, 5 > 2		
ECBI intensity score	4 > 1, 2, 3, 5		
CSBI-3 score	4 > 1, 2, 3, 5		
CBCL Total T-score	4 > 1, 2, 3, 5	5 > 1, 2	3 > 1, 2
CBCL Internalizing T-score	4 > 1, 2, 3		
CBCL Externalizing T-score	4 > 1, 2, 3, 5	5 > 1, 2	
CBCL Sex Problems T-score	4 > 1, 2, 3, 5	3, 5 > 1	
TRF Total T-score	1, 4 > 2		
TRF Eternalizing T-score	4, 5 > 2, 3		
PSI parental attachment to child[a]	3, 4 > 1, 2, 5		
PSI child demandingness	4 > 1, 2		
PSI-child domain score	4 > 1		
STAIC–trait anxiety	3 > 1		

Note. The five types of children are 1 = sexually aggressive; 2 = nondisordered; 3 = highly traumatized; 4 = rule breakers; and 5 = abuse reactive. *DSM–IV = Diagnostic and Statistical Manual of Mental Disorders* (4th ed.); ODD = oppositional defiant disorder; PTSD = posttraumatic stress disorder; ECBI = Eyberg Child Behavior Inventory; CSBI-3 = Child Sexual Behavior Inventory–3; CBCL = Child Behavior Checklist; TRF = Teacher's Report Form; PSI = Parenting Stress Index; STAIC = State–Trait Anxiety Inventory for Children.
[a] Higher score signifies lower level of attachment.

treatment-induced change on a measure of sexualized behaviors in children: the Child Sexual Behavior Inventory–3 (CSBI–3; Friedrich, 1995). The analysis revealed that, after only 16 weeks in treatment, three of the five child types (i.e., highly traumatized, abuse reactive, and rule breakers) derived significantly more benefit from the SAST than from expressive therapy. SAST was most effective with highly traumatized children, 75% of whom manifested clinically significant change (i.e., a reduction of >2 standard deviations from their intake CSBI score). The other two child types, conduct disordered and nonsymptomatic, benefited similarly from SAST and expressive therapy.

Our research demonstrated that distinct types of children with sexual behavior problems exist, that they can be distinguished on a wide range of clinically relevant variables, and that identification of child type is relevant to choice of treatment modalities and outcome. Despite this finding, children with sexual behavior problems tend to be referred to the most intensive treatment regardless of their personal or familial characteristics. Based on our own research (Pithers et al., 1998b) and supported by the research of others (Huke, Scovel, & Magnuson, 1999), we strongly believe that it is not advisable to refer all children and families to intensive treatment. Some children and families may require lengthy and intensive intervention, but many may benefit from brief, educational interventions.

We offer the following tentative suggestions for treatment selection, but additional research is needed before these suggestions might be considered clinical guidelines. Nonsymptomatic children do not appear to need intensive intervention and, at least with some of these children, it may be counterproductive. Nonsymptomatic children exhibited no evidence of profound or enduring pathology. Instead of intensive treatment for these children, intervention should focus on parenting skills and the context within which the family lives. Effective intervention might consist of parental training to foster closer oversight of children's behaviors, positive disciplinary practices, boundary setting within the extended family, and an educational program about the children's premature or developing sexuality. The children may need to be seen briefly in formal therapy, if at all.

In contrast to nonsymptomatic children, sexually aggressive children exhibited the hallmark characteristics of early-onset, lifelong conduct disorder that has a poor prognosis. Parents of sexually aggressive children exercised little oversight over their children's behaviors. An effective intervention for sexually aggressive children may need to focus on parental or ecological characteristics that impede parental attachment to their child and promote coercive parent–child interactions. It is plausible that the parents of sexually aggressive children witnessed their children's unacceptable behaviors but elected not to disclose it to a child care agency, possibly to evade a closer examination of their own conduct. If so, implementing interventions that might prevent the development of such a predisposition would be important (e.g., home visiting programs). Based on an analysis of risk factors for child abuse (e.g., low birth weight, history of parental violence or substance abuse), multicomponent home-visiting programs, which offer support, education, and intervention, may play a vital role in fostering a more prosocial course (Kitzman et al., 2000).

In our experience, favorable treatment outcomes will occur with most children and families if treatment (a) involves, at a minimum, the child and the child's primary caregiver; (b) is delivered in a parallel group format (i.e., separate and simultaneous groups for children and caregivers); (c) is tailored to the developmental needs of the child and family; (d) is responsive to the strengths and deficits evident in each child; (e) promotes a high level of participation by the child, family, and therapist in the process of change; (f) extends beyond the therapy suite to include the participation of professionals in schools and other social agencies, as well as trusted others; (g) is conducted by service providers with graduate degrees in recognized health care professions; and (h) is provided by health care professionals who have been trained to competence in this therapeutic model and who receive ongoing clinical supervision.

CONCLUSION

We believe that developing carefully designed treatments for specific types of children and families is important. At least of equal importance is the spirit in which the work is conducted. Professionals dedicated to preventing child maltreatment must nurture respect for the preciousness of children in every citizen, among all families, in every school, inside the medical community, among law enforcement professionals, in the therapeutic milieu, within social services agencies, and throughout the continuum of care. The principle of respect for the wondrous potential of children must *resonate* loudly. Children sense its presence in others, feed off its rhythm, and may adopt respect for others as their own song. Belief in the potential of children must endure, indeed, must grow stronger, when we encounter the numb face of extensive maltreatment, the ravaging effects of poverty on the human spirit, the haunting memory of domestic violence, the bone-chill of rejection by those whom society says should love us the most, or the silence of parental absence. Recognition of the preciousness of children must be modeled again and again and again in each act of social service, no matter how objective or administrative it might appear. Compassion for the whole person, whether overwhelmed or resilient, must win the day. The spirit with which we conduct our work is an ingredient in our effectiveness, particularly when the spirits of the people with whom we work ache. Never give up hope that people, most of all children, can make dramatic changes in their lives.

REFERENCES

Abel, G. G., Becker, J. V., Mittelman, M. S., Cunningham-Rathner, J., Rouleau, J. L., & Murphy, W. D. (1987). Self-reported sex crimes of nonincarcerated paraphiliacs. *Journal of Interpersonal Violence, 2,* 3–25.

Abel, G. G., & Rouleau, J. L. (1990). The nature and extent of sexual assault. In W. L. Marshall, D. R. Laws, & H. E. Barbaree (Eds.), *The handbook of sexual assault: Issues, theories, and treatment of the offender* (pp. 9–21). New York: Plenum.

Abidin, R. R. (1995). *Parenting stress index* (3rd ed.). Charlottesville, VA: Pediatric Psychology Press.

American Bar Association. (1994). *The state of criminal justice: An annual report.* Washington, DC: Author.

American Psychiatric Association. (1994). *Diagnostic and statistical manual of mental disorders (4th ed.).* Washington, DC: Author.

Araji, S. K. (1997). *Sexually aggressive children: Coming to understand them.* Thousand Oaks, CA: Sage.

Beck, A. J., & Mumola, C. J. (1999). *Prisoners in 1998.* Washington, DC: Bureau of Justice Statistics.

Berliner, L. (1991). Effects of sexual abuse on children. *Violence Update, 1,* 10–11.

Burton, D. (2000). Were adolescent sexual offenders children with sexual behavior problems? *Sexual Abuse: A Journal of Research and Treatment, 12,* 37–48.

Butts, J. A., & Snyder, H. N. (1997, September). The youngest delinquents: Offenders under age 15. *Juvenile Justice Bulletin,* 1–11.

Classen, C., Fielf, N. P., Atkinson, A., & Spiegel, D. (1998). Representations of self in women sexually abused in childhood. *Child Abuse and Neglect, 22,* 997–1004.

Friedrich, W. N. (1995). The clinical use of the Child Sexual Behavior Inventory: Frequently asked questions. *The APSAC Advisor, 8,* 1–20.

Furby, L., Weinrott, M., & Blackshaw, L. (1989). Sex offender recidivism: A review. *Psychological Bulletin, 105,* 3–30.

Gray, A., Busconi, A., Houchens, P., & Pithers, W. D. (1997). Children with sexual behavior problems and their caregivers: Demographics, functioning, and clinical patterns. *Sexual Abuse: A Journal of Research and Treatment, 9,* 267–290.

Gray, A. S., & Pithers, W. D. (1993). Relapse prevention with sexually abusive adolescents: Expanding treatment and supervision. In H. E. Barbaree, W. L. Marshall, & S. Hudson (Eds.), *The juvenile sexual offender* (pp. 289–319). New York: Guilford.

Gray, A., Pithers, W. D., Busconi, A., & Houchens, P. (1999). Developmental and etiological characteristics of children with sexual behavior problems: Treatment implications. *Child Abuse and Neglect, 23,* 601–621.

Huke, S. C., Scovel, D., & Magnuson, L. (1999, October). *Children with sexual behavior problems: Empirical support for clinically relevant subtypes.* Paper presented at the annual conference of the Association for the Assessment and Treatment of Sexual Abusers, Orlando, FL.

Kendall-Tackett, K. A., Williams, L. M., & Finkelhor, D. (1993). Impact of sexual abuse on children: A review and synthesis of recent empirical studies. *Psychological Bulletin, 113,* 164–180.

Kitzman, H., Olds, D. L., Sidora, K., Henderson, C. R., Hanks, C., Cole, R., et al. (2000). Enduring effects of nurse home visitation on maternal life course: A 3-year follow-up of a randomized trial. *Journal of the American Medical Association, 283,* 1983–1989.

McClellan, J., McCurry, C., Ronnei, M., Adams, J., Eisner, A., & Storck, M. (1996). Age of onset of sexual abuse: Relationship to sexually inappropriate behaviors. *Journal of the American Academy of Child and Adolescent Psychiatry, 34,* 1375–1383.

McLeer, S., Deblinger, E., Atkins, M., Ralphe, D., & Foa, E. (1988). Posttraumatic stress disorder in sexually abused children. *Journal of the American Academy of Child and Adolescent Psychiatry, 27,* 650–654.

Meddin, J., & Hansen, I. (1985). The services provided during a child abuse and/ or neglect case investigation and the barriers that exist to service provision. *Child Abuse and Neglect, 9,* 175–182.

Patterson, G. R. (1982). *Coercive family process: A social learning approach.* Eugene, OR: Castalia.

Pithers, W. D. (1982). [Tally of sex offenders in the Vermont Department of Corrections: Underestimation resulting from official records versus analysis of criminal behavior.] Unpublished data.

Pithers, W. D. (1990). Relapse prevention: A method for enhancing maintenance of therapeutic change in sexual aggressors. In W. L. Marshall, D. R. Laws, & H. E. Barbaree (Eds.), *The handbook of sexual assault: Issues, theories, and treatment of the offender.* New York: Plenum.

Pithers, W. D. (1997, November). *Treatment of adult sex offenders.* Paper presented at the meeting of the Center on Sex Offender Management, Washington, DC.

Pithers, W. D. (1999). Empathy: Definition, enhancement, and relevance to the self-management of sexual abusers. *Journal of Interpersonal Violence, 14,* 257–284.

Pithers, W. D., & Gray, A. (1998). The other half of the story: Children with sexual behavior problems. *Psychology, Public Policy, and Law, 4,* 200–217.

Pithers, W. D., Gray, A., Busconi, A., & Houchens, P. (1998a). Caregivers of children with sexual behavior problems: Psychological and familial functioning. *Child Abuse and Neglect, 22,* 43–55.

Pithers, W. D., Gray, A., Busconi, A., & Houchens, P. (1998b). Children with sexual behavior problems: Identification of five distinct child types and related treatment considerations. *Child Maltreatment, 3,* 384–407.

Pithers, W. D., Gray, A., & Davis, M. E. (in press). *Children with sexual behavior problems: Assessment and treatment of the children and their caregivers.* American Psychological Association: Washington, DC.

Pithers, W. D., Sonderegger, N., Gray, A., Busconi, A., Houchens, P., & Friedrich, W. N. (2001). *Factors differentiating sexually abused children who display sexual behavior problems from those who do not.* Manuscript submitted for publication.

Salovitz, B., & Keys, D. (1988). Is child protective service still a service? *Protecting Children, 5,* 17–23.

Schlosser, E. (1998, December). The prison-industrial complex. *Atlantic Monthly, 282,* 51–77.

Steiner, H. (1999, October). *Modern approaches to the management of disruptive behavior disorders.* Workshop presented at the Management and Intervention of Adolescents With Disruptive Behavior Disorders conference, Barrett Center, Brisbane, Australia.

U.S. Department of Education. (1994). *Sixteenth annual report to Congress on the implementation of the Individuals With Disabilities Education Act.* Washington, DC: Author.

Widom, C. S. (1995). Victims of childhood sexual abuse: Later criminal consequences. In *National Institute of Justice: Research in brief* (pp. 1–8). Washington, DC: National Institute of Justice.

Widom, C. S. (2000, January). Childhood victimization: Early adversity, later pathology. *National Institute of Justice Journal,* 3–9.

14

CHEMICAL CASTRATION OF SEX OFFENDERS: TREATMENT OR PUNISHMENT?

ROBERT D. MILLER

Over the years, various legal approaches have been used to deal with the perplexing problem of sexually violent offenders, including civil commitment with forced treatment, largely psychodynamic therapy and behavioral treatment. However, these treatment approaches proved largely ineffective in reducing recidivism (Furby, Weinrott, & Blackshaw, 1989; Group for the Advancement of Psychiatry, 1977; Harris, 1995). Consequently, these civil commitment approaches fell into disfavor and were repealed[1] or little used after the 1970s (Erickson, 1995; Group for the Advancement of Psychiatry, 1977).

Portions of this chapter were published in Miller (1998). Copyright © 1998 by the American Psychological Association (APA). Reprinted with permission.
I would like to thank Kelli Evans of the California ACLU, Katherine Becker of the American Psychiatric Association's Division of Governmental Relations, and the staff of the *American Bar Association Journal* for providing information allowing me to track the chemical castration bills discussed in this chapter.
[1]Most mentally disordered sex offender laws of the 1950s were eventually repealed because of civil libertarian attacks on indefinite commitment, their high cost compared with imprisonment, and minimal reduction in recidivism with the psychodynamic therapy

In the late 1980s and early 1990s, however, there has been a resurgence of interest in confining sex offenders for "treatment" (see this volume, chapter 1). Because of the failures of previous treatments, one technique that has caught on recently has been treatment with medications that reduce the intensity of sexual drives (Miller, 1998). Requiring offenders to take prescribed medication as a condition of probation, parole, or conditional release from insanity commitments is not new (*United States v. Bryant*, 1978). What is new about these "chemical castration" laws is that they *require* judges to impose treatment for entire classes of offenders defined solely by crime committed. Often judges order offenders to take these drugs without any medical evaluations to determine if the medications are clinically indicated, safe, or effective for a particular offender. These laws remove all judicial discretion in determining whether the treatment is medically safe or appropriate or whether it is likely to be effective; the medications must be a part of any probation or parole plan for all offenders in the prescribed legal class.

This chapter discusses the history of biological treatments for sexual violence and the legal responses to them. After discussing surgical castration, I focus on evolving techniques of chemical castration. I then examine the effectiveness of these drugs and their side effects. Recent legislative efforts to impose chemical castration on sex offenders are then discussed, followed by a discussion of the medical, legal, and ethical problems these new statutes raise.

BIOLOGICAL TREATMENTS THAT AFFECT SEXUAL BEHAVIOR

Surgical Sterilization and Castration

Under the "eye-for-an-eye" principle, rapists have been castrated as punishment for centuries. As torture and mutilation lost favor as legitimate methods of punishment, the retributive justification for castration virtually disappeared, to be replaced in the first part of the 20th century by eugenic sterilization (*Buck v. Bell*, 1927; Cynkar, 1981; Stuerup, 1972). Thirteen states continue to have eugenic sterilization laws, although they are rarely used (Cynkar, 1981).

Surgical castration is occasionally used to reduce inappropriate sexual behavior. However, because the procedure is irreversible and is not always effective (Cynkar, 1981), and because reversible medications are now widely available, it has largely fallen into disfavor (Letterie & Fox, 1990).

treatments available at the time. The remaining laws were little used after the 1970s; although new behavioral techniques had been developed, they also have not proved effective in reducing recidivism for incarcerated sex offenders. (See this volume, chapter 5, for a discussion of treatment efficacy for sex offenders.)

In 1910, the U.S. Supreme Court referred to castration (as opposed to sterilization) as "barbaric" and disproportionate to the offense involved (*Weems v. United States*, 1910). The courts have also generally frowned on forced surgical sterilization (*Davis v. Berry*, 1914/1917; *Mickle v. Henricks*, 1918; *Skinner v. Oklahoma*, 1941; *State v. Brown*, 1985; *Williams v. Smith*, 1918). Coerced surgical sterilization and castration have virtually disappeared, only to be replaced by recent chemical castration laws, which provide for sex-drive-reducing medications as an alternative.

Chemical Castration

In 1944, Foote first reported the use of progesteronal hormonal compounds with men. The progesterone agent medroxyprogesterone acetate (MPA) was first tried with sex offenders in the United States by Money and his colleagues (Money, 1970, 1972). Its clinically appropriate use is to reduce abnormal levels of sex drive or sexual fantasies to normal levels, to permit patients to control their socially prohibited urges, and to allow them relief from the intrusive fantasies and urges that they have great difficulty in controlling; it is *not* to render them impotent. Berlin and Malin (1991) reported that over 2,000 patients treated with MPA had a sexual recidivism rate of less than 3% over 10 years. It is important to note that the percentage of sex offenders with abnormal levels of sex drive or fantasies is small, perhaps 10% of offenders. Thus, the medications would not be effective with the remaining offenders unless used in such large doses that it would castrate them.

MPA works by accelerating the breakdown and elimination of testosterone and by inhibiting the secretion of luteinizing hormone, which stimulates the testes to secrete testosterone (Bradford, 1983). Many offenders with abnormally high sex drives do not have abnormally high levels of testosterone but still respond to the treatment. Experts believe that the testosterone receptors may be unusually sensitive in such offenders.

A number of side effects have been reported from these drugs: weight gain, hyperinsulinemic response to glucose, diabetes mellitus, irregular gallbladder functioning, diverticulitis, fatigue or lethargy, testicular atrophy, sweats, nightmares, dyspnea, hypogonadism, hot and cold flashes, leg cramps, hypertension, thrombosis, and insomnia (Berlin & Meinecke, 1981; Bradford, 1983). All side effects are reported to disappear after discontinuation of MPA, although it may take up to 6 months for full sexual functioning to return.

Another class of medications has recently shown promise in the treatment of offenders with abnormally intense or frequent sexual drives. Synthetic analogues of gonadotropin-releasing hormones (GnRH; those that stimulate the production of testosterone) reduce levels of testosterone by inhibiting the secretion of natural GnRH. Preliminary anecdotal reports appear promising, and side effects appear to be limited to reduction in size of the testes, erectile failure, decreased libido, and decreased body hair (Robert, 1992; Rosier & Witztum, 1998; Thibaut, Cordier, & Kuhn, 1996).

Other medications also reduce excessive sexual drives. Most promising are the selective serotonin reuptake inhibitor antidepressants; there is mounting evidence that they are also effective in reducing excessive sexual drive or fantasies (Bradford, 1996). It is important to recognize (as too many legislators have not) that the only clinically appropriate use of all these medications with sex offenders is to reduce abnormally excessive sexual drives or fantasies, not to render patients impotent. Although none of the laws specify how the medications should be used, "chemical castration" implies a medically inappropriate use of the medications, because their goal is social control, not treatment, and because the laws analogize the medications with surgical castration.

RECENT LEGISLATIVE EFFORTS TO REQUIRE CHEMICAL CASTRATION

California was the first state to pass a law requiring certain convicted sex offenders to submit to treatment with MPA as a condition of probation (California Penal Code § 645, 1996). A number of other states have followed suit. Most of these statutes are simply clones of the California legislation, although some consider legal issues in greater detail. As of the date of this writing, three other similar bills have passed (Florida, Georgia, and Montana), nine others have been defeated or were withdrawn (Colorado, Hawaii, Iowa, Maryland, Mississippi, New Hampshire, New Mexico, Oklahoma, and Tennessee), and two were ultimately not reintroduced (Maine and Texas). Wisconsin ultimately passed a much more reasonable statute (Wis. Rev. Stat. § 980.12.062(b)(c), 980.08.(4)(5), and 980.12(2), 1998) that places the responsibility for deciding on treatment with the mental health department; however, it authorizes the use of these drugs only after a medical evaluation has established that this treatment is appropriate. It also provides for the department to contract with community agencies to fund services, including antiandrogen treatment.

Of the 28 bills introduced, only 6 require any medical evaluation before the treatment is imposed (Colorado, Florida, Iowa, Nevada, Washington, and Wisconsin), and none except Wisconsin's require a judge to consider medical advice in ordering the treatment. While all list MPA as a drug that can satisfy the probation conditions, several mention alternative medications. Six bills (California, Colorado, Hawaii, New Mexico, Oklahoma, and South Carolina) do recognize the dilemma in which such laws may place physicians by providing that courts cannot force them to prescribe the medications against their wills. California's is the only one of the five that have passed that includes the exception.

None of the bills clearly define what is meant by "chemical castration"; from the tenor of the bills (except Wisconsin's), the most likely interpretation is that the medications should be used to render offenders completely impotent, which, of course, is the pharmacological equivalent of surgical castration, although reversible.

Offenders can reject the proposed treatment if they elect to complete their sentences in prison; but if they wish to be released before the end of their sentences, they must comply with the treatment. Although this treatment is mandated, no provisions are made to ensure that professionals are actually available who are knowledgeable in its use and willing to administer it and monitor the offenders on these drugs.

DISCUSSION

The requirement that whole classes of (legally defined) sex offenders take powerful medications as an absolute condition of parole or probation, without medical evaluation to determine efficacy or safety, raises serious clinical concerns about the medical interests of the patient, informed consent, privacy, and the integrity of the medical profession itself. In addition, forced administration of sex-drive-reducing medications raises (or ought to raise) legal concerns about constitutional issues of due process, privacy, and cruel and unusual punishment. This section will present these concerns, and argue that since the legal community (including legislatures and too many courts) does not appear to be interested in the clinically appropriate treatment of sex offenders, it is up to clinicians to advocate for that treatment.

Medical Interests of the Patient

The Task Force Report of the American Psychiatric Association (American Psychiatric Association, 1998b) supports the use of sex-drive-reducing medications, but only after a thorough clinical evaluation and as part of a comprehensive treatment plan. The task force authors acknowledge that informed consent is problematic when the treatment is court ordered but conclude that such medications should be part of the community treatment plan for at least some serious offenders. They specifically state: "Laws which predicate release from prison on 'chemical castration' . . . for broad classes of sex offenders are objectionable because they are not based on adequate diagnostic and treatment considerations and because they improperly link medical treatment with punishment and social control" (p. 117). The American Academy of Psychiatry and the Law (1998) approved an opinion of its Ethics Committee, which states that a psychiatrist should provide treatment only if clinically indicated and not because it is court ordered. Thus, even if judges order such treatment, ethical physicians should not implement it unless it is shown to be clinically indicated.

Courts have held that the use of medications for purposes other than to treat a patient's mental disorder is unconstitutional (*Knecht v. Gillman*, 1973; *Mackey v. Procunier*, 1973; *Nelson v. Heyne*, 1974/1984). A major issue in the chemical castration laws is the purpose for which these drugs are to be used. None of these statutes require that these drugs must be medically appropriate for these offenders. Given the political pressure behind passage of the laws and their failure to provide any parameters for treatment, it appears obvious that many legislators are not concerned about medically inappropriate use of the medications. Not only are there no provisions in most of the bills for medical evaluation and no requirement in any of them that medical opinions should override mandated treatment, but also they are all silent on the credentials or experience of the physicians who would prescribe the treatment. Nor does any state, except Wisconsin, provide any funding for these medications, which cost an average of \$200–\$400 a month. Thus, even if medically appropriate, it would be impossible for the great majority of offenders to comply with their conditions of probation in practice.

None of the medications, which have been shown to be effective in reducing excessive sex drive or fantasies, has been approved by the U.S. Food and Drug Administration (FDA) for that purpose for two reasons. First, the cost of obtaining FDA approval would be economically prohibitive, given the very limited market. Second, the drug companies are wary of litigation stemming from the use of their products with sex offenders. Although there are no "official" guidelines for prescribing the medications for sex offenders, practical guidelines have been established by experienced practitioners in the field and published in the professional literature. Nonetheless, most jurisdictions lack any knowledgeable and experienced psychiatrists who are capable of evaluating offenders for appropriateness of treatment, prescribing it correctly, or monitoring the effects of medication and the necessary associated psychotherapy (John M. W. Bradford, personal communication, May 21, 1997).

As written, these bills apply to whole classes of sex offenders. These classes are defined by the crime committed by the offender. Consequently, there are a number of reasons why these laws require many, if not most, offenders to take medications that are not medically appropriate for them. For example, there are a number of medical contraindications to treatment with all of these drugs; thus, these drugs will not be medically appropriate for all offenders. Also, many jurisdictions lack any experienced psychiatrists who are willing to provide this type of treatment to sex offenders in the community (State of Connecticut, 1983). In sum, these laws would force the great majority of offenders to choose between continued incarceration and medically inappropriate treatment—even assuming they could afford these drugs and that physicians could be found who were willing to prescribe and monitor their use.

Informed Consent

Few sex offenders lack the cognitive capacity to give informed consent, unless they suffer from other mental disorders that affect cognitive capacity (Miller, Stava, & Miller, 1988). Assuming that the physician possesses and provides adequate information about the procedures, the thorny issue is voluntariness. Those who argue that *no* incarcerated person can give consent to experimental treatment to get out of prison (Green, 1986; Marco & Marco, 1980; Vanderzyl, 1994) are certainly not representing their supposed clients' interests. If an offender is determined by an experienced psychiatrist to be appropriate for a trial of medication, understands the risks and benefits, and wants to try the medication to reduce his intrusive fantasies, he should certainly have access to the treatment, in or out of prison. If the medication works, there should be no problem with making it a condition of probation or parole, as long as the offender is informed as part of the consent process. The fact that the offender is incarcerated at the time of consent and that such consent would bring about release are factors that might justify an inquiry into voluntariness but, in themselves, do not render voluntary choices impossible (Winick, 1997a).

These arguments should not be taken to mean that sex offenders should be treated with these medications against their wills. A blanket requirement that all offenders in a given legal (not clinical) class be forced to take them in order to be released from prison, regardless of their clinical conditions, may be constitutional given the Supreme Court's attitude toward sex offenders but is neither sound social policy nor acceptable medical practice.

Due Process

In dealing with involuntary treatment with psychotropic medications, the Supreme Court has held that such treatment must be medically appropriate (*Riggins v. Nevada*, 1992; *Washington v. Harper*, 1990). Because the laws as written would inevitably force a number of offenders to accept medically inappropriate treatment (if they could find physicians willing to provide it), substantive due process would appear to be violated. In addition, because no hearings are required to determine the medical appropriateness of the medications, procedural due process would also appear to be violated (*Riggins v. Nevada*, 1992; *Washington v. Harper*, 1990), although the Supreme Court's cavalier approach to the rights of sex offenders (*Kan-*

sas v. Crane, 2002; *Kansas v. Hendricks*, 1997) would suggest that the Court might also not be concerned with due process challenges.

First Amendment

Although sex-drive-reducing medications do affect freedom of thought (e.g., sexual thoughts), some lower courts have rejected, in cases involving antipsychotic medication, the concept that the freedom to have abnormal thoughts caused by mental disease is protected by the First Amendment (*Rogers v. Okin*, 1980), although some courts have accepted the contention (*Bee v. Greaves*, 1984). The Supreme Court has never directly addressed the issue (Winick, 1997b).

Eighth Amendment

As discussed earlier, courts have invoked the Eighth Amendment's ban on cruel and unusual punishments to reject the involuntary use of medications with prisoners when not used for direct treatment of a medical condition (*Knecht v. Gillman*, 1973; *Mackey v. Procunier*, 1973; *Nelson v. Heyne*, 1974). In the case of sex-drive-reducing medications, one state appeals court even rejected the trial court's granting of probation on the condition that the sex offender take Depo-Provera, holding that the treatment was experimental and citing practical problems, such as the difficulty of enforcing the order, side effects, and informed consent (*People v. Gauntlett*, 1984).

Winick (1997a) argued that the Eighth Amendment could be used to invalidate rehabilitation of criminals if the treatment were disproportionate to the offense, indecent or inhumane, or insufficiently related to transforming the offender into a law-abiding member of society. In the current legal climate, however, few courts are likely to extend their protections to sex offenders that far.

Privacy and Bodily Integrity

Courts have generally shown great deference to personal privacy and bodily integrity, especially as it concerns the right to procreate (*Carey v. Population Services Int'l*, 1977; Note: "Compulsory contraception as a condition of probation: The use and abuse of Norplant," 1992). If sex-drive-reducing medications are used in a medically appropriate fashion, they do not interfere with procreation (and in fact may facilitate a man having normal sexual relations with an appropriate partner). When used as chemical castration, however (i.e., to render an offender impotent), they would certainly prevent procreation as effectively as surgical castration, which (as discussed earlier) has been found to be constitutionally impermissible as punishment.

Integrity of the Medical Profession

Psychiatrists are comfortable with prescribing psychotropic medication under involuntary conditions, as long as they are knowledgeable about the proposed treatments and are convinced that those treatments are appropriate for the patients involved. Their professional organization has presented amicus briefs in support of the involuntary administration of antipsychotic medications to patients with psychotic disorders who cannot make informed decisions about treatment (American Psychiatric Association & Washington State Psychiatric Association, 1990).

With chemical castration, however, the situation is significantly different in several respects. First, although all psychiatrists are trained to diagnose psychotic patients and prescribe antipsychotic medication for them, very few training programs provide any experience with sex offenders (Felthous & Miller, 1987). Most psychiatrists are therefore not competent to provide adequate evaluations or treatment for this population. Second, although managed care has forced a growing number of psychiatrists to provide treatment to seriously mentally ill patients in the public sector, there is no comparable economic pressure to encourage them to treat sex offenders. Third, although laws in most states explicitly provide an avenue for psychiatrists to obtain authority to treat patients involuntarily with antipsychotic medication, none of these laws authorize judges or any other nonmedical official to *order* their administration without a petition from a physician.

Legislatures have certainly not been concerned with physicians' ethics or the integrity of their profession in drafting chemical castration laws. Although none has authorized judges to order physicians to prescribe medication per se, all of the bills require that the medication be started while the offender is still in the state's Department of Corrections; correctional physicians typically have much less professional freedom than their colleagues outside the state correctional systems and may be subject to considerable pressure to provide the treatment, regardless of their competency to administer it or any ethical objections that they may have.

The Supreme Court has not been impressed with clinical ethical issues or with practical issues such as the availability of knowledgeable physicians to administer and monitor the medications or the ability of the offender to pay for them. State courts may be more sympathetic to clinical concerns. For example, the Washington State Supreme Court held, in a case involving forced medication of prison inmates, that the "State's interests justifying forced medication include maintenance of the ethical integrity of the medical profession" (*Harper v. State*, 1988). The Louisiana

Supreme Court, in a case involving forced medication to restore competency for execution, held that

> Consequently, medical treatment cannot occur when the state orders a physician to administer antipsychotic drugs to an insane prisoner in an attempt to render him competent for execution. Because the physician is required by his oath both to alleviate suffering and to do no harm, the state's order forces him to act unethically and contrary to the goals of medical treatment. (*State v. Perry*, 1992, p. 752)

The Louisiana Supreme Court further held that

> When antipsychotic drugs are forcibly administered to further the state's interest in carrying out capital punishment, and therefore not done in the prisoner's best medical interest, the intrusion represents an *extremely severe* interference with that person's liberty. The object of the intrusion is hostile in the utmost instead of beneficent, and the trustful, communicative doctor–patient relationship essential to the effective humane administration of antipsychotic drugs cannot exist. (*State v. Perry*, 1992, p. 758)

Citing the Louisiana decision and ethical statements of the American Medical Association and the American Psychiatric Association with approval, the South Carolina Supreme Court (*Singleton v. State*, 1993) also barred the forced use of antipsychotic drugs solely to restore competency for execution. The Massachusetts Supreme Judicial Court considered the ethical integrity of the medical profession as one of the state interests in compelling medical treatment, but in a case in which the physicians felt that the treatment (hemodialysis) was medically essential (*Commissioner of Corrections v. Myers*, 1979), the court went on to hold that "The court's order accords fully with medical ethics . . . and does not require treatment contrary to good medical practice" (*Myers*, 1979, p. 458).

Not all courts have been so willing to defer to professional ethics, however. In *Gary v. Hegstrom* (1987), the court held that it went too far for a court to require adoption of the standards of professional organizations. The 9th Circuit held in *Hoptowit v. Ray* (1987) that

> In determining whether challenged prison condition violates evolving standards of decency, courts may consider opinions of experts and pertinent organizations, but these opinions will not ordinarily establish constitutional minima since what experts may consider desirable may well constitute appropriate goals to which other branches may aspire but do not usually establish those minimums below which the Constitution establishes prohibition.

Some clinicians are concerned that the risks from a utilitarian approach are that the definition of deviance might be expanded to impose social control over harmless or violent people without mental illness (Halleck, 1981; Tancredi & Weisstub, 1986). Those concerns appear justified if the control of the process is taken out of the hands of responsible and experienced clinicians. Too many so-called "sex offender treatment programs" are so concerned with victims' rights and protection of society that they give short shrift to effective treatment, and these are the programs that are most likely to be given the responsibility for administering medications and the psychotherapy that is supposed to accompany it. For example, the initial report of the Colorado Sex Offender Treatment Board (which is mandated by the legislature's standards for evaluating and treating sex offenders) contained fewer than 2 pages concerning treatment in 87 pages, and no mention of physicians at all (Colorado Department of Public Safety, 1996). The Board subsequently changed its name to the (more appropriate) Sex Offender Management Board.

As physicians, psychiatrists have an ethical obligation to oppose laws that are contrary to the best interests of their patients (American Psychiatric Association, 1998a). Despite the recent American Psychiatric Association Task Force Report, there is still little evidence of any organized efforts to discharge that obligation. Generally when physicians' prerogatives have been usurped by the legal system, there is an immediate outcry, which has not occurred with this issue. With advocacy groups (as well as the public in general), sex offenders do not inspire much sympathy; neither do they provide reimbursement. In addition, so few psychiatrists have chosen to work with sex offenders that most can afford to ignore the issue.

Halleck (1971) argued that society uses psychiatry to salve its conscience; by seeming to provide special consideration for a few mentally disordered offenders, it permits deflection of attention from the larger problem of crime. In addition, by using psychiatrists and their medications, the criminal justice system attempts to legitimize and sanitize what are underneath punitive programs. Psychiatrists should not lend credibility to such efforts and should actively oppose them in the courts and legislatures.

CONCLUSION

The new chemical castration laws raise serious legal and ethical dilemmas. Although a small percentage of offenders may be helped by these drugs, most will not, and the new laws fail to require a clinical determination of the appropriateness of chemical castration for the particular offender. As a result, serious problems are raised under the Eighth Amendment, substantive due process, and procedural due process. Given the disinclination of the courts to protect the rights of sex offenders, however, it may be unlikely that courts will invalidate these laws. The use of medically inappropriate treatment for social control purposes raises grave ethical concerns for psychiatrists and other physicians asked to participate in their administration. Physicians are duty bound to attempt to do good and to avoid doing harm. To preserve the integrity of the medical profession, physicians should avoid participation in the administration of any form of chemical castration that is not medically appropriate for the patient and should oppose legislative attempts to enact these questionable provisions. Such attempts can be effective if knowledgeable professionals explain the appropriate (and inappropriate) use of sex drive medications. For example, colleagues were able to convince the sponsors of a chemical castration bill in the Colorado legislature to withdraw it after simply explaining what the medications can and cannot do.

REFERENCES

American Academy of Psychiatry and the Law. (1998). *Involuntary drug treatment of sex offenders*. Bloomfield, CT: Author.

American Psychiatric Association. (1998a). *Principles of medical ethics* (with annotations especially applicable to psychiatry, Section 3). Washington, DC: Author.

American Psychiatric Association. (1998b). *Task force report on sexually dangerous offenders* [*draft*]. Washington, DC: Author.

American Psychiatric Association and the Washington State Psychiatric Association. (1990). Brief as *Amici Curiae*, Washington v. Harper, 494 U.S. 210 (1990) (No. 88-599).

Bee v. Greaves, 744 F.2d 1387 (10th Cir. 1984).

Berlin, F. S., & Malin, H. M. (1991). Media distortion of the public's perception of recidivism and psychiatric rehabilitation. *American Journal of Psychiatry, 148*, 1572–1576.

Berlin, F. S., & Meinecke, C. F. (1981). Treatment of sex offenders with antiandrogenic medication: Conceptualization, review of treatment modalities, and preliminary findings. *American Journal of Psychiatry, 138*, 601–607.

Bradford, J. M. W. (1983). The hormonal treatment of sex offenders. *Bulletin of the American Academy of Psychiatry and the Law, 11*, 159–169.

Bradford, J. M. W. (1996). The role of serotonin in the future of forensic psychiatry. *Bulletin of the American Academy of Psychiatry and the Law, 24*, 57–72.

Buck v. Bell, 274 U.S. 200, 207 (1927).

California Penal Code § 645 (1996).

Carey v. Population Services Int'l, 431 U.S. 678 (1977).

Colorado Department of Public Safety, Division of Criminal Justice. (1996). *Standards and guidelines for the assessment, evaluation, treatment and behavioral monitoring of adult sex offenders*. Denver: Author.

Commissioner of Corrections v. Myers, 390 S.E.2d 452 (Mass. 1979).

Cynkar, R. J. (1981). *Buck v. Bell*: "Felt necessities" v. fundamental values? *Columbia Law Review, 81*, 1418–1461.

Davis v. Berry, 216 F.413 (S.D. Iowa 1914), *rev'd on other grounds*, 242 U.S. 468 (1917).

Erickson, W. D. (1995). "Northern lights": Minnesota's experience with sex offender legislation. *Newsletter of the American Academy of Psychiatry and the Law, 20,* 3–4.

Felthous, A. R., & Miller, R. D. (1987). Health law and mental health law courses in U.S. medical schools. *Bulletin of the American Academy of Psychiatry and Law, 15,* 319–327.

Foote, R. M. (1944). Diethylstilbestrol in the management of pathological states in males. *Journal of Nervous and Mental Disease, 99,* 928–935.

Furby, L., Weinrott, M. R., & Blackshaw, L. (1989). Sex offender recidivism: A review. *Psychological Bulletin, 105,* 10–27.

Gary v. Hegstrom, 831 F.2d 1420 (9th Cir. 1987).

Ginzberg, J. F. (1992). Compulsory contraception as a condition of probation: The use and abuse of Norplant [Note]. *Brooklyn Law Review, 58,* 979–1019.

Green, W. (1986). Depo-Provera, castration, and the probation of rape offenders: Statutory and constitutional issues. *University of Dayton Law Review, 12,* 1–26.

Group for the Advancement of Psychiatry. (1977, April). *Psychiatry and sex psychopath legislation: The 30s to the 80s* (Vol. IX, Publication No. 98). Washington, DC: Author.

Halleck S. L. (1971). *The politics of therapy.* New York: Harper & Row.

Halleck, S. L. (1981). The ethics of antiandrogen therapy. *American Journal of Psychiatry, 138,* 642–643.

Harper v. State, 759 P.2d 358, 364 (Wash. 1988).

Harris, P. M. (1995). Prison-based sex offender treatment programs in the post sexual psychopath era. *Journal of Psychiatry and Law, 23,* 555–581.

Hoptowit v. Ray, 682 F.2d 1237, 1238 (9th Cir. 1987).

Kansas v. Crane, 534 U.S. 407 (2002).

Kansas v. Hendricks, 117 S. Ct. 2072 (1997).

Knecht v. Gillman, 488 F.2d 1136 (8th Cir. 1973).

Letterie, G. S., & Fox, W. F., Jr. (1990). Legal aspects of involuntary sterilization. *Fertility and Sterility, 53,* 391–398.

Mackey v. Procunier, 477 F.2d 877 (9th Cir. 1973).

Marco, C. F., & Marco, J. M. (1980). Antabuse: Medication in exchange for a limited freedom—Is it legal? *American Journal of Law and Medicine, 6,* 295–330.

Mickle v. Henricks, 262 F. 687 (1918).

Miller, R. D. (1998). The forced administration of sex-drive reducing medications to sex offenders: Treatment or punishment? *Psychology, Public Policy, and Law, 4,* 175–199.

Miller, R. D., Stava, L. J., & Miller, R. K. (1988). The insanity defense for sex offenders: Jury decisions after the repeal of Wisconsin's Sex Crimes Law. *Hospital and Community Psychiatry, 39*, 186–189.

Money, J. (1970). Use of an androgen-depleting hormone in the treatment of male sex offenders. *Journal of Sex Research, 6*, 165–172.

Money, J. (1972). The therapeutic use of androgen-depleting hormone. In H. L. P. Resnik & M. E. Wolfgang (Eds.), *Sexual behaviors, social, clinical and legal aspects* (pp. 351–360). Boston: Little, Brown.

Nelson v. Heyne, 491 F.2d 352, 356 (7th Cir. 1974), *cert. denied*, 417 U.S. 976 (1974).

People v. Gauntlett, 352 N.W.2d 310 (Mich. App. 1984).

Riggins v. Nevada, 112 S. Ct. 1810 (1992).

Robert, R. (1992). The management of a case of treatment-resistant paraphilia with a long-acting LHRH agonist. *Canadian Journal of Psychiatry, 37*, 567–569.

Rogers v. Okin, 634 F.2d 650 (1st Cir. 1980).

Rosier, A., & Witztum, E. (1998). Treatment of men with paraphilia with a long-acting analogue of gonadotropin-releasing. *New England Journal of Medicine, 338*, 416–422.

Singleton v. State, 437 S.E.2d 53 (S.C. 1993).

Skinner v. Oklahoma, 316 U.S. 535 (1941).

State v. Brown, 326 S.E.2d 410 (S.C. 1985).

State v. Perry, 610 So. 2d 746 (La. 1992).

State of Connecticut Department of Corrections. (1983, October). *Report of Depo-Provera study group.* Wethersfield: Author.

Stuerup, G. K. (1972). Castration, the total treatment In H. L. P. Resnik & M. E. Wolfgang (Eds.), *Sexual behaviors, social, clinical and legal aspects* (pp. 361–382). Boston: Little, Brown.

Tancredi, L. R., & Weisstub, D. (1986). Technology assessment: Its role in forensic psychiatry and the case of chemical castration. *International Journal of Law and Psychiatry, 8*, 257–271.

Thibaut, F., Cordier, B., & Kuhn, J.-M. (1996). Gonadotrophin hormone releasing hormone agonist in cases of severe paraphilia: A lifetime treatment? *Psychoneuroendocrinology, 21*, 411–419.

United States v. Bryant, 670 F. Supp. 840, 843 (Minn. 1978).

Vanderzyl, K. A. (1994). Castration as an alternative to incarceration: An impotent approach to the punishment of sex offenders [Comment]. *Northern Illinois University Law Review, 15*, 107–140.

Washington v. Harper, 110 S. Ct. 1028 (1990).

Weems v. United States, 217 U.S. 349, 377 (1910).

Williams v. Smith, 262 F. 687, 690-91 (D. Nev. 1918).

Winick, B. J. (1997a). Coercion and mental health treatment. *Denver Law Review*, *74*, 1145–1168.

Winick, B. J. (1997b). *The right to refuse mental health treatment*. Washington, DC: American Psychological Association.

Wis. Rev. Stat. § 980.12.062(b)(c), 980.08.(4)(5), and 980.12(2) (1998).

15

COMMUNITY CONTAINMENT OF SEX OFFENDER RISK: A PROMISING APPROACH

KIM ENGLISH, LINDA JONES, AND DIANE PATRICK

In a growing number of jurisdictions nationwide, criminal justice professionals are working hard to adopt innovative methods for handling adult sex offenders on probation or parole. The most promising model, called a *containment approach*, reduces or *contains* the probability of reoffense by convicted sex criminals living in the community (English, Pullen, & Jones, 1996). A systemwide, multidisciplinary focus on public safety is the hallmark of this model, which includes the following components: (a) a victim-

The findings presented in this chapter are based on research consisting of two national telephone surveys of a representative sample of over 700 probation and parole supervisors (1994 and 1998), an extensive literature review on victim trauma and sex offender treatment, a systematic review of scores of criminal justice agency documents, field interviews of hundreds of professionals working in 27 jurisdictions in 11 states, and detailed on-site data collection on sexual assault incidents from 232 convicted sex offender case files from areas in 4 states. This research was funded by the National Institute of Justice, U.S. Department of Justice, under Grant Nos. 92-IJ-CX-K021 and D97LBVX0034. Points of view expressed herein are those of the authors and do not necessarily represent the official position of the U.S. Department of Justice. We gratefully acknowledge the assistance of Diane Pasini-Hill and Sydney Cooley-Towell of the Division of Criminal Justice, Office of Research and Statistics, in the conduct of this national study.

265

centered philosophy, (b) multidisciplinary collaboration, (c) containment-focused risk management, (d) consistent multiagency policies and protocols, and (e) quality control mechanisms.

Although many people believe that convicted sex abusers are sent directly to prison, more often these offenders are actually living with us in our communities. In Colorado, for example, between 50% and 60% of convicted sex offenders receive sentences to probation. Likewise, nearly all sex offenders sentenced to prison return to the community, either under official parole supervision or without any supervision after serving their maximum prison terms. In fact, the containment approach developed as a direct result of practitioners' struggles to reduce inconsistencies in the way criminal justice professionals work with community-based sex offenders. During field interviews, probation and parole officers and their supervisors, treatment providers, judges, police officers, victim advocates, and other concerned experts recounted many anecdotes that demonstrated one consistent finding: Despite everyone's good intentions, gaps and inconsistencies in the criminal justice system allowed many sexual perpetrators to reoffend. When, for example, supervising probation and parole officers and treatment providers were not aligned with a consistent intervention strategy, sex offenders capitalized on these inconsistencies.

In the containment model, a specially trained case management team carries out the day-to-day work of risk reduction. The team includes a probation or parole officer, a treatment provider, and a polygraph examiner, who act together to decrease or eliminate an individual's privacy, opportunity, and access to potential or past victims. Limiting opportunities for reoffending requires that the team have accurate information about an individual's past and potential victims and high-risk behavior unique to that sexual abuser. To solicit and verify this information, postconviction polygraphs are added to the sex-offense-specific treatment of the probationer or parolee. The combination is powerful. The threat or actuality of the polygraph exam increases the scope and accuracy of sexual history information the offender gives in treatment, provides a method to verify whether he or she is currently engaging in high-risk or assaultive behavior (English, Jones, Pasini-Hill, & Patrick, 2000), and contributes to breaking through the denial many sex offenders demonstrate as part of their offense pattern. The supervising probation or parole officer supports this combined treatment–polygraph process by using the information to manage risk and to levy consequences.

FIVE COMPONENTS OF THE CONTAINMENT APPROACH

In this chapter, we describe the five components of the containment approach (see English et al., 1996), incorporating new empirical findings that demonstrate the unique contributions of a combined treatment–polygraph process to this approach.

Victim-Centered Philosophy

The containment approach begins with an explicit philosophy that embraces victim protection and community safety as its primary mission. Research indicates that the effects of sexual assault on victims are often profound and long-lasting (see Wyatt & Powell, 1988). Sexual assault victims are at significantly higher risk than nonvictims to abuse alcohol and drugs; to suffer from depression, anxiety, nightmares, and social isolation; and to attempt suicide (Briere & Runtz, 1988; Kilpatrick, Edmunds, & Seymour, 1992; Peters, 1988). Because most sexual assaults occur in the context of a relationship established and manipulated over time, the victim is often confused and made by the perpetrator to feel responsible. The *Rape in America* report (Kilpatrick et al., 1992) found that one out of five victims was raped by a stranger, whereas nearly half (46%) were raped by someone very close to them: a father, stepfather, boyfriend, husband, ex-husband, or other relative. Sixty-one percent were raped before the age of 18; many of those raped as children were raped by trusted caretakers. The presence of a relationship may partly explain the fact that four out of five victims did not report the rape to law enforcement. Experts on sexual abuse explain that this violation of a trusting relationship may cause nearly unbearable confusion and trauma to the victim (Herman, 1992).

Summit (1988) acknowledged the psychological damage inherent in the full range of sexually abusive behaviors when he emphasized not just rape but touching: "Sexual touching, so often trivialized by words such as fondling or molestation (annoyance), is only the physical expression of a climate of invasion, isolation and abandonment" (p. 55). A victim-centered philosophy, then, assumes that every sexual assault, from a violent stranger rape to voyeurism by a family member, represents a significant act of betrayal. Thus, addressing the victim's fear and need for safety and empowerment is a system priority.

If the societal response to an attack is to place the victim at fault, the experience of trauma is magnified, and recovery may be delayed (Hindman, 1988). Explaining that sexual abuse is a process rather than an act or series of acts, Finkelhor (1988) stated: "Clinicians have often observed that the harm of some sexual abuse experiences lies less in the actual sexual contact than in the process of disclosure or even in the process of intervention" (pp. 77–78). Many of the women in Kilpatrick et al.'s (1992) survey of over 4,000 women reported that fear of being blamed for the attack was a reason they did not report the crime. Understanding this point is vital for professionals interested in implementing the containment strategy. The power and authority of police officers, lawyers, judges, and social workers can weigh as heavily on the victim as on the perpetrator. For instance, well-intentioned community notification laws (see this volume, chapter 12) may have a devastating effect on the victim if the perpetrator is a family member, as often is the case (see this volume, chapter 8). In situations like this, the healthy recovery of the victim and the well-being of the community should guide policy development, program implementation, and the actions of staff working with both sexual assault victims and perpetrators.

Adopting a victim-centered philosophy may require a significant shift in values, as every case management decision will require considering the dangerousness the abuser presents to past and potential victims. Probation and parole agencies are challenged to dissolve the usual job and agency boundaries so that risk can be quickly assessed. Typically, the criminal justice system focuses on the conviction crime—a rapist is only a rapist, and so is considered a danger only to adult women (and not children); a man convicted of molesting a little boy is considered fixated only on little boys and so is safe to be with little girls. But research indicates that many sex offenders have a history of hurting many types of victims (Ahlmeyer, Heil, McKee, & English, 2000), so the crime of conviction may not reflect current or future danger to victims.

Multidisciplinary Collaboration

The development of teams of professionals who specialize in sex offender cases improves communication and contributes to efficiency and positive morale in the face of very difficult casework. Collaborating agencies can include sex offender treatment programs, law enforcement, probation, parole, schools, social services, rape crisis centers, hospitals, prisons, polygraph examiners, researchers, and victim advocate organizations. In a call to collaborate across disciplines and within communities for the purpose of addressing the epidemic of sexual assault, the American Medical Association (1995) also added these to the list above: attorneys, emergency room staff, universities, and victim assistance centers.

Our field research indicates that interagency and multidisciplinary collaboration occurs in many ways. In Colorado, for example, a state-level Sex Offender Management Board with multidisciplinary membership is defined in legislation and meets monthly. The Board has issued guidelines for the evaluation, treatment, and behavioral monitoring of adult sex offenders, including perpetrators with developmental disabilities, and it recently identified release criteria for sex offenders serving lifetime probation or parole sentences (Colorado Sex Offender Management Board, 1999). In Oregon, quarterly meetings are held for all the probation and parole officers from across the state who specialize in the supervision of adult sex offenders. Metropolitan Dallas probation and parole officers, treatment providers, and polygraph examiners meet monthly for cross-training and information sharing. In Ohio, a parole officer took it upon herself to meet her colleagues working in the local police department's sex crime unit. They now work together to solve cases. Often, these types of relationships are forged by line staff, with one committed professional seeking out the expertise of another, and regular meetings and communications ensuing thereafter. These small and large acts of collaboration have begun to change the way work gets done in many regions across the United States.

Containment-Focused Risk Management

The containment approach depends on the team members—probation or parole officer, treatment provider, and polygraph examiner—obtaining and sharing key pieces of information about the abuser and then systematically and consistently responding to that information to minimize access to victims. The team must be philosophically aligned, well trained, empowered to make case-specific recommendations to the court or parole board, and given sufficient discretion and resources (guided by clear protocols) to investigate the likelihood of reoffense and to invoke consequences.

Laws in most areas define community supervision as a privilege, and a condition of this privilege in the containment approach is the waiver of confidentiality. Waivers allow the containment team, offender, and family members or significant others (including, sometimes, the victim's therapist) to share and utilize the same information.

When a sex offender first begins to serve a sentence of probation or parole, what is known about him is generally limited to information from police reports, the presentence investigation, sometimes a psychosexual evaluation or risk assessment, and some criminal history information. To effectively contain or lower risk, the team needs to know much more: information about the sexual abuser's preferred victim types, sexual assault history, the frequency and extent of deviant sexual arousal and behaviors, and events or emotional states that are precursors to reoffense (see this volume, chapters 3 and 12, for discussions of risk assessment and risk management issues). This information becomes the basis of establishing the *modus operandi* for each sex offender who is under supervision in the community. Knowledge of these details provides the foundation for surveillance and supervision plans customized to lower risk by denying the offender the access and privacy necessary to harm victims.

Most of this information will be obtained though sex-offense-specific treatment, with the accuracy of the defender's self-reports, past and current deviant behavior being validated and the information expanded by polygraph examinations, and consequences for deceptive results being issued through the authority of the criminal justice system. Full disclosure of a lifetime of sexual deviance and abuse is the expectation and the norm. Early in the treatment process, the client will be assigned the job of writing the details of his sex history. The resulting log or journal includes all sexual activity, with consenting and nonconsenting partners, a description of each victim (e.g., age, gender, relationship to offender), and the circumstances surrounding the assault. In this exercise, the person must reveal the lifestyle he has carefully designed to deceive others and promote deviant sexual activity. The information is verified by a polygraph examination, and deceptive findings on the exam lead to a variety of consequences. These prior victimizations, typically not readily disclosed by the perpetrator, will be used to assess current and future risk and also to assure that treatment is appropriately directed at real patterns of behavior. Sufficient information to determine a sex offender's present and future risk is incomplete unless the treatment, polygraph, and criminal justice containment team work together to obtain *full* disclosure.

Should past crimes uncovered in this manner be prosecuted? This complicated issue dissuades some officials from fully implementing the containment approach. However, many locations have implemented options that minimize the likelihood of an individual's arrest for past crimes, including limited immunity agreements and treatment practices that encourage disclosure of prior victims without obtaining identifying information. Policymakers and team members must work with prosecutors and victim advocate organizations in their communities to develop acceptable plans and practices about how this sex history information will be handled.

Each of the three anchors in the containment triangle—supervision, therapy, and polygraph examinations—benefits from the distinct job performed by other members: "The criminal justice supervision activity is informed and improved by the information obtained in sex-offender-specific therapy, and therapy is informed and improved by the information obtained during well-conducted post-conviction polygraph examinations" (English, 1998, p. 225). The three functions must be perceived by the offender as separate yet aligned with the others. Each of these activities is discussed further below, along with new empirical findings on the unique contribution of the combined treatment–polygraph process to risk management practices.

Criminal Justice Supervision

The team is empowered primarily through the criminal justice system exercising its authority in a number of ways. Specialized terms and conditions for sex offenders, lengthy probation and parole sentences, restrictions on risky behaviors, restrictions on contact with children, random home visits, urinalysis testing, electronic monitoring, and verified law enforcement registration are some of the external controls that can be levied.

The criminal justice system can also invoke consequences for an offender's nonparticipation in treatment, violation of supervision conditions, and behaviors that represent a danger to any potential victim. Consequences for failure to follow consistently the directives of treatment and supervision can take a variety of forms. At a minimum, surveillance can be increased (e.g., house arrest, electronic monitoring, additional home visits by the supervising officer, requirements to phone the officer or others with location information) and orders for additional treatment sessions (with a corresponding increase in treatment fees assessed against the offender) can be imposed. Intermediate sanctions include community service activities, short-term jail sentences, or placement in a halfway house for sex offenders. At the most serious end of the sanctions continuum is revocation of the community sentence and placement in prison. The anticipation of these consequences provides incentives for the offender to participate actively in treatment, obtain frequent polygraph examinations, and comply with conditions of supervision.

Not surprisingly, sanctions must be invoked immediately. Failing to short-circuit the abusive pattern may prolong risk to the community or, more likely, to a particular victim. Many treatment providers and polygraph examiners have reported that, without the leverage of the criminal justice system's consequences for noncompliance, they could not work with sex offenders. Without consistent pressure on an offender to adhere to the behavioral expectations detailed in his conditions of supervision and treatment contract, community safety becomes dependent on the offender's goodwill and self-control. According to trauma expert Dr. Judith Herman (1989) of Harvard, "Vigorous enforcement of existing criminal laws prohibiting sexual assault might be expected to have some preventive effect since both the compulsive and opportunistic offenders are keenly sensitive to external controls" (p. 188). "Vigorous enforcement" translates into supervision and surveillance strategies customized to each offender's idiosyncratic assault patterns. Once these patterns are known, the officer can restrict employment (e.g., working around children), disapprove certain leisure time activities (e.g., cruising the streets in an automobile), monitor the offender's telephone bills for use of 1-900 numbers, restrict the offender's use of alcohol and drugs, prohibit or confiscate items that are used to entice children (kittens, puppies, toys, and video games) or to stimulate deviant fantasies.

Pithers's (1990) description of the assault pattern is a reminder of the need to be alert for what may, at first, appear to be accidental or occasional victim access:

> Many aggressors, seeking to minimize their responsibility for offenses, would also have us believe their behaviors are the product of irresistible impulses overwhelming their self-control. . . . In reality, many offenders

carefully plan offenses so that they appear to occur without fore-thought. (p. 334)

Amir (1971) found that 75% of rapes involved some degree of planning, whereas Pithers, Kashima, Cumming, Beal, and Buell (1988) reported that 90% of their sample of sex offenders reported experiencing specific, strong, emotional states before reoffending. Hudson, Ward, and McCormack's (1999) study of sexual offense pathways reflects the planning components in the description of the 6-stage offending process. Fortunately, this very attention to planning can increase the likelihood of detection. Equipped with adequate information, the criminal justice agent is well positioned to identify precursor behaviors that can be modified when sufficient structure and appropriate consequences are applied.

The intensity of supervision required of the probation or parole officer is significant, and collaboration with individuals in other disciplines takes time and care. Case-specific supervision requires planning, documentation, and on-site meetings with the offender at home and at work. Often, safety considerations require that fieldwork be conducted in teams of two officers. Ongoing training is also necessary to keep staff members up to date. Probation and parole officers should have caseloads limited to 20 or 25 sex offenders, and they should have flexibility in work hours to monitor the offender's activities at night and on weekends. Halfway houses with 24-hour monitoring of the facility and the offender's location should be available in all regions so a safe, residential option is available to criminal justice officials managing these cases. Criminal justice policymakers must explore the reallocation of resources if they intend to take the leadership role necessary to implement a containment approach.

Sex-Offense-Specific Treatment

Sex offender treatment targets the thoughts, feelings, denial, minimizations, motivations, justifications, and lifelong behaviors and thought patterns that are, in fact, fused to the sexual assault itself (see this volume, chapter 5). The supervising officer works closely with the treatment provider to learn the offender's long-term patterns that *precede* actual assaults. These details, vitally necessary to assess risk but historically outside the scope of criminal justice system intervention, are at the center of therapy.

Sex-offense-specific treatment of offenders differs from traditional therapy in a number of important aspects. First, in sex-offense-specific treatment, the therapist best cares for the client by not accepting the client's description of his or her sexual past as complete or even true. The therapist relies heavily on corroborative information contained in the police report and presentence information, while encouraging and confronting the offender's disclosure of sexually abusive or deviant behavior. In addition, the therapist's primary commitment is to the community at large:

Public safety is paramount. The focus of the treatment is on the assaultive behavior that harms others. The offender's manipulation and rationalizations that precede or follow the assault are considered part of the crime, not an explanation for the assault. Treatment providers understand that the offender must disclose the full extent of his or her deviant sexual history. Holding on to these powerful secrets is not therapeutic and, if allowed by the therapist, will perpetuate the very secrecy that is at the core of the offender's lifestyle, feeding the next assault.

Sex-offense-specific treatment occurs primarily in group therapy settings. Working in a group, therapists are less likely to succumb to the subtle manipulations that individual offenders have perfected over a lifetime. A group of offenders, coached by the therapist, can recognize and confront these familiar manipulations by others in the treatment program. Descriptions of cognitive distortions and psychological defense mechanisms, the step-by-step sexual assault cycle, and the development of a concrete prevention plan provide the working material of treatment.

An essential role of treatment is to obtain the method-of-operation details needed by criminal justice officials to develop risk management plans as well as to assist sex offenders in developing internal controls over their offending behaviors. Offenders are expected to assume full responsibility for the damage they cause their victim(s) and to take measures necessary to prevent future abusive behaviors. The threat or actuality of postconviction polygraphs and criminal justice consequences help motivate these nonvoluntary clients to fully engage in treatment, complete homework assignments, and learn and use the tools of behavior modification.

Postconviction Polygraphs

The postconviction polygraph examination strengthens the treatment and supervision of sex offenders by verifying the accuracy and completeness of the sexual history information gained in treatment and by periodically monitoring the offender's compliance with criminal justice and treatment conditions. Regular polygraph examinations are conducted by an examiner who specializes in this type of exam. Our 1998 telephone survey of a nationally representative sample of more than 600 probation and parole supervisors across the nation indicated that between 15% and 20% of the jurisdictions contacted were using postconviction polygraph examinations with sex offenders.

The postconviction polygraph must be used in conjunction with sex-offense-specific treatment. These two components, acting together and consistently supported by criminal justice supervision and consequences for noncompliance, provide a powerful incentive for an offender to be truthful and to refrain from behavior for which he or she will surely be caught. Without the use of the polygraph examination process, the information necessary to control the risk of offenders is incomplete, and the offender's risk to the community remains uncertain.

Treatment–Polygraph Process

Risk management can be only as effective as the information on which it is built. Case file analysis for our 1998 study confirmed the multiplicity of paraphilic and high-risk behaviors that other researchers have found. The data, which were organized to describe the additional victims, paraphilias, and risk behaviors documented when a combined treatment–polygraph process is added to traditional criminal justice supervision practices, yielded the following selected findings: The proportion of sex offenders who admitted to committing incest increased by half (38% to 58%) after treatment and polygraph tests were administered. One third (34.6%) of self-reported incest perpetrators disclosed a history of sexually assaulting strangers, and over half (56.7%) disclosed sexually assaulting victims from a position of trust (excluding incest victims). Approximately twice as many offenders admitted having male victims (20% to 36%) and having adult victims (19% to 44%). Three times as many offenders admitted to having victims of both genders (10% to 29%), to engaging in the "hands-off" offenses of exhibitionism, voyeurism, and stalking (22% to 67%), and to engaging in high-risk behaviors (27% to 80%). The size of the group admitting to *more than one type of* "hands-off" offense increased tenfold (3% to 35%). Despite the significant increase in deviant behavior reported by this sample of offenders during the treatment–polygraph process, the information presented here does not fully reflect the deviant and risky behaviors of these men. Only one third of them were found non-deceptive on at least one polygraph examination, indicating a lack of full disclosure of sexual history or high-risk behavior.

Treatment providers who work with sex offenders on relapse prevention plans indicate that high-risk activities are usually integrated into the sex offense cycle as precursors to sexual assault. Incomplete knowledge of these behaviors masks the offender's risk to specific victims and to the larger community. When we examined the files for information obtained during maintenance examinations (which monitor the offender's current behavior on probation or parole and test for compliance with the conditions of supervision and treatment), we found that the treatment–polygraph process also detected new offenses: 21 of 180 offenders revealed crimes against new victims while under supervision in the 12 to 24 months since sentencing. Most frequently, the new crime was fondling, frottage, exhibitionism, or voyeurism. In one instance, sex with a minor child was disclosed. Without the postconviction polygraph, it is unlikely that these new crimes would have been detected. Without intervention, public safety would be increasingly jeopardized.

These data provide compelling evidence that the addition of the polygraph to the other tools of criminal justice supervision and sex offender treatment is having an important effect on long-term, effective risk-monitoring practices. Simply put, sex offenders give up more information when the polygraph is used. And more information means better risk management.

Informed and Consistent Public Policies

The fourth component of the containment approach requires local criminal justice practitioners to develop public policy at all levels of government that institutionalize and codify the containment approach. These policies should be based on research, should hold offenders accountable, and, to be effectively implemented in the field, must empower those who work closely with sexual perpetrators. Policies must define and structure the discretion authorities need to supervise and treat each offender individually. Criminal justice practitioners must also codify local and agreed-on practices that support a victim-oriented approach to sex offender risk management. Written guidelines for the uniform processing of sex assault cases should include, at a minimum, the following (English et al., 1996):

- Acceptance or rejection of plea agreements in cases of sexual assault
- The weight given in sentencing to an offender's continued denial of the crime
- Use of polygraph information
- Family reunification assessment protocols
- Presentence investigation report information
- Failure to progress in treatment
- Revocation procedures
- Third-party liability/duty to warn potential victims
- Employment restrictions for sex offenders under criminal justice supervision
- Length of community supervision (i.e., lifetime)

Clear, consistent, and documented agreements on sex offender policies, combined with the cooperation of agencies responsible for managing sex offenders, are essential to enable the containment process outlined here to proceed. Written procedures and protocols should describe how these team interactions will occur. The range of activities that require such documentation is quite large, but primary among them is the need for open communication and information sharing at all stages of the process.

Quality Control

The containment approach requires broad discretion on the part of the criminal justice system staff, treatment providers, polygraph examiners, and others collaborating for the purpose of public safety. Such discretion must be systematically monitored to ensure fairness and justice. For this reason, quality control is fundamental to the administration of any sex offender program, project, or systemwide process. Quality control activities should include, at a minimum: regular, multiagency case review meetings to ensure prescribed policies and practices are implemented as planned; videotaping of all polygraph examinations to avoid recanted statements and to enable periodic review by a quality control team; and the collection of case data describing the characteristics of offenders who fail in treatment or commit new sex crimes.

Sexual abuse cases are difficult to deal with, and the offender will attempt to manipulate the criminal justice system just as he or she did the assault victim(s). Professionals can burn out, get soft, miss red flags, turn cynical, and otherwise become ineffective. Empathy toward victims and repeated exposure to traumatic material can also result in *compassion fatigue* (Figley, 1995; Stamm, 1995) by experts who work with sexual offenders. Police, firefighters, and other emergency workers report that they are most vulnerable to compassion fatigue when dealing with the pain of children (Stamm, 1995). In addition, "trauma is contagious" (Herman, 1990, p. 180). Compassion fatigue, a near certainty in this area of work, presents a significant threat to the quality of the program and the well-being of the dedicated professionals who are working to make our world safer.

Working together as a team is the primary defense against this common phenomenon. Honest communication among team members is the first step in creating a continuum of quality control mechanisms. The next step is a process that brings together agency administrators who actively support the protocols and stand behind the staff who enforce the protocols and make difficult decisions in the field. Ongoing training, flexible hours, a supportive environment, and safe working conditions are important ways that administrators can help fight compassion fatigue.

A final aspect of quality control consists of clearly defined and agreed-on measures of success. It is challenging to identify measures of detection, detention, and revocation that target offenders *before* the commission of a new assault. Addressing these issues requires the allocation of resources for monitoring and evaluation. Indeed, resource allocation is a key to quality control.

CONCLUSION

Sex offenders have been the subject of enormous publicity and concern in the last decade. Heinous crimes are televised globally. This has led the way for states to implement civil commitment laws for sexually violent predators, require registration of sex offenders with local law enforcement, and pass laws that require some degree of community notification when a sex offender is living in the community. Well-supported and sensibly implemented, these broad laws and policies have their place in the menu of sex offender management tools. Summit (1988) reminded us that children will be victimized as long as adults allow it. We must reform our official systems of response to truly impact what the American Medical Association (1995) called "the silent-violent epidemic of sexual assault."

The new legal responses to sexually dangerous offenders cannot succeed in isolating and incapacitating all potential recidivists from the community. Nor can inpatient sex offender treatment succeed in changing the behavior patterns of sex offenders. How offenders behave in institutional settings does not always predict how they will behave once released to the community. Given the inevitability that many sex offenders will be released to the community from prison and from the hospital, we need to develop systematic ways of monitoring their behavior in the community that manage the risk that many will continue to present and that provide postinstitutional treatment opportunities that can increase the likelihood of rehabilitation when the individual is subjected to the stresses and temptations of resuming life in society. This chapter has proposed an innovative program of individualized risk management that involves a multidisciplinary effort in which criminal justice, treatment, and polygraph professionals can work together to monitor and treat discharged sex offenders and contain the risk they may continue to present.

REFERENCES

Ahlmeyer, S., Heil, M., McKee, B., & English, K. (2000) The impact of polygraph admissions of victims offenses in adult offenders. *Sex Abuse: A Journal of Research and Treatment, 12*(2), 123–138.

American Medical Association. (1995). *Sexual assault in America* (Position paper). Chicago: Author.

Amir, M. (1971). *Patterns of forcible rape.* Chicago: University of Chicago Press.

Briere, J., & Runtz, M. (1988). Post sexual abuse trauma. In G. E. Wyatt & G. J. Powell (Eds.), *Lasting effects of child sexual abuse* (pp. 85–99). Newbury Park, CA: Sage.

Colorado Sex Offender Management Board. (1999). *Standards and guidelines for the assessment, evaluation, treatment, and behavioral monitoring of adult sex offenders* (Revised). Denver: Colorado Division of Criminal Justice, Department of Public Safety.

English, K. (1998). The containment approach: An aggressive strategy for the community management of adult sex offenders. *Psychology, Public Policy, and Law, 4*(1/2), 218–235.

English, K., Jones, L., Pasini-Hill, D., & Patrick, D. (2000). *The second national telephone survey on the community management of adult sex offenders.* Washington, DC: U.S. Department of Justice, National Institute of Justice.

English, K., Pullen, S., & Jones, L. (Eds.). (1996). *Managing adult sex offenders: A containment approach.* Lexington, KY: American Probation and Parole Association.

Figley, C. R. (Ed.). (1995). *Compassion fatigue: Coping with secondary traumatic stress disorder in those who treat the traumatized.* New York: Brunner/Mazel.

Finkelhor, D. (1988). The trauma of sexual abuse: Two models. In G. E. Wyatt & G. J. Powell (Eds.), *Lasting effects of child sexual abuse* (pp. 61–80). Newbury Park, CA: Sage.

Herman, J. (1989). *Trauma and recovery.* New York: Basic Books.

Herman, J. L. (1990). Sex offenders: A feminist perspective. In W. L. Marshall, D. R. Laws, & H. E. Barbaree (Eds.), *Handbook of sexual assault: Issues, theories, and treatment of the offender* (pp. 177–194). New York: Plenum.

Herman, J. L. (1992). *Trauma and recovery.* New York: Basic Books.

Hindman, J. (1988). *Just before dawn.* Boise, ID: Northwest Printing.

Hudson, S. M., Ward, T., & McCormack, J. C. (1999). Offense pathways in sexual offenders. *Journal of Interpersonal Violence, 14*(8), 779–798.

Kilpatrick, D. G., Edmunds, C. N., & Seymour, A. (1992). *Rape in America: A report to the nation.* Charleston: Medical University of South Carolina, National Victim Center and Crime Victims Research and Treatment Center.

Peters, S. D. (1988). Child sexual abuse and later psychological problems. In G. E. Wyatt & G. J. Powell (Eds.), *Lasting effects of child sexual abuse* (pp. 101–117). Newbury Park, CA: Sage.

Pithers, W. D. (1990). Relapse prevention with sexual aggressors: A method for maintaining therapeutic gain and enhancing external supervision. In W. L. Marshall, D. R. Laws, & H. E. Barbaree (Eds.), *Handbook of sexual assault: Issues, theories, and treatment of the offender* (pp. 343–361). New York: Plenum.

Pithers, W. D., Kashima, K., Cumming, G. F., Beal, L. S., & Buell, M. (1988). Relapse prevention of sexual aggression. In R. Prentky & V. Quinsey (Eds.), *Annals of the New York Academy of Sciences* (pp. 244–260). New York: New York Academy of Sciences.

Stamm, B. H. (Ed.). (1995). *Secondary traumatic stress*. Lutherville, MD: Sidran.

Summit, R. C. (1988). Societal avoidance of child sexual abuse. In G. E. Wyatt & G. J. Powell (Eds.), *Lasting effects of child sexual abuse* (pp. 39–60). Newbury Park, CA: Sage.

Wyatt, G. E., & Powell, G. J. (Eds.). (1988). *Lasting effects of child sexual abuse*. Newbury Park, CA: Sage.

VI

EVALUATING THE WISDOM OF SEXUALLY VIOLENT PREDATOR LAWS

16

THE COSTS OF ENACTING A SEXUAL PREDATOR LAW AND RECOMMENDATIONS FOR KEEPING THEM FROM SKYROCKETING

JOHN Q. LA FOND

In 1990 Washington State enacted the first sexually violent predator (SVP) law. It allows prosecutors to civilly commit dangerous sex offenders to a secure mental health facility for an indefinite period, but only after they have served their complete prison terms (La Fond, 1992). Since 1990 many other states have enacted a similar law, and others are considering it. (Chapters 1 and 2 of this volume describe these laws in detail and explain how they work.)

Several states have had extensive experience implementing SVP laws. Their experiences are important for policymakers considering enacting SVP laws and for decision makers who must determine if these laws are a cost-effective means of making communities safer. This chapter describes

This chapter has been expanded from La Fond (1998). Copyright © 1998 by the American Psychological Association (APA). Adapted with permission of the author and the APA. I wish to express my gratitude to W. L. Fitch and D. Hammen for allowing me to use in this chapter selected information on costs, which they had compiled.

the costs of implementing SVP laws—they are very expensive. It then identifies measures that states can take to keep these costs from becoming unsustainable.

COSTS OF IMPLEMENTATION

Screening

States must establish new bureaucracies to compile and screen the records of sex offenders about to be released from prison to see if they qualify under the state SVP law for commitment. New software programming may have to be written for this task. Personnel will have to be hired to ensure that records are complete and accurate; often, out-of-state conviction records must be obtained. This can be tedious and time consuming (La Fond, 1998).

California's SVP law took effect on January 1, 1996. As of February 1, 2002, the records of 4,054 sex offenders were referred to the California Department of Mental Health (DMH) for a records review. On the basis of this review, the DMH found that 2,226 offenders met the statutory criteria for an SVP, while 1,756 did not. Record review was pending in 72 cases. Thus, significant resources must be invested to screen sex offenders about to be released from prison (Sex Offender Commitment Report, 2000).

Florida's SVP law took effect on January 1, 1999. In the first year after enactment, the files of 4,377 sex offenders about to be released from prison had been referred to the state screening agency to determine if they met the statutory criteria. Of these, 2,808 were recommended for further assessment by a court (Office of Program Policy Analysis and Government Accountability, 2000).

Clinicians

Qualified mental health professionals (MHPs) must be hired to conduct clinical evaluations of those identified by the screening process or by a probable cause hearing as possible SVPs. Instructional material on how to conduct SVP evaluations may also have to be prepared. Some states, like California, require thorough clinical evaluations (usually conducted in the prison where the offender is located) by at least two MHPs and sometimes by as many as four. Other states, like Washington, will send these individuals to a central state facility for at least 30 days (and usually much longer) for evaluation by the state-employed staff.

Conducting a professionally appropriate evaluation is time consuming. Of course, the clinician must be well versed in the state SVP law and its definitions. The clinician must also obtain a wide range of records relating to the individual. These include prior treatment records and prison history and materials related to the qualifying offense(s), such as police reports, victim statements, and hearing transcripts. In addition, evaluators need to spend a fair amount of time directly with the offender obtaining sexual history and conducting a mental status exam. Evaluators may also need to conduct additional tests. (This volume, chapter 4, describes in detail how MHPs should conduct various evaluations under an SVP law.)

To have sufficient personnel to conduct these evaluations, states will have to either contract with private MHPs or hire them permanently. Private MHPs in California charge about $100 per hour (including travel time) and expenses to conduct these evaluations. The cost of hiring a state MHP as a full-time employee in California is approximately $90,000 including benefits. Defendants may retain their own expert at state expense if indigent. Because most of these individuals have been in prison, most of them are indigent.

These additional costs can be substantial. As of February 2, 2002, California had conducted 2,226 clinical evaluations. Clinical evaluations were positive in 944 cases and negative in 1,230 cases; evaluations were pending in 52 cases (Sex Offender Commitment Report, 2000). For the fiscal year 1999–2000, California expected to spend approximately $2.3 million on initial DMH assessments, evaluations, and costs related to evaluator court testimony (California SVP Cost Summary, 1999).

Florida has incurred substantial costs in providing pretrial screening. The cost of a prepetition screening and evaluation that ultimately results in a recommendation for filing an SVP petition is about $4,000 (G. Venz, Director of the Sexually Violent Predator Program, Florida Department of Children and Families, personal communication, January 24, 2002). Reportedly, a psychologist in Gainesville, Florida has a 3-year, $6.6 million dollar contract to conduct personal evaluations in that state (Sterghos Brochu, 2001a).

Trials and Appeals

If the prosecutor seeks to commit an individual as an SVP, a trial will be held in most cases. (Most states underestimated how long it would take to bring these cases to trial. As a result, states must pay for housing many individuals for long periods of time while they await trial.) Often there will be pretrial motions and extensive discovery. In California, a probable cause hearing is really a "minitrial"; it can easily take at least 1 day and, in some cases, 2 or 3 days. Trial preparation includes extensive review of documents and the preparation (and in some states deposition) of many witnesses, including MHPs who will testify as expert witnesses. For the fiscal year 1999–2000, California estimated it would spend approximately

$3.97 million on local costs for probable cause hearings and trials. These costs include prosecutors, defense counsel, court costs, transportation, and local housing (California SVP Cost Summary, 1999). Because the state of California, like Washington State, pays most of the local costs, there is little financial incentive for prosecutors not to file. In 1997 Minnesota officials estimated that each commitment proceeding cost about $100,000 for attorneys and experts alone, not including other costs (National Association of State Mental Health Directors & Health Services Research Institute, 1999).

Under most state SVP laws, either the defendant or the prosecutor can request a jury trial. In Washington State, prosecutors almost always request a jury trial. Thus, jurors must be selected and jury trials conducted. This adds time and expense. Prosecutors may decline to accept the defense counsel's offer to stipulate that their client has been convicted of a qualifying sex crime. Instead, prosecutors often have the victims of the offender's earlier crimes testify at the SVP trial. SVP trials in Washington State can last from 1 to 6 weeks. Defense counsel and their clients often treat these trials like "death penalty" cases because indefinite commitment as an SVP is, to many people, a death sentence.

In addition, many appeals involving SVP trials will be taken. In implementation of a new law, there are invariably a number of important constitutional, evidentiary, and procedural issues that appellate courts must resolve. In some instances, SVP cases may have to be retried in light of appellate court decisions (La Fond, 1998). Thus, states incur legal costs beyond simply trying SVP cases. In addition, many state SVP laws permit trials to determine if an SVP is entitled to release or must stay in confinement. Thus, multiple trials for SVPs can be expected.

SVP Census Projections

Census projections for SVPs are extremely problematic. Because most SVP statutes only require conviction of a single qualifying crime and do not require a serious mental disorder recognized by authoritative medical texts or organizations, the number of sex offenders eligible for commitment is very large (see this volume, chapter 7). Many sex offenders qualify for the diagnosis of antisocial personality disorder, a subtype of personality disorder, which is a diagnosis used in many SVP laws. Antisocial personality disorder is based primarily on an individual's criminal history.

It appears that screening by state agencies is the most important determination in eliminating sex offenders from potential SVP commitment. In a few states, notably California, probable cause hearings also remove many offenders from possible commitment. Hearings in California result in a finding of no probable cause in approximately 20% of the cases. In other states, like Washington, probable cause is almost always found, thus virtually ensuring a trial. In many states, most offenders who actually go to trial are committed as SVPs. In Washington, the government has won most SVP trials. In Florida, 47 of the 61 men actually brought to trial as of December 2, 2001, were committed; prosecutors had a 77% success rate (Sterghos Brochu, 2001a). In California, prosecutors appear to prevail in about 83% of the cases; 342 individuals were committed to treatment programs, while 72 were released as of February 1, 2002.

State projections for the number of SVPs in their institutions vary. Washington State projected a census of 150–200 by the end of 2000. As of October 30, 2001, it had 143 male offenders committed to its Special Commitment Center (SCC) for SVPs and 2 female offenders committed elsewhere. Because there is no facility in Washington State that can serve SVPs under 18, one youth has been placed in an out-of-state residential facility at a cost of $120,000 per year (Special Commitment Center 2001–2003 Biennium Funding, 2002). Kansas, which enacted its SVP law in 1994, projects a census of 132 by the year 2015. As of January 16, 2002, it had more than 60 SVPs (Rizzo, 2002). It projects a court commitment rate of 95% and an average length of stay of 4 years (Testimony of Janet Schalansky, 1999). California projects a maximum census of about 1,500 SVPs. As of February 2, 2002, California had committed 342 offenders to treatment as SVPs. Probable cause has been found in 520 other cases, and 116 individuals were awaiting trial. Minnesota hopes to cap its census at 350, whereas Wisconsin projects a maximum population of 600 committed offenders.

A number of states appear to be running ahead of projections made when their law was first enacted. In December 1999, Florida projected that 614 offenders would be committed by the year 2009 even though commitments were currently running at about 11 per month (132 per year). More recently, this estimate was increased; in early 2002 Florida estimated that it would have between 1,000 and 1,200 individuals committed under its law by the end of 2010 (G. Venz, personal communication, January 24, 2002). As of December 2001, there were 382 offenders confined under the law; many of them are awaiting trial (Sterghos Brochu, 2001a). Thus, this initial projection may be extremely understated, perhaps reaching 600 by 2004. In January 2002, Florida revised its initial estimate and expected that it would have approximately 450 SVPs in confinement by July 2002 (G. Venz, personal communication, January 24, 2002). This estimate appears on target.

Florida expected to build a 600-bed facility to be opened by March 2002. However, Governor Jeb Bush vetoed construction of the facility when the construction bids came in between $75 and $100 million. As of December 2001, a private company, Liberty Behavioral Corporation, a Pennsylvania corporation, was being paid about $1 million a month to run the treatment program at a renovated facility in Desoto County. When the

SVP program was moved there from Martin County, 78 of its 118 staff quit (Sterghos Brochu, 2001b). New staff members had to be hired and trained.

On a national basis, Fitch and Hammen (2001) reported that a total of 1,208 individuals have been committed as SVPs as of fall 2001 and that another 866 individuals were awaiting trial (see this volume, chapter 1). Thus, the number of individuals committed as SVPs will surely increase.

Perhaps the most important—and unknowable variable—in the calculus is the release rate of SVPs after commitment to treatment programs. As of the end of 2001, Washington State had released fewer than 10 SVPs to a transitional community release program. It had yet to grant final release to *anyone* even though its law has been in effect since August 1990. Kansas projects a release rate of 50% after 4 years of treatment. This seems unduly optimistic. As of February 2002, Kansas had released only three SVPs to a "transitional release" status even though it enacted its SVP law in 1994. It took 5 years for Kansas to release its first SVP to a least-restrictive alternative placement, or LRA (see this volume, chapter 4). Because officials were unable to find placement in a community willing to accept the initial offender given transitional release, he was housed in the beginning in a cottage on the grounds of the SVP hospital. Nationally (excluding Texas), only 49 SVPs have been released on LRAs as of June 2000 (see this volume, chapter 2). Thus, only about 5% of individuals committed as SVPs since these laws went into effect have been released to community transition programs. One would hope that this percentage increases after states have had a reasonable opportunity to provide treatment to SVPs.

Decisions to place SVPs in community release programs are difficult. As chapter 3 of this book shows, there is evidence indicating that experts, using actuarial instruments, can predict sexual dangerousness with some accuracy and reliability. This approach uses past historical facts, such as the age of first offending, gender of victim, and number of offenses, as the basis of this prediction. Thus, many experts have confidence in their ability to identify which sex offenders should be committed as SVPs.

However, we know very little about predicting when someone committed to a treatment program is safe to be released. This prediction is based on variable factors such as alteration of attitudes toward their conduct and their victims, changes in sexual preferences, and other dynamic factors that can change during the course of treatment. Consequently, experts are more confident of their decisions to *commit* than of their decisions to *release*. The predictable political backlash that will materialize *when* an SVP on transitional or final release reoffends—an inevitable event—undoubtedly makes officials even more reluctant to recommend release. Thus, one would expect that the commitment rate would far exceed the release rate for SVPs.

This has certainly been the case so far. Fitch and Hammen (2001) reported that as of fall 2001, only 20 SVPs were committed as outpatients, whereas 1,208 were committed as inpatients. This is simply astounding! Since 1990, only 20 patients were placed in outpatient commitment more than 11 years after the first SVP law was enacted. Given this ratio, it seems inevitable that the SVP census in every state will continue to grow well beyond initial projections.

Female SVPs

Although most sex offenders committed as SVPs will be men, women have already been committed under these laws in several states, including Washington, California, and Missouri. It is likely that female SVPs and adolescent SVPs will have to be housed and treated in separate facilities. A federal court in Washington State, noting that commingling of male and female SVPs presented both safety and treatment issues, ruled that the state must place Washington's female SVPs in a separate facility suitable for treatment (La Fond, 1998). Most treatment professionals believe that segregation and treatment by gender is required to prevent new victimization of females by male sex offenders and to prevent psychological harm to female SVPs that participation in treatment sessions with male sex offenders can cause. Thus, states should be prepared to provide separate suitable housing and treatment programs for female SVPs. Because the number of female SVPs is likely to be very small (at least initially), economies of scale are unlikely. Consequently, the per capita costs for female SVPs may be extremely high.

Right to Treatment

Most state SVP laws provide a right to treatment for SVPs (Washington Sexually Violent Predators Act, 1999). (This volume, chapter 6, also describes the constitutional role that treatment plays.) The Supreme Court upheld the Kansas law, in part, because Kansas was providing treatment to SVPs and the attorney general for Kansas told that Court that treatment was an important goal of its law (*Kansas v. Hendricks*, 1997).

In 1994 a federal court in Seattle held that SVPs have a constitutional right to treatment and issued an injunction ordering Washington to upgrade its SVP program (*Turay v. Weston*, 1994). In general terms, the state was ordered to provide treatment in a therapeutic environment, implement a treatment program that conformed to prevailing professional standards, prepare an individual treatment plan for each SVP, and hire and train a professionally qualified staff. The court hired a special master to evaluate the program, make recommendations for improvement, and to report back to the court on problems the special master identified and the state's solutions.

Through the end of 1999, Washington State had spent approximately $44.5 million on operations on the SCC, which houses and treats SVPs. Nonetheless, as of May 2000 (6 years after the initial court order and after numerous on-site evaluations of the program by the special master, which also included 17 reports to the court), Washington State's SVP program still did not comply with the court order. The program has been plagued by its inability to find a suitable permanent facility; to hire, train, and retain staff knowledgeable in treating sex offenders; to provide a community transition release program; and, generally, to implement a bona fide treatment program that exists not only on paper but also in reality.

Finally exhausted by Washington State's deliberate failure to provide constitutionally required treatment to SVPs, the court ruled in November 1999 that, as of May 1, 2000, it would fine the state $50 per day per SVP if it has not complied with the court's order. As of November 26, 2001, these fines have accumulated to $3.5 million; the judge has suspended payment as long as progress is being made by the SCC in complying with his orders. As a result of this severe sanction, the legislature budgeted a supplementary expenditure of $14 million to construct the first stage of a new SCC facility. The state also provided an additional $5 million for staff hiring and training. Thirty new staff positions were created in December 1999, improving the staff-to-resident ratio.

After an extended hearing, the court ruled on May 5, 2000, that Washington had not yet complied with its earlier orders to provide constitutionally required treatment but that it had made "substantial progress." After another hearing held on December 5, 2000, the court ruled again that Washington State had still not complied with its order to provide constitutionally required treatment. Because the state was making progress, however, the court did not impose any fines. In August 2001, the special master appointed by the court in 1994 to monitor Washington's compliance with court orders resigned after 7 years on the job (Duran, 2001).

As a result of this litigation, a permanent 404-bed SCC facility is being constructed on McNeil Island to house Washington's SVP program (Special Commitment Center 2001–2003 Biennium Funding, 2002) The state's 2001–2003 budget proposes spending $33.5 million on the SCC.

Every state that enacts an SVP law will have to provide constitutionally adequate treatment. They must hire and train staff who are qualified to treat sex offenders. Most staff will learn "on the job." As noted by a Michigan mental health official concerning sex offender treatment professionals:

> Michigan does not have a reservoir of trained clinicians in this specialized field, does not have minimum standards of certification, and has few recognized treatment programs for sex offenders, either in state juvenile, adult, or mental health institutions, or in the private sector. (La Fond, 1998, p. 492)

Providing treatment that conforms to prevailing professional standards is complicated by the fact that SVPs are very diverse with different characteristics, including mental disability, varying diagnoses, sexual attractions, and arousal patterns (see this volume, chapter 2). Thus, some aspects of treatment will have to be tailored to meet the unique needs of each individual.

In addition to providing professionally qualified staff and individualized treatment, states will have to renovate or build new facilities, establish treatment programs, prepare individualized treatment plans, and establish a self-contained functional institutional bureaucracy. Eventually, every state will also have to develop and fund transitional release programs.

Failure to provide constitutionally required treatment and humane conditions of confinement will result in prolonged and expensive litigation that may require expenditure of significant additional funds to upgrade programs. These lawsuits may also result in fines and payment of attorneys' fees. Washington State has paid 16 individuals committed to its SVP program $10,000 each and has paid their attorneys $250,000 to settle their right-to-treatment lawsuits. It also incurred significant litigation costs defending various lawsuits, including the salaries and fees of special masters appointed by the federal court. Lawsuits seeking enforcement of the right to treatment and seeking to improve the conditions of confinement have reportedly been brought in Wisconsin (*West v. Macht*, 1999), Illinois (*In re Traynoff*), and California (*Hydrick v. Wilson*, 1998). Simply put, it is impossible to run SVP programs "on the cheap."

Confinement and Treatment Costs

Running an SVP facility is doubly challenging and doubly expensive because the state must maintain a facility that is both *secure* and *therapeutic*. SVP facilities must perform the function of a prison and of a hospital. In 2001, states reported an average annual inpatient treatment cost per patient ranging from $70,000 in Arizona to $165,000 in the District of Columbia. Minnesota estimated a per patient cost of $150,000 annually, while Wisconsin's estimate was $87,000. California estimated those costs at $107,000, while Florida's estimate was $85,700 (Fitch & Hammen, 2001).

SVP programs can have significant impact on other state programs. California initially placed its SVPs in Atascadero State Hospital. To make room for them, the state had to send seriously disturbed forensic patients at Atascadero to other DMH facilities. This hydraulic effect required renovations at other facilities to add secure accommodations for these displaced patients. For the fiscal year 1999–2000, California expected to spend a total of $38.574 million on inpatient SVPs (328 SVPs full year and 65 SVPs half year; California SVP Cost Summary, 1999). But, $47.393

million was allocated to its SVP program in 1998 (Fitch & Hammen, 2001).

Currently, California plans to construct a new inpatient facility to house 1,500 inpatient SVPs. The facility is estimated to cost approximately $300 million to construct and is expected to open in July 2003 (California SVP Cost Summary, 1999). This date may be optimistic because officials encountered predictable "not in my backyard" opposition from local communities who do not want the facility sited near them.

Washington State reportedly pays $130,000 a year for each SVP at the SCC (Carter, 2000). Washington State is building a new SVP facility with a 400-bed capacity at McNeil Island. Initially estimated to cost $40 million, this estimate was increased to $81 million dollars. It is scheduled to be completed in 2005. The *Seattle Times* reported:

> With an estimated 25 new residents coming in each year—and few, if any, getting out—the new center would soon be well over capacity, with a projected 550 residents in the year 2013. And, even at today's cost per resident, that would require an operating budget alone of at least $72 million a year. (Carter, 2000, p. A1)

As of fall 2001, Minnesota had committed 175 offenders as SVPs (see this volume, chapter 1). It currently has 150 beds and is requesting funding for 200 more beds. The admission rate has been running about 16–18 per year. A Minnesota Department of Corrections report projects a total cost for the current practice of SVP commitments to be about $76 million per year in 2010 compared with $17 million in 1998—a 450% increase in a 12-year period. Minnesota is trying to develop strategies to reduce its SVP treatment expenditures. It may start trying to identify potential SVPs in the prison system and offer them treatment while they serve their prison terms, hoping that in many cases SVP commitment will not be necessary at the end of their sentences.

Missouri, which enacted its SVP law in 1999, had 22 offenders committed as SVPs and another 29 awaiting trial as of January 9, 2002; it expects to add another 20 to 30 next year (Dreiling, 2002). As of April 2000, its SVP facility had 24 beds and a treatment staff of 57. Thus, it had to expand its bed capacity significantly. It projects a census of 150 SVPs. In early 2000, Florida Governor Bush asked that $8.8 million in addition to the $23 million proposed by the legislature be set aside to help build a new or renovated SVP facility (Samolinski, 2000). Only 3 years after its enactment, Florida had spent $45 million on it (Sterghos Brochu, 2001a).

States may be able to reduce treatment costs somewhat below those of a major state psychiatric hospital. Unlike many civilly committed patients in most state hospitals, most SVPs do not receive extensive medication. Thus, SVP facilities may not need as many professional staff qualified to prescribe or dispense drugs as other state hospitals. Florida has privatized the treatment program at its primary SVP facility. Other states have been reported to be exploring privatization of SVP programs. Although this strategy might reduce costs, states would still have to ensure that treatment required by law is being provided. Thus, states would still have to monitor these facilities, their staffs, and their treatment programs.

Release and Community Transition Programs

Conditional release of SVPs can require intensive supervision, including 24-hour supervision by security guards, equipping a home with electronic monitoring and security systems, visits to a probation officer, alcohol and drug counseling, and sex offender treatment. The costs can be substantial, although they are, in most cases, lower than the cost of institutional care.

Officials from Wisconsin, which has the most SVPs on outpatient commitment (9), reported an average annual cost of $27,500, with a high of $129,000 and a low of $0. Illinois (4 outpatients) estimates a cost of $91,000 per case. California predicts that its first outpatient commitment from institutional care will cost $115,000. Washington with 6 SVPs on outpatient commitment reports a range from $25,000 to $105,000 (Fitch & Hammen, 2001). In one particular case, however, Washington State officials estimated that providing these services would cost $150,000 a year to provide LRA housing (Fisher, 2000). In another case Washington State is reported to have paid over $10,000 a month to place an SVP in a community transition program.

The Washington State governor proposed a budget for the 2001–2003 biennium that included $9.5 million for placing SVPs into community LRAs. It includes construction of a 24-bed facility on McNeil Island, $2 million for community safety mitigation, and $800,000 for additional law enforcement on McNeil Island (Special Commitment Center 2001–2003 Biennium Funding, 2002).

In most states, prosecutors can object to a decision by the treatment staff to release an SVP and insist on another trial. In many states, they can ask for a jury trial. Because of the fierce public antagonism toward SVPs, there is often intense public pressure against releasing an SVP. Prosecutors often object to their release. Washington State has concluded that an SVP does not have a right to judicial review of the staff's determination that he is not safe to be released (*In re Petersen*, 1999). Release without staff support and the prosecutor's acquiescence is extremely difficult. In the first 10 years in which the Washington SVP law was in effect, only 6 SVPs were released on LRAs as of March 2000. Judges ordered all of these releases over the objection of staff. Even with staff support, prosecutors in Washington State have successfully blocked conditional release of an SVP by insisting on a jury trial (Morris & Carter, 2000). Ironically, this was the *first* case in which SCC staff had *recommended* release of a SVP and the prosecutor called *no* witnesses!

All experts agree that sex offenders in SVP programs should be placed in a community transition program before final release (La Fond, 1992). During this phase, offenders continue treatment and are closely monitored in the community. This program allows experts to make a more realistic risk assessment because it is based on the offender's behavior in a real-life situation rather than in a secure facility.

Most states, including California, Kansas, Minnesota, and Washington, have not yet provided a systematic program for community release. The court in a Washington right-to-treatment case concluded: "Without LRAs, the constitutional requirement of treatment leading, if successful, to cure and release, cannot fully be met" (*Turay v. Seling*, 2000). It noted that "ad hoc negotiations for [SVP] placement are no substitute for a systematic transition program with adequate LRA facilities." As of February 2000, Minnesota had placed only one individual in transitional release. In many states the SVP (invariably his lawyer) must design and arrange for community release on an ad hoc basis.

States probably need a "critical mass" of offenders ready for transitional release before it is financially feasible to consider building and staffing a transitional release facility. Even then, it may be difficult to site the facility because of community opposition. The absence of a structured program and a permanent facility with professional staff to facilitate transitional release inhibits release decisions, making it more likely that the census of SVPs in institutions will remain high.

At least one state, Florida, will not place released SVPs into a community facility under an LRA or conditional release program. Its statute does not authorize LRAs. Instead, SVPs will be released without supervision if they qualify under the law. However, most of them will then have to register with the Florida Department of Law Enforcement (G. Venz, personal communication, January 24, 2002). (See this volume, chapter 12, for a discussion of sex offender registration laws.)

Many states have enacted sex offender notification laws, which require or authorize state officials to notify a community when a dangerous sex offender about to be released from custody intends to reside in that community. (See this volume, chapter 12, for a description of these laws.) Local communities often object to the state placing an SVP near them on transitional release. This often complicates arranging for community release.

To date, states have not spent much money on transitional release programs. If they have any realistic expectation of releasing SVPs and thereby keeping their inpatient census at a reasonable level, states will have to spend substantial funds on community transition programs. Simply put, a major unavoidable cost of implementing an SVP law has yet to be incurred.

In many states, treatment staff cannot release SVPs on their own authority (see this volume, chapter 2). Courts must approve each release, and, in many states, prosecutors may object to release and seek continued commitment, including requesting another trial. Thus, the release decision is not primarily a clinical decision, even though additional clinical evaluations are usually required and can be expensive (see this volume, chapter 4). Rather, it is a judicial decision, often subject to objections by prosecutors and to intense political pressure.

There is another confounding phenomenon that may inflate the number of offenders who remain committed indefinitely as SVPs. Some offenders are not participating in treatment. This is especially true in Washington State where, as of March 2000, 45 of the 106 individuals then confined at the SCC were not participating in treatment (Carter, 2000). In Missouri, some SVPs are considered not suitable for treatment. The release prospects for these offenders remain very low because a change in their mental status is unlikely. Over time these individuals will simply accumulate in the system, significantly adding to the census and to costs. (It is possible, however, that these individuals might be placed in a less expensive custodial facility. Even then, SVPs cannot be placed in prisons or other correctional facilities.)

If SVPs are not released in sufficient numbers, census in SVP institutions will increase. As many of these individuals get older, their general medical needs will increase. In January 2002, California spent close to $1 million for a heart transplant for a state prison inmate. Its annual health care costs for its almost 157,000 criminal inmates increased from $282 million in 1998 to $663 million in 2002 (Sterngold, 2002). Although SVPs will constitute a much smaller confined population, states should expect increased spending to provide a wide range of medical services to this population as it ages. It is not clear whether states are taking such costs into account in determining the amount of funding that will be required by SVP programs.

Money spent on confining and treating SVPs is money *not* spent on many other pressing social needs (see this volume, chapters 1 and 13). In his 2001–2003 budget, Washington State Governor Gary Locke proposed spending $43 million on the SCC, which houses and treats SVPs. This is an increase of $18.8 million in spending over his 1999–2001 budget for the SCC—a 78% increase! Meanwhile, Governor Locke's 2001–2003 budget proposes *cutting* the state's funding for children's services, juvenile rehabilitation, mental health, aging and adult services, alcohol and substance abuse, medical assistance, and vocational rehabilitation (Washington State Department of Social and Health Services, 2002).

KEEPING COSTS FROM SKYROCKETING

Although problematic in a number of important ways, policymakers can roughly estimate the per capita cost of evaluating potential SVPs and trying SVP cases. They can also estimate with some confidence the per capita costs of building secure and therapeutic facilities to house SVPs and staffing them with qualified professional staffs and providing appropriate treatment programs. Estimating the costs of providing transitional release programs, an essential component of an SVP law, is more difficult because, so far, states have had limited experience with them. But with additional experience, it should be more manageable.

Undoubtedly, the most difficult calculation is to accurately project a steady-state census over time. That is, what is the maximum number of SVPs a state should expect to house and treat? Several significant variables come into play here, including the number of eligible sex offenders about to be released from prison, the rate of referral, the rate of filing, the rate of successful commitments, and the length of commitment—which of course requires an estimate of the rate of release. Other variables, such as changes in sentencing laws and incidence of sex crimes, are also important. It is fair to say that, as of now, no state really has a firm basis for predicting how many SVPs will actually be institutionalized under these laws. In any event, the costs of enacting and implementing an SVP law will be significant.

How, then, can states contain these costs within reasonable bounds? There are a number of reforms that need to be made in drafting and implementing SVP laws.

First, states must do a more thorough job of screening potential SVP cases, reducing the number of sex offenders identified as probable SVPs. Second, the filing decision should not be left solely in the hands of prosecutors, especially local prosecutors who are elected. The political pressures to file, both initially and at conditional release, can be enormous. States should consider broadening participation in the decision to file SVP petitions, specifically by including experts in diagnosing and treating sex offenders. Third, clinical evaluations should be conducted before the probable cause hearing rather than after. California's experience indicates that a significant number of SVP trials and commitments will thereby be avoided. Fourth, judges must take probable cause hearings seriously. Washington State's experience indicates that, in some states, this screening device simply does not work. Fifth, sex offenders should not languish in confinement for several years before the SVP trial is held. Pressure should be brought to bear both on the state and on defense counsel to resolve the crucial issue of whether the individual is—or is not—an SVP.

Sixth, only individuals whose commitment as an SVP is being sought should be allowed to request a jury trial. Prosecutors should not be allowed to insist on jury trials. Juries in these cases do not serve as a protector of individual liberty against government tyranny as envisioned by the framers of our Constitution. Rather, they will invariably err on the side of community safety and vote to commit. Seventh, SVP laws should authorize commitment to an LRA from the outset. This will allow SVP laws to use a risk management approach in appropriate cases to protect the community (see this volume, chapter 15) while reducing costs. Eighth, states should revise their SVP laws to authorize treatment staff to grant conditional release without allowing objection by prosecutors. Ninth, states must establish viable transitional release programs that provide community security, effective treatment, and ongoing risk assessment. Without such placements, the pressure to keep SVPs in perpetual confinement will be intense.

CONCLUSION

Most important, policymakers must decide whether the primary purpose of the law is to provide sex offenders with a realistic opportunity to change and to earn their release or whether the real purpose is to simply confine them for as long as possible. Ultimately, a state must decide whether it will establish a bona fide therapeutic commitment program or an indeterminate confinement scheme masquerading as therapeutic hospitalization (La Fond, 1999). If states are willing to provide constitutionally required treatment, to offer community transition placements, and to release offenders when they have successfully completed the treatment program, then more SVPs will be released and the number of SVPs in confinement should eventually stabilize. If, however, states are intent simply on quarantining SVPs, then the number of SVPs in confinement will steadily increase. Who knows how much that will cost?

REFERENCES

California SVP Cost Summary, Fiscal Year 1999–2000. (1999, November 3). [On file with John Q. La Fond].

Carter, M. (2000, March 21). Sex-offender center: 10 years of trouble. *Seattle Times*, p. A1.

Dreiling, G. (2002, January 9). Fallen angel. *Riverfront Times*. Retrieved on November 13, 2002 from http://www.riverfronttimes.com/issues/2002-01-09/features.html/1/index.html

Duran, S. (2001, November 26). Judge may not need sex center adviser. *News Tribune* (Tacoma, Washington), p. B1.

Fisher, D. (2000, August 16). Predator's supervised release is proposed. *Seattle Post-Intelligencer*, p. B1.

Fitch, W. L., & Hammen, D. (2001). *Sex offender commitment: A survey of the states*. Unpublished manuscript.

Hydrick v. Wilson, C.D. Cal. Cause No. CV 98-7167TJH (RNB) (1998).

Kansas v. Hendricks, 117 S. Ct. 2072 (1997).

La Fond, J. Q. (1992). Washington's sexually violent predator law: A deliberate misuse of the therapeutic state for social control. *University of Puget Sound Law Review, 15*, 655–708.

La Fond, J. Q. (1998). The costs of enacting a sexually violent predator law. *Psychology, Public Policy, and Law, 4*, 468–504.

La Fond, J. Q. (1999). Can therapeutic jurisprudence be normatively neutral? Sexual predators laws: Their impact on participants and policy. *Arizona Law Review, 41*, 375–415.

Morris, K., & Carter, M. (2000, August 19). Jurors reject request to free eight-time rapist. *Seattle Times*, p. A1.

National Association of State Mental Health Program Directors & Health Services Research Institute. (1999). *Evaluation center survey on the civil commitment of sexually violent criminal offender legislation*. Alexandria, VA: National Association of State Mental Health Program Directors.

Office of Program Policy Analysis and Government Accountability. (2000, February). *The Florida Legislature Report No. 99-36*. Tallahassee, FL: Author.

In re Petersen, 980 P.2d 1204 (1999).

Rizzo, T. (2002, January 16). Prosecutors want KCK man classified as sexual predator. *Kansas City Star*, p. B2.

Samolinski, C. J. (2000, April 16). Post-release supervision falls through the cracks. *Tampa Tribune*, p. 9.

Sex Offender Commitment Report. (2000). Retrieved May 15, 2000, from http://www.dmh.cahwnet.gov/socp/facts-figures.asp.

Special Commitment Center 2001–2003 Biennium Funding. (2002). Retrieved from http://www.wa.gov/dshs/budget

Sterghos Brochu, N. (2001a, December 2). Sex-offender law flawed, critics say; civil rights, costs are debated. *Fort Lauderdale Sun-Sentinel*, p. 1A.

Sterghos Brochu, N. (2001b, December 3). Treatment program's effectiveness debated. *Fort Lauderdale Sun-Sentinel*, p. 1A.

Sterngold, J. (2002, January 31). Inmate's transplant prompts questions of costs and ethics. *New York Times*, p. A18.

Testimony of Janet Schalansky, Secretary of Kansas Department of Social and Rehabilitation Services, Kansas (1999, October 19). [On file with John Q. La Fond].

In re Traynoff, Kane County, Ill., Cause No. 98 HR 456.

Turay v. Seling, 108 F. Supp. 2d 1148 (W.D. Wash. 2000).

Turay v. Weston, No. C91-664WD (W.D. Wash. 1994).

Washington Sexually Violent Predators Act, Wash. Rev. Code § 71.09 (Supp. 1999).

Washington State Department of Social and Health Services. (2002). *Budget, 2001–2003*. Retrieved from http://www.app2.wa.gov/dshs/budget

West v. Macht, 197 F.3d 1185 (7th Cir. 1999).

17

MANAGING THE MONSTROUS: SEX OFFENDERS AND THE NEW PENOLOGY

JONATHAN SIMON

The U.S. Supreme Court often writes as if the social meaning of punishment were exhausted by the traditional purposes of criminal sanctions: retribution or vengeance, deterrence, reform, and incapacitation (*United States v. Ursery*, 518 U.S. 267, 1996). Seen in this way, the recent decades have witnessed rapid cycles of preference among these purposes. Rehabilitation was the cutting-edge philosophy of the late 19th century, but as late as 1968, the President's Commission Report on crime policy emphasized improvements in rehabilitation as the central task in the future of corrections (Presidential Commission on Law Enforcement and the Administration of Justice, 1967). Yet a decade later, Allen (1981) could declare the decline of the rehabilitative ideal. In the 1980s just desert, retribution, and deterrence seemed to be back, whereas in the 1990s

This chapter is a revised and updated version of material first published in Simon (1998b). Copyright © 1998 by the American Psychological Association (APA). Adapted with permission of the author and the APA.

incapacitation and open appeals to vengeance have emerged as leading rationales for a much expanded penal state (Caplow & Simon, 1999).

In a series of papers, Malcolm Feeley and I (see Feeley & Simon, 1992, 1994; Simon & Feeley, 1995) have argued that a different kind of historical change is unfolding in our contemporary penal practices that cuts across many of these philosophical differences. What we have described as the *new penology* is marked more by changes in the targets, strategies, and discourses of the penal establishment than by purposes in a formal sense. These shifts are discontinuous and not always all present, but three broad patterns have emerged as defining characteristics of the new penology.

First, the new penology abandons the priority of the individual in penality. From the end of the 18th century at least, Anglo American and Continental criminal law were increasingly focused on the individual offender, albeit in very different postures. The target was sometimes the responsible agent behind the heinous act; at other times, it was the delinquent individual, whose later crimes were thought to be foreshadowed in minor transgressions. By the 20th century, the target of efforts to scientifically study the origins of crime focused on the personality and social conditions of the offender (Garland, 1985; Rothman, 1980). This lent priority to forms of expertise that could plausibly claim to produce knowledge at the level of the person (Simon, 1998a). Today this priority of the individual in both knowledge and power is being displaced in favor of groups, categories, and classes. An important dimension is the priority given to the language of risk in the administration of justice.

A second shift has taken place in the master narratives of penology: Offenders formerly defined as aberrant and in need of transformation are now seen as high-risk individuals in need of management (Logan, 1999; Steiker, 1998). The rehabilitative ideal was a development of the 20th century, but transformative and reformative goals of punishment have longer roots going back to the Enlightenment reformers of the 18th century and even earlier to cannon law. It is not that transformation has disappeared as a goal, but increasingly it amounts to little more than gestures, whereas the central focus has increasingly come to be on managing members of a population likely to be in and out of penal custody for a large portion of their lives. Latent in this managerialism is a growing sense that little or nothing can be done to change offenders. The optimism that informed 18th- and 19th-century penal theorists has been replaced by a pragmatic pessimism that assumes little effectiveness to efforts at transformation. This pessimism reflects broader social shifts in both social conditions and the production of knowledge. The growth of a seemingly permanent poverty class in American cities, often referred to as an "underclass," feeds the perception that transformational strategies aimed at offenders are both futile and useless (Simon, 1993). The pessimistic sense that expert-guided interventions in the lives of individuals for social improvement are unlikely to succeed is a common one today.

A third major shift has been the displacement of evaluative norms rooted in real communities by operational parameters rooted in the penal system itself as evaluative guides (Simon, 1993). Criminal justice decision making (e.g., pardons, paroles, and probation) were traditionally attuned to signals from those in the community in a position to fear or control the offender, including employers, family members, and neighbors. In recent decades this community focus has lessened and largely been replaced by technocratic forms of knowledge, such as drug tests and compliance with administrative rules.

The new penology is only one important determinate of criminal justice practice today. It describes ways of thinking and responding most evident among penal managers, their staffs, and the penumbra of academic and policy workers involved in the production of penal discourse. Public and political discussion of penality has been pulled in a very different direction, indeed one that clashes strikingly with the new penology (Simon & Feeley, 1995). This public discourse emphasizes what can be called *populist punitiveness*. The death penalty, "three-strikes-and-you're-out" laws, and mandatory sentences for drug dealing all reflect a new primacy of vengeance seeking. For example, recent opinion surveys have found that supporters of the death penalty are more likely to cite vengeance and retribution as justifications than a decade ago, when utilitarian objectives like deterrence were the prime justifications cited (Ellsworth & Gross, 1994).

Populist punitiveness operates uneasily with the new penology. The new penology is concerned with high-risk populations; populist punitiveness is as obsessed as ever with specific dangerous individuals. The new penology treats crime as a normal fact of life to be managed; populist punitiveness insists on a zero-tolerance approach and believes that with severe enough sanctions, crime can and should be completely eliminated. The new penology speaks the language of managerialism and systems theory; populist punitiveness remains rooted in normative judgments about aberrational evil. For the most part, the new penology and populist punitiveness coexist through a tenuously maintained acoustic divide. Politicians pass laws expressing populist punitiveness while relying on the managerial skill of penal professionals to keep the costs down by applying the techniques and strategies of the new penology. However, when the public learns that a new penology-minded bureaucracy often moderates its punitive mandates, the response is generally one of falling back on punitiveness.

Recent sex offender laws provide a compelling picture of how the new penology and populist punitiveness are being merged in the creation of penal policy. In the old penology, with its focus on transforming aberrant individuals, the sex offender, along with the alcoholic, the mentally impaired, and the like, provided central examples of how crime was rooted in individual deviation. Treatment and rehabilitation coexisted with incapacitation and preventive measures like sterilization, but all of these presupposed expertise acting through individualized judgment. These exemplary figures also helped justify the penetration of psychological and psychiatric professionals into the criminal justice system.

One of the most compelling aspects of the new generation of sex offender laws is precisely the degree to which they permit a blending of the new penology with populist punitiveness. The new penology is generally agnostic toward treatment. (See this volume, chapter 5, for a discussion of whether treatment for sex offenders is effective in reducing sexual reoffending.) The goal is waste management (Logan, 2000). Populist punitiveness is exceedingly hostile toward medicalization. The result is an important transformation of the sex offender from the most obvious example of crime as disease back to an earlier conception of crime as monstrosity. Sex offenders are our modern-day monsters.

Decisions handed down during the 1990s by the U.S. Supreme Court and the Supreme Court of New Jersey have opened a window into the new-style sex offender laws and their constitutional significance. In *Kansas v. Hendricks* (1997), the Supreme Court per Justice Thomas upheld the Kansas Sexually Violent Predators Act (Kan. Stat. Ann. § 59-2901 *et seq.*, 1994), a law permitting the civil commitment of "violent sexual predators," including those who have already served their complete prison sentence for the underlying crimes. (This volume, chapters 1 and 2, describe these SVP laws. Chapter 11 analyzes the *Hendricks* decision in detail.) In *Doe v. Poritz* (1995), the Supreme Court of New Jersey upheld Megan's Law, a statute mandating a system of registration and selective community notification of convicted sex offenders.

The next section of this chapter describes the preventive detention law upheld in *Hendricks*. Then I discuss the new community registration laws enacted by many states under the title "Megan's Law" in New Jersey. (This volume, chapter 12, also discusses these registration and notification laws.) Both laws are fairly typical of statutes adopted in many states. The conclusion offers a critique of the terms under which the new penology is being constitutionalized in such cases and a plea for courts to recognize the distinctive features of contemporary penal practices in contrast to presuming continuity with the traditional goals of punishment.

THE CASE OF *KANSAS V. HENDRICKS*

In *Kansas v. Hendricks* (1997), the U.S. Supreme Court upheld the Kansas Sexually Violent Predator Act. A majority opinion by Justice Thomas reversed the holding by the Kansas Supreme Court that the act violated Hendricks's right to due process because it made "mental aberration" a predicate finding for confinement rather than "mental illness," with its implication of psychiatric and psychological expertise. Justice Thomas, writing for a majority of six, upheld the statute. He found that the concept of "mental abnormality" appropriately limited the range of persons subject to confinement to those whose previous acts of sexual violence were combined with an objective mental characteristic supporting an inference of propensity to future crimes of sexual violence. The majority opinion also rejected Hendricks's cross-claim that the act violated the Constitution's double jeopardy and *ex post facto* prohibitions. Justice Thomas found that the act was neither intended to be punitive nor so punitive in effect as to constitute an additional term of punishment.

From Individual to Aggregates

The target of the Kansas statute is explicitly framed in terms of dangerous categories or classes of persons. The act's preamble names its target as a subpopulation or group rather than a type of behavior or form of individual aberration: "A small but extremely dangerous group of sexually violent predators exist who do not have a mental disease or defect that renders them appropriate for involuntary treatment pursuant to the [general civil commitment statute]" (*Kansas v. Hendricks*, 521 U.S. 346, 351).

The Kansas procedure, to be sure, appears to solicitously protect the individual by insisting on both a probable cause finding by a judge and ultimately a finding by a jury that the defendant was, in fact, a sexually violent predator. The trial is to include examination by mental health professionals. But these procedural gestures toward the individual cannot change the fact that the underlying inquiry is rooted in a group concept. Once the jury found Hendricks a "sexually violent predator," the conclusion was foregone that he would be transferred to the custody of the Secretary of Social and Rehabilitation Services.

From Normalization to Management

The Kansas Act further defines its goals as ones of management rather than transformation: "The Kansas Legislature enacted the Sexually Violent Predator Act in 1994 to grapple with the problem of *managing* [italics added] repeat sexual offenders." Indeed, the premise of the whole legislation is that managing sexual offenders under existing laws is difficult precisely because of the inapplicability of normal treatment assumptions to the act's "sexual predators." (This volume, chapter 5, describes treatment for sex offenders, and chapter 6 explores the constitutional role that treatment plays in SVP laws.)

The legislature further finds that the sexually violent predators' likelihood of engaging in repeat acts of predatory sexual violence is high. The existing involuntary commitment procedure ... is inadequate to address the risk these sexually violent predators pose to society. (*Kansas v. Hendricks*, 521 U.S. 346, 351)

From Social Norms to Systems

The displacement of decision-making criteria grounded in social judgments by technocratic system imperatives is one way of understanding the difference between "mental illness" and "mental abnormality" at the heart of the Court's due process analysis. The former is a concept grounded in sources of expertise relatively autonomous of the penal system, whereas the latter appears to be a far more flexible concept shaped by the system's own knowledge of the offender. Indeed, Justice Kennedy's concurrence underlined precisely this problem by worrying out loud that further implementation might show that the concept of "mental abnormality is too imprecise a category to offer a solid basis for concluding that civil detention is justified" (*Kansas v. Hendricks*, 521 U.S. 346, 373, Kennedy, J., concurring).

Populist Punitiveness

The Kansas Act also reflects the role of sexual offenders as the new monsters haunting the American public. The majority opinion fully accepts the state's interpretation of the act as an act of risk management. But the very centrality of the term *predator*, which has no foundation in either human science or criminal jurisprudence, indicates the implicit reference to popular emotions, including fear and the desire for vengeance. Along with the act's elimination of an emphasis on treatment and expertise, this makes the Kansas Act a potent symbol of the state's willingness to exercise power, unmediated by treatment motivations or scientific norms, on those deemed "monstrous." This is further emphasized by the role given to the prosecutor and the jury. The Kansas Act places the decision to seek post-sentence civil confinement on the prosecutor. The ultimate decision as to whether such a prisoner should be considered a "sexually violent predator" is to be made at a trial by a jury.

Prosecutors are generally among those state officials most vulnerable to and sensitive to public pressures and fears. The jury is, of course, an even more direct way to embody popular consent in acts of state power. Indeed, the development of the old penology through mechanisms such as the indeterminate sentence and parole had the effect of removing the duration of punishment away from the influence of prosecutors and juries in favor of quasi-autonomous bodies supposedly grounded in professional expertise (e.g., parole boards and juvenile court clinics). By equipping its prosecutors with the power to confine "sexually violent predators" and inviting juries to consent, Kansas has emphasized the importance of populist fears and demands for punishment in its management of sex offenders.

MEGAN'S LAW

Megan's Law (alternatively titled the Registration and Community Notification Laws) was enacted in New Jersey in 1994 in response to public outrage over the rape and murder of a 7-year-old girl, Megan Kanka, by a previously convicted sex offender who was living across the street along with two other sex offenders (N.J. Stat. Ann. § 2C:7-1 to 7-11). Megan's murder became a rallying point for victims' rights activists, and her parents became prominent spokespeople for the victims' rights movement. These groups, prominently featured by the media, framed the issue as one of the betrayal of parents by a state unable to control predators and unwilling to empower citizens to protect themselves. The New Jersey legislature responded with a law defining those convicted of a long list of sex offenses as "sexual predators" and establishing a process for registration, risk assessment, and community notification of those deemed to be of moderate or high risk of further sex crimes. In 1994 the federal government enacted a law requiring states to have at least registration requirements if not notification (the Jacob Wetterling Crimes Against Children and Sexually Violent Offender Registration Act, 42 U.S.C. § 4071, 1994). Today every state has a registration law, and nearly 20 have notification of citizens, some under the name Megan's Law while others have attached the name of local child victims.

The design and implementation of Megan's Law reflect the imperatives of the new penology and populist punitiveness that we have discussed earlier. In this section, I examine the New Jersey version, because it was the first and has received the most administrative and judicial development.

From Individuals to Aggregates

First, in place of the old penology's concern with individuals, and like the Kansas Sexually Violent Predator Act, Megan's Law names a subpopulation or category of persons as its target. The statute defined its target as "sex offenders . . . offenders who commit other predatory acts against children . . . and . . . persons who prey on others as a result of mental illness" (*Doe v. Poritz*, 662 A.2d 367, 374–75). The logic of the classification is one based on statistical evidence about recidivism rather than on clinical judgments about individual proclivities.

The laws represent a conclusion by the Legislature that those convicted sex offenders who have successfully, or apparently successfully, been integrated into their communities, adjusted their lives so as to appear no more threatening than anyone else in the neighborhood, are entitled not to be disturbed simply because of that prior offense and conviction; but a conclusion as well, that the characteristics of some of them, and the *statistical information concerning them* [italics added], make it clear that despite such integration, reoffense is a realistic risk, and knowledge of their presence a realistic protection against it. (*Doe v. Poritz*, 662 A.2d 367)

Megan's Law also reflects the priority given to risk, and especially actuarial constructions of risk, by the new penology. (This volume, chapter 3, discusses actuarial instruments for assessing risk for sex offenders.) Once a person qualifies as a "sexual predator" for purposes of Megan's Law, he must be assigned to one of three grades of relative risk. Even the lowest tier involves some notification, to local law enforcement, and implies some level of risk. Thus, nobody classified by Megan's Law exists outside of a grid of risk. The statute mandated the state to create a process for assigning registrants to one of the three risk levels. In response, the state created a device known as the Registrant Risk Assessment Scale for the purpose of assessing all registrants under Megan's Law. The scale is actually a complex hybrid of specific risk factors. The assessor must grade the registrant 1 to 3 on a range of factors dealing with prior offense severity and frequency, current treatment potential, and support network. These assessments are then combined on a weighted formula to produce a single index number. In upholding the Registrant Risk Assessment Scale, the New Jersey Supreme Court recognized the supremacy of actuarial knowledge about risk and the diminished role of individualizing the offender.

Although using both the Scale and clinical interviews of registrants may on some occasions provide a more accurate prediction of risk of reoffense than use of the Scale alone, the Committee decided that clinical interviews of each registrant were not necessary. That decision was based on scientific literature that showed that the use of actuarial concrete predictors is at least as good, if not in most cases better, in terms of reliability and predictability than clinical interviews. After conducting a cost–benefit analysis of requiring clinical interviews of each offender, the Committee determined that the minimal improvement in predictability that might be gained by using clinical interviews could not justify the high cost associated with conducting such interviews for each registrant. (*In re C.A.*, 679 A.2d 1153, 1170)

More recently, the New Jersey Supreme Court has explicitly noted the distinction between risk assessment, which involves group classifications, and individualized judgment, and the court affirmed that the registration and community notification law focuses on the former.

> Registrant urges a more particularized showing by the prosecutor before notification is given to the schools and community organizations located within a half-mile radius of his home. He contends that the State must show that it is "reasonably certain" that he will show up at those locations and thus encounter potential victims there. In effect, he argues that there must be that specific a showing with regard to schools and similar organizations for a Tier Two offender in each and every case. In support, he cites to the Guidelines' reference that contact with the offender be "reasonably certain" as set forth in the explanation of "fair chance to encounter" the offender. The Appellate Division was persuaded by the registrant's argument. We do not agree. To accept that analysis would render meaningless the presumptive effect of the Legislature's language that decreed that once a registrant is classified as a Tier Two offender, notification shall be given to organizations in the community that are in charge of the actual care or supervision of women or children unless there are presented limiting circumstances affecting the presumptive assessment of risk of re-offense. (In re M.F., 776 A.2d 780, 790, New Jersey, 2001)

In shifting the focus to group predictions, the government has escaped the heavy burden of predicting individual behavior.

From Normalization to Management

Although the old penology focused on transforming offenders, Megan's Law is premised precisely on the futility of that effort with sex offenders. In its first opinion upholding the basic registration and notification requirements of Megan's Law, the Supreme Court of New Jersey noted:

> Concerning the basic facts [about sex offenders], however, there is no dispute: as far as society is concerned, sex offenses of the kind covered by the law are among the most abhorrent of all offenses; the relative recidivism rate of sex offenders is high compared to other offenders; treatment success of sex offenders exhibiting repetitive and compulsive characteristics is low; and the time span between the initial offense and re-offense can be long. (Doe v. Poritz, 662 A.2d 367, 374 note 1)

The "overall purpose of the law," according to the Supreme Court in a later opinion further approving the implementation of Megan's Law, "was to protect the community from the dangers of recidivism by sex offenders" (In the matter of Registrant G.B., 685 A.2d 1252, 1256). In short, sex offenders, as defined by Megan's Law, constitute a population of persons who pose a long-term risk of inflicting horrible costs on society. In this sense Megan's Law is actually premised on the failure of other efforts, including deterrence and treatment in prison. Although treatment measures may or may not be part of the state's primary response to sex offenders, Megan's Law reflects the imperative of providing a long-term strategy for managing a permanently dangerous class.

We can also observe this flattening of the task of governance to the merely managerial in the very name by which the subjects of Megan's Law are called (i.e., "registrants"). As registrants, offenders can expect little more than proper administration of the rules under which they are registered. The state denied any intent to punish sex offenders through registering and in some cases notifying their neighbors of their criminal history. Rather, the state is providing a risk management service for the benefit of the community. This marks an important shift in quality of state power asserted in penal law. The old penology was a vehicle for relatively unbridled visions of state competence. The new penology, in contrast, is shaped by a pervasive skepticism about the power of the state to fundamentally change offenders. Megan's Law goes further by treating this as a problem not for the state but for the community. Megan's Law is, in effect, an unfunded mandate to community groups and parents to take responsibility for protecting children against sexual offenders.

From Social Norms to Systems

Despite its superficial appeal to popular concerns (addressed later), the administrative structures of Megan's Law emphasize technocratic forms of knowledge that further distance decision making from the community. The legislation that enacted Megan's Law required the attorney general to develop guidelines for local prosecutors and listed a host of factors to be included. The attorney general convened a committee of "mental health experts" to produce a scale to be used throughout the state to assess the risk of each registrant (*In re* C.A., 679 A.2d 1153, 1158). The committee agreed on two conditions for accepting risk factors identified in the professional literature. All factors had to have empirical support somewhere in that literature, and all had to be "concrete criteria that could be gathered in a consistent and reliable manner" (*In re* C.A., 679 A.2d 1153, 1169). The two principles amount to the institutional needs of the mental health and correctional fields, respectively. The factors must be ones endorsed by the professional literature of risk assessment and must be ones easily implemented by the existing correctional information system. The development of these factors reflects a clear preference for knowledge that is produced by the criminal justice system itself.

Populist Punitiveness

The populist nature of Megan's Law is readily apparent in its timing, naming, and operation. The law was enacted shortly after the murder of

Megan Kanka and well before her killer had been convicted. There was little doubt that it reflected the need felt by politicians to respond to an act that horrified many in the state rather than a considered police strategy. The naming of the law is even stronger evidence of its populist logic. By placing Megan Kanka's presence literally in front of the law, the legislature assured that any consideration of it would have to confront Megan's death and popular feelings about it. This produced a number of different kinds of effects. It clearly raised the cost of political opposition. Even to discuss Megan's Law, one has to come immediately into the presence of Megan Kanka, her youth, her suffering, and her mortality. Indeed, the first two decisions by the Supreme Court of New Jersey on the law both recounted the fact of Megan's murder.

The Supreme Court of New Jersey acknowledged the centrality of popular sentiments regarding the horror of the young victim's murder: "Clearly, both the Legislature's and the public's increasing awareness of the dangers posed by sex offenders triggered laws here, and elsewhere, as the understanding of the problem was accelerated by the occurrence of highly publicized and horrific offenses" (*Doe v. Poritz*, 662 A.2d 367, 376).

But while recognizing the populist aspect of this strategy, the majority refused to acknowledge the likely punitiveness that would inform private response. Instead, the court thought it had

> no right to assume that the public will be punitive when the Legislature was not, that the public, instead of protecting itself as the laws intended, will attempt to destroy the lives of those subject to the laws, and this Court has no right to assume that community leaders, public officials, law enforcement authorities will not seek to educate the public concerning the Legislature's intent. (*Doe v. Poritz*, 1995, 662 A.2d 367, 376)

The opinion strikes a defensive tone—"no right to assume"—in the presumed presence of the popular will that marks a kind of judicial populism in addition to the more obvious legislative populism of the hastily enacted law itself. The development of modern institutions, particularly the prison, was aimed at displacing popular emotions from the center of punishment by extending the control of state-based professionals. From a spectacle of solidarity between state and people against their common enemies, punishment became a vehicle for inculcating habits of social order suitable to a democratic society (Foucault, 1977; Rothman, 1971). Megan's Law is a shift away from this process of modernization. Starting with its name, and with the central role given to local prosecutors in applying the risk classification, Megan's Law advertises itself as a new hybrid of public and private vengeance.

CONSTITUTIONALIZING THE NEW PENOLOGY

Both *Hendricks* and the trio of New Jersey cases on Megan's Law reflect the relative indifference of the Constitution to substantive shifts in penal strategy. The major issues of dispute on these high courts have concerned whether to classify these particular practices as punishments. But as Justice Kennedy pointed out in his concurrence to *Hendricks*, the question of how to classify such laws often will be of interest only to a limited number of people who can take advantage of *ex post facto* or double jeopardy claims (*Kansas v. Hendricks*, 521 U.S. 346, 370). It is not surprising that broad constitutional norms should leave sovereign states largely free to pursue different kinds of responses to crime, but the constitutionalization of the new sex offender laws also marks a substantive lessening in the rigor of constitutional review. This lessening in rigor, doctrinally located in due process analysis, is linked to the courts' own incomplete recognition of the new penology operating within these laws.

Justice Thomas's opinion in *Hendricks* reaches its conclusion by recasting the complex precedents on civil confinement as a story of unambiguous power by the state to deprive of liberty those deemed dangerous to good public order. Reaching back behind the era of due process expansion, Thomas invoked one of the strongest constitutional images of state police power, that in *Jacobson v. Massachusetts* (1905). This little-discussed case was decided the same year as *Lochner v. New York* (1905) and presented a very different picture of state power and individual rights in the early 20th century than that often denounced decision. *Jacobson* unanimously affirmed the power of states to compel citizens to undergo vaccination against small pox, despite acknowledged risks and real medical controversy at the time regarding the benefits of vaccination. In *Hendricks*, Justice Thomas argued that this venerable power to address dangerous individuals has no necessary relationship to treatment strategies or the role of psychiatric and psychological expertise. Noting that terms such as *mental illness* have no "talismanic significance," Thomas held that the critical issue was the adequacy of the criteria designed to separate those targeted for confinement from "other dangerous persons who are perhaps more properly dealt with exclusively through criminal proceedings," and he held Kansas's criteria adequate (*Kansas v. Hendricks*, 521 U.S. 346, 360).

Justice Thomas also rejected Hendricks's claim that the statute was a punishment being imposed in violation of his right against double jeopardy and *ex post facto* punishment. Here the Court followed the pattern of other recent punishment cases and treated Kansas's intent to produce a civil sanction as having a strong presumption behind it. But even after granting this strong presumption, the Kansas Act came in for remarkably little scrutiny of the risks facing those defined as in need of confinement in terms of its administrative structures. Here the logic of the new penology worked to insulate the state from the burdens of the criminal process. In the context of the Kansas Sexually Violent Predator Act, Hendricks's past crimes were not justifications for punishment but present indicators of risk. The state's goal was only delivering risk management services to the public, not performing rituals of sovereign domination on deserving enemies of the people.

Justice Thomas and the majority reduced treatment to a secondary concern for due process. (This volume, chapter 6, discusses the role treatment plays in the Supreme Court's decision in *Hendricks*.) The centrality of treatment under previous readings of the due process clause made the constitutionality of confinement turn on the institutional priority of treatment and treatment professionals (i.e., those with a grounding in forms of knowledge and power independent of the penal system). In *Hendricks*, treatment was reduced to a gesture. Justice Thomas's opinion allowed the state to obtain the constitutional immunity of "treatment" without compromising its own organizational autonomy in this way.

More recently in *Seling v. Young* (2001), the Court made clear that it has no intention of requiring real efforts at treatment as a condition of allowing the state to confine a civil subject under prisonlike conditions. The plaintiff in that case, confined under a scheme "patterned" after the Kansas statute approved in *Hendricks*, complained that for 7 years he had been "subject to conditions more restrictive than those placed on true civil commitment detainees, and even state prisoners" (*Seling v. Young*, 531 U.S. 250, 259). The plaintiff's expert, a court-appointed resident advocate and psychologist, wrote regarding the treatment promises of the program that "the Center [where Seling and other sexual predators were confined] had not fundamentally changed over so many years, he had come to suspect that the Center was designed and managed to punish and confine individuals for life without any hope of release to a less restrictive setting" (*Seling v. Young*, 531 U.S. 250, 260). The Court held that such claims presented no contested issue of fact in the face of the Washington Supreme Court's earlier holding (*In re Young*, 857 P.2d 989, 1993) that the act was civil in nature. "The civil nature of a confinement scheme cannot be altered based merely on vagaries in the implementation of the authorizing statute" (*Seling v. Young*, 531 U.S. 250, 263).

The opinions of the Supreme Court of New Jersey in reviewing that state's pioneering version of Megan's Law also reflect a failure to recognize the new penology and an incorporation of its values into constitutional review. While purporting to balance the harm to the registrants against the interests of the community, the court stepped away from demanding anything more than the appearance of rationality. Having affirmed the power of actuarial judgment, it would be consistent to require the state to undertake the validation studies necessary to support them over time. Instead, the New Jersey Supreme Court dismissed validation as "neither feasible nor practicable" (*In re C.A.*, 679 A.2d 1153, 1171) while approving the Registrant Risk Assessment Scale as "useful and rational." The New Jersey Supreme Court has, however, indicated a real concern with the potential for abuse and left room in the system for the registrants to obtain hearings and produce expert testimony beyond the scale, at least where they can purport to show reasons why the scale might not predict well for the individual registrant (*In the matter of Registrant G.B.*, 685 A.2d 1252, 1262). It remains to be seen whether the New Jersey trial courts will ultimately maintain close scrutiny on the tier assignments of prosecutors.

CONCLUSION

A new generation of sex offender laws is being produced that reflects a profound change in contemporary penality. This change is taking place on a number of different levels, including the targets of penal efforts, the forms of expertise that provide them with authority, and the image of state power these laws communicate. Behind the superficially consistent object of sex offender, a distinctly new and far more pessimistic vision has emerged. Sex offenders are the embodiment not of psychopathology, with the potential for diagnostic and treatment knowledge to provide better controls over such offenders, but of the monstrous and the limits of science to know or change people.

Behind the seeming heterogeneity of laws such as the Kansas Sexually Violent Predator Act and Megan's Law is a common set of transformations in the quality of state power, the demands the law places on its rationality, and the promises it makes to the community. Retreating from its historic claims to exercise scientific expertise to normalize the dangerously deviant, the state increasingly offers instead evidence of its identification with the fears of victims. Avoiding any real accountability for public safety, these new policies transfer the risk to two groups—sex offenders themselves, who may face permanent confinement or the risks of public lynching, and the individual citizens, community organizations, and families, who are expected to police themselves against sex offenders—with the role of the state reduced to that of facilitating protection through warnings (Pratt, 1997). In both schemes, scientific expertise, now in the form of risk prediction, is once again crucial to the exercise of state power but now with virtually no externally testable performance claims or standards.

Recent cases upholding these laws against a variety of constitutional challenges provide little real scrutiny of this transformation. Instead, the U.S. Supreme Court has begun to redefine downward constitutional expectations of state penal strategies. Not only has the logic of the new penology escaped direct review, but also its features have helped mask the decline of constitutional standards. Ironically, the more the state disavows the benevolent goals of individualized treatment, the more deference courts are willing to pay to the exercise of that power.

REFERENCES

Allen, F. A. (1981). *The decline of the rehabilitative ideal: Penal policy and social purpose.* New Haven, CT: Yale University Press.

In re C.A., 679 A.2d 1153 (New Jersey 1996).

Caplow, T., & Simon, J. (1999). Understanding prison policy and population trends. In M. Tonry & J. Petersilia (Eds.), *Prisons: Crime and justice* (pp. 63–120). Chicago: University of Chicago Press.

Doe v. Poritz, 662 A.2d 367 (New Jersey 1995).

Ellsworth, P. C., & Gross, S. R. (1994). Hardening of attitudes: Americans' views on the death penalty. *Journal of Social Issues, 50,* 19–52.

Feeley, M., & Simon, J. (1992). The new penology: Notes on the emerging strategy of corrections and its implications. *Criminology, 30,* 449–474.

Feeley, M., & Simon, J. (1994). Actuarial justice: Power/knowledge in contemporary criminal justice. In D. Neikin (Ed.), *The future of criminology* (pp. 173–201). London: Sage.

Foucault, M. (1977). *Discipline and punish: The birth of the prison* (Alan Sheridan, Trans.). New York: Pantheon.

Garland, D. (1985). *Punishment and welfare: A history of penal strategies.* Brookfield, VT: Gower.

Jacob Wetterling Crimes Against Children and Sexually Violent Offender Registration Act, 42 U.S.C. § 4071 (1994).

Jacobson v. Massachusetts, 197 U.S. 11 (1905).

Kansas v. Hendricks, 521 U.S. 346 (1997).

Kansas Sexually Violent Predators Act, Kan. Stat. Ann. § 59-2901 *et seq.* (1994).

Lochner v. New York, 198 U.S. 45 (1905).

Logan, W. A. (1999). Liberty interests in the preventive state: Procedural due process and sex offender community notification laws. *Journal of Criminal Law and Criminology, 89,* 1167–1231.

Logan, W. A. (2000). A study in "actuarial justice": Sex offender classification practice and procedure. *Buffalo Criminal Law Review, 3,* 593–637.

Megan's Law, or Registration and Community Notification Laws, N.J. Stat. Ann. § 2C:7-1–7-11 (1994).

In re M.F., 776 A.2d 780, 790 (New Jersey 2001).

Pratt, J. (1997). *Governing the dangerous: Dangerousness, law and social change.* Sydney, Australia: Federation Press.

Presidential Commission on Law Enforcement and the Administration of Justice. (1967). *The challenge of crime in a free society.* Washington, DC: U.S. Government Printing Office.

In the matter of Registrant G.B., 685 A.2d 1252 (New Jersey 1996).

Rothman, D. J. (1971). *The discovery of the asylum: Social order and disorder in the new republic.* Toronto, Ontario, Canada: Little, Brown.

Rothman, D. J. (1980). *Conscience and convenience: The asylum and its alternatives in progressive America.* Toronto, Ontario, Canada: Little, Brown.

Seling v. Young, 531 U.S. 250 (2001).

Sexually Violent Predators Act, Kan. Stat. Ann. § 59-29a01 *et seq.* (1994).

Simon, J. (1993). *Poor discipline: Parole and the social control of the underclass, 1890– 1990.* Chicago: University of Chicago Press.

Simon, J. (1998a). Ghosts of the disciplinary machine: Lee Harvey Oswald, life-history and the truth of crime. *Yale Journal of Law and the Humanities, 10,* 75–113.

Simon, J. (1998b). Managing the monstrous: Sex offenders and the new penology. *Psychology, Public Policy, and the Law, 4,* 452.

Simon, J., & Feeley, M. (1995). True crime: The new penology and public discourse on crime. In T. G. Blomberg & S. Cohen (Eds.), *Punishment and social control: Essays in honor of Sheldon Messinger* (pp. 24–52). New York: Aldine de Gruyter.

Steiker, C. S. (1998). Supreme Court Review Foreward: The limits of the preventive state. *Journal of Criminal Law and Criminology, 88,* 771.

United States v. Ursery, 518 U.S. 267 (1996).

In re Young, 857 P.2d 989 (1993).

18

A THERAPEUTIC JURISPRUDENCE ASSESSMENT OF SEXUALLY VIOLENT PREDATOR LAWS

BRUCE J. WINICK

Some 15 states have now adopted sexually violent predator laws, a civil commitment approach for dealing with repetitive sex offenders (see this volume, chapters 1 and 2). In the wake of the Supreme Court's decision in *Kansas v. Hendricks* (1997) upholding the constitutionality of these laws, many other states are considering their adoption. Designed to protect the public from sex offenders who repeatedly reoffend, these laws authorize the commitment of previously convicted sex offenders about to be discharged at the expiration of their prison terms if determined to be suffering from a mental abnormality or personality disorder that makes it likely that they will reoffend (Winick, 1998). The analogy to civil commitment for those with mental illness suggests that these statutes are designed to provide needed treatment to sex offenders, but in practice, treat-

This chapter is a revised and updated version of material first published in Winick (1998). Copyright © 1998 by the American Psychological Association (APA). Adapted with permission of the author and the APA.

ment has taken a back seat to their principal purpose—the isolation of these offenders through preventive detention.

Are these statutes wise? Is this the best approach to protect the community? Is this new form of commitment the best way to provide sex offender treatment? A variety of factors must be considered in addressing these questions, including those of cost, community safety, treatment efficacy, and morality, and the debate about these laws has largely focused on these considerations (see this volume, chapters 2, 5, 7, 9, 10, and 16). One consideration that is rarely addressed is the therapeutic impact of these laws on sex offenders, clinicians assigned to work in these programs, and nonsexual offenders suffering from mental illness. This chapter uses the approach of therapeutic jurisprudence (Stolle, Wexler, & Winick, 2000; Wexler & Winick, 1996; Wexler & Winick, 1991; Winick, 1997b; see also this volume, chapter 12) to analyze this often overlooked dimension of the debate over sexually violent predator laws.

CRIMINAL VERSUS ILLNESS MODELS FOR DEALING WITH SEX OFFENDERS

Our policy toward sex offenders has fluctuated between two polar approaches. Before the 1930s, sex offenders were treated as criminals, were held responsible for their actions, and were subjected to criminal punishment for them (Winick, 1998). Starting in the late 1930s, states experimented with sexual psychopath legislation that authorized a special form of civil or criminal commitment for those found, after a hearing, to be dangerous or "sexual psychopaths." Rather than treating child molestation and other types of sexual acts as criminal, these statutes treated them largely as symptoms of illness and labeled their perpetrators as "sexual psychopaths." Rather than being punished, these offenders were committed to specialized facilities designed for treatment and rehabilitation. These two different approaches to sex offenders may be seen as reflecting two very different conceptions of the problem: a criminal model and an illness model.

Sexual psychopath statutes were in widespread use in the 1940s through the 1970s but thereafter began to fall into disfavor. Treatment provided in sexual psychopath programs was regarded as ineffective, and the sexual psychopath approach came to be seen as an experiment that had failed (Committee on Psychiatry and Law, 1977). Many states repealed their sexual psychopath statutes, and by the 1980s, those states that continued to retain them rarely used them. In general, the illness model was replaced by the traditional criminal model. In the early 1990s, in response to a number of high-profile sexual mutilations and murders of children, Washington State and a number of other states adopted a new model: the sexually violent predator law (see this volume, chapter 1). In effect, these new sexual predator laws are a recycled version of the former sexual psychopath statutes. They seek to incapacitate through long-term civil commitment repetitive sex offenders and label them "sexually violent predators." Although motivated primarily by the desire to incapacitate these offenders and thereby protect the public from their dangerous propensities, these statutes commit them to psychiatric facilities where treatment is supposed to be provided. These statutes thus represent a retreat from the criminal or punishment model and a return to the illness or treatment model for dealing with sex offenders.

Which model is preferable? An analysis of this question calls for consideration of a number of normative and economic factors. One factor that should be considered in assessing the relative merits of the criminal versus illness model for dealing with sex offenders is the therapeutic dimension. Based on a therapeutic jurisprudence analysis of these laws, I conclude that, on balance, a criminal approach that offers treatment in prison on a voluntary basis is preferable to the new sexual predator statutory schemes (Winick, 1998).

Labeling Effects

The criminal or punishment approach to sex offenders labels offenders as criminals and imposes criminal incarceration as a means of incapacitation, deterrence, and retribution. Sex offenders are told that their conduct violates our society's basic rules, that they are responsible for their conduct and are properly subject to blame and condemnation, and that they will suffer serious deprivations of liberty and other hardships as a result of their inexcusable actions. If after completion of their prison terms, they choose to reoffend, the punishment model tells them that they will be dealt with even more harshly, receiving lengthier periods of incarceration and perhaps even a life sentence under habitual offender laws.

In contrast, the new illness model labels sex offenders as being "mentally abnormal" or having a "personality disorder" and links that abnormality or personality disorder to their propensity to engage in repeated sexual offenses. They are mentally abnormal or disordered in some sense, offenders are told, and their mental abnormality renders them unable to control their strong urges to engage in violent sexual conduct. Indeed, the U.S. Supreme Court recently reaffirmed the requirement that, to be subject to sexually violent predator commitment, the offender's mental abnormality or personality must be shown to render it difficult for him to control his behavior (*Kansas v. Crane*, 2002). They cannot help themselves, they are told, because they are ill and need hospitalization to protect the community from them and to attempt to treat their abnormality.

Both criminal and illness models thus label individuals and in so doing give them important messages. The criminal label tells offenders that they have committed bad acts; that they could have controlled their conduct but chose not to for reasons that we find inexcusable; and that if they reoffend, they will be dealt with even more harshly. The illness label, in contrast, tells them that they are largely not responsible for their conduct; it is their illness that is responsible, because it prevents them from controlling their actions. Ironically, the criminal model may be more therapeutic for sex offenders, and the illness model may produce serious antitherapeutic effects. General principles of cognitive psychology suggest that treating people who violate the law as ill and hence not in control of their conduct may be counterproductive. People who commit sex offenses indulge their propensity to act in ways that are harmful to others rather than attempting to control it. These individuals undeniably have problems, but allowing them to think of themselves as "mentally abnormal" or suffering from a "personality disorder" may have the unintended effect of encouraging their antisocial conduct. Self-control often requires a high degree of discipline and willpower that may be difficult to muster if individuals regard themselves as suffering from an illness that causes them to lose such control. Self-attribution and self-efficacy studies consistently show that people reframe their world experiences, expectations, and explanations for their behavior on the basis of their self-concept and their understanding of what they are "suffering" from (Bandura, 1997). Their self-perceptions contribute significantly to their performance and behavior (Arkin & Baumgardner, 1985). Their sense of what symptoms they have influences their behavior independent of their abilities. People who attribute their lack of self-control and their antisocial conduct to illness may tend to feel that self-control is not possible, a type of "self-handicapping" that can undermine determination and inhibit future attempts to exercise self-control behavior (Arkin & Baumgardner, 1985). People who believe they lack the capacity to control their harmful conduct because of an internal deficit that seems unchangeable predictably develop expectations of failure. As a result, they may not even attempt to exercise self-control, or may do so without any serious commitment to succeed. The illness label thus can be a self-fulfilling prophecy (Jones, 1984).

Labeling sex offenders as sexually violent predators therefore may reinforce their antisocial sexual behavior. The label may function to get in the way of change and provide these individuals with an excuse for giving in to their sexual urges. As a result, it may make it more difficult for sex offenders to exercise the self-control that society would like to encourage. In contrast, treating these individuals as responsible and making them face responsibility for their actions through criminal punishment may produce a positive cognitive restructuring. It can help them come to view themselves as in control of their actions and thus exercise a greater degree of self-control, conforming their conduct to the requirements of the criminal law.

Effects on Treatment Outcome

Labeling people as violent sexual predators and thereby communicating to them the message that they are mentally abnormal in ways that prevent them from controlling their antisocial conduct may also undermine the potential of the treatment they are offered. People who believe they suffer from a condition that renders them unable to control or resist their sexual desires for children when under stress may come to feel that there is little they can do when they feel stressed out except to give in to their sexual urges. These people need to learn methods of stress control, a common component of any sex offender treatment program (see this volume, chapter 5). Both the value of learning these techniques and the potential for success would seem diminished if individuals think they suffer from an illness that prevents self-control in these circumstances. In fact, to succeed in treatment, individuals must regard themselves as changeable and as capable of learning how to control their behavior (Harris, Rice, & Quinsey, 1998; see also this volume, chapter 5).

Cognitive–behavioral therapy seems to be the most effective treatment approach in the sex offender treatment arsenal (Becker & Murphy, 1998; see also this volume, chapter 5). Many sex offenders are in denial concerning the reality of their actions, the extent to which their victims consented to or desired their actions, and the degree of their responsibility for them. A first step in effecting a positive cognitive restructuring is breaking down such denial. Labeling sex offenders as morally blameworthy criminal offenders who are responsible for their actions, rather than as mentally ill persons who suffer from a mental abnormality that makes self-control impossible, is more likely to lead these individuals to take responsibility for their conduct.

Sexually violent predator laws, by concentrating treatment resources on the postprison civil commitment period and by providing disincentives for sex offenders to take advantage of prison treatment programs, may drain treatment resources away from prison programs and otherwise undermine their ability to be effective. Sex offender treatment should be made available within the prison, and such treatment should be encouraged. Some states offer sex offender treatment in prison. Treatment delivered nearer in time to the offense is more likely to be effective. Inasmuch as some sex offenders have a false ideation concerning the circumstances of their crime, the passage of a long period of time only solidifies this self-deception in ways that make it more difficult to break down. A delay in treatment or legal rules that provide a disincentive to engage in treatment while in prison can further reinforce the offender's deviant attitudes and behavior patterns, making them more chronic.

Many sex offenders, probably most, plead guilty to their crimes. An important insight of therapeutic jurisprudence has been that judges given the discretion to accept *nolo contendere* (no contest) pleas or Alford pleas (in which individuals plead guilty but refuse to admit that they committed the offense) should decline to accept them and insist, instead, on a plea of guilty (Wexler & Winick, 1992). A plea of guilty is an acceptance of responsibility for the offense, whereas a *nolo* or Alford plea allows individuals to remain in denial, evading responsibility for their actions. Sexual predator laws may provide a strong disincentive for sex offenders to plead guilty to their crimes. Because such statutes will authorize civil commitment of repeat sex offenders once they finish their prison terms, often for periods that will be extremely long (perhaps a lifetime), the individual may have a greater incentive to fight the charges or at least not to provide an admission of guilt that will be admissible in the sex predator commitment hearing. To the extent that guilty pleas are deterred, these new statutes will have the antitherapeutic effect of perpetuating denial and cognitive distortions. Particularly if individuals choose to plead not guilty and go to trial, their advocacy of their own innocence may foster a form of cognitive dissonance that makes it even more difficult for them to come to accept responsibility for their actions.

Many states may offer some treatment or counseling programs to sentenced sex offenders, encouraging them to participate in rehabilitative efforts designed to decrease the likelihood of their recidivism. The leading form of sex offender treatment is cognitive–behavioral therapy, which includes several components (Winick, 1998; see also this volume, chapter 5). Behavioral therapy is used to block or reduce inappropriate sexual arousal and to reinforce nondeviant sexual arousal. Another component involves social skills training, designed to remedy deficiencies in social abilities that may hinder the sex offender's capacity to initiate and sustain normal sexual relations. An additional component involves the attempt to change the cognitive distortions that often perpetuate paraphiliac behavior and empathy training designed to bring a greater awareness of the consequences of victimization. Finally, such treatment involves relapse prevention training, designed to alert the offender, the offender's family and support network, and the offender's therapist or case manager to the behavioral cues that might precede relapse and to take appropriate steps to avoid it.

For these approaches to work in a prison sex offender program, the offender must communicate openly with the therapist, making a full and frank disclosure of prior sexual offenses and behavioral patterns. Ironically, violent sexual predator statutes might undermine this essential condition for effective treatment. In states in which violent sex predator laws have been enacted, offenders will be aware of the risk of civil commitment after expiration of their prison term if it has been determined that they are likely to recidivate. This alone will make them reluctant to divulge information to their therapists concerning their past sexual behavior unless there is clear protection for the confidentiality of such disclosures. Washington, the first state to enact the sexually violent predator statute, actually requires an express waiver by the offender of confidentiality and an acknowledgment that information disclosed in treatment may subsequently be used in determining the propriety of sexually violent predator civil commitment (La Fond, 1998). Even in states that do not insist on an express waiver of confidentiality, offenders may fear that this information will be used against them in commitment decision making after they are discharged from prison. This actual or perceived lack of confidentiality can seriously burden the therapeutic relationship by destroying trust and confidence in the therapist. By discouraging a full and frank disclosure of past sexual behavior, the lack of confidentiality also can prevent offenders from accepting responsibility for their behavior, thereby reinforcing cognitive distortions that contribute to a perpetuation of their antisocial actions. Sexually violent predator laws may therefore discourage sex offenders in prison from accepting treatment or from participating in it with the full candor that may be necessary for treatment to succeed.

When an individual is subjected to civil commitment pursuant to a sexual predator statutory scheme, treatment will be imposed on a mandatory basis. In contrast, when an individual is sentenced to prison as a sex offender, treatment (to the extent it is offered) will be made available largely on a voluntary basis. Treatment programs that pose a potential for rehabilitation should be made available, either in prison or as part of the civil commitment scheme. Whether treatment is offered on a voluntary basis or imposed coercively may itself have an important impact on treatment outcomes (Winick, 1997a, 1997c). People coerced into treatment often respond with a negative psychological reactance that may diminish the potential for treatment success. People forced into treatment against their will may go through the motions of the treatment program but derive little benefit. Absent intrinsic motivation to succeed in treatment, genuine compliance with treatment measures and real attitudinal change are unlikely. Sex offenders coerced into treatment thus may behave appropriately while institutionalized and even master the vocabulary of attitudinal change. Once discharged from the institution, however, they may return to their old attitudes and behavior patterns.

Cognitive–behavioral approaches indicated for sex offenders require a high degree of motivation on the part of the individual to succeed. People given a choice whether to participate in a treatment program may refuse treatment, but they also may accept it. For those who accept it, the psychological value of having made the choice may play an important role in increasing treatment efficacy. It may allow individuals to internalize the treatment goal and increase their commitment to attaining it. It may increase motivation, effort, and compliance and set up expectancies of positive results that can help to produce such a therapeutic response.

Moreover, because positive treatment outcome will increase the likelihood that the prisoner will be released on parole, the individual will be given an incentive to participate and succeed. In contrast, once individuals are labeled sexually violent predators and committed as a result, they will realize that their ultimate release is extremely unlikely. Release will be difficult as a result of the program staff's inevitable disinclination to predict nonrecidivism, given the general difficulties of making predictions in this area (see this volume, chapter 3), as well as the high costs to the clinical evaluator of false-negative predictions and the low cost of making false-positive ones. Release from such programs is unlikely even if the individual participates earnestly in treatment and experiences positive attitudinal and behavioral changes (see this volume, chapter 16). This can only dampen the motivation to succeed that may be an essential component of positive results.

Trust and confidence in the therapist also predictively will be enhanced when sex offenders voluntarily choose treatment rather than being coerced into accepting it. Moreover, voluntariness is more likely to enable sex offenders to experience the clinical staff as being benevolently motivated, whereas coercion may make them question their motives. Having trust and confidence in the therapist and believing that he or she is benevolently motivated seem to be significantly related to treatment success (Winick, 1997a).

A variety of factors inherent to sexually violent predator statutory schemes therefore may actually hinder treatment effectiveness. Treatment provided at an earlier time and on a voluntary basis in a prison program may be more likely to succeed. Perhaps ironically, criminal or punishment models that make treatment available on a voluntary basis and encourage individuals to accept responsibility for their wrongful conduct may have greater potential for the rehabilitation of sex offenders than do sexually violent predator illness models that mandate treatment for offenders labeled as having a mental abnormality that prevents them from controlling their conduct.

IMPACT ON CLINICIANS WHO PROVIDE SEX OFFENDER TREATMENT

Sexually violent predator laws may also have a negative effect on clinicians asked to play the role of therapists in sex offender treatment programs. As previously indicated, the possibility of sexually violent predator civil commitment after the expiration of a prison term may undermine the willingness of patients in prison treatment programs to participate in these programs with the full candor that may be necessary for treatment success. In addition, sexually violent predator laws mandate treatment rather than simply offering it on a voluntary basis. Patients who are required to undergo treatment may participate in it in only a formal way, failing to bring to treatment the degree of commitment and motivation that might be essential for treatment success. Some will display a form of psychological reactance that will make treatment frustrating for both the therapist and patient as well as unlikely to succeed.

Requiring clinicians to participate in a coercive treatment program also will present an ethical dilemma. The codes of ethics of the various clinical disciplines emphasize voluntary treatment and raise serious questions about participation in treatment imposed coercively (Winick, 1997c). Involuntary treatment may not be unethical in cases in which it has been judicially ordered for a patient who is incompetent to appreciate the need for treatment and to participate in treatment decision making. Sex offenders, however, do not suffer from cognitive impairments that render them incompetent in these ways. Treatment provided in a sexually violent predator treatment program is not paternalistically motivated. Sexually violent predator commitment plays essentially a social control function. Clinicians forced to work in these programs may therefore perceive themselves more as jailers than as therapists (Winick, 1998). As a result, the ability of these programs to recruit and retain ethical and talented clinicians will be considerably reduced.

Clinicians who are employed in these programs may experience a high degree of frustration in working with unmotivated patients. Those labeled as sexually violent predators presumably have had a long history of recidivism and may be the least likely to succeed in sex offender treatment. Even if treatment is successful, community protection pressures will make it unlikely that such repeatedly reoffending "predators" will be released. This reality, known to both therapists and patients, may make the treatment process seem to be a pretense, an empty ritual rather than a genuine treatment alliance designed to produce meaningful improvement. Participating in such a treatment program may be demoralizing for clinicians, producing emotional conflicts, lowered self-esteem, and even depression, rather than the sense of professional satisfaction that comes from helping others. In short, sexually violent predator laws can pose negative effects on the mental health and psychological functioning of the clinicians who work in these programs.

IMPACT ON PEOPLE WITH GENUINE MENTAL DISORDERS

Civil commitment of sexually violent predators is expensive and could involve a potentially large number of individuals, draining resources away from people with genuine mental disability. To assure safety and protection from escape, the facilities in which sexually violent predators are placed need to duplicate the security measures of correctional facilities and require additional treatment, evaluation, and processing costs (Zonana, 1997). La Fond (1998; see also this volume, chapter 16) estimated the cost of sexually violent predator commitment at $107,000 to $112,000 per patient per year and probably even higher. The yearly cost per inmate in these facilities is estimated to be at least twice as high as comparable costs in correctional facilities.

Not only is the per-inmate cost of such confinement exceedingly high, but the potential number of candidates for such commitment is large and apparently growing exponentially. More than 10% of the U.S. prison population is estimated to be composed of sex offenders (Zonana, 1997). Ten percent of these are estimated to qualify for commitment as sexual violent predators. If these estimates are accurate, more than 11,000 sex offenders would qualify for sexually violent predator commitment. Moreover, because sexually violent predators are unlikely to be released from confinement for many years, these numbers will swell over time, imposing extraordinarily high expenses for their custodial confinement (see this volume, chapter 16).

The high expenses imposed by sexually violent predator commitment will inevitably reduce the treatment resources available for sex offenders in prison as well as for civil mental patients who are not sex offenders. Using scarce psychiatric hospital beds and clinical resources for repetitive sex offenders who probably will be difficult to treat, rather than for people suffering from severe mental disorder who would benefit significantly from such treatment, is a misuse of the mental hospital (American Psychiatric Association, 1999). By depriving people with severe mental illness of needed hospital resources, the sexually violent predator laws can be viewed as imposing antitherapeutic effects on the mentally disabled population generally.

Sexually violent predator laws impose antitherapeutic consequences on the general population of people with mental illness in another respect. By using an illness rather than a criminal model and labeling sexually violent predators as people who are "mentally abnormal" instead of as bad, these laws could impose a profound effect on public attitudes toward those with mental illness and ultimately on the way those with mental illness perceive themselves. People with mental illness already are stigmatized in ways that impose serious social and psychological disadvantages that are long-lasting (Fink & Tasman, 1992). The labeling theory of mental illness associated with Thomas Scheff and others posits that the effect of the mental illness label on the way others perceive and respond to the labeled individual sets in motion attitudes and behavior patterns in the individual that confirm stereotyped images of mental illness (Scheff, 1966). The label produces in the individual a damaged self-concept that brings about a self-fulfilling prophecy (Jones, 1984). The mental illness label thus historically has been thought of as stigmatizing individuals, coloring the way others regard and interact with them and the way they conceive of themselves.

"Stigma" has been defined as "an attribute that is deeply discrediting" (Goffman, 1963, p. 3). People who are labeled as mentally ill already are discredited, marginalized, and excluded from a variety of social, educational, and occupational opportunities. When people learn of the application of a mental illness label to an individual, they sometimes are led to engage in actions that tend to confirm their expectations about the mentally ill person by restricting the individual's behavioral and learning opportunities (Jones, 1984). The "mental illness" label often produces social ostracism and difficulty in obtaining employment and housing.

One traditional stereotype concerning those with mental illness is that they are violent and prone to criminality. Sexually violent predator laws, by labeling sex offenders as mentally abnormal, perpetuate this unfortunate stigma. They may cause members of the public to confuse people with mental illness with sex offenders, attributing to mental patients generally the highly negative attitudes, fears, and hatreds associated with sex offenders. The label "mental illness" already carries the baggage of dangerousness (Link & Cullen, 1986). The public has traditionally associated mental illness with violence. Although there appears to be a relationship between mental disorder and violent behavior, and mental disorder may be a risk factor for the occurrence of violence (Monahan, 1993), this relationship is only a modest one (Monahan, 1993). Only people currently experiencing psychotic symptoms may be at increased risk of violence (Link, Cullen, Frank, & Wozniak, 1987). In actuality, approximately 90% of those with mental disorder are not violent (Monahan, 1993). The risk of violence presented by mental disorder is modest compared with the risk presented by other factors, such as male gender, young age, and lower socioeconomic status, and especially when compared with that presented by alcoholism and drug abuse (Monahan, 1993). As John Monahan, the foremost scholar of the relationship between mental illness and violence, concludes, "[n]one of the data gives any support to the sensationalized caricature of the mentally disordered served up by the media, the shunning of former patients by employees and neighbors in the community, or regressive 'lock them all up' laws proposed by politicians pandering to public fears" (Monahan, 1993, p. 299). Sexually violent predator laws can only reinforce and exacerbate this unfortunate and largely unjustified stigma.

CONCLUSION

Sexually violent predator laws are antitherapeutic in a number of respects. They impose labeling and other effects that can undermine the potential that sex offenders will be rehabilitated. They can impose negative psychological effects on clinicians who work in such programs. In addition, they can deprive people who suffer from serious mental illness of needed treatment resources and perpetuate the stigma of dangerousness that mental patients have long been subjected to.

The sex offender label applied under the sexually violent predator statutes seems to signal that the possibility of redemption by the community is foreclosed. The way these laws currently are administered, sexual predators will be hospitalized for an indefinite period that predictably will be quite lengthy. In addition, discharged sex offenders will be branded with a public sex offender label that suggests that a mental abnormality is responsible for their conduct and that they suffer from a deficit that is beyond their control and seems unchangeable. This is a message of hopelessness that can only diminish the individual's motivation and ability to change. Instead, a sex offender law should be rewritten and applied in such a way as to offer a message of hope.

Under our present practices, when sex offenders are predicted to be likely to recidivate, they are cast off, either indefinitely committed to a psychiatric hospital for a lengthy period of incapacitation or released to the community with a brand that will prevent or seriously encumber their rehabilitation and redemption. If we genuinely wish to effectuate the rehabilitation of sex offenders, sex offender treatment should be made readily available in the community on a confidential basis to anyone wishing to engage in it. Such treatment also should be offered to convicted offenders in the prison. Offenders should be encouraged to accept such treatment but not coerced into doing so. Behavioral techniques, social skills training, cognitive restructuring approaches, empathy training, and relapse prevention training should be offered and encouraged for anyone who would like help in learning how to control his or her sexual desires. Preventative approaches in the community also should be offered (see this volume, chapter 13). Offenders who opt to participate in prison treatment programs should be assured confidentiality in their communications with clinical staff. Offenders should not be denied treatment until the expiration of their prison term. When offenders are released, adequate postrelease programs should be available that include community treatment and probation or parole supervision.

Sexually violent predator laws should be repealed or not adopted in states that do not presently have them. Although constitutional, they are unwise. The high fiscal costs and antitherapeutic consequences of these laws mandate this conclusion. These laws were adopted as stop-gap measures in states that had relatively short determinate sentences for sex offenders (see this volume, chapter 2). Most states now have lengthier, indeterminate prison terms for sex offenders, rendering the need for these statutes obsolete. Thus, the negative effects of these laws far exceed their positive value inasmuch as community protection can be accomplished through reliance on a criminal punishment model with enhanced penalties for repeat offenders.

Even if these laws are not repealed, they should be revised in several important respects. We should rethink the label "sexually violent predator," the imposition of which can have strongly negative effects on the offender's willingness to engage in treatment and ability to respond favorably to it. If civil commitment after expiration of a prison sentence is deemed warranted for some sex offenders, it can be accomplished without the necessity of this unfortunate label. If preventive detention is warranted for a small number of sex offenders deemed highly likely to repeatedly reoffend, such detention should be accomplished in secure facilities that are not psychiatric hospitals. Psychiatric hospitals are not needed for the provision of sex offender treatment, which consists largely of counseling and behavioral approaches. These treatment approaches should be offered to sex offenders housed in secure preventive detention, but, again, on a voluntary basis. Offenders should be encouraged to accept such treatment but not coerced into doing so, because coercion might backfire, producing psychological reactance and other negative psychological effects that diminish the likelihood that such treatment will succeed.

Sexually violent predator statutory schemes should be restructured to convert them from prediction to risk management models (see this volume, chapter 12). Gradually reduced tiers of risk should be used, governing conditions of confinement and the availability of temporary and partial-release options, and ultimately leading to supervised release for those who have demonstrated rehabilitation and minimal risk of reoffending.

If implemented, these reforms could do much to minimize the present antitherapeutic consequences of this new model for dealing with sex offenders and increase its therapeutic potential. Instead of subjecting sex offenders to psychologically damaging labeling and perpetual stigmatization, we should offer meaningful treatment and incentives that motivate them to accept treatment and to learn how to control their behavior. Instead of hopelessness and continued ostracism, we should extend to sex offenders who are motivated to change a meaningful opportunity for rehabilitation and redemption.

REFERENCES

American Psychiatric Association. (1999). *Task force on sexually dangerous offenders.* Washington, DC: Author.

Arkin, R. N., & Baumgardner, A. H. (1985). Self-handicapping. In J. H. Harvey & G. Weary (Eds.), *Attribution: Basic issues and applications* (pp. 169–198). Orlando, FL: Academic Press.

Bandura, A. (1997). *Self-efficacy: The exercise of control.* New York: Freeman.

Becker, J. V., & Murphy, W. D. (1998). What we know and do not know about assessing and treating sex offenders. *Psychology, Public Policy, and Law, 4,* 116–137.

Committee on Psychiatry and Law of the Group for the Advancement of Psychiatry. (1977). *Psychiatry and sex psychopath legislation: The 30's to the 80's.* New York: Group for the Advancement of Psychiatry.

Fink, P., & Tasman, A. (1992). *Stigma and mental illness.* Washington, DC: American Psychiatric Press.

Goffman, E. (1963). *Stigma: Notes on the management of spoiled identity.* Englewood Cliffs, NJ: Prentice-Hall.

Harris, G. T., Rice, M. E., & Quinsey, V. L. (1998). Appraisal and management of risk in sexual aggressors: Implications for criminal justice policy. *Psychology, Public Policy, and Law, 4,* 73–115.

Jones, E. E. (1984). *Social stigma: The psychology of marked relationships.* New York: Freeman.

Kansas v. Crane, 122 S. Ct. 867 (2002).

Kansas v. Hendricks, 521 U.S. 346 (1997).

La Fond, J. Q. (1998). The cost of enacting a sexual predator law. *Psychology, Public Policy, and Law, 4,* 468–504.

Link, B. G., & Cullen, F. T. (1986). Contact with the mentally ill and perceptions of how dangerous they are. *Journal of Health and Social Behavior, 27,* 289–302.

Link, B. G., Cullen, F. T., Frank, J., & Wozniak, J. F. (1987). The social rejection of former mental patients: Understanding why labels matter. *American Journal of Sociology, 92,* 1461–1500.

Monahan, J. (1993). Mental disorder and violence: Another link. In S. Hodgins (Ed.), *Mental disorder and crime* (pp. 287–302). Newbury Park, CA: Sage.

Scheff, T. J. (1966). *Being mentally ill: A sociological theory.* Chicago: Aldine.

Stolle, D. P., Wexler, D. B., & Winick, B. J. (Eds.). (2000). *Practicing therapeutic jurisprudence: Law as a helping profession.* Durham, NC: Carolina Academic Press.

Wexler, D. B., & Winick, B. J. (1991). *Essays in therapeutic jurisprudence.* Durham, NC: Carolina Academic Press.

Wexler, D. B., & Winick, B. J. (1992). Therapeutic jurisprudence and criminal justice mental health issues. *American Bar Association Physical and Mental Disability Law Report, 16,* 225–231.

Wexler, D. B., & Winick, B. J. (Eds.). (1996). *Law in a therapeutic key: Developments in therapeutic jurisprudence.* Durham, NC: Carolina Academic Press.

Winick, B. J. (1997a). Coercion and mental health treatment. *Denver University Law Review, 74,* 1145–1168.

Winick, B. J. (1997b). The jurisprudence of therapeutic jurisprudence. *Psychology, Public Policy, and Law, 3,* 184–206.

Winick, B. J. (1997c). *The right to refuse mental health treatment*. Washington, DC: American Psychological Association.

Winick, B. J. (1998). Sex offender law in the 1990s: A therapeutic jurisprudence analysis. *Psychology, Public Policy, and Law, 4*, 505–570.

Zonana, H. (1997). The civil commitment of sex offenders. *Science, 278*, 1248–1250.

CONCLUSION

BRUCE J. WINICK AND JOHN Q. LA FOND

This book has critically examined new legal approaches for protecting society from sexually dangerous offenders. These approaches—sexually violent predator (SVP) laws, sex offender registration and community notification laws, and chemical castration laws—use a variety of innovative strategies designed to protect society from dangerous sex offenders. What can we learn from our experts about the wisdom and effectiveness of these new schemes?

SEXUALLY VIOLENT PREDATOR LAWS

SVP laws isolate and incapacitate sex offenders presenting the greatest risk of future violence through long-term civil commitment at the expiration of their prison terms. These statutes, enacted in at least 15 states and upheld by the U.S. Supreme Court, fill gaps in the law that previously had allowed dangerous sex offenders to be released from prison. Other states are actively considering enacting an SVP law. On balance, these laws, though constitutional, are unwise.

Preventive Detention

Though merely a special form of civil commitment, these SVP laws are in reality a special form of preventive detention. Their mission is to confine as long as possible rather than to treat and release as soon as possible. The inadequate clinical resources too often provided in these programs and the lack of confidentiality provided offenders make this very clear. The failure of states to grant even conditional release to any significant number of SVPs some 12 years after these laws went into effect also confirms this.

Perverts Justice

Lengthy civil commitment will protect the community from some of the most dangerous repetitive sex offenders. However, resorting to this subterfuge blurs the line between criminal punishment and civil commitment and distorts the nature of the psychiatric hospital in ways that threaten principles of justice, therapy, and constitutional values. Moreover, these laws provide disincentives for sex offenders facing criminal charges to accept criminal responsibility for their conduct and for sentenced offenders to engage in treatment within the prison or to do so in earnest. As a result, these laws may actually undermine the potential of prison treatment, which has greater potential for success because it is offered nearer in time to the offense.

Antitherapeutic Effects

SVP laws may have antitherapeutic effects that undermine the potential for rehabilitation. By labeling offenders as sexually violent predators, these laws reinforce the conception of many sex offenders that they are "sick" and, therefore, unable to control their conduct. This self-conception may diminish the significant potential that cognitive–behavioral and relapse prevention treatment models have in teaching offenders effective strategies for controlling their sexual behavior. Ironically, by embracing a medical model of sexual offending, SVP laws may also diminish the rehabilitative potential of the criminal law's punitive moral model. This accountability model makes sex offenders take responsibility for their conduct and provides incentives for them to meaningfully participate in treatment.

SVP laws may also pose antitherapeutic effects for clinicians who work in SVP programs, thereby decreasing the probability that highly qualified clinicians will seek this work. These laws will also have antitherapeutic consequences for people who suffer from serious mental illness. They will be deprived of needed hospital and clinical resources because money must now be spent on SVPs rather than on people with serious mental disabilities. Truly mentally disabled people may be subject to further stigmatization because the public may confuse them with dangerous sex offenders.

Too Expensive

The SVP commitment model is extremely costly. Although we may have actuarial tools that permit identification of a *group* of offenders who are most likely to offend, we do not know which *individuals* among the group will or will not reoffend. Thus, we will surely commit many sex offenders who would *not* have reoffended if released from prison. To compound the problem of overcommitment, we do not yet have tools that can accurately identify when risk has decreased sufficiently to permit someone to be released from an SVP institution under supervision to the community. As a result, SVP commitment may in practice be the equivalent of a life sentence for many SVPs.

Alternative Solutions

Legislators considering whether to adopt SVP laws need to balance whether the marginal protection of the community they bring is worth the threat to principles of justice and constitutional values, potential antitherapeutic consequences, and extremely high fiscal costs. Thoughtful analysis is made all the more difficult by the intense political climate in which such legislation often is considered.

Community concern about personal safety is legitimate and important. But legislators should consider alternative methods of protecting the community. In most states, lengthy criminal penalties exist for sex offending, and enhanced penalties are available for repetitive offenders. In states where the penal law is inadequate to authorize sufficiently lengthy imprisonment for repetitive sex offenders, this problem can easily be remedied through statutory amendment.

If a punishment or moral model of sex offending is adopted instead of the medical model represented by the SVP laws, the message sent to sex offenders will be loud and clear. Their conduct is wrong and will be subjected to severe punishment. Offenders can control their antisocial behavior; if they refuse to do so, they will be sent to prison for a long time. Legislatures relying on the punishment model should provide prison treatment opportunities for sex offenders who choose to change. These programs are designed to teach them how to control their behavior. While the empirical research on sex offender treatment efficacy is inconclusive, emerging cognitive–behavioral and relapse prevention models hold much promise, at least for motivated offenders. It is in everyone's interest that prison-based treatment is available and subjected to methodologically sound evaluation.

SEX OFFENDERS RELEASED FROM PRISON

What should be done with sex offenders after they are released from prison? All states have sex offender registration laws, which require most sex offenders to register with the police. Many states also have community notification laws, which provide information to the community that allows people to take protective measures.

Community Notification Laws

Community notification laws that use only one tier of risk should be rethought. Three or more tiers of risk should be used, with offenders who show progress being enabled to move from high-risk to lower risk categories when appropriate. So revised, these notification laws can function as a form of risk management and can provide meaningful incentives to offenders to participate in and respond favorably to treatment. Several graduated tiers of risk therefore should be used, and the risk that a discharged sex offender presents should be subject to periodic reevaluation in light of changing circumstances, including the results of community monitoring and successful participation in rehabilitative programs.

In addition, hearings should be used for risk classification and reclassification decisions. Such hearings can provide offenders with a sense of participation that can have therapeutic advantages, including breaking down the cognitive distortions many sex offenders have that perpetuate their reoffending patterns.

A broad rethinking of registration and notification laws and how they should be applied thus is warranted. Reshaping these laws as our experts suggest could convert them into a useful risk management approach that can better achieve their community protection purposes and better foster rehabilitation.

Community Containment

Sex offenders paroled from prison before the expiration of their penal terms who pose little further risk of reoffending should be subject to moderate parole supervision. Sex offenders released after serving the full confinement sentence who pose a serious risk of reoffending should be subjected to intensive control in the community. The community containment approach used in Colorado is an effective model that should be replicated elsewhere. This model involves an interdisciplinary effort in which law enforcement officials, sex offender treaters, and polygraph professionals work together to manage the risk of reoffending and to provide offenders with incentives to participate meaningfully in treatment.

CHEMICAL CASTRATION LAWS

Chemical castration laws, which require administration of sex-drive-reducing drugs as a condition for release on probation or parole, raise grave constitutional and ethical concerns. Although these drugs may be effective in reducing violence in a small percentage of sex offenders, chemical castration laws do not require individual clinical evaluation of the offender. Instead, they impose medication based on the offense rather than on whether these drugs are medically appropriate for the person.

More research is needed to determine when these drugs are appropriate and to measure their effectiveness and safety. The U.S. Food and Drug Administration has not approved these drugs for eliminating sex drive in a broad class of sex offenders. In the absence of more information, psychiatrists asked to participate in the administration of these drugs will face serious ethical dilemmas relating to the use of medication for social control purposes. At a minimum, these drugs should be used only following a thorough medical evaluation and as part of a comprehensive treatment plan. States considering enacting a chemical castration law should proceed with caution, awaiting further research. Any state that insists on enacting such a law should at the very least require a medical evaluation prior to requiring sex offenders to take these drugs. There really is no need for these laws, however, because community containment and other intensive supervision models can always be used for offenders who pose a serious risk of reoffending.

A RESEARCH AGENDA

The new legal models that have emerged in the 1990s for dealing with sexually violent offenders raise serious empirical, legal, and ethical questions and pose significant challenges for mental health professionals who evaluate and treat sex offenders. Although we have learned much more in recent years about risk assessment and treatment of sex offenders, there remains much that we do not know. The chapters in this volume document the need for new research initiatives in a variety of areas.

Much more research is needed concerning the etiology of sexual offending. Knowing what causes sex offending should significantly advance strategies for preventing and eliminating it. We also need to continue to test and improve risk assessment instruments for predicting which *individual* is likely to engage in sexual violence and refine the way clinical evaluations are conducted. Tools for determining when individual sex offenders no longer pose a serious risk of reoffending are sorely lacking. New and innovative treatment techniques must be developed and their efficacy rigorously evaluated.

More research is also required on the reforms proposed in this book to restructure many of the new strategies enacted since 1990 to provide better community protection and offender rehabilitation. Therapeutic jurisprudence provides a very useful perspective for studying these laws to ascertain whether they produce antitherapeutic effects that can be minimized. It also suggests how these laws may be reshaped and applied differently to maximize their therapeutic potential.

COST–BENEFIT ANALYSIS AND ALTERNATIVE STRATEGIES

These new legal approaches to dealing with sexual violence may inadvertently impose additional social costs on society that, in the long run, may increase rather than decrease sexual violence. By diverting public attention and resources to punishing sex crimes committed by strangers *after* they have occurred, these laws may neglect the important problem of how sex crimes can be *prevented*.

Helping Sexually Abused Children

An especially important but neglected focus of our societal attention is children who have been sexually abused, and who, as a result, pose a high risk of abusing others in the future. Early intervention and preventive approaches that target this category of potential sex offenders may be considerably more cost-effective than SVP programs that focus on the indefinite incarceration of adult offenders. Research on these children and their families can provide important information that can help to prevent future sexual offending. Our policies concerning sexual violence, therefore, should place much more emphasis on primary and secondary prevention rather than merely on tertiary prevention.

Targeting Sex Crimes Committed by Familiars

By overemphasizing sex crimes committed by strangers, our new legal approaches mistakenly ignore the fact that the overwhelming majority of sex offenses are committed by family members and others known to the victim. These include rapes of adults and crimes committed by sexually abusive children. Emphasizing SVP laws, community registration and notification laws, and chemical castration laws has distracted us from dealing effectively with the more extensive problem of preventing sexual violence by offenders who know their victims. We need to refocus our research, treatment, prevention, and law enforcement resources to deal with this area of sexual violence if we are to succeed in protecting the community from sexual abuse.

RETHINKING THE PREVENTION OF SEXUAL VIOLENCE

This book challenges many of the new strategies and practices enacted since 1990 to prevent sexual violence. It calls for important reforms, more research, and new initiatives. Some of our conclusions may be controversial and provocative. We sincerely hope that they will stimulate further dialogue and debate among legislators, policymakers, law enforcement officials, judges, lawyers, and mental health professionals performing evaluation and treatment in this area, as well as undergraduate and graduate students preparing for careers in these fields. Much more creative work remains to be done if we are to succeed in protecting our society from sexual violence.

TABLE OF AUTHORITIES

Numbers in italics refer to listings in the reference sections.

Knecht v. Gillman, 488 F.2d 1136 (8th Cir. 1973), 254, 256, *261*
Lindsley v. Natural Carbonic Gas Co., 220 U.S. 61 (1911), *210*
In re Linehan, 557 N.W. 2d 171 (Minn. 1996) ("Linehan III"), 202, *209*
In re Linehan, 594 N.W. 2d 867 (Minn. 1999), ("Linehan IV"), 127, *129*,
     210
Lochner v. New York 198 U.S. 45 (1905), 312, *315*
Mackey v. Procunier, 477 F.2d 877 (9th Cir. 1973), 254, 256, *261*
Mayock v. Martin, 245 A.2d 574 (1968), 137, *145*
McGowan v. Maryland, 366 U.S. 420 (1961), *210*
McKune v. Lile, 122 S. Ct. 2017 (2002), 169n, *181*
In re M.F. 776 A.2d 780, 790 (New Jersey 2001), 309, *315*
Mickle v. Henricks, 262 F. 687 (1918), 251, *261*
Minnesota v. Pearson, 309 U.S. 270 (1940), *210*
Nelson v. Heyne, 491 F.2d 352, 356 (7th Cir. 1974), *cert. denied*, 417 U.S.
     976 (1974), 254, 246, *262*
New Orleans v. Dukes, 427 U.S. 297 (1976), *210*
N.J. Stat. Ann. § 2C:7-1–7-11 (1994) Megan's Law, or Registration and
     Community Notification Laws, *315*
O'Connor v. Donaldson, 422 U.S. 563 (1975), *210*
People v. Gauntlett, 352 N.W.2d 310 (Mich. App. 1984), 256, *262*
In re Petersen, 980 P.2d 1204 (1999), 293, *298*
Powell v. Texas, 392 U.S. 514 (1968), 169, *181*
Regina v. Reynolds, Crim. L.R. 679 (C.A.) (1998), 204, *210*
Riggins v. Nevada, 112 S. Ct. 1810 (1992), 255, *262*
Matter of Registrant G.B. 685 A.2d 1252, 1256, 1262 (New Jersey 1996),
     309, 314, *316*
Rogers v. Okin, 634 F.2d 650 (1st Cir. 1980), 256, *262*
Rouse v. Cameron, 373 F.2d 451 (D.C. Cir. 1967), 207, *210*
Seling v. Young, 531 U.S. 250 (2001), 123, 126, *129*, 172, *182*, 313, *316*
Singleton v. State, 437 S.E. 2d 53 (S.C. 1993), 258, *262*
Skinner v. Oklahoma, 316 U.S. 535 (1941), 251, *262*
State v. Brown, 326 S.E. 2d 410 (S.C. 1985), 251, *262*
State v. Perry, 610 So.2d 746 (La. 1992), 258, *262*
State v. Post, 541 N.W. 2d 115 (Wis. 1995), 127, *129*
In re Traynoff, Kane County, Ill., Cause No. 98 HR 456, 291, *298*
In re Turay, 139 Wash. 2d379 (1999), *210*
Turay v. Seling, 108 F. Supp. 2d 1148 (W.D. Wash. 2000), 293
Turay v. Weston, No. C91-664-WD (W.D. Wash. 1994), 55, 59, 289, *298*
United States v. Bryant, 70 F. Supp. 840m 843 (Minn. 1978), 250, *262*
United States v. Salerno, 481 U.S. 739 (1987), 127, *129*
United States v. Ursery, 518 U.S. 267 (1996), 301, *316*
Washington v. Harper, 110 S. Ct. 1028 (1990), 255, *262*
Weems v. United States, 217 U.S. 349, 377 (1910), 251, *262*
West v. Macht, 197 F.3d 1185 (7th Cir. 1999), 291, *299*
Williams v. Smith, 262 F. 687, 690-01 (D. Nev. 1918), 251, *263*
Wisconsin v. Post, 541 N.W.2d 115 (1995), *210*

AUTHOR INDEX

Numbers in italics refer to listings in the reference sections.

SUBJECT INDEX

"Behavioral abnormality," in Texas com-
mitment law, 37
Behavioral quarantine, 170, 179
Behavioral therapy, 107–109, 322
Beneficence principle, 10, 123, 128
  and treatment-amenability require-
  ment, 125
Biological treatments affecting sexual be-
  havior. *See* Antiandrogen treat-
  ment; Castration (surgical);
  Chemical castration
Blame-the-victim mentality, in rape cases,
  154
Bodily integrity, and chemical castration,
  256–257
Breyer, Stephen G., 207
Brown v. Mayle, 171
Buck v. Bell, 250
Burt Rape Myth Acceptance Scale, 86
Bush, Jeb, 287, 292

California
  and chemical castration, 252, 253
  commitment law of, 27n, 30
  and evaluators, 77
  prison health care costs in, 295
  sexual predator (commitment) law of,
  27n, 30, 45, 46, 53
    costs of clinicians for, 285
    costs of hearings and trials for, 285–
    286
    costs of release and transition pro-
    grams under, 293, 294
    costs of screening for, 284
    and costs of secure and therapeutic
    facility, 291–292
    and less restrictive alternative or re-
    lease, 52
    number of persons held, 45
    and provision of services, 33, 34, 35
    and SVP census projections, 286–
    287
  sexual psychopath law of, 42
Carey v. Population Services Int'l, 256
Case management
  in containment approach, 19, 266,
  268–270 (*see also* Containment
  approach)
  in Texas program, 37
Castration (surgical), 104–105, 121,
  250–251, 256–257

Castration, chemical. *See* Chemical castration
Causation, vs. excuse, 176
Certificate of confidentiality, 232
Chapman v. United States, 199
Chemical castration, 4, 4–5, 18, 251–
  252, 259–260, 337
  American Psychiatric Association Task
  Force Report on, 136
  cost of, 254
  and due process, 255–256
  and Eighth Amendment, 256
  and First Amendment, 256
  and informed consent, 253, 255
  and integrity of medical profession,
  257–259
  legislative efforts to require, 252–253
  as mandatory for defined class, 250
  and medical interests of patient, 253–
  255
  and privacy or bodily integrity, 256–
  257
Child protective services (CPS), 236–
  237, 241
Children
  sex crimes against, 150–151
  sexual abuse prevention education for,
  156
Children with sexual behavior problems,
  17, 231–234
  age of first abuse as predictor for, 237
  empirically derived types of, 242–244
  etiology of problems of, 237–238, 239
  interventions for, 240–242, 244–245
Child sexual abuse, 235, 338
  and child protective services (CPS),
  236–237
  and children with sexual behavior
  problems, 231, 232, 237–238
  and posttraumatic stress disorder, 238–
  240
  quality control in containment of, 276
  traumatic influences of, 233
Child Sexual Behavior Inventory–3
  (CSBI), 243
Civil commitment (for mentally ill in
  general), 171
  American Psychiatric Association on,
  137–139
  calculus for, 205
  and commitment under sexual predator
  statutes, 192

constraints on misuse of, 139

and danger of *Hendricks* and *Crane* cases, 178–180, 197, 206

distinction of from criminal punishment needed, 202–203

historical perspective on, 136–137

and insanity defense, 140–141, 174 (*see also at* Insanity)

libertarian model of, 137, 138

and moral model, 170

parens patriae power as basis of, 123

personality disorders as justification of, 142

police power as basis of, 123–124

and respect for persons, 193–194

Civil commitment laws (for sexual offenders), 3, 27–31, 37, 192

as "abuse of psychiatry," 131, 135

alternatives to, 15–19, 35–37, 52, 53, 288, 294, 335–336

American Psychiatric Association Task Force Report on, 35, 135

and constitutional values or ethical theory, 12–15, 18

cost of, 325–326 (*see also* Costs of sexual predator laws)

as criminal incarceration, 206–207, 334

and criminal punishment vs. mental health treatment, 13–14, 29n, 36, 318–319

(*see also* Criminal model; Illness model)

extension of to other categories

and kleptomania, 206

and lack of treatment, 206

PMDD, 204–205

pyromania, 203–204

and extrastatutory considerations, 31–32

indefinite period for, 172

of Kansas, 11, 47, 142, 173–174, 192, 304–307 (*see also under* Kansas)

and *Kansas v. Hendricks*, 122–123, 175, 176–177, 192 (*see also Kansas v. Hendricks*)

as limited protection, 173

and nexus between mental abnormality and sexual dangerousness, 77

and offenders known to victims, 12

and offenders' self-concept, 21

as preventive detention, 171, 174, 180, 334

and punitive intent, 126

and responsibility of sexual predators, 174, 178

and risk assessment, 63–64 (*see also* Risk assessment)

without "sexually violent predator" label, 329

as threat to liberty, 180

time period of disfavor toward, 249, 249–250n

and treatment, 10, 119–120, 127–128

right to treatment, 123, 125–127

of Washington State, 4, 7, 28–30, 41, 43–44, 51, 54–56, 192, 283 (*see also under* Washington State)

Cliffhanger analogy, 177–178

Clinical judgment, on recidivism risk, 66, 67

Clinicians providing sex offender treatment

cost of, 284–285

impact of sexual predator laws on, 324–325, 334

See also Psychiatry

Cognitive-behavioral therapy, 107–109, 122, 127, 321, 322, 323, 335

Colorado

antiandrogen treatment in, 5

and chemical castration, 252, 260

community containment approach in, 336–337

sex offenders on probation, 266

supervision mandated in, 36

Colorado Sex Offender Management Board (previously Sex Offender Treatment Board), 259, 268

Commissioner of Corrections v. Myers, 258

Commitment laws. *See* Civil commitment laws

Community, and registration or notification laws, 216–219

Community containment. *See* Containment approach

Community notification law(s), 3–4, 213, 214, 226–227, 277, 336

and federal government, 307

Megan's Law, 4, 44, 159, 213, 215, 217, 304, 307–311, 313–314

negative effects of, 15–16

of New Jersey, 4

and redemption, 226

American Psychiatric Association
Model Civil Commitment Law
criteria for, 139n
Humphrey v. Cady, 198
Hydrick v. Wilson, 291

Illinois, sexual predator (commitment)
law of, 27n, 30, 45, 46
and frequency of commitment, 33
and less restrictive alternative or release, 52
number of persons held, 45
and provision of services, 34
Illness, and reoffending risk, 91
Illness model, 318–319
and labeling effects on offenders, 319–
321
and labeling of mentally ill, 326
and treatment outcome, 321–324
Incest offenders, 110
Indefinite commitment, as death penalty,
286
Indeterminate sentencing arrangements,
43, 135–136, 143, 235, 306–307,
328
in Colorado program, 36
in Washington program, 55–56
Indiana, commitment legislation stalled
in, 35
Information gathering, in initial evalua-
tion, 80–81
Informed consent, 253
for chemical castration, 253, 255
Innovative state program for, 235–236
In re Blodgett, 198, 202
In re C.A., 308, 310, 314
In re Gault, 137, 199
In re Hendricks, 192
In re Linehan (Linehan III), 198, 201, 202
In re Linehan (Linehan IV), 127, 199
In the matter of Registrant G.B., 309, 314
In re M.F., 309
In re Petersen, 293
In re Traynoff, 291
In re Turay, 199
In re Young, 187, 192, 313
Insanity acquittees
confinement of (O'Connor), 205
vs. sexual predators, 141
Insanity defense
vs. civil commitment, 174

and culpability, 190
Insight-oriented psychotherapy, as treatment component, 107
International Classification of Diseases
(ICD-10), 142
Internet, registration information on, 214
Interventions for children with sexual behavior problems, 240, 244–245
different levels of, 244
STEP program for, 240–242
Involuntary confinement
desert vs. disease rationale for, 170–
173
See also Civil commitment laws
Iowa
and chemical castration, 252
sexual predator (commitment) law of,
27n, 47
and frequency of commitment, 33
and less restrictive alternative or release, 52
number of persons held, 45
Irresistible impulses, false claims of, 271–
272
and cliffhanger analogy, 177–178

Jackson v. Indiana, 127, 172, 198
Jacobson v. Massachusetts, 312
Jacob Wetterling Crimes Against Chil-
dren and Sexually Violent Of-
fender Registration Act, 28, 307
Janet D. v. Carros, 208
Joint Commission on the Accreditation
of Hospital Organizations
(JCAHO), 34
Jones v. United States, 171, 179, 198
Jurisprudence, therapeutic, 15, 21, 157,
159, 223, 318
Justice
civil commitment as perverting, 334
retributive, 170
Justification, vs. excuse, 191

Kanka, Megan, 4, 213, 216, 307, 310–
311. *See also* Megan's Law
Kansas
and evaluators, 77
petition for release in, 78
sexual predator (commitment) law of,
11, 27n, 47, 173–174, 192, 304–
307

Kansas (*continued*)
    as confinement, 142
    costs of release and transition pro-
       grams for, 294
    and frequency of commitment, 33
    and less restrictive alternative or re-
       lease, 52
    and "mental abnormality," 173,
       174–176, 178, 306
    number of persons held, 45
    and prognosis, 28
    and substantive due process, 198
    and SVP census projections, 287,
       288
    and treatment, 120, 289
  and time needed for release, 89
  and Washington State law, 29
Kansas v. Crane, 6, 142–143n, 177, 209
  and due process, 255–256
  and evaluation, 80
  extended danger of, 178–180
  and predators' control problems, 29,
    78, 93, 123, 166, 178, 192, 201,
    319
Kansas v. Hendricks, 11, 13, 14–15, 29n,
    122–123, 142–144, 208–209,
    304–307, 312–313
  and control theory of excuse, 176–177
  on creation of legal criteria, 175
  and criminal vs. civil confinement,
    175, 192
  and dangerousness as confinement cri-
    terion, 170
  and definition of mental disorders, 84
  and deterrence, 127
  and due process, 255–256
  and examples of sexual assault, 187
  expansion of civil commitment power
    from, 178–180, 197, 206
  as expansion of state power, 21
  and incapacitation rationale, 172
  and medical vs. moral model, 166
  and mental abnormality, 200–203
    as relevant to other categories, 203
  and nonpunitive intent, 126
  and other state laws, 37–38
  preventive detention permitted in,
    174, 180
  and standard of scrutiny, 198–200, 209
  and treatment-amenability require-
    ment, 122, 124–125

and treatment rationale, 10, 206–208,
    289
and Washington State law, 29
and widespread adoption of sexual
    predator laws, 317
Kendra's Law, 139
Kennedy, Anthony M., 29n, 202, 203,
    205, 206, 207, 306, 312
Kleptomaniacs, and sex offenders, 206
Knecht v. Gillman, 254, 256

Labeling effects, 319–321
  on mentally ill patients, 326–327
Lack-of-control requirement, 6, 29, 29n,
    78, 177, 178, 201, 319
La Fond, John, 174
Law reform
  context for, 4–5
  of sexual predator laws, 328–329
Laws against sexual predators. See Civil
    commitment laws; Community
    notification laws; Registration
    laws; Sexual predator laws
Least-restrictive alternative placement
    (LRA), 288, 294
Legal institutions of social control
  expressive function of, 188–189
  practical and expressive functions of
    (three examples), 190–191
  self-determination protected by, 189–
    190, 193
Legal policies on sex offenders. *See* Sex
    offender legal policies
Liability
  fear of, 140
  Oliver Wendell Holmes on, 185
Liberal tradition of political morality,
    189–190
Liberty Behavioral Corporation, 287
Liberty right, 169, 170. *See also* Auton-
    omy principle
Lifetime confinement, 127
Lindsley v. Natural Carbonic Gas Co., 199
Linehan III, 198, 201, 202
Linehan IV, 127, 199
Lochner v. New York, 312
Locke, Gary, 295
Locus of control, 217
LRAs (least-restrictive alternative place-
    ments), 288, 294

Mackey v. Procunier, 254, 256

Maine, and chemical castration, 252
Managed care, 139, 142, 257
Managerialism, in new penology, 302
    and Kansas sexual predator law, 305
    and Megan's Law, 309–310
Manual for the Sexual Violence Risk–20
    (SVR–20), 87
Marshall, Thurgood, 169
Maryland
    and chemical castration, 252
    commitment legislation stalled in, 35
Massachusetts, sexual predator (commit-
    ment) law of, 27n, 45, 47
    and frequency of commitment, 33
    and less restrictive alternative or re-
        lease, 52
    number of persons held, 45
    and provision of services, 32
Mayock v. Martin, 137
McGowan v. Maryland, 199
McIntyre, John, 132
McKune v. Lile, 169n
Medical model of deviance, 11, 12–13,
    135, 165, 166–167, 169–170,
    180
Medical profession, integrity of, and
    chemical castration, 257–259
Medical tests, in initial evaluation, 87
Medications
    anti-Parkinsonian, 87
    to restore competency for execution,
        258
    sex-drive-reducing, 5, 18, 85, 105–107,
        121, 250, 253, 337 (*see also*
        Chemical castration)
Medroxyprogesterone acetate (MPA),
    105–106, 251, 252
Megan's Law, 4, 44, 159, 213, 215, 217,
    304, 307–311, 313–314. *See also*
    Community notification law(s)
"Mental abnormality"
    and antisocial conduct, 320
    and civil commitment laws, 12, 13, 29
    courts' interpretation of, 142
    and discharged sex offenders, 328
    and evaluation as sexually dangerous,
        77
    extended danger in definition of, 178–
        179
    and illness model, 319
    in initial evaluation, 83–84
    and *Kansas v. Crane*, 177, 319

in *Kansas v. Hendricks*, 29n, 200–203,
    305
in Kansas statute, 173, 174–176, 178
    and causation vs. excuse, 176
    vs. "mental illness," 306
and labeling, 321
as relevant to other categories, 203–
    206
and state sexual predator laws, 45, 46,
    47, 48, 49, 50, 51, 317
Mental health professionals (MHPs). *See*
    Clinicians providing sex offender
    treatment; Psychiatry
Mental health treatment
    vs. criminal punishment, 13–14, 29n,
        36
    See also Psychiatry; Treatment of sex
        offenders
Mentally ill persons
    and labeling of sexual predators, 326–
        327
    and sex predator laws, 22, 38
        as taking funds from treatment of,
            143–144, 295, 326
Mental status examination, in initial
    evaluation, 83–85
Meta-analysis, 103
MHPs (mental health professionals). *See*
    Clinicians providing sex offender
    treatment; Psychiatry
Michigan
    and costs of treatment, 290
    postsentence commitment for variety
        of offenders in, 38
Mickle v. Henricks, 251
Minnesota, sexual predator (commit-
    ment) law of (Sexually Danger-
    ous Persons Act), 27n, 28, 30,
    45, 48, 53, 201
    costs of hearings and trials for, 286
    costs of release and transition programs
        for, 294
    costs of secure and therapeutic facility
        for, 292
    and frequency of commitment, 32, 33
    and less restrictive alternative or re-
        lease, 52
    number of persons held, 45
    and provision of services, 33, 34
    and SVP census projections, 287
    and treatment, 120

Oklahoma
and chemical castration, 252
commitment law repealed in, 38
"One strike" laws, 71
Oregon
probation/parole officer meetings in,
268
"Outpatient commitment" statutes, 139
Overcommitment, 335

Packard, Elizabeth, 137
Paraphilias, 134, 225. *See also* Sex offenders
Parens patriae interventions, 10, 123, 124,
138
Parentalism, and imposed treatment, 167
Parole
chemical castration as condition of, 4,
4–5
in Colorado program, 36
Paternalistic model of civil commitment,
132, 137, 138, 139
PCL–R (Psychopathy Checklist–
Revised), 68, 69, 86
Pedophilia
and evaluation of sex offenders, 84, 87,
92
as paraphilia, 134
psychotic symptoms lacking in, 225
question of continuation of, 92
test of cognitive distortion in, 86
See also Sex crimes; Sex offenders
Penile plethysmography (PPG), 86
Penology, new. *See* New penology
People v. Gauntlett, 256
Personality disorder, 175, 319
antisocial, 103, 179, 202, 203, 205,
286
and antisocial conduct, 320
and sexually violent predator laws, 317
Phallometric assessment, 65, 112
Pharmacological treatments, 105–107
Physical examination, in initial evaluation, 87
Plea bargains, by sex offenders 234
PMDD (premenstrual dysphoric disorder)
and sex offenses, 204–205
Police, and registration or community
notification laws, 217
Police power commitments, 123–124
as alternative social control institution,
193

under American Psychiatric Association's Model Law, 139–140
and psychiatry, 142
and treatment, 10, 124, 167
See also Civil commitment laws
Polygraphy
in containment approach, 266, 269,
270, 271, 273–274, 274
in initial evaluation 86
in release-related evaluation, 91
in risk-assessment model, 224
Populist punitiveness, 303–304
and Kansas sexual predator statute,
306–307
and Megan's Law, 310–311
Postconviction polygraphs, 273–274
Posttraumatic stress disorder (PTSD), and
child sexual abuse, 238
Powell v. Texas, 169–170
PPG (penile plethysmography), 86
Prediction model, 16, 221–222, 223
Premenstrual dysphoric disorder (PMDD),
and sex offenses, 204–205
President's Commission Report on crime
policy, 301
Prevention lifestyle, for families, 238
Preventive approaches, 17
in community, 226–227, 328
vs. new legal approaches, 338
See also Interventions for children with
sexual behavior problems
Preventive detention (confinement), 171,
174, 180
sexual predator laws as, 133, 317–318,
334
Prisons, sex offenders in, 234, 235
Privacy, and chemical castration, 256–
257
Probable cause, in Kansas statute, 305
Probable cause hearings, 76, 286
Probationary sentences, 235–236
Psychiatry
fear of undermining of confidence in,
133
and medication of sex offenders, 259
and personalilty disorders as commitment basis, 142
and sex offender commitment laws,
121, 131, 135
See also Clinicians providing sex offender treatment

Psychological testing, in initial evaluation, 85–86

Psychology, Public Policy and Law, special symposium issue of, 6

Psychopathy, as recidivism predictor, 103, 112

Psychopathy Checklist–Revised (PCL–R), 68, 69, 86

Psychotherapy
insight-oriented, 107
nonbehavioral, 103–104

PTSD (posttraumatic stress disorder), and child sexual abuse, 238

Public morality, conventional. *See* Conventional public morality

Public policies, in containment approach, 275

Punishment
expressive function of, 188–189
vs. mental health treatment, 13–14, 29n, 36
and new penology, 302–304
popular emotions vs. state-based professionals in development of, 311
sexual predator laws as, 10
social purposes of, 301–304
in three examples of culpability, 185–186, 187
and treatment of sex offenders, 168–169
See also Populist punitiveness

Punishment (moral) model of deviance, 13, 165, 167–170, 180, 335

Punitive intent, and treatment, 126–127

Pyromania, sex offenses compared with, 203–204

Quality control, in containment approach, 275–276

Quarantine, behavioral, 170, 179

Rape, 12, 151
and Burt Rape Myth Acceptance Scale, 86
castration as punishment for, 250
doubts about credibility of victims of, 155–156
fear from publicizing of, 155
hidden, 151–152, 267
juror decisions in cases of, 154
paucity of information on, 156

by perpetrators known to victims (nonstrangers), 12, 151, 267
planning of, 272
police processing of cases of, 152–153
prosecutor processing of cases of, 153–154
recidivism rate for, 64
and victim-centered philosophy, 267
victim perceptions of, 152

Rape in America (Kilpatrick et al.), 267

Rapid Risk Assessment for Sex Offence Recidivism (RRASOR), 68, 69, 88

Rationality
and indefinite commitment, 171
and responsibility for sexual conduct, 168

Raven Progressive Matrices, 86

Reasonable medical certainty (RMC), in initial evaluation, 89

Recidivism
accuracy in prediction of, 63 (*see also* Risk assessment)
base rates for, 64–65
factors in, 112
hearings as reducing, 225
measure of, 102
and new legal strategies, 4
psychopathy as predictor of, 112
rate of, 235
registration and community notification laws as furthering, 220–221
risk factors for, 65–66
dynamic and static, 64, 70–71, 72
treatment effectiveness for, 111 (*see also* Evaluation of treatment; Treatment of sex offenders)
See also Evaluation of sex offenders; Evaluation of treatment

Record review, in initial evaluation, 80–81

Redemption, for sex offenders, 226

Registrant Risk Assessment Scale, 308, 314

Registration and Community Notification Laws (New Jersey), 307. *See also* Megan's Law

Registration laws, 3, 213, 214, 226–227, 276–277
as federal requirement, 4, 307

increase in numbers required to register under, 5
Megan's Law, 4, 44, 159, 213, 215, 217, 304, 307–311, 313–314
negative effects of, 15–16
and redemption, 226
restructuring of, 221–226
therapeutic implications of
for community, 216–219
for offenders, 219–221
three-tiered system of, 214–216, 221, 223
See also Community notification law(s)
Rehabilitation, and registration or community notification laws, 219
Relapse prevention, as treatment component, 107, 108, 122, 226, 322, 335
Release decisions, 140
costs of, 293–295
Research
agenda for, 337–338
American Psychiatric Association Task Force Report on, 134–135
on links between violence toward women and victim-offender relationship, 158
and medical model, 170
Responsibility, 167
and civil commitment, 173, 180
definition of under criminal law, 190
and expressive function of legal institutions, 189
in *Hendricks* case, 192
and Kansas statute, 174, 175, 176
and legislators, 175
and medical model, 13, 166, 169
and moral model, 167–168, 169
and preventive detention, 174
and sexual predators, 125, 167, 174, 178, 180
and social-control gap, 125
See also Culpability
Retributive justice, 170
Riggins v. Nevada, 255
Risk, and new penology, 302, 303
Risk assessment, 8, 16, 63–64, 71–72
actuarial methods of, 88, 222
and actuarial risk scales, 66–70
and community notification, 218
and decision to release, 288

dynamic and static factors in, 64, 70–71, 72, 88, 90
and evaluators, 77
and initial evaluation, 87–89
and management of sex offenders, 111
and new penology, 314
and recidivism base rates, 64–65
and recidivism risk factors, 65–66
and screening process, 58
Risk management, 16–17, 22
community notification laws as, 218, 336
containment-focused, 19, 269–270
criminal justice supervision in, 270–272
postconviction polygraphs, 273–274
sex-offense-specific treatment in, 272–273
treatment-polygraph process, 274–275
and *Kansas v. Hendricks*, 313
and Megan's Law, 310
in restructuring of sexual predator laws, 329
of registration and community notification laws, 221–226
RMC (reasonable medical certainty) in initial evaluation, 89
Rogers v. Okin, 256
Rouse v. Cameron, 207–208
RRASOR (Rapid Risk Assessment for Sex Offence Recidivism), 68, 69, 88

SAC–J (Thornton's Structured Anchored Clinical Judgement scale), 69
SAST (Sex Abuse Specific Treatment), 241–242, 242, 243–244
Scarlet Letter, The (Hawthorne), 226
Scheff, Thomas, 326
Screening, 76
costs of, 284
need for thoroughness in, 296
Selective serotonin reuptake inhibitors (SSRIs), 121, 252
Self-attribution, 320
as sex offender, 220
Self-deception, 321
Self-determination
and liberal institutions, 189
See also Autonomy principle

Sexual assaults
    effect of on victim, 267
    and high-risk activities, 274
    prosecutor processing of cases of, 153
    victim perceptions of, 152
    See also Rape; Sex crimes
Sexual crimes. *See* Sex crimes
Sexual dangerousness, 8. *See also* Danger-
    ousness; Risk assessment
Sexual deviance or offending
    etiology of, 337–338
    as recidivism risk factor, 65, 66, 103
    See also Sex crimes; Sex offenders
Sexual history
    in containment approach, 270
    in initial evaluation, 82–83
"Sexually violent predators" (SVP)
    in commitment laws, 29, 319
    definition of, 75, 77
Sexually violent predator laws. *See* Sex-
    ual predator laws
Sexual offenders. *See* Sex offenders
Sexual predator evaluations. *See* Evalua-
    tions of sexual offenders
Sexual predator laws (sexually violent
    predator, SVP, laws), 7, 19–22,
    142–143, 144, 192–194, 197,
    283, 317–318, 333
    as "abuse of psychiatry," 131, 135
    as antitherapeutic, 16, 327–328, 334–
        335
    and conventional public morality, 193
    costs of, 283–284, 297, 325–326
        for clinicians, 284–285
        containment of, 296–297
        estimation of, 296
        and female SVPs, 289
        and funding for other programs,
            143–144, 295, 326
        and overcommitment problem, 335
        for release and community transition
            programs, 293–295
        and right to treatment, 289–291
        for screening, 284
        for secure and therapeutic facility,
            291–293
        and SVP census projections, 286–
            289, 296
        for trials and appeals, 285–286
        in Washington State, 54–55
    and evaluation, 75 (*see also* Evaluation
        of sexual offenders)

    and *Hendricks* decision, 15
    impact of on clinicians, 324–325, 334
    and insanity acquittees, 141
    of Kansas, 11, 27n, 47, 173–174, 192,
        304–307 (*see also under* Kansas)
    as missing offenses by nonstrangers,
        149–150, 159 (*see also* Nonstran-
        ger sex offenders)
    new penology plus populist punitive-
        ness in, 303–314
    as preventive detention, 334
    and public morality, 14 (*see also* Con-
        ventional public morality)
    question of real purpose of, 297
    repeal or revision of called for, 328–
        329
    and treatment, 10
        right to treatment under, 120 (*see
            also* Treatment of sex offenders)
    state policy perspective on, 41, 57–58
        comparison of statutes, 44–53
        issues emerging from, 54–56
        lessons for, 56–57
        and prison/mental health hospital
            distinction, 58
    status of persons undermined by, 194
    and therapeutic jurisprudence, 318
    of Washington State, 4, 7, 28–30, 41–
        44, 51, 54–56, 192, 283 (*see also
        under* Washington State)
    See also Civil commitment laws; Com-
        munity notification laws; Regis-
        tration laws
Sexual predator programs, Council on
    Psychiatry and Law on, 133
Sexual preferences, as predictor, 112
Sexual psychopath legislation, 132, 318
Sexual psychopath program, of Washing-
    ton State, 42
Sexual psychopathy laws, 56–57
Sexual reoffending
    and community containment, 19
    See also Containment approach; Recid-
        ivism
Sexual violence, rethinking prevention
    of, 339
    by strangers vs. nonstrangers, 150 (*see
        also* Nonstranger sex offenders)
    victim-attacker relation in, 6
    See also Sex crimes
Shipley-Hartford test, 86

Washington v. Harper, 255

Washington State

and chemical castration, 252

insanity defense and civil commitment statutes of, 174

sexual predator (commitment) law of, 4, 7, 28–30, 41, 51, 54–56, 192, 283

and confidentiality waiver, 323

costs of (2001–2003), 295

costs of clinicians for, 284–285

costs of hearings and trials for, 286

costs of release and transition programs under, 293–294

costs of secure and therapeutic facility for, 292

and filing considerations, 31, 53

and frequency of commitment, 32, 33

historical background of, 42–44

and laws in other states, 5

and less restrictive alternative or release, 52, 53

on list of states, 27n

number of persons held, 45

and offenders not treated, 295

predatory crime defined in, 150

and previous laws, 132

and probable-cause hearings, 296

and prognosis, 28

and provision of services, 32, 33, 34, 35

and publicizing of sex crimes, 149, 318–319

and recidivism, 172

strict scrutiny applied to, 199

and SVP census projections, 286–287, 288

and treatment, 120, 289–290

Weems v. United States, 251

West v. Mach, 291

Williams v. Smith, 251

Wisconsin

and chemical castration, 252, 253, 254

sexual predator (commitment) law of, 27n, 30, 45, 51, 142

and frequency of commitment, 33

and less restrictive alternative or release, 52

number of persons held, 45

and provision of services, 33

and SVP census projections, 287

Wisconsin v. Post, 198

Women, sex crimes against, 151–152, 157, 159. *See also* Rape

World Wide Web, risk literature on 77

Youngberg v. Romeo, 123, 126, 127, 179, 208

Young v. Weston, 198

Zadvydas v. Davis, 127

ABOUT THE EDITORS

Bruce J. Winick, JD, is professor of law at the University of Miami School of Law in Coral Gables, Florida, where he has taught since 1974. He is cofounder of the school of social enquiry known as *therapeutic jurisprudence.* He is the author of the books *The Right to Refuse Mental Health Treatment* (American Psychological Association [APA], 1997) and *Therapeutic Jurisprudence Applied: Essays on Mental Health Law* and he is the coauthor or coeditor of *Judging in a Therapeutic Key: Therapeutic Jurisprudence and the Courts, Practicing Therapeutic Jurisprudence: Law as a Helping Profession, The Essentials of Florida Mental Health Law,* and *Law in a Therapeutic Key.* He also has authored more than 80 articles in law reviews and interdisciplinary journals.

He is the coeditor of the APA book series, *Law and Public Policy: Psychology and the Social Sciences.* He is legal advisor and a founding member of the board of editors of *Psychology, Public Policy, and Law* and serves on the editorial board of *Law and Human Behavior.* He has guest edited numerous symposia in academic journals, including one coedited with John Q. La Fond on sex offenders and the law.

Professor Winick previously served as New York City's Director of Court Mental Health Services and as General Counsel of its Department of Mental Health.

John Q. La Fond holds the Edward A. Smith/Missouri Chair in Law, the Constitution, and Society at the University of Missouri–Kansas City School of Law. A graduate of Yale College and Yale Law School, Professor La Fond is an internationally recognized scholar in mental health law, criminal law and procedure, and constitutional law. He has written extensively on involuntary hospitalization of the mentally ill, the criminal responsibility of mentally ill offenders, substantive criminal law, mental health law and policy in the United States, control and treatment of sex offenders, and therapeutic jurisprudence. He is coauthor of *Back to the Asylum: The Future of Mental Health Law and Policy in the United States* and *Criminal Law: Examples and Explanation* (1st and 2nd editions).

Professor La Fond was a legal consultant to a major National Institute of Mental Health (NIMH) study on the impact of expanding the statutory criteria for civil commitment and another NIMH study assessing outcome measures in the public welfare domain for people with serious mental disorders. He has convened a national symposium, "On Preventing Intimate Violence: Have Law and Public Policy Failed?" La Fond also wrote and argued briefs challenging the constitutionality of Washington State's novel sexual predator commitment law. He was coeditor of "Sex Offenders: Scientific, Legal, And Policy Perspectives," published in *Psychology, Public Policy, and Law.*